Biography of a Buffoon

On the most "interesting" man in black America: The Reverend Al Sharpton

M. Paul Sinclair

ISBN: 0999474308
ISBN 13: 9780999474303

Contents

Prologue

The "racial racketeer" might be a politician, minister, teacher, director of a community center, or head of a "social uplift agency." As long as he did certain things and expressed the popular opinions on questions, he lacked nothing, and those who followed him found their way apparently better paid as the years went by. His leadership, then, was recognized and the ultimate undoing of the Negroes in the community was assured.[1]

THERE IS A pyramid of tyranny at the heart of the village that, much like the tower of Babel, can be seen from any point on earth. To see it up close, though, you're guided down a retrograde path of tutelage that snakes its way through many miles of mangrove proscription to an area of stealth decadence in the center of town, where it stands tall in the village square. There, many are oppressed in one form or another, and dissonance pervades, as the villagers cope primarily by focusing on that which is external to their condition, on that to which the entire village is subjected—its wholesome oppression.

In this beautiful, happy, angry, "all important," yet often ignored and maligned little village, we find a struggle playing out among three primary classes of villagers. There's a fierce struggle of existence among the masses, characterized by survival of the fittest and the meanest while the meek fly under the radar. There's a struggle for adaptation among the middle classes that do the heavy lifting, characterized by the advancement of the disciplined, the cautious, and the measured. Finally, there's a difficult struggle for variation and dominance among an elite and bourgeois class that straddles a *form-over-substance* dialectic,

---

1 Carter G. Woodson, *The Mis-Education of the Negro* (ASALH Press, Washington, D.C., 2005), 64–65.

characterized by frustration from imitation and identity-subjugation, if not out-right self-renunciation in a deft effort at far-fetched assimilation.

Form ranges from the serious—clergy, politics, and activism—to the frivolous—money, athleticism, entertainment, celebrity, the celebrated of any kind, or other attributes of prestige instead of intelligence, legitimacy, power, or any substantive relevance. In the world of imitation, few things are real or relevant. But as all of this provides a vicarious escape from the daily realities of the village at large, *form* has gained considerable importance among the masses, having become the *raison d'être* of most villagers.

Across these three classes, we find the charlatan's paradise; it's a rich and fertile pasture wherein the commoditization and commercialization of racial oppression see the exploitation of the village by fellow villagers in politics, in the clergy, in the media, in the intellectual and literary realm, and in social and civil rights activism. Invariably, the village views these exploiters as advocates and leaders, as they best articulate its pain and suffering, even while exploiting both.

Introduction

BIOGRAPHY OF A *Buffoon (Biography)* is a tragicomic sketch of America's "premiere" black leader not named Obama or Jackson—the Reverend Al Sharpton (the Rev.). It examines the oppression-driven emotional embrace of unreason in many parts of black America that often facilitates the ascendance of indecency and gives rise to contemporary racial racketeers.

Racial Racketeers

The racial racketeers Dr. Carter Woodson had identified are practitioners of race exploitation. Usually the caste of "professional blacks" as opposed to African American professionals, they're mostly the politicians, activists, writers, journalists, television commentators, and preachers who make a living off of racism, discrimination, the second-class citizenry, victimization, and the overall disenfranchisement of African Americans across the spectrum.

Many (though not all) serve their particular interests in the fertile domain of collective activism for profit. Some fleece black folk in churches while others use marches and protests as shakedown tools. Others in politics negate the value of the black vote in cash-for-endorsement electioneering schemes. Writers and others in the media excel at programming and literature that strikes the dominant emotion of race. Collectively, they cultivate an emotional and a reactive populace through various means of exploitative conditioning. They're African Americans for whom there would be no livelihood in a society free of racism and racist oppression of the masses of their people. Their bread and butter is race and, as a consequence, they're empowered because they're black—on the backs of other blacks.

Headed today by the Reverend Sharpton and others, they believe that black America would be nowhere without them, therefore owing much to them. To speak to them of trailblazing African Americans in business, in the military, in science & technology, and so on is anathema. Their sole deference is to big money athletes and entertainers or to the otherwise publicly celebrated, through whom they elevate their own statures and prestige by association—a variant of *fusion without integrity* [Fromm][2].

These men and women excel at profiting from black pain. They lead movements that are businesses that have long degenerated into outright rackets [Hoffer[3]]. The economic interpretation of their activism (business-racket) requires a massive black underclass and widespread disenfranchisement on which to trade. So, while they profess to be in the service of their people, they're more often in service to themselves, with little interest in improving the lot of the former. In fact, they have as much interest in equality of the races as white racists, because *equality* would render them no more powerful than the masses of their people that they exploit. More importantly, there is no wealth to be gained from widespread *equality*. Opportunities lie in the pain and suffering of their own, in stoking the passions and emotions of victims—of those feeling frustrated, deprived, disaffected, or oppressed—but to no avail.

Take this June 4, 1990, piece from *People Magazine*, "The Racial Murder of Yusef Hawkins Inflamed New York City, Forcing His Parents to Relive Their Anguish," by writer Montgomery Brower. In speaking of losing their son, Yusef Hawkins, who was killed by racists in 1989, Moses Stewart, father of the young Hawkins, recalled the efforts by former race leader, Reverend Jesse Jackson, to exploit his son's death for political purposes:

> A host of politicians and black leaders, including the Rev. Jesse Jackson, came to pay their respects. Moses was less than flattered by some of the attention. "I had made it known to everybody that I was not going to allow my son to be used for any political game because I didn't want them bouncing him around between

---

2 Social Psychoanalyst Erich Fromm's description of disingenuous unions based on domination, submission, and exploitation, among other factors.

3 Social Philosopher Eric Hoffer's description of the usual progression of mass movements.

them for votes. Then Jesse shows up and comes in with his entourage, and he takes his shoes off, and he says. 'That boy in there could be the next reason why [David] Dinkins could be elected Mayor of New York City.' So I said, 'Hold it, don't do that. I want him buried with dignity and respect.' [Later] Jesse apologizes, and we say a little prayer, and he tries to get us to walk him outside. So, the only thing he wanted was to come outside with the family, with the click, click, click and the camera bit. But we were wise to that, so he kind of lost that battle."

As the family grieved their dead son, the insensitive Reverend Jackson had seen in its loss an opportunity to elect David Dinkins, mayor, by stoking the passions of black New Yorkers.

Throughout his books we see that Reverend Sharpton had learned the tricks of the trade from Jackson, only to take them to a higher level and to use them with less tact over the years. But in his years atop activism, Sharpton hasn't brought about any tangible change in the condition of his people, and has been bereft of any new ideas beyond regurgitating the moral suasion of Dr. King's "dream" a half-century ago. Like Jackson, the Rev. has professionalized marching and protesting while nixing the real work of lobbying and legislative engagement to change the landscape for his people. Sharpton has come to see himself as the center of power in black America—believing that, but for his marches and protests, the black community would've long gone the route of the dinosaurs.

But this diminishes the history of black progress in the last few decades. In periods when black America was uniformly nonintegrated, overtly disenfranchised, and universally oppressed, previous generations of civil rights leaders had combined direct action with legislative lobbying and litigation to tear down barriers. However, in today's bifurcated black America, that universality of the black condition is no longer the case. For example, television mogul Oprah Winfrey and a few rap stars can now buy up every square mile and the entire economies between Selma and Montgomery if they so choose. The Sharpton marches and protests therefore no longer wield the same power or the same effectiveness as in the past. As African Americans have excelled in all domains in the last few decades, there are vast stratifications along wealth, class, ideologies, religious and political affiliations, and so on. So, the march and the protest—when not "celebritized" (free of celebrity involvement)—no longer hold the same appeal, reverence, or effect.

For example, established national politicians and celebrities didn't show up in Cleveland to protest the killing of young Tamir Rice—the twelve-year-old shot and killed by a police officer two seconds after being told to drop a toy gun. It was hardly a cause célèbre for the national black sociopolitical elite. Nor, for that matter, did we see any such protests for the numerous other black men uselessly cut down by police across the land. But symbolic acts of resistance by celebrities or athletes, such as footballer Colin Kaepernick's anthem demonstration, become immediate *appels à la guerre*—calls to war—a measure of the extent to which black America has become "celebritized" but not necessarily any more consciously concerned.

In fall 2017, the sight of former New York City black police officers protesting Mr. Kaepernick's continued unemployment was stunning. Given that there were no such demonstrations by this group after any of the other numerous and even less publicized incidents of police abuse and killings of innocent black men, protesting Mr. Kaepernick's unemployment was just an effort to jump on a celebrity's bandwagon. In New York alone, Eric Garner's death by suffocation and young Kalief Browder's induced suicide, following his release after abandonment in the New York City jail system, should have merited some consideration by this esteemed group of former black officers. Simply put, in the black community, the march and protest are not what they used to be—neither in purpose nor effect—as the black condition is no longer universal and activist causes are now driven more by their celebrated nature than by any conscious need to manifest.

So, although in the past he has had to hire people from homeless shelters to stage his "rent-a-protests," this change in the landscape has been lost on Reverend Sharpton. He has come to believe that "black power" in America is Al Sharpton and has failed to accept the contradiction of his realities—that his staple of marching and protesting isn't an indication of freedom or power but precisely of the absence of both. The Rev. cannot understand that the powerful do not have to perpetually march or picket their continued existential weakness and abuse.

In exploring the irony of the bumbling and mostly ignorant preacher-activist atop black leadership during the presidency of a black intellectual—former President Barack Obama—*Biography* speaks to the level to which inferiority and inequality as phenomena aren't just white-imposed realities of black life in America. It shows that instead, they're often uniquely reserved conditions by black leadership for its people, who then willingly accept and embrace such conditioned destinies.

From childhood to the present, Reverend Sharpton's grandiosity has given us a kind of tragic activism, infused with treachery, deceit, narcissism, and megalomaniacal ostentation at each stage of his public life. He claimed to have begun serving his people through preaching at age four, after which he then insisted that the children and teachers in his school refer to him as "the Reverend Alfred Charles Sharpton Jr." As a sixty-year-old adult, he was still enough unsophisticated and egotistical to include this in a book in which, among other things, he regaled himself for being on his way to the "greatness" that he'd always sought.

In high school, the Rev. staged protests that shut down the entire institution, just because he didn't like the food they served in the cafeteria. In college, he dropped out just because he was "too brilliant" for the curriculum they taught in the classroom. On his way up the ladder, he claimed famous heroes— Marcus Garvey, Congressman Adam Clayton Powell Jr., and Jesse Jackson— he'd needed while climbing up, only to abandon or eviscerate them in his books once he thought he was atop and had no longer needed their association. As a man in his forties, he wrote a book telling young activists not to emulate Dr. Martin Luther King Jr., because he thought Dr. King wasn't as great as the media had made him out to be. Nonetheless, for the past several decades, Sharpton has made a living converting King's civil rights activism into a fertile pasture of civil rights profiteering.

The Rev. has hustled corporations by taking residents out of homeless shelters to stage rent-a-protests and has pocketed money as a pitchman for a predatory financing organization that targeted the black community he claimed to have represented and served. In recent years, some have even accused him of being paid to suppress cries of corporate racism. Elsewhere he has posited himself as the payoff point and absolver of sins of white public figures or celebrities who run afoul of racial sensitivity and as the redeemer of the black ones who run afoul of the law.

Although never elected even to any public office by his people, Sharpton appointed himself as a black leader, hijacked police brutality in staging his fiefdom, and has since made a career off the pain and suffering of black victims of racism in New York City and beyond. In both terms of the Obama administration, he arrogated himself to VIP overseer to police black criticisms of the president, effectively imposing a stealth dictatorship over black America's freedom of thought and speech.

Yet his role and past injections into racial conflicts have often produced catastrophic results—as in the early 1990s Crown Heights riots in Brooklyn, New York, and the tragedy at Freddie's Fashion Mart in Harlem a few years later. But even before any of those disasters, his 1980s *nom de guerre*—the Tawana Brawley hoax-affair warrior—had brought a level of tension to New York City and the nation that was almost reminiscent of Alabama's Scottsboro Boys affair in 1931. Where the Rev.'s involvements weren't directly disastrous, they still ended up fomenting much of the very racism against which he claims to have fought. He has proven over and over again that he has neither the power nor the influence about which he has often boasted. He has shown that his very existence isn't a symbol of strength but precisely the opposite, one of abject weakness—his and black America's.

In the early '90s, many believed that the Rev. had worked behind the scenes with the Republican opposition in its defeat of New York City's first black mayor, fellow Democrat David Dinkins. Since then, Sharpton has mounted several political runs for offices that he had neither intention nor chance of winning but simply to accumulate votes, which he then bartered for endorsing his primary opponents for hard cold cash. In 2004, he took deceit to a new level (high or low) when as a Democrat, he was financed and managed by Republican operative Roger Stone in mounting what many believed to have been a mole presidential bid solely intended to weaken the eventual Democratic nominee, John Kerry. This act of treachery then forced the Democrats to co-opt and use the Rev. as a mouthpiece in the years that followed, which then elevated his profile and further legitimized his imposition upon black America as its leader. In 2014, at the high point of his prestige as a leader, news magazine the *Smoking Gun*, outed the Rev. as a former FBI informant. Through Freedom of Information releases, the magazine revealed that Sharpton was "CI-17"—an '80s era FBI confidential informant who'd spied on mobsters for the government, just as he'd long been rumored to have done on black activists during that time as well.

Over the years, the Rev. has written three pieces of fiction, portraying himself as a child prodigy—placing himself as a youth among the famous, the celebrated, and the otherwise infamous. He has invented stories of "lessons learned" from the famous and has reinvented and denied his old self by retroactively claiming involvement in historical events to which he was a stranger. In fact, he has invented so much fiction on paper that by the end of his last book, *The Rejected Stone (Stone)*, he ended up placing himself at a famous historical event while he was sixty-four hundred miles away—a lie he then made the centerpiece of a 2016 book by another author.

Elsewhere, Sharpton used his books to wage an internecine war to discredit his former mentor, Jessie Jackson, who'd stood in the way of his activism for profit. As the Rev. sought to lay exclusive claim to the privileges and profit of activism, then principal profiteer Jackson was a stumbling block, thereby becoming the target of his protégé's scorn. In his first book, *Go and Tell Pharaoh (Pharaoh)*, Sharpton vilified Jackson—accusing him of having conflicts of interests and of forsaking his obligations as a civil rights activist to wrap himself in the cloak of Bill Clinton's presidency. Yet a decade later, when the Rev. had become fully entrenched among the black middle class and elites he'd once scorned, he functioned primarily as an adjunct communication arm of the White House for the duration of the Obama administration. He'd complained that white America had opposed him because "the people" had chosen him, whereas it had become used to choosing other black leaders. But although making several runs for elected office without ever being chosen by any black electorate, his ascendancy during the Obama years was as the chosen one (for the moment) of a white media organization that deemed him good for its business model of progressive advocacy. Comcast-MSNBC, the network that employs him and gave him that ascendant path as a power player, is neither owned nor led by African Americans. So, white America hadn't really opposed the Rev. in the past, as he'd claimed; it just hadn't gotten around to choosing him as yet.

For Reverend Sharpton, there would be no livelihood in a society free of a massive black underclass subject to racism and oppression. He, more than any other, has shown that his bread and butter is race and, as a consequence, he's empowered only because he's black, in an America whose bread is buttered by race—now a perfectly commoditized business like any other. But Sharpton's empowerment also highlights the moral impairment of black America in her struggle for advancement. And this is a principal focus of *Biography of a Buffoon*.

Among its highlights, *Biography* explores that moral impairment and to some extent, the decadence that has allowed the elevation of men like Reverend Sharpton. It largely ignores media accounts and publicly known Sharpton buffoonery of the last three decades. Using his words across three books, it's a composite based on Reverend Sharpton—as he has shown himself in his books. To provide a better context of the Rev.'s interactions in local New York City political campaigns, it cites comments by local New York City reporter Andrew Kirtzman, as well as former New York City political operative Evan Mandery's book, *The Campaign*. In a chapter on the Rev.'s 2004 presidential bid, it cites reporter Juan Williams' book *Enough*, which lamented the overall decrepit black leadership in America and pointed to the Rev.'s emotional blackmail of the Democratic Party in 2004 as an example. *Biography* also cites The *Village Voice's* Wayne Barrett's reporting that had exposed Sharpton's 2004 Democratic presidential bid as cynical subterfuge with the aid of Republican operative Roger Stone. The details of his 2004 presidential campaign remain unknown to most Americans—black and white.

All in all, contents not based on Reverend Sharpton's own words are less than two percent of this book. *Biography* is the world of the Reverend Alfred Charles Sharpton Jr. according to *the Rev.*

Act I: Piston-Era Barnstormer

The average human being is a perverse creature;
and when he isn't, he is a practical joker.

—MARK TWAIN[4]

Reverend Al Sharpton smiles and holds his arms up as he poses for a portrait while campaigning for political office. (Photo by James Marshall/Corbis via Getty Images.)

---

4 *Following the Equator- The Wit and Wisdom of Mark Twain, 3.*

1

PSYCHIATRIST CAMILLA ANDERSON once said, "Few of us would ever wind up feeling like turds if we didn't start off with the grandiose assumptions that we must be great and noble."[5] Behavioral psychologist Dr. Albert Ellis added, "Grandiosity is one of the most common of disturbed human feelings, and often compensates for underlying feelings of slobhood."[6] It is in this sense that we might call Reverend Sharpton a poster boy for "turdish slobhood." With childish fantasies of being everything from a "freedom fighter" to aspirations of being a "great leader," his grandiose tendencies have often shown us a complete turd that was neither:

> It dawned on me, reading about these great men, that if I wanted to go to the next level, I needed to take control of my mouth—both what I put into it and what I allowed to come out of it. What I ate and what I said. And I could only do that by controlling my mind, controlling my appetites. To me, that became the path to greatness; it was the only way I could go from being a famous leader to being a great leader.[7]

As they're usually oblivious to their comical projections and grandiosity, turds end up being ignored by the rest of us, out of exhaustion. Most of us couldn't care less about understanding them or their motivations; instead, we merely take note of their neuroses and diabolic impulses and have a good laugh. For example, who but the diabolically neurotic would tell us that on the road to greatness in American politics lies the path of being skinny? As consumers of such comedy, few among us could escape having a good laugh.

But then there is also the issue of demagogues and charlatans and the likelihood that turds in slobhood are often one masking as the other. Demagogues aren't that bad if they're authentic. You know that you're dealing with a particular type, so you develop the tools and mechanisms to either deal with it or to avoid it. Charlatans, though, are bad news, because they're inauthentic—not real. They're enhanced chameleons that go with the flow just to gain an advantageous position. They might be Christians today and Muslims or Jews

---

5 Albert Ellis, *The Case against Religiosity* (American Atheist Press, 1976), 35.

6 Ibid.

7 Reverend Al Sharpton with Nick Chiles, *The Rejected Stone: Al Sharpton and the Path to American Leadership* (Cash Money Content & Massenburg Media, 2013), 209.

tomorrow, whites this moment and light-skinned blacks with frizzy hair the next—if it suits their bank accounts and social circumstances. They're convincing because before convincing others, they first convince themselves. So, there is little to trust in charlatans as their only consistency is inconsistency, their only sense of decency, indecency. Therefore, while the charlatan masking as a demagogue might be a practical joker, where unmasked, he or she is often a genuinely perverse creature.

Perverse Creature or Practical Joker?

African American professor Manning Marable once wondered how the black church that produced men like Dr. Martin Luther King Jr. could have also produced men like Reverend Ike—the former a great man of honor and the latter a charlatan and so-called prosperity preacher.

Of course, this was straight posture or at least a naïve thought, given that the black church's evolution in America has always seen the pious and the impious charlatan competing for center stage. So, let's assume that naïveté for the moment in speaking of contemporary black America. The same question could be posed—of President Barack Obama and Reverend Al Sharpton sharing the stage: how could the same black community see and accept two men so different, as leaders in the same millennium, the same century, the same decade, the same time-period?

While a question that might provoke some soul-searching among many African Americans, others will just as quickly dismiss it as nonsense. Taking offense at the thought of Reverend Sharpton in the same league as President Obama, some will exclaim outright, *No comparisons to be made!* The educated and those with a "black card" to protect, might tell you straightforward: *Al Sharpton is not a black leader. Nobody respects him in the grassroots community*—meaning he has no "street cred," no legitimacy, as they view "legitimacy" as coming from the grassroots. Others who feel the opposite will readily tell you: *The black community didn't produce the two,* with the more precise among them revealing their subconscious; *Black America didn't produce Barack Obama,* they might say. But then the lights immediately go on, and on realizing that this would mean having to accept the Rev. as the representative of blackness, they might immediately do a double take and run back to stealthily reclaim Mr. Obama, without explicitly rejecting the Rev. *Well, that's a good question,* they might say. *I'll have to think about that one for a minute.*

This scenario has played out among some of my friends and a few times even with strangers in the streets in the last few years. No one knew that I was writing a book about Reverend Sharpton or that I was conducting my mini-nonscientific research. Where I've had time on my hands or space in my lungs, I've occasionally shot back by asking, "Then, if he's not a black leader, why is he the go-to guy on TV for all things black?" As I said though—only with time and enough lung capacity because invariably, an exercise in dissonance or connivance will follow. I'll get all the reasons why the Rev. isn't the leader of black America—none of which will generally make much sense because for as long as he's that go-to guy for white politicians and the media, black leadership is flushed down the toilet—deprived of oxygen. Plain and simple, the Rev. is the self-appointed black leader who has since been anointed by the mainstream and to whom so-called black leadership and its leading institutions have since subordinated themselves.

So, in appropriating the Marable irony to contemporary times, it is true that while a black intellectual was completing his second term in the Oval Office, a black rabble-rouser was sitting atop national black leadership in America as no less than a prestigious television host. It was brilliance and debonair sharing the stage with the antithesis of brilliance and the essence of unrefined that was long rumored to have been on the payroll of authorities seeking to entrap, arrest, and decapitate grassroots black leadership and activists. Reverend Al Sharpton, known as much for exploiting racial conflicts as for an unusual ability at the advancement of self-interests, had come to represent the high point of dissonance in black America during the Obama reign.

In a culture where tutelage and proscription find comfort in systemic (and systematic) racism, and where the cognoscenti of the black political and activist class masks its betrayal and opportunism behind the curtains of real racism in society, Reverend Sharpton had ironically peaked in the shadows of President Barack Obama—a leader with no such "street cred" in the modern pantheon of bellicose civil rights activism. Today, the Rev. sits atop a long list of charlatan black leaders, not because he has fleeced black America in the traditional sense—via the church, a community savings & loan bank, elected office, or through propagandist platforms (literature and media)—but because he has fleeced a generation of African Americans of its right to dignified and morally untainted leadership.

It has sometimes been tough to paint the Rev. in a box, given the choices he has made. He's been mired in debt and unpaid taxes for years, which shows the fiscal irresponsibility of a poor man living as wealthy. He could've easily been counting the unbridled flow of cash from behind a pulpit—like the Lear and Gulfstream traveling zillionaires who'd taken that path. Yet early on he'd chosen the path of activism out of a desire for power and acceptance rather than take the easy road to money by preaching. Ironically, in the broader scheme of things, he might have served a better (and "higher") purpose and might have done less collateral damage to black leadership and to his people's material conditions had he indeed opted to chase the money from behind a pulpit. But he was smitten by power and kingmaker syndromes from an early age. Since then, where he has not done direct damage, his very presence has often served to undermine progress in a black America. While undertaking direct actions to challenge continued racism and discrimination, as with any disfavored minority in society, the black community nonetheless needs to engage the empowered ruling classes through social and legislative means—contrary to Sharpton's bellicosity and underlying narrow self-interests.

So then, how did the Rev., a talented yet unknown writer of fiction, rise atop black leadership in an America in which he has long been unmasked as a race-baiting charlatan wearing the mask of a demagogue? These are the questions that I endeavor to answer in the following chapters.

The 2016 Election Cycle

To believe yourself brave is to be brave.

—MARK TWAIN[8]

Donald Trump, Al Sharpton, and Don King attend the Art of the Deal book party at Trump Tower in New York City in December 1987. (Photo by Sonia Moskowitz/Getty Images.)

AS THE 2016 election cycle kicked into high gear in the summer of 2015, I, like most Americans, was interested in figuring out the candidates' positions on

---

8 *Joan of Arc – The Wit and Wisdom of Mark Twain* (Dover Publications, New York, 1999), 15.

relevant issues but having a non-running dark horse in the electioneering, my interest was also elsewhere. Even more than the candidates' domestic agenda and foreign policy positions, I was interested in seeing the role that Reverend Sharpton would be playing in the Democratic contest ahead. I was nearing the end of this book and was unusually preoccupied with Sharpton's post-Obama role, especially after reading his last book, 2013's *Stone*, in which he'd boasted of an omnipotent role in the 2008 elections and of his increasing importance and newfound status as an Obama-era Democratic Party VIP.

Since scratching his way to the peak of the mountaintop, many of his African American detractors were then of the opinion that the Rev. was poised to trip up, tumble, and plunge back into the valley with the winding down of the Obama presidency. Online, many free-thinking radicals were echoing the opinion that the so-called Obama-bump that had translated into so-called Obama-jobs for many black media personalities—the Rev. included—had already seen its last ex-dividend date, with few benefits left to be accrued to its remaining holders. For this election cycle, I was curious whether or not it would be business as usual with the Rev. and the Democratic Party: Would the party continue to unleash him as the vote-broker extraordinaire to stitch up the black vote by any means necessary (campaigning and endorsing)? Or would 2016 be the year the Democrats finally summoned the courage to rid themselves of their most persistent albatross?

In both books and behind the scenes, the Rev. had revealed a relationship with the Democratic Party that was fraught with hypocrisy, deception, and backstabbing. Former First Lady and then-presidential candidate Hillary Clinton is the wife of former president Bill Clinton, whom Sharpton had once called a white supremacist who commanded the submission of his "niggers" (Reverend Jesse Jackson). But as a senator, she'd still kowtowed to him over the years, so it was anyone's guess. So, with President Obama leaving office, I was thinking, *What now for the Rev.?*

Infectious and Contagious

A July 21, 2015, *Washington Post* article by writer Jonathan Capehart—written after a meeting between the newspaper's editorial board and Reverend

Sharpton—was but one point of departure to an election cycle laced with comedy, buffoonery, historical ironies, and contradictions.

The electoral landscape was changing. American politics was seeing an upending of the traditional dynamics of political campaigning. Billionaire Donald Trump, quite possibly the most controversial candidate since segregationist George Wallace, had made a boisterous entrance to the race with incendiary comments about Mexicans and immigration, among other things. To the chagrin of many on both sides of the aisle, his candidacy was catching fire. Some within his own Republican Party had pulled a page from the playbook used against African Americans in the past: they styled Mr. Trump's core white rural supporters as "low information voters" who didn't fully understand the issues. In the Trump's candidacy, Democrats saw the underpinnings of white nationalism, racism, and xenophobia and they cried foul. They'd failed to note that much of America, in particular, middle America and its dying ghost towns, were sick and tired of politicians of both stripes who cared more about bailing out Wall Street than about rebuilding factories and businesses on Main Street—issues that Mr. Trump was successfully articulating. On both sides of the political spectrum, nearly everyone had become overnight experts at "advising" Trump's "doomed" candidacy, while proving themselves neophytes whose expectations he defied at each turn.

So, the *Post* article, "What Al Sharpton Learned from James Brown That Donald Trump Hasn't," had pointed to the possibilities of at least one assigned role for the Rev.—that of respectable elder statesman with valuable expertise to impart during the process. And here, he seemed to have believed that he'd had the gravitas to give a few lessons of the game on the upstart Donald Trump, via the *Post*'s erstwhile editorial writer Jonathan Capehart.

But where suggestive advice or rebukes to the grand Mr. Trump should've registered to anyone of sound mind as just plain silly, "Lessons Al Sharpton had learned from James Brown that Donald Trump hadn't" was downright buffoonery. What lessons? What synthesized information, insights, or relevant knowledge could Reverend Sharpton impart to the greatest salesman in all of Manhattan and by extension, on planet earth? What expertise could singer James Brown have possibly taught the Rev. that could've been of any benefit to Donald Trump in his political campaign? *Trump learns lessons from the man in the mirror,*

I thought to myself. But then there were also the Sharpton books in which the Rev. had chronicled four decades of relationships with famous mentors James Brown, Adam Clayton Powell Jr., and others by writing of so-called lessons learned from these individuals. These recollections, written by Sharpton in one moment and denounced and discredited by him in the next, often appeared to have been well-crafted inventions that oscillated between conflicting iterations of his lessons learned in life while showing us those he hadn't. In the end, his revisions and contradictions of "lessons learned" from one book to the other had left good reasons to be doubtful of any lessons learned from his mentors. But poor Jonathan Capehart was none the wiser.

As I read the *Washington Post* article, it was like Groundhog Day. It seemed a memorable piece for the upcoming campaign season, precisely because it was likely to be forgotten by the very next day. But according to Mr. Capehart, Reverend Sharpton had "perfectly assessed" Donald Trump's character and was, therefore, best placed to give the candidate advice:

> The Rev Al Sharpton perfectly assessed the character of Donald Trump's death-defying campaign for the Republican presidential nomination. "What plays at Lincoln Center don't play at the Apollo," Sharpton said about Trump. "And I think that he is an Apollo act in Lincoln Center."

Attempting to appropriate center stage from Donald Trump at a stadium, in a concert hall, in the open skies, on the high seas, or in a newspaper column was indeed the height of silly season, the abundance of oxygen notwithstanding. Where Reverend Sharpton was the source of comedy, Jonathan Capehart had enjoined himself to our very amusement. Here was an African-American writer at one of the nation's premier newspapers quoting America's central black leader as effectively suggesting that the expropriated African American jazz that plays at Lincoln Center in New York City will not play too well for the supposedly urban (maybe even "ghettoized") patrons of the Apollo Theatre in Harlem.

What exactly did the Rev. mean by that? A weak attempt at paraphrasing might read like this: *Although white and rich, the crude, crass, white trash Donald Trump was more like the rowdy black folks at the Apollo Theater in Harlem. But to*

9

become president, he now needs to step up the game and adopt a genteel, polite, and dignified persona, more in line with the refined and cultured white folks who go to Lincoln Center.

Anecdotally, for some reason, African Americans are forever longing to tell white folk how to behave. Leave it to the infectious Reverend Sharpton to tell Mr. Trump that he should act less like Harlem's Leroy and more like the Upper West Side's Ludlow. Leave it to affected Jonathan Capehart to write it in his newspaper. At that point, it wasn't hard to imagine the pale-faced head of a white writer who'd written a similar piece of nonsense under a guillotine—being chased to his death by a Sharpton-led posse demanding his "white racist" head.

(L–R) Jonathan Capehart, Margaret Capehart, and Reverend Al Sharpton attend the cocktail party celebrating Jonathan Capehart's appointment as senior vice president at Hill & Knowlton, USA, at the home of Darren Walker on February 15, 2005, in New York City. (Photo by Billy Farrrell/Patrick McMullan via Getty Images.)

Bearing witness to such wanton literary vulgarity had indeed signaled the onset of what President Obama used to call the political silly season. The Sharpton factor in the upcoming election then became evident. For better or for worse, the forces of Democratic political inertia had once more decided to legitimize his imposition upon our consciousness in one way or another. As a subject matter expert, he was now being dispatched to enlighten the readers of broadsheets like the *Washington Post*.

Jonathan Capehart, a man who'd made a number of cognitively scripted and highly cerebral appearances on Sharpton's television show, *Politics Nation*, had known the Rev. from the mid-1990s New York social scene. In fact, as an aide to former New York City mayor Michael Bloomberg, Capehart had once played go-between for Bloomberg and Sharpton back in the 2001 New York City mayoral election.[9] In using Reverend Sharpton as his source, the erudite Mr. Capehart was no doubt throwing his old friend a bone. But he'd either never read a Sharpton book (three works of art with bucket lists of his so-called lessons learned) or had done so without an appreciation for their inherently fictional quality and comedic value—thereby eliminating the Rev. as a credible source to be quoted in the *Washington Post*.

Having read the Sharpton books over the last two decades, I'd noted his attempts at social elevation through claimed associations with famous people he'd known. Lessons he'd learned from them—appropriations of the same events and circumstances into polar opposite versions across three different books over nearly twenty years—were thrown about to legitimize his intimacies with the famed and celebrated. But since the same event can't be true and false at the same time, it means that, in many cases, at least two out of three stories written were embellishments, while yet in other cases, all three were complete fabrications.

"We Don't Want Sinatra"

"We don't want Sinatra" and "I am not Sinatra" are two different versions of the same event told across two books. I cover the Rev.'s relationship with singer James Brown at length in a later chapter, so this is a quick sampling of why his "lessons learned" from James Brown could hardly have been seriously considered, even by a better man than candidate Donald Trump.

---

9 Al Sharpton with Karen Hunter, *Al on America* (Dafina Books/Kensington, New York, 2002), 174.

The filming of a 1980s-era movie scene had given rise to a fantastic and pointless piece of Sharpton storytelling in support of the Rev.'s contention of two distinct lessons learned from James Brown. Some might recall the electrifying moment when Jake and Elwood Blues walked into Reverend Cleophus James' Chicago church to sheer electricity. A glowing halo enveloped these gentlemen, and in no time, it was game-on. The choir sang and clapped; the men did backflips up to the altar, and the entire congregational prostration that followed signaled being in the midst of the black Holiness-Spiritualists experience. The movie was *The Blues Brothers*, which starred actors John Belushi, Dan Aykroyd, and the legendary soul singer and Sharpton mentor, James Brown, as the enigmatic Reverend Cleophus James.

Behind this comedic experience, Reverend Sharpton, who in those days was somewhat of a James Brown sidekick, surrogate son, and road groupie, wrote of another piece of comedy that had unfolded behind the scenes on the movie set. In 1996's *Pharaoh*, the Rev. had told of accompanying Brown during the filming of the movie, giving us the backdrop of how things had played out on set:

> I thought about a time I was with James Brown and he was working on the Blues Brothers movie. They asked James to sing a gospel song, and he was being all polite and everything, very proper, and John Belushi interrupted him and said, "Mr. Brown, with all due respect, we want you to put your soul into it, we want the screams, the wow. We want James Brown. If we wanted Frank Sinatra, we would have booked him." That's what I realized at Abyssinian. If they wanted Cornel West, they would have asked him. They wanted Al Sharpton.[10]

The James Brown he described was modesty incarnate in the midst of Hollywood. He was the genteel southern black gentleman soaking up the white man's adulation when the white man had wanted the "wow"—the authentic kicking, screaming, singing, and dancing immodesty of the black man doing his *thang*. But unknown to readers then, it was really a pointless

---

10 Reverend Al Sharpton and Anthony Walton, *Go and Tell Pharaoh* (DoubleDay, New York, 1996), 78–79.

12

attack on Dr. Cornel West and the black elites by the then firebrand Reverend Sharpton, recalling his decision to preach a certain way to ordinary black folks at a church in Harlem. To mask his full intent, the Rev. then made it into a "lesson learned" from singer James Brown.

"I'm Not Sinatra"

Six years later, by the time of his second book, 2002's *Al on America*, the Rev. and Dr. Cornel West, who would be an adviser to Sharpton's 2004 presidential campaign, were back on the mend, and so Dr. West was no longer an object of scorn. This time, the Rev.'s purpose wasn't to belittle Dr. Cornel West or to show us a humble and modest James Brown but instead to project a James Brown who was fiercely black and proud of it—one who "didn't take no mess."

A chapter in honor of Brown was entitled, "I'm Black and I'm Proud." In it, we got a revision of the same event on *The Blues Brothers* movie set that couldn't have been more different. Those white Hollywood guys had now wanted James Brown to be "white-lite"—modest, demurred, and polite. They wanted Ole Blue Eyes instead of Soul Brother No.1. But the proud black man stood his ground, telling them that what they saw was what they would get. They'd asked for and would get James Brown, not Frank Sinatra:

> James Brown taught me to be myself. After James Brown had gone through a rough period in his career, John Belushi and Dan Aykroyd reached out to him for a movie they were doing called The Blues Brothers. They wanted him to play a preacher in their movie. James Brown took it and I even helped him rehearse for the part…James Brown was to come out in his preacher's robe and deliver his sermon. He came out and did the famous James Brown slide out to the pulpit. He did his spin and his split and was dancing during the song. The director stopped him and said, "Wait a minute, Mr. Brown, you have to calm down." James Brown looked and him and said, "If you wanted Frank Sinatra, you should have booked him. If you want James Brown, this is what you get."[11]

---

11 Sharpton with Hunter, *Al on America*, 209–10.

In doing so, Brown had supposedly taught Sharpton what was yet another trite lesson—to always be himself and to never let others define him. The profundity of this second recollection of the events (six years after the first) was breathtaking, in particular, because it was such a valuable lesson Reverend Sharpton had learned from his idol James Brown. But it's hard to imagine that the aging singer—then fighting the times to stay relevant while dealing with his many personal demons—gets a shot at movie stardom and reinvention, only to tell those who were kind enough to throw him a life jacket that, "If you want James Brown, this is what you get!" But accordingly, the Rev. was so impressed (or enthralled) that he went on to tell us in great detail of the powerful impression this had made on him:

> Those were defining moments for me. James Brown taught me never to let people define who you are. I asked him later why he stood his ground with those Hollywood people. He said, "If you start letting people define who you are, people will then decide what is credible and what is not. And you never give them that, Rev. You may suffer, but you never give them that."[12]

The Rev. had reworked the story with enough details and accompanying visuals that it was very convincing as a "defining moment," unless of course, you'd read *Pharaoh* six years earlier. So, the basis on which he was being pitched as an eminent expert to rebuke Donald Trump with "lessons learned" from James Brown didn't have a leg to stand on. That he was now disseminating advice to a presidential candidate, based on lessons learned from James Brown, was the mainstreaming of idiocy. Yet the *Post* article continued,

> I asked Sharpton for his view of what's going on with The Donald and why he's doing what he's doing at a meeting with editors and reporters at The Post this morning. There was no better person to ask. Sharpton and Trump are both New Yorkers who have known each other and done battle with each other for years. And they are both targets and survivors of the Big Apple tabloids that make sport

---

12 Ibid.

of high-flying folks like them. That's why Sharpton's assessment of Trump's campaign and its future is as vivid as it is correct.

Jonathan Capehart did have a basis for using Reverend Sharpton as a source of intelligence on Donald Trump, although he didn't explore this, possibly out of ignorance of the facts. The truth is that the parallel universes inhabited by Reverend Sharpton and Donald Trump have harmoniously intersected for decades. The Rev. has a history with Mr. Trump, going back to the days when Sharpton was an underling of boxing promoter Don King—a longtime friend of Donald Trump and an associate in Trump's efforts to develop business and promote his Atlantic City ventures in the 1980s. In fact, Donald Trump and the Rev. were so tight at one point that on James Brown's death, in the wee hours of the night before the funeral service at the Apollo Theatre in New York, the Rev., unable to find a plane to transport Brown's body from South Carolina to New York, had reached out to Donald Trump, seeking to borrow his plane (at the time indisposed).

Even more important though, is the intersection of the two men via Republican operative Roger Stone. Mr. Stone, another Trump associate of several decades, had led Mr. Trump's short-lived 2000 campaign for president on the Reform Party ticket. He was also a key adviser to the 2016 Trump election campaign (activities for which Stone now figures into intelligence investigations and the search for sordid characters with names like Guccifer 2.0). The Republican Roger Stone had also financed and managed "Democrat" Al Sharpton's 2004 presidential bid (covered in depth in a later chapter). Seen through this prism, the *Washington Post's* editorial board and Mr. Capehart weren't too far off the mark in seeking Sharpton's expertise on Trump. The Rev. might have been in a position to criticize Mr. Trump to a newspaper but not to deliver the type of critique that could ultimately have been of any value. Because in the long Sharpton-Trump friendship, Donald Trump was the one holding the cards and likely much of Sharpton's own secrets and "lessons learned" as well. A man in perpetual hunt for money and donors is a man with secrets and, indeed, of which there's much to learn.

So, on any given day, there is likely a limit to what Al Sharpton can really say about Donald Trump without exposing Sharpton himself as a fraud. But in the eyes of Jonathan Capehart, a part of that "perfectly assessed character" was the preacher man's apocalyptic assessment of the billionaire's political future—based on Sharpton's upbringing by James Brown:

> What followed was a lesson imparted to Sharpton by James Brown, the legendary singer who was a mentor to the preacher and now-MSNBC host, that was so rich in imagery that I dare not chop it up into quotes. In short, Trump is a lounge act who hasn't realized that he is now performing on the main stage. The rules are different. The expectations are higher. And his failure to make the transition will doom him.

The Rev.'s literary visuals had so impressed Mr. Capehart that in refusing to chop them up into quotes, the writer plunged full frontal into the realm of naked buffoonery by quoting the buffoon in the first instance and by paraphrasing him in the second:

> First time I went to Vegas...[James Brown] took me there. And [he] said to me, "Reverend, let me tell you something...There's a difference between the lounge act and the acts that play the main room." We're at Caesar's Palace. I'm about 19–20 years old. And I said, "What do you mean?" And he said, "When you're in the lounge, you're competing with the bars and the barmaids and the slot machines and people gambling. So you do whatever you can to get attention. But when you're in the main room, they paid to see a show. You've got to be ready. You gotta have choreography. You gotta be rehearsed. You gotta have polish." He says, "When you get on the main stage, Reverend, whatever you did to get out the lounge don't do that on the main stage."

Sharpton had now moved from the Apollo and Lincoln Center to lounges and main rooms in Vegas gambling halls. As James Brown was known for his meticulous dedication and discipline, it isn't beyond the realm that he might have taught numerous lessons to his protégé-sidekick on the business of show business and of performing in general. But whether it was from James Brown or from Adam Clayton Powell Jr., the telling of Sharpton's "lessons learned" from his mentors was mere performance art. That the *Washington Post* had thought him credible enough to give advice to a current presidential candidate was an example of the infectious Reverend Sharpton at work. Jonathan Capehart had rightfully cited the Rev.'s 2004 presidential campaign to legitimize his source, as no one is better placed to offer commentary on a political race than one who has actually run such a race, or so it would seem:

> Sharpton said he never forgot that when he prepared to take the debate stage in 2004 with Kerry and other Democrats. "I didn't get up there and say, 'No justice, no peace,'" he said. "I'm at the main stage now." Sharpton said not recognizing the venue change is Trump's problem. "When you run for president, in my opinion, you run either to win or you run to further a cause," Sharpton said. He said he believes that Jeb Bush (R) and Hillary Clinton are running to win. The candidate for the Democratic presidential nomination in 2004 pointed out that "I ran to further a cause." While he said he knew he wasn't going to beat President George W. Bush in the general election or then-senator John F. Kerry in the primary for that matter, he said he ran because he felt issues "we wanted to raise like criminal justice and all were not going to be in the center stage if we didn't have a candidate."

But again, as this was a Democratic campaign run by dedicated Donald Trump loyalist, Republican Roger Stone, Donald Trump was likely to have long learned any lessons to be had from Reverend Sharpton's 2004 presidential campaign.

History is rarely as kind to us as we would like it to be. Its rebuke of Jonathan Capehart's belief in the Rev.'s "vivid and correct assessment" of Donald Trump's candidacy, campaign, and its future, is emblematic of all things Sharpton. Where past is the prologue, the Rev. was likely to be as credible in predicting, in imparting advice, or in serving any useful purpose as a subject-matter expert, as he had been in convincing us of any real lessons he'd learned from James Brown.

Kingmaker

One never ceases to make a hero of one's self.

—MARK TWAIN[13]

Democratic presidential candidate Senator Bernie Sanders (D-VT) meets with Reverend Al Sharpton at Sylvia's Restaurant on February 10, 2016, in the Harlem neighborhood of New York City. The meeting comes after a strong victory for Senator Sanders in the New Hampshire primary. (Photo by Andrew Renneisen/Getty Images.)

---

13 *The Gilded Age-The Wit and Wisdom of Mark Twain*, 3.

2002's *AL ON America's* chapter 15 was entitled, "Kingmaker." There, the Rev. had described his omnipresent role in the 2001 New York City mayoral race that Democrat Mark Green had lost after Sharpton had refused to support Green. Mark Green and Reverend Sharpton had a back and forth tit for tat in which Green had sought his endorsement by wining and dining him but then publicly renounced him in front of conservative and Jewish constituents. Sharpton then threw his support to Green's opponent Fernando Ferrer, after which Green—like Peter to Jesus—then denied knowledge of Sharpton or of ever seeking his endorsement.

The Rev. then wrote an epistle of his overwhelming courting by powerful film producer Harvey Weinstein and former president Bill Clinton,[14] among many, to get him to support Green. But it was to no avail as the Rev. stood his ground against the scoundrel Mark Green. Missing from his written account though, was that he'd supported Mark Green three years earlier in 1998 for senator—then stating that Green had been consistent on issues affecting working-class people, that he had integrity, and that he would've been an excellent senator for all New Yorkers.

Nonetheless, this was the beginning of Sharpton, the kingmaker in New York City politics. Although Green had defeated the Rev.'s candidate, Fernando Ferrer, in the primary, Michael Bloomberg then went on to beat Mark Green in the general election. In the end, Reverend Sharpton had "arrived," carrying with him the ability to scuttle Mark Green's chances after Green had supposedly disrespected him, or so he'd told us.

So, in 2016, the Rev. was at it again or at least attempting to insert himself as such. As candidate Donald Trump burned through his Republican rivals like fire through a cane field, Vermont Senator Bernie Sanders' campaign too was catching fire for much of the same populism as Mr. Trump. Bernie spoke to people in the heartland of America about the need to bring back factories and blue-collar jobs, while Secretary Hillary Clinton "misspoke" of her desire to kill West Virginia's coal industry but without speaking of any concrete plan to subsidize the development of green industries and replacement jobs. The

---

14 Sharpton with Hunter, *Al on America*, 173.

people of West Virginia and elsewhere across the Rust Belt wondered aloud, *How do you misspeak about killing jobs?*

As Bernie hammered away at the need to reverse middle-America's decimation, machinations to undermine him from within the Clinton-dominated Democratic establishment intensified. But another surprise of the election cycle had emerged: a sizeable chunk of young, educated African Americans chose Sanders—the senator from one of the whitest states in the Union—as their best option for moving forward. Whether they had retained then-candidate Barack Obama's and his wife Michelle's 2008 speeches vehemently extolling Hillary Clinton's untrustworthiness or her husband Bill Clinton's adverse 1994 Crime Bill or other Clinton fauxpas over the years, these educated black youths abandoned her and threw their support behind Bernie. But this wasn't enough to take Sanders across the line. With older African Americans and the plurality of the black political establishment solidly in the Clinton camp (Congressman John Lewis still believes she was actually elected), Bernie Sanders needed to do something to get some of those older and less educated black voters, while consolidating his gains among the youth. The black vote was as much a path to victory for him as it was for Secretary Clinton.

But with his former endorsee, Jesse Jackson, whom Sanders had endorsed for president in 1988, relegated to the *has-been* column, the senator surprised and disappointed many by resorting to the all-too-familiar page from the playbook of the black vote and the white politician. Fresh off a primary win in New Hampshire, he set out to court Reverend Sharpton in Manhattan. It was yet another example of Sharpton's staying power in the election cycle underway. On seeing the picture in the newspapers of the two men having breakfast at Sylvia's Harlem restaurant, many black Bernie loyalists initially reacted with complete disbelief. The *ick* factor was palpable. It was difficult not to feel the senator's discomfort sitting there alongside the Rev. In fact, Bernie had the posture of a westerner along the China-North Korea frontier who'd just made a wrong turn only to end up staring "Big Kim" dead in the face.

Bernie Sanders wasn't among the usual Democratic supplicants of Reverend Sharpton, quite possibly because as the senator of lily-white Vermont, he didn't have to be. His campaign might have rightfully answered critics by asking, *What was Bernie to do in the face of the avalanche of black officials who'd pledged their support to Secretary Clinton?* But given history, that couldn't have blunted the disappointment among many of the black millennials who were supporting him.

The politics of the black vote and the white politician still bear tinges of the Reconstruction era. In the aftermath of Reconstruction, the engineers of late nineteenth-century disenfranchisement of African Americans across the South had used the ease of procuring the black vote by corrupt politicians and their brokers behind pulpits and in civic organizations as the main pretext for disenfranchisement. To date, the black vote that interests all politicians come election time belongs to voters who interest few after November. As a result, it suffices for the beneficiary Democratic Party to outsource its engagement with the black community to vote-brokers like Reverend Sharpton and others, by which the party becomes chief enabler of many of these so-called black leaders whose leadership is effectively a racket.

As a result, for many Sanders supporters in the black community, the sight of the two men together was less than welcomed. They wanted to see national politicians engage directly with their communities, to speak directly to their concerns, rather than by the usual outsourcing of their engagement.

But with an eye to the upcoming primary election in South Carolina—the state where the numerical significance of blacks had given way to some of the early origins of Southern disenfranchisement—Senator Sanders was facing the same numerical significance, but of an enfranchised black primary voting bloc in the clutches of his opponent, Secretary Clinton. Bernie was neither a black man named Obama nor a white man named Clinton with a saxophone in hand. Poor Bernie was incapable of serenading black churchgoers in North Charleston on Sunday morning with the type of rhythmic catechistic whooping sermons that captivates or that might have pushed him over the top. It seemed he'd had little choice in the matter after all.

So, convinced of Reverend Sharpton's national prowess, Bernie reached out and threw a Hail Mary pass to the god of the metropolis. It was fait accompli for both. Bernie had needed a photo op with a notable black leader before heading South. With a new diet and newfound prestige, it had been a while since the Rev. had feasted at Sylvia's restaurant in Harlem; it was time for a hearty breakfast. By sitting there with Sharpton for the cameras, Bernie was telegraphing his "legitimacy" to black South Carolinians; Sharpton was telegraphing his continued ability to be a kingmaker to the Democrats.

The Pugilist

Do good when you can, and charge when
you think they will stand for it.

—MARK TWAIN[15]

*Reverend Al Sharpton confronts NYPD at Black Workers' demo in midtown, New York,
New York, August 28, 1990. (Photo by Allan Tannenbaum/Getty Images.)*

15 *More Maxims of Mark-The Wit and Wisdom of Mark Twain,* 10.

IN MY LIFETIME, black men in New York had never known an existence free of being targeted by the police. At a certain point in the 1980s, those of us in Brooklyn, Queens, Manhattan, and the Bronx, only had the Rev. to defend us—a point he has not since failed to remind us of in his books. It was, therefore, impossible to understate his presence and his importance in the boroughs back in those days. He was our fearless and dutiful servant *a la* Isaiah. The New York City Police Department's (NYPD) history of brutality against African Americans—later enshrined in infamy with names like Abner Louima, Amadou Diallo, and Sean Bell—had given the Rev. prominence and preeminence in those days. But the acts of the racist citizenry had made him equally invaluable to many of us as well.

"Subway vigilante" Bernard Goetz had unloaded a hail of bullets on suspected muggers around Christmas time during my first break from college in 1984, which had me fear to ride the subways. The victims were black youths like me. But Reverend Sharpton was there challenging Mayor Ed Koch and demanding that a jury send "Bernie" to prison. On my return home from college in Christmas 1986, New York City was rife with racial tension. The incidents were many, but the big one had surrounded the death of Michael Griffith. Griffith was a young African American who was struck and killed by a car after being chased by a group of racist white youths into oncoming traffic on a major Brooklyn parkway. When Sharpton led a march in Howard Beach, Brooklyn, to protest Griffith's death, the "distinguished" citizens gave him a payday with their grotesque and racist behavior for the camera; they showered Sharpton and the marchers with the *n*-word and watermelons.

The Rev. had already become a household name for his marches and protests when, by the end of 1987, his notoriety exploded with the Tawana Brawley affair. Ms. Brawley, a black teen from a suburban county outside of New York City, had alleged to have been raped by four white men and left defiled in feces by her attackers. As her representatives, Reverend Sharpton and two cohorts—attorneys Alton H. Maddox and C. Vernon Mason—accused an assistant district attorney in the locality of being one of the rapists and the local prosecutor's office of leading a cover-up. More importantly, though, the Rev. used the affair, later revealed to have been a hoax known to him, to bring

New York City to a near race war, in the hopes that the city would then have to negotiate with him for calm, thereby empowering and legitimizing him as a community leader.

In 1989 there was yet another racist killing—that of the earlier mentioned black teen Yusef Hawkins—by a white mob in Bensonhurst, Brooklyn. The Rev. led a January 1991 march in protest, during which a deranged man tried sending him to hell at the tip of a blade but failed miserably. It was Sharpton's moment of martyrdom, so much so that he later took pleasure in declaring forgiveness of his attacker in front of the cameras, while filing a lawsuit accusing New York City of failure to protect him—a lawsuit he settled with the city for $200,000 in 2003.

In 1990 New York State then opted for less ambitious objectives by trying to send him to prison for life, but that too failed miserably. A seventy-count indictment by the state attorney general that was meant to sideline the Rev. for a long time saw him acquitted on all sixty-seven of the more serious counts. Another three resulted in later misdemeanor pleadings.

In 1991, he was at the center of the Crown Heights riots in Brooklyn that erupted after an accident in which Jewish driver Yosef Lifsh had struck and killed a young black boy, Gavin Cato, and injured his cousin Angela. A series of events, including speculation whether the driver might have ignored the needs of the injured black children, sparked days of rioting. On his release from jail, Lifsh was spirited out of the country to Israel after a New York grand jury had failed to indict him for a crime. The circumstances added to the complexities and the tensions between the African American and Hasidic communities of Crown Heights that were exploited and recklessly stoked by the Rev. and others. The tension and spiraling violence culminated with the murder of innocent rabbinical student Yankel Rosenbaum.

Four years after that, the Rev. was a "co-sponsor" of a 1995 protest against Jewish-owned clothing store Freddie's Fashion Mart in Harlem. A rental dispute between a Jewish tenant and an African-American sub-tenant soon devolved into open verbal race-baiting by Sharpton and others. In that melee, a suicidal madman then entered Freddie's and torched the establishment, murdering several employees in the process. Many blamed Reverend Sharpton for the intensity of the incitement that led to the mayhem and murder in Harlem, but he disagreed, claiming an involvement solely as a negotiator between the disputing parties.

But as with his involvement in the Brawley affair and the Crown Heights riots, the pugilistic Reverend survived the recriminations for his involvement in Freddie's Fashion Mart to live to fight another day. Travails that might have driven others into obscurity ended up cementing his *bona fide* status as the black activist and community leader with whom to be reckoned. By the end of the 1980s and into the 1990s, he'd become a fixture in New York, confounding political and media types at all levels. He'd beaten public opinions and the long arms of the state, only to later "mainstream" himself with runs for political offices—even challenging his onetime prosecutorial nemesis, state attorney general Robert Abrams, for a Senate seat in 1992.

Departure Point

Given his long history as a societal lightning rod, it is understandable that his detractors are of one opinion while his supporters are of another. I'd started my journey as a serious Sharpton fan in the early 1980s. I first saw him around that time somewhere in downtown Brooklyn. His then massive figure seemed ideal for the monumental task of tackling the sad realities we'd faced—a mission he'd set out to undertake on our behalf, or at least that is how it had appeared to us back then. I was a black teenager living in East Flatbush, Brooklyn. After 7:00 p.m., a weekend bicycle ride to Kings Plaza was often a dangerous exercise south of Avenue D on into the Canarsie area. This was the pre-political correctness era when racism was much more overt and casual in New York City; then, no one lost his or her job or was filmed and put to shame on social media for yelling, "N-word, go home."

By the mid to late 1980s, in addition to his marches and protests, the Rev. had gotten into physical brawls with opponents on pre-reality television shows. He'd "occupied" subway tracks in the middle of Manhattan, interrupting train traffic to protest the absence of black employees in the Metropolitan Transportation Authority; and he'd fought the mayor and governor on various aspects of institutional racism in the city. A little later when I discovered that, separated by about a dozen years, he and I had also attended the same high school—Samuel J. Tilden High School in Brooklyn—I came to idolize him.

His "direct actions" weren't the civil disobedience of earlier generations of civil rights leaders but were instead brusque, in-your-face confrontations that flowed from a blunt, in-your-face personality. This had earned my adoration as a young man. Having claimed both Queens and Brooklyn as his native homes, he'd become sort of a BQE (Brooklyn-Queens Expressway) polecat—a Brooklynite who couldn't get past reminding us of his Queens nativity. Queens was considered a more upscale borough in those days.

On television, he'd obfuscated and equivocated at each turn, never backing down from a fight. Admittedly, at times when the bars of acceptable behavior were too difficult for him to scale, he merely placed them on the ground, enabling an easy walk-over to then run out and declare "decisive" victory. As he plunged in moral turpitude, he hoisted himself in moral standing—to himself. But none of that had mattered to us as young black men back then. The Rev. had become someone special for very special reasons—not least of which was the way he'd tackled the system on our behalf. Many of us had distrusted the police for the way they treated us, and he was able to articulate that distrust, while saying, *Enough is enough!*

To the extent that he was a polarizing figure, it was only to white people and a few place-holding blacks, and that had endeared him to us even more. In those days, "polarizing" had meant nothing more than opposing wanton police abuse, racial profiling, and the killing of young black men in Brooklyn and Queens and old black women like Eleanor Bumpers in the Bronx. Those who'd deemed the Rev. a polarizing figure were often the ones who didn't care about us—those who couldn't have cared less about our humanity. Many were the types who either called us the *n*-word at the drop of a hat or thought it in private anyway. They'd dismissed the Rev. as a joke at different points, but he was the joke they had to contend with. Nothing beats skunks like polecats; their scent is equally foul but where the former might be friendly and cunning, the latter are aggressive and offensive, and they always survive the test of time. The establishment had its many skunks, and we had our polecat.

Saint or Sinner?

As some of us would later discover, the Rev. was less of an activist for humankind and more of an activist for mankind Sharpton. He wasn't working for his people, as he'd always claimed but was instead working for Al Sharpton. He was a man disposed solely to elevate his stature and to empower himself, and activism was just a means to an end. For me, disgust at his more exploitative and thuggish behavior would only come many years later in adulthood, as hubris would have him treat us as the "poor lowly black folk" who might well have been obliterated and extinguished by white racism but for the grace of his presence and advocacy. We'd become his *chasse gardée*—his private hunting ground, his domain of patronage. My fascination turned to disappointment over the years, and I soon started to cost-benefit the Rev., to question whether he was a net benefit or net cost to black America. Was he a saint or sinner?

Keeping up with his activism and antics—a distinction that soon evaporated with the years—resulted in somewhat of a running profile sketched out over nearly three decades. By the time he was forty, the Rev. had been through numerous confrontations, perhaps more than most leaders in corporate America, and he'd faced them with his innate bellicosity—denying those in power the ability to stop or even to slow him down at any point. For this reason, there are few people in America with more experience in standing up, fighting back, and leading the charge (or the march), as he. But there are also few who've had as many opportunities to learn, grow, and redeem themselves, yet heeding none.

But knowledge is rarely gained from the fringes of the extreme—that natural dwelling place of emotions, having triumphed over reason. As both the well- and the mal-intended are often misconstrued, I'd set out to find out about Reverend Sharpton from Reverend Sharpton, the writer. I wasn't much interested in knowing how he felt about himself, as I knew he naturally thought himself the best thing since sliced bread, but I wanted to understand him from what he showed us through his words and thoughts. I'd seen what he'd done but still needed to hear what he'd thought. I wanted to understand him through his written testimonies and his sentiments on the totality of his experiences. As the world had watched the force of his cult personality, I'd followed what he'd put on paper. He'd become kind of an enigma to me, much like, say, a Robert Mugabe of Zimbabwe—a man who'd liberated his people from the yoke of colonial fascism and taken his country to independence, only to later impose his own form of oppressive authoritarianism on the "liberated."

Even for Sharpton's detractors, it's hard to dispute that like former president Mugabe, the Rev. was at some point very effective and might have held genuine concerns for the well-being and "freedom" of his people. But also like Mugabe, he'd shown that those with missions of freedom for their people are sometimes the least likely to want it for their masses. On closer inspection, it was in this sense that he couldn't have been more different from Robert Mugabe. Although he touted himself as such, the Rev. was never a freedom fighter. The trenches of his youth were paved with shady characters, gangsters, government informers and their handlers, recording devices, corporate and political shakedowns, power-driven protest marches and rallies, fake political campaigns, endorsement hustles, and personal ambitions for which nefarious machinations and subterfuge were often breakfast, lunch, and dinner.

The Rev. had done so much to tarnish his stated aims over the years that it made me want to find out what really drove him. What had happened to the Reverend Al I'd admired as a young man? What were his real motivations and inspirations? Was he in it for fame, fortune, or just for power and personal aggrandizement? But just as important, I needed to understand how he was able to rise atop black leadership and gain "respectability," given all that I had discovered about him.

The Sadist

<hr>

Man was made at the end of a week's work, when God was tired.

—MARK TWAIN[16]

IN HIS BOOK, *The Art of Loving*, German psychologist and writer Dr. Erich Fromm tells us that sadism (domination) is the active form of symbiotic fusion—the passive form being the submission (masochism) through which we escape our aloneness and sense of imprisonment. Key to sadistic conduct is making others part and parcel of themselves, thereby enhancing and inflating their self-image at the expense of others.[17] While this is generally thought of in the context of sexual relationships, sadists are more than often movement leaders—political, religious, and cult leaders, who command by customs, doctrines, laws, or religious edicts. They thrive on the masochistic submission of constituents or adherents driven to submit out of their fears, emptiness, fanaticism, frustrations, meaninglessness, desires for self-renunciation, fervent hope, and so on. It's the messiah complex in those who command submission.

For community, movement, and political leaders, the holding out of a utopian future ensures constituent idolatry that fuels their sadism. For preachers, they hold out the keys to a promised land, to rebirth, and to "paradise" that attracts the submissive flock who regards them as prophets, as reincarnations, as messiahs, or as God's representatives on earth, through which they, in turn, fuel their sadism. For the celebrity preachers bereft of pulpit and submissive

<hr>

16 *Notebook - The Wit and Wisdom of Mark Twain*, 1.

17 Erich Fromm, *The Art of Loving* (1954; repr., Continuum International Publishing Group, 2000), 18.

flock, it's the mental incorporation of those around them—public figures and celebrities they know, through whose association they inflate and enhance their image of themselves in order to fuel their sadism. As Eric Hoffer tells us, all are seeking full renunciation of, and death to, the miserable and meaningless self.

Crafting Fiction

The sadist doesn't just command an audience through fusional fiction; he or she often insists on writing and articulating real fiction as well. I first read a Sharpton book, then as an ardent fan back in the late 1990s. Three books later—with three different points of view, three different target audiences, three different messages to convey, three different purposes to serve, and with three entirely different Al Sharptons to contend with—I was able to sketch a summary composite beyond the piecemeal love-hate, friend-foe prism through which the Rev. is known to the public. The difficulty was figuring out which best approximated the real Reverend Sharpton. At times, he seemed no less than a multipurpose, multi-headed hydra out to devour all in his path, while at other times, a single purpose-driven machine disposed solely of the need for approbation and acceptance from the white society he often vilifies—largely a function of self-renunciation through a desire for assimilation. The former, readily observed over time while the latter has been an infinitely tricky labyrinth to navigate, starting with life as a child preacher.

In the first place, the Rev. sought adulation, respectability, and acceptance, after which he sought fame and money. This then gave way to status and power, which then saw him back to a visceral hunt for money to support the lifestyle of his newly found status. 2013's *Stone*, for example, was the work of a bloviating buffoon who wasted much ink telling us not to envy his first-class flights and dinners in fancy restaurants, because he'd now deserved it. Accordingly, it was his time.

Key to the buffoonery, though, was a brilliant talent for crafting fiction while presenting it as nonfictional and autobiographical. Take this fantastic story, told as a matter of fact in *Pharaoh*, of an event that had obviously not taken place: After being indicted and charged, the Rev.'s big tax trial had come to an end on July 2, 1990, when a jury had acquitted him. Less certain, though, was the outcome for the poor black man he'd encountered, whose fate was left in the mouth of a howling dog:

> Maddox [his attorney] asked for an immediate trial, and we had to decide wheth-
> er to hold the New York City or Albany one first. This led to our returning to
> Albany one day, and while we sat in the courtroom, waiting to see Judge Turner,
> there was another trial going on, a black man accused of some crime. The black
> man was sitting there with a white defense attorney in front of an all-white jury
> being prosecuted by a white prosecutor, and they call as a witness a white cop
> and a dog from the canine squad. The prosecutor would ask the cop a question,
> and then the cop would ask the dog, and the dog would howl once for "Yes"
> and two howls for "No." I looked at Maddox and said, "If I'm in a place where a
> black man can be put in jail on the word of a dog, then I'll take my chances in
> Manhattan.[18]

With the entire New York political establishment trying to send him to prison, the Rev. showed us a court process that was set up to ensure maximum harassment by forcing him to shuttle between Manhattan and Albany (145 miles) for court appearances. He was facing charges in Manhattan and indictments in Albany. But it was the howling-dog incident that made him eventually request a trial in Manhattan rather than upstate.

That a black man might have spent even a night in jail on the basis of a dog's howl had completed Sharpton's portrayal of an uncivilized and racist America willing to stop at nothing to incarcerate African Americans. But as there was no record of Reverend Sharpton ever leading a protest to prevent the use of howling dogs as witnesses against blacks anywhere in the state of New York, there was no need to research Supreme Court rulings on the issue. His were the real talents of a humorist at work. But in this case, the comedic construction had a single flaw: Sharpton had forgotten to tell us that the dog was white as well. After all, if a dog were being used to put away black men,

---

18 Al Sharpton and Walton, *Go and Tell Pharaoh*, 148.

that would've been the equivalent of the all-white Southern jury, meaning the howling dog would have to have been white and racist as well.

A few years back, a friend asked me, "How did Al Sharpton become Al Sharpton?" She was as surprised at his ascendance as many in the silent black majority who've long regarded him as a buffoon. But I was not; I retrieved *Pharaoh* and showed her the story of the howling dog. "There!" I said. "That's how!"

Diagnoses

From the Rev's early writings, we saw the *psychosis of deficiencies* at work. He was busy compensating for inadequacies across the psychological spectrum. There were the typical elements that have kept psychologists, psychiatrists, and social philosophers occupied since the days of Sigmund Freud: supreme aspirations, delusions of grandeur, hubris, narcissism, aggression, ingratiation, low tolerance for ambiguity, and an insecurity that drives frequent mean-spirited attacks on detractors. Today, a dysfunctional youth is still the owner of much retail space in a supremely dysfunctional adult—the likely result of maladaptation and an affective-deficient childhood and bearing all the signs of hatred for a miserable and undesired "self."

The Rev.'s first significant book, *Pharaoh* was a collection of grandiose embellishments and outright fiction that enhanced him vis-à-vis those famous people incorporated into his orbit. That mental incorporation of others had created what Dr. Fromm had described as *fusion without integrity*, meaning just for selfish motives. Most of this was easily recognizable but enjoyable to read—precisely for those very reasons. Nonetheless, it read like the work of a sadist.

That late 1990s "messenger" to *Pharaoh* was a rabble-rousing blowhard determined to kick the feet out from under any table where he'd felt denied a place. *Pharaoh* was also an overt attack on the black bourgeoisie, the elite black political establishment, its principal institutional agents—the National Association for the Advancement of Colored People (NAACP), the National Urban League—and even on the civil rights movement and its leaders, in particular, Dr. Martin Luther King Jr. As a man of forty-two, the Rev. had held up a spotlight for us to witness the spectacle of an empty vessel attempting to belittle and reduce others around him and some who'd come before him, to elevate himself and to make himself appear more substantial. He'd made significant efforts to frame his life in historical perspectives, giving us a Jesus-like childhood that had placed him amid important people and at the center of magnanimous events. He then gave us an adulthood in which others were generally juxtaposed next to him in ancient *Manichean* terms: his enemies and detractors were invariably nefarious white devils or devious black sell-outs, while he remained the sole bright light, guided by purity in service to *his people* and their causes.

Pharaoh was *Infallible Al*, as it was all about legitimizing indefensible past behaviors—none of which he'd seen as indefensible. At one point, he recalled an appearance on the 1980s-era *Phil Donahue Show*. I didn't see the show, but even in reading about it many years later, I got goosebumps recalling the days when the Rev. was "the man"—the days when I'd also seen his black critics as treasonous sell-outs. Like many, I'd believed, hook, line, and sinker, the Brawley story of abduction and rape by white racists:

> On the Phil Donahue Show, Phil Donahue said to me, "How can you possibly believe that these men you've accused could do such a thing?" And I pointed out to the crowd and said, "How can you ask me that, when you are sitting in a church with five hundred black people and every one of us has a different complexion? Where did that come from? How could I not think it possible that white men might rape black women?"[19] What I don't think that most white people understand was that there is some Tawana in most black people, almost like a collective memory, as Jung described it, that corresponds to the event.[20]

Who would or could have argued with this? The history of slave rape in the feudal slavocracy of the American South is well known, though insufficiently documented. Property ownership had conferred rights to do whatever, including rape, beat, torture, and to trade. Multitudes of women were indeed thrown into workhouses, beaten, humiliated, and yes, raped, for refusing the master's conjugal visits. There's also a valid argument that conduct under bondage can

---

19 Ibid., 136.
20 Ibid.

never be of free will, but that's judging by today's standards and not by the standards of times when the deprivation of civil recognition and rights of sub humanization were the law of the land. But the sad truth is that as products of miscegenation (the once-prohibited interracial relations), not all mixed-race blacks were the result of slave rape; some were indeed the result of consensual conjugal visits. Some black women had embraced this aspect of antebellum life and had willingly availed themselves as mistresses and concubines to white masters—a phenomenon that would have a profound impact on the future black race and culture in America and beyond, in both skin-tone gradation, physical attributes, and behavioral attitudes.

In fact, the first criterion of the early black gentry in the enslaved and colonized world was the presence of white blood in the veins, much of which was the result of voluntary nighttime integration that elevated the status of the black women involved and of the offspring of such unions. In *Pharaoh*, Reverend Sharpton himself didn't fail to remind us of the white blood flowing through his own veins from none other than Confederate hero Robert E. Lee:

> My mother is fair-skinned...There was a legend in my mother's family that my great-grandmother Minnie was the slave child of General Robert E. Lee. We grew up believing we had this Confederate general's blood in us. I've sometimes thought that might account for the extremely light skin color of some of my mother's people.[21]

Cohabitation between owners and slaves was sometimes based on mutual attraction. At other times, it was based on the conferred status and privilege from the perceived prestige to the real tangible advantages of free movement, housework instead of fieldwork, better food and clothing, having "mulatto" children, and above all, the prospects of freedom for the women and their biracial children (manumission). By the mid-eighteenth century, it was a way of life across much of the South. In Louisiana, for example, the planters' mulatto concubines and mistresses had become so influential that in 1786 the Spanish governor, Esteban Rodriguez Miró, in an effort to curb their

---

21 Ibid., 18.

prestige, had barred them by decree (Tignon Laws) from wearing jewels and feathers in their hair when they came into town. Unfortunately, it was an early form of "slut-shaming" that had painted all black women who'd adorned themselves in the popular fashions of the era as indecent, which had then led to a revolt by black women of all stripes, who'd taken it as a badge of honor and endearment.

The Octoroons, Quadroons, and other mixed-race classes of the era had formed a new and proud mulatto aristocracy—the "Free Men of Color." In fact, the New Orleans region had become a mecca for fellow mulattos fleeing a revolutionary and predominantly black-African Saint Domingue, leading up to and in the aftermath of its 1804 independence declaration to become the country of Haiti. Mixed race counterparts in places like North Charleston, South Carolina, had their "Brown Men's" clubs, where they practiced their own form of segregation from, and oppression of, dark-skinned blacks—even engaging in commercial slave buying and trading for profit—a historical fact that most mainstream black scholars are still loathed to accept.

More importantly, though, the ban on interracial marriage in America (up until 1960s Supreme Court decision in *Loving v. Virginia*) wasn't to prevent white slave owners from raping or from marrying their slaves to rape them. Nor was it, for that matter, to prevent black men from marrying white women—then, a life-threatening act. It was solely to prevent voluntary marriages between white men and black women, from fear of the emergence of a so-called "mongrel race" that had posed a threat to white purity, white numerical dominance, and white supremacy, especially in places like South Carolina and Louisiana where blacks were numerically significant.

So, the sad truth is that the rape narrative commonly admitted isn't the sole means of the African's evolution into a race of many gradients but an acceptable narrative that avoids dealing with an unpleasant aspect of a murky history. In fact, this was not unique to American slavery but has been a phenomenon of African evolution since the Portuguese first set up shop on Africa's west coast around the early 1440s. But putting the rape narrative forward is always a winning argument because, in the macro sense, it was indeed true on a large scale. But in this case, putting it forward to legitimize the Brawley hoax of kidnap and rape that he'd used to fuel a near race war in New York was an example of

Reverend Sharpton's tactical brilliance. We all ate it up. What white or black person would've dared to argue such facts against him on national TV, especially in a studio audience of African Americans?

The Rev. knew this very well; he's best at quick hits and catch-phrases. He also knows a winning argument when he has one. Referencing Carl Jung's "Collective Memory Theory" to reinforce the point had simply pulled us all emotionally into the raping of Ms. Brawley. At once, he touched all black women in America and all the black men who cared about them. For those who'd doubted the events, Sharpton's message was clear: *Tawana Brawley is your mother, your aunt, your sister, your niece, your cousin, your daughter!* Her experience was "slave-creep" threatening to overrun black America anew. So, we all had an obligation to support her (him) in the fight against this scourge before it happened to one of our women. He was really appealing to the audience, saying in effect, *These racist white men were doing what they've always done to our women because they've always gotten away with it. They were still raping our black women!*

Brooklyn's Beguiled

Reverend Sharpton has had a natural style of drawing parallels between himself and great religious figures like Jesus and Moses, with enough in-depth details that are as compelling and persuasive as they're fictional. It was almost the telling of the Sharpton story by the evangelists Matthew, Mark, Luke, and John—predicated on the social status he momentarily sought at the time of writing.

Pharaoh was his Gospel of Mark (the original story, according to most scholars), in which the quasi-Pharisaic Reverend Sharpton—like Jesus up against the Sanhedrin—was up against the genteel Sadducaic establishment of feckless black elites, their institutions, and their Democratic Party sponsors (the Romans). The Rev. had written it when society—both fans and detractors alike—had viewed him as a buffoon, and it showed. He'd paid little attention to how he was perceived and had set out to laugh at those who'd mistakenly thought he should have. Speaking of the white Democratic political machine in New York that had attempted to thwart his attempt at a statewide run, he said,

> They never thought I would become a force they would have to reckon with. But how could they? I was a fool, a Buffon without a serious thought in my skull. They were so busy calling me fat and mocking my hair (something I mocked myself, another thing that no one noticed) they never noticed that I had won a partial victory against Bernard Goetz, clear cut victories in Howard Beach and Bensonhurst, and even in the controversy of the Brawley affair, I hadn't backed down.[22]

2002's *Al on America* was his Gospels of Matthew and Luke combined, building on the Mark story but with a few updates and replete with imaginative and incisive embellishments. It was an affirmation of the Messiah in our midst—the one with gravitas and with enough crossover appeal to become president of the United States in 2004. It was a *Pharaoh* redux, but with the softening edge of a man with a different agenda and target audience in mind. Then, he was seeking a crossover mainstream appeal, and this was a book written for a white audience. Here, he distanced himself from, and eviscerated, his previous heroes. At the same time, he dropped his critique of Dr. King and instead embraced him. As African Americans were unlikely to run out and buy a Sharpton book, they were likely to remain oblivious to what he'd had to say to white people about them, and the Rev. knew it. So, with much introspection and criticism of the black community, he attempted to charm the socks off white America, after having told them to go to hell six years earlier in *Pharaoh*.

His third book, 2013's *Stone*, was his Gospel of John, the pure non-synoptic Reverend Al. It is a combined *Pharaoh* and *Al on America* redux, tinged with updates sourced from completely different times—the Obama era. It's laced with new idols and mentors, in keeping with the times of the now progressive

---

22 Ibid., 213.

and enhanced Reverend Sharpton. It's effectively the presentation of a "Made Man"—cocksure in a sort of messianic way: once cast away as a *rejected stone* but now returned as the indisputable savior to lead his people out of the wilderness. We should recall that some scholars believe that the evangelist John might have written Revelations as well.

But the messianic Al was also the picture he had writer James McBride complete in a whimsical Sharpton depiction in McBride's 2016 book on singer James Brown. Whether taken from Matthew 21, Mark 12, Luke 20, Acts 4, 1 Peter 2, or Psalm 118, the Rev. has always seen himself as the stone that the builder had wrongly refused. He told us that, like Jesus, he was the *rejected stone* that ultimately became the chief cornerstone, hence the full title of the book— *The Rejected Stone: Al Sharpton and the Path to American Leadership.*

Nonetheless, *Stone* is Reverend Sharpton at the pinnacle of success and power, moved by the momentous change in the country and draped in the ascendance of the first black president of the United States. Here we had the nexus of low emotional intelligence, high-hubris, and supreme narcissism manifest to produce an acute lack of self-awareness that obliterated the bounds of credulity in the stories told. Marking a note of distinction between the present and the past, the Rev., oblivious to the irony of a perpetually insane and vain condition, spoke of those good ole days when "vanity got the better of my sanity."

Written in his effort to legitimize himself as an accepted political insider in the Obama era, he was consistent in claiming responsibility for various advancements in black America over the years. He was also consistent in his life's goal to be part of the black elites he'd once vilified and consistent in his pursuit of acceptance by the white establishment—its patrons and power brokers. Most important, he also showed his paramount lifelong objective—to establish himself as the next Reverend Jesse Jackson. While making mea culpa for his old life as a buffoon, he was also consistent in blaming his father for a broken childhood and an irreparable manhood as well.

As he boasted of his newfound status, he shared his belief that it was high time for others to get in line and kiss his sizably reduced posterior. *Stone* showed Sharpton's extensive efforts to make himself appear suitable for his new role of a respectable statesman, but instead, it ended up resonating the scream of an almost cartoonish character, yelling, *I'm still the same old buffoon.* His many decades in the public eye had had less to do with improvements in the condition of his people than with improvements in Al Sharpton's conditions, and he'd felt confident enough to tell us, *Begrudge me not!*

While we all mature, develop differences in tastes and preferences, recognize the errors of our youth, adopt different social, religious, and political ideologies and affiliations, this wasn't the case with the Rev. His has been a maturation in opportunism. His life, as presented in his books, has been somewhat of a purified reincarnation—not the mere shedding of the skin by a snake but the genetic engineering and birth of an entirely new and enhanced species, from say, a python in one book to an enhanced cobra in another.

In the end, it painted a picture of black America's de facto leader as mentally unwell, which might have also been a metaphor for contemporary black America as well—if indeed Reverend Sharpton were indeed its leader.

Moving Targets

Before exhaustion had set in, it was fun to read his moving and changing realities through time as his circumstances changed. With each successive book, he ignored the previous one, as if he'd neither lived the past nor once or twice written about it. The same stories were told, but differently, at times even attributing the same dialogues to different people. He wrote of mentors in one book while denying them in another. As they fell out of favor with history, they fell out of favor with the Rev. As others, including his enemies, came into favor and power with time, they came into favor with him. His *pharaonic* heroes (1996's *Pharaoh*) were African American strong men he'd claimed as mentors and role models, men who were his idea of greatness, men who had the public adulation for which he'd yearned. This included Pan-African nationalist Marcus Garvey, former Harlem congressman Adam Clayton Powell Jr., and civil rights leader Reverend Jesse Jackson, whom Sharpton had then claimed as a surrogate father.

Six years later, though, in *Al on America*, he eschewed the high-octane testosterone-driven black men and ran to Dr. King. A decade later in *Stone*, he went even further by exculpating himself for his youthful indiscretions in admiring his original heroes who were no longer *en vogue*. As a near six-ty-year-old man, he then finally added women to his repertoire, presenting us with Sharpton the life-long progressive—barely missing out on Susan B. Anthony and Mother Mary Jones as his youthful heroines. Marriage equality had yet to become the law of the land, so at the time of writing *Stone*, Harvey Milk had also missed out on being mentioned as a Sharpton childhood hero. But stay tuned for his next book.

In vehemently castigating black elites, black politicians, the NAACP, the National Urban League, and their principal sponsor, the Democratic Party, the Rev. of *Pharaoh* had accused them of fecklessness, excoriated them for not recognizing his greatness, and blamed them for having persecuted him in one way or another over the years. But that was before getting into the club. With his rise atop the black elite establishment by the writing of *Stone*, he became the prime defender of the NAACP and the National Urban League and an outspoken siren for the Democratic Party. As a reader of his books, it was sheer comedy seeing him on television denying and disavowing his past self—at least, as he'd written it.

I've already mentioned his infinitely different versions of the same lessons learned from his male mentors to support arguments in one book while render-ing them baseless in supporting different ones in another. But most memorable is that, in one section of a book, he placed himself on location sixty-four hun-dred miles away for an event, only to put himself at home for that same event in another section of the same book, for the sole purpose of associating himself with two different celebrities at the same time.

He'd opened *Pharaoh* with a comical take on his own career as an activist, claiming to have taken many risks that could've damaged his career, such as en-gaging the political process—that dreaded tightrope through which charlatans and scoundrels alike elevate their public profile in American politics. But note how he pretty much told us who he thought he was, albeit ascribing it to the media:

The next year, in 1992, I ran as a candidate for the United States Senate in the New York Democratic primary. In many ways, I risked my career to do so,

because the media painted me as a loudmouth, a walking sound bite, a con artist, a charlatan, and worst of all, an imposter, with no real constituency and no
true issues, a self-created media manipulator.[23]

A few pages later in the same book, he reiterated this by telling us that it was his
need to act out of "resolve" that made him enter electoral politics:

After I was stabbed, I decided to try to begin acting out of resolve, out of an
overall plan, to become proactive, that's why I entered electoral politics: I realized that running around from problem to problem, chasing phone call after
phone call, would never move society. We have to change the broad socioeco-
nomic conditions in this society and will require change in the body politic.[24]

Six years later, in 2002's *Al on America*, he took umbrage at any suggestion that
he was unqualified to run for president or that he should consider running for
local office instead:

To even question why I'm running is insulting. Pundits ask me why not run for
Congress [*sic*] or local office, an office they say I might have a better chance of
winning. That question, too, is insulting. If I'm good enough for Congress, why
aren't I good enough for the highest office?[25]

In the opening of the same book, he'd told us why America had needed him as
president:

The next leader for this country must be able to look at all America and see her
for what she will become and then work tirelessly to see her become it. I am that
leader.[26]

---

23 Ibid., 2.
24 Ibid., 3.
25 Sharpton with Hunter, *Al on America*, 5.
26 Ibid., xix.

Toward the end of that same book, he told us, "If I win this next race [the presidency]—and I am running to win. That's what I'll be [*meaning* "president"]."[27] Yet a few paragraphs before the passage above, he'd recalled his meetings with his buddies, Congressman Gregory Meeks and former New York governor David Paterson, back in the old days to discuss their public roles:

> Their job was to go inside the system. Mine was to help set a climate so they could operate inside that system. My job has been to try to create a climate around issues like police brutality so they could create police brutality legislature. But if they did what I did, they couldn't get inside to make laws. They couldn't get elected.[28]

In other words, although writing an entire book telling us of his qualifications to be, and of his seriousness about becoming president, the Rev. started by telling us that he was unelectable, yet taking umbrage a few passages later at anyone who would question his electability. In 2013's *Stone* he came clean about his fake political campaigns, affirming the validity of the very criticisms he'd once decried and implied to have been racist. But in doing so, he masked his motivations under his usual guise of running "issues campaigns."

> I never aspired to be a politician. I saw running for office as a way of bringing issues that had been marginalized into the mainstream. It's part of the job of an activist...So I ran for US Senate, I ran for mayor, I ran for president. I never ran to win. If I actually wanted to hold office, I could have run for seats that were more attainable.[29]

In one moment, he told us he risked his career to enter politics, and in another, he entered politics to further what looked very much like a career—but out of "resolve." Finally, in his third book, he showed that his real reasons had to do

---

27 Ibid., 201–2.

28 Ibid., 201.

29 Al Sharpton with Chiles, *The Rejected Stone*, 126.

with neither resolve nor risk-taking but purely out of opportunism. Depending on the particular social ladder he'd sought to climb at the time of writing, his rhetorical objectives varied. Additionally, his appropriation of the same events across time into vastly different versions suitable to new circumstances and new audiences often took on historical or even biblical proportions. If by rhetorical design, it's fair to say that not since first-century writers like Flavius Josephus—who'd given us differing versions of the same events in *War of the Jews*, *Jewish Antiquities*, *Life of Josephus*, and *Against Apion*—have we seen such a deft appropriation of the same subject matters across different books.

It Started in Babel

———~———

Circumstances make man, not man circumstances.

—Mark Twain[30]

A KEY FEATURE of adaptation under American slavery was the idealization of the white master (and by extension, of his wife and children), who, while often feared and loathed for his brutality, was nonetheless the protector of his merchandise. While less so among the masses, we still see this in black leadership and in middle-class black America—both in perpetual search for approbation and acceptance in their efforts to assimilate. For both, the social interpretation of success and *equality* just means a certain level of denial of identity and self, validated by a feeling of acceptance by white America. Fortunately for both, dissonance and denial have also been key features of their adaptation.

But adaptation has also manifested another critical feature—the disparagement of the black male, who posed a threat to the white master's relationship and omnipotent role in the black woman's life.[31] Many will dispute this, but the truth is that much of the neurosis in black familial life today can be traced back to any number of these and other factors of our cultivation out of slavery. The disparagement of the black male, for example, has been so mainstreamed in the contemporary black culture that at times, he has just resigned himself to live up to what is "expected" of him.

In the Sharpton household, Alfred Sharpton Sr. had lived up to, and even surpassed, such expectations—so much so that his son's contempt for him drove

---

30 *Notebook - The Wit and Wisdom of Mark Twain,* 2.

31 Abraham Kardiner and Lionel Ovesey, *The Mark of Oppression* (W. W. Norton, 1951), 46.

44

the junior Sharpton, as a fifty-nine-year-old man, to use a segment of his book to negate the entire existence of the black male as a factor in the evolution of the black culture in America. Although it was also a disingenuous attempt to show the Rev.'s progressive credentials by putting forward his support for the new "non-nuclear" family, it highlighted the folly of a black America that arrogates itself to whites in the social realm. White single parents are often more affluent, and their children do not face the same social perils as the average inner city black child raised by a single mother.

Yet in 2013's *Stone*, the Rev. declared the two-parent black family in America a myth—something that has never existed. He then went to great lengths to tell us that black fathers were never needed while showing the dysfunction caused by the absence of his own father in his young life. To support his belief, Sharpton then dug up a now outdated yet still partly relevant 1965 report, written when he was about eleven—"The Negro Family"—issued by the then assistant secretary of labor, Daniel Patrick Moynihan. He attacked its position that "at the heart of the deterioration of the fabric of Negro society is the deterioration of the Negro family. It is the fundamental source of the weakness of the Negro community at the present time"[32]:

> I was born in the middle of the twentieth century, and I grew up in a Brooklyn community surrounded by kids who came from single-parent families…My mother, Ada Sharpton raised me on strong family values with no father in the home; most of my friends in Brooklyn had strong family values and came out of so-called broken homes…we may have come out of broken homes, but we didn't have broken families.[33]

While many—in particular, bourgeois black intellectuals who are yet to accept or value the family structure as requisite in building strong communities—have attacked the Moynihan report over the decades for a variety of reasons, in Sharpton's attack, we could see the opposite of what he was trying to convey. We could see how fundamental are the events of childhood and the level of

---

32 Al Sharpton with Chiles, *The Rejected Stone*, 46.
33 Ibid., 65.

affectivity nurtured or hindered. We could see that, in his case, cultivating a well-balanced boy in a two-parent home would've been infinitely easier than the insurmountable task of fixing a maladaptive adult male later in life. The Rev. created a "straw man"—that two-parent homes were solely the purview of white America and not of his own people—against which to argue for no reason at all. He told us, "By using the white family and white society as his point of comparison, Moynihan essentially missed the fundamental truth of black American life: Black success has always derived [*sic*] from community, not family."[34]

It was indeed, the *ebonics* (black ignorance) of sociology by a man deep in the throes of ignorance. His community has been weakened because it's been ravaged by single-parents having to struggle to raise children in complex and challenging modern environments. But Sharpton chose to give legitimacy to anecdotal stereotypes and the permissible nonscientific racism of earlier times— primarily that social differences in society have roots in biological differences (inferiorities) of the races, which then drive differences in social behaviors:

> I've never known a time when we didn't have serious issues in the black family... As Moynihan pointed out correctly, much of it emanated from our history. It was against the law for my great-grandfather to name his children after himself and to marry his wife legally. So when was this period of the thriving black families? It certainly wasn't during slavery, when the idea of the black family by law couldn't even exist. Was it during Reconstruction, when the first generation could marry legally? I don't think so.[35]

We've had decades of psychological evidence (from Fromm and many others) that shows that while a mother's unconditional love comforts a child and shapes its inner world—giving it a sense of being, a sense of existence, and a sense of security, a father's conditional love shapes its perception of the outer world—providing it the basis for external thought, knowledge, and discipline, which are all required for social integration and future adaptation within our patriarchal system. Fathers' love mimics the larger society, which holds strong individual expectations,

---

34 Ibid., 64.

35 Ibid., 64–65.

especially of its male members. Like society at large, fathers impose conditions on the child in exchange for affection. But in black America, even in the face of dire decadence that rots the very fabric of society, many still insist on clinging to ignorance; they insist on feeling rather than thinking, unable to get beyond the frontier of sensitivity. The Rev., therefore, took it upon himself to champion ignorance.

So, back on the farm, we had the race leader of a community that sees upwards of seventy percent of children being born to single mothers in some areas, declaring the father's role and his own—as the father of two daughters—irrelevant in black America. His maladaptation as a child then forced the adult to go way back into slavery to advance perplexingly idiotic ideas, while once more making false claims on a sketchy history to support generalized ignorance. Besides, by referencing slavery to support his argument, Sharpton had inadvertently advanced the demagogic comparisons implied by white racists who often dare to suggest that social conditions for blacks were better during slavery.

But to the Rev.'s dismissal of fathers itself, it's not just that the normalization of the single-parent home is debilitating to black women who struggle to raise children without fathers, but that the overall disastrous result of absent fathers across black America is quite evident for the world to see. Many things—from losing value for education, gang-memberships, criminal involvements, the emasculation of young men, the masculinization of young women, dysfunctional sexual relationships to many other inter-familial neuroses—can sometimes be traced back to the normalized absence of fathers. By emasculation, I mean to point out the numerous sons who grow up with no sense of male civic responsibility or paternal instincts. By masculinization, I am speaking of the countless daughters who grow up with paternal prejudices—having no value for the male's relationships with their children and thereby assuming the attitude that they can be both mother and father. Excluded here are the single mothers who have no choice in the matter, having been forced to take on the responsibilities of both, in the absence of useless fathers. But in the broader context, both men and women who are the victims of this element of black decadence are then destined to bequeath vicious cycles of intra-familial dysfunctionalities to their children as their lasting legacies.

Although I had taken it for granted, I realized the importance of my own role as a father in my son Romain's life when he was about nine years old. I had to take a plane and then rent a car to go see him perform in his school play while he was away at boarding school. I'd arrived late and didn't want to make a commotion to reach my seat in the parents' section up front, so I stood in the back and watched him on stage. I could see that he was distressed and distracted as he performed. He kept on looking over at his mother sitting there in the parent section, and she would wave to him. But I knew that wasn't the reason he'd kept on glancing over at her; he was looking at my empty seat next to her. After a few minutes I thought, *what the hell!* I pushed my way forward, caused a little commotion, and took my seat. I had my camera in hand pointed at the stage, clicking away as I moved forward, and was able to capture a blurry picture of the smile on his face once he'd seen me. At the end of the performance, the parents went backstage, and Romain rushed by his mother straight over to me, grabbed my feet, and buried his head between my legs while crying. I picked him up and told him his performance was great, and I asked him why he was crying. "Papa," he said. "I thought you weren't going to come." Even though I'd arrived, the thought that I might not have shown up had still overwhelmed and saddened him.

Although our individual personal experiences do not make for scientific facts, can anyone in civil society really doubt the importance of both parents in a child's life? Above all else, the single-parent / absent-father phenomenon is an acute form of tyranny exacted on children in any society—to experience life bereft of fatherly or motherly love and guidance, either from not knowing their fathers or mothers or from having either parent absent and not playing any role in the children's lives. The absent father phenomenon is particularly acute in the black community. Yet as a black leader, the Rev. used his book to advocate decadence by effectively sending a message to absent black fathers that their behavior is the norm to be expected. To black mothers who see no value in paternal relationships—for themselves or their children, once they're no longer involved with the fathers—he also told them that this is a norm to be expected.

As further proof that there had never been such a thing as the two-parent black family, the Rev. cited his great-grandfather's prohibition from legally marrying his wife. But this was Sharpton seeking to legitimize himself in the eyes of an ignorant choir—those unaware that while this was true during certain stages of slavery, at other stages, African Americans did indeed marry and do have a history of strong two-parent families. Although marriages were then restricted, it was still important to the religious and social integrative beliefs of the itinerant black community.

Additionally, once the Northern abolitionists had gained traction with Christian arguments of the devastation wreaked on the enslaved, many plantation owners had even cynically countered by allowing some proliferation of marriages, which was the most "Christian" of traditions. Beyond that, though, through the middle of the 20th century, African American rates of marriage were on par with, and in some cases, had exceeded, rates of marriage in white America. But then hardly anyone in their right mind would argue a point in 2013 and use standards of slavery to support it.

But slave marriage and two-parent black families seemed the least of Reverend Sharpton's concern in writing this. His discussion was really the abnegation of the father of whom he'd felt deprived. At the same time, he was currying favor with that segment of the wealthy progressive white community that embraces, as a concept, the inutility of two-parent families. Much like the criminal born into a life and environment of crime who grows up to believe that everyone is a criminal at heart or the thief who thinks that everyone else steals as he does, the Rev. took the social functioning of his home life and that of his limited social milieu as the norm. This led him to express himself accordingly: *I never had a father, most of my friends didn't have any; so they don't exist; they don't matter!* But here again, it's worth reminding that this is from a man who is a father to two daughters.

Abandonment and Resentment

Not only had his father abandoned the family but the elder Sharpton had also absconded with his stepdaughter (the Rev.'s half-sister)—his wife's first child by a previous marriage, who was also carrying his child:

> My father abandoning my family when I was nine was one of the most devastating and consequential events of my childhood. It also instilled in me a desire to break the generational curse of father abandonment that haunts so many families, particularly in the African-American community.[36]

This incestuous family upheaval obliterated the middle-class life of a big Hollis, Queens home with new Cadillacs in the garage each year. It sent the young

---

36 Ibid., 15.

Reverend and his mother to live in the projects in Brooklyn, which he, having known what it was like to have regular municipal services in Hollis, had resented:

> What bothered me about moving to the ghetto wasn't that I was going to an all-black situation. I'd known that in the church and enjoyed and respected it. The troubling thing was that I knew from living in Hollis Queens, what it was like living in a community where the garbage was picked up on time, where the police would come when you called, where hospitals took care of you in the emergency room...I think that is why Marcus Garvey and Adam Clayton Powell and later Martin Luther King captivated me so.[37]

We might infer here that Garvey, Powell, and King, unlike the wider black community, had appreciated the value of on-time garbage pickup, prompt police response, and adequate hospitals. The "all-black situation," as he termed it, was a clear indication that in spite of his declared comfort with them in church, and his future lifelong toil in their service, the Rev. wasn't at all thrilled to live among fellow African Americans in his decidedly black housing project in Brooklyn. Moving to black Brooklyn from presumably mixed Hollis, Queens had left him with as much disdain for his father as it had for his new circumstances there:

> And I couldn't believe the conditions that black people not only lived in but accepted as inevitable in the projects. I knew better...I had lived on the other side of the tracks, at least the other side of the black tracks...And I knew that what we were getting in the projects and on Lincoln Place meant we were getting, quite frankly, shafted, because I had seen better, with my own eyes. I hadn't heard about better. I hadn't read about being better; I had lived better...I've always felt that I deserved better than what was proffered because I had known a more fulfilling, more satisfying, more rewarding life.[38]

---

37 Al Sharpton and Walton, *Go and Tell Pharaoh*, 36.
38 Ibid., 36–37.

Nothing is wrong with embracing natural aspirations of wanting a good life or a better one in the pursuit of happiness, and we couldn't help feeling some pity for the young boy, even as he related the story in adulthood. How awful it must have been to have been around so many black folks in that "all-black situation"? But this discomfort wasn't all that unusual. While the Rev. is often a master of the incoherent thought, the ignorance of his own history prevented him from seeing that he was showing the usual affliction of being black in America at a certain time.

As late as the mid-twentieth century, black America was awash in overt self-hatred and internal prejudices based on skin-tone gradients and numerical concentration in certain areas. The pressures of assimilation were then out in the open. In *The Mark of Oppression* (1951), a psychosocial study of black communities of that era, psychoanalysts Abraham Kardiner and Lionel Ovesey pointed to the shame and self-esteem crisis among many African Americans, brought on by living among their fellow brothers and sisters in Harlem. One subject studied had stated,

> I resented being a Negro in a Negro neighborhood. It was such a contrast from having lived in a good building in the Bronx and having gone to a good school. I will never forget how horrible that first night in Harlem was…I hated it, and I rejected it completely. I'll tell you what Harlem represents to me. It represents, "these are your people."[39]

The writers saw this as resulting from the struggle for status, which in every way, shape, and form, sums up the Sharpton life. But in all fairness, it's still a phenomenon of contemporary life, albeit one that's denied. Without knowing his past, though, the Rev. had divulged a present state of mind that was the seeds harvested from that very past. Simply speaking, he'd resented being black and living in a black neighborhood—purely a symptom of the struggle for adaptation and assimilation to which he was subjected.

---

39 Kardiner and Ovesey, *The Mark of Oppression*, 285–86.

His father's abandonment had also affected him in other ways. It appeared to have been at the core of a lifetime's need for acceptance—an acceptance he thought was owed to him, although he'd failed to understand how his behavior had shaped his public persona as a demagogue, or how it had impacted his reception and fueled his rejection. The Rev. refused to accept that he was the cause of how others had viewed him, and he has held to the idea that he was wronged— giving credence to his *rejected stone* complex and a belief that, like Jesus, he was unjustly persecuted. This rejection hardened him over the years and cultivated a resolve for a payday—Reverend Sharpton's own reparations project, which has seen him spend a lifetime straddling a transactional dialectic of perpetual child and victim all at the same time, all in an effort reclaim that social approbation he believes is due to him.

Acceptance

As human beings are social mammals, we're generally desirous of approbation and acceptance by others—family, friends, social or religious groups, tribes, ethnic groups, communities, or even the larger national culture. Although no one will admit this, for the plurality of the oppressed or victimized classes, the need for acceptance by the dominant, powerful, rich ruling-classes is even acuter. This is because of a *psychosis of deficiencies* and *inadequacies* that accompanies group oppression of any kind, which then leaves its subjects with a certain unbearable heaviness of meaninglessness. A key measure of assimilation, therefore, lies in the feeling of acceptance through which the oppressed seeks to rid itself of that dreadful "self" that's riddled with that *psychosis of deficiencies* and *inadequacies.*

In his book *The Colonizer and the Colonized*, French writer Albert Memi, a North African Jew, wrote of the Maghrebin colonization of his youth in much the same way a midcentury African American might have described the American experience or a Caribbean or West African colonial might have characterized early-century colonial life. Memi's depiction of the colonized's aspiration to be part of the colonizing class and to partake of its privileges is no different from the former so-called plantation mentality in places like North Charleston, South Carolina or different parts of Louisiana—epicenters of the earlier mentioned Free Men of Color.

As Memi illustrated, the colonials and their way of life soon became the benchmark of humanity in the eyes of the dehumanized colonized—much the same way that "white" was idealized as, and to some extent remains, the benchmark of black America's and the former enslaved or colonial diaspora's humanity. Today's popular discourse about "white privilege" goes back to that same arrogation of the oppressed in their desired efforts to assimilate and shrug off the psychosis. After all, dominance and supremacy can hardly be viewed as "privileges," unless of course, we worship an awful God with a manifestly sinister sense of humor.

According to Memi, this is because the power castes of colonials had always ended up imposing *psychosis of deficiencies* and *inadequacies* upon the colonized and disenfranchised—on those with neither money, land, class, stature, nor power. In his case, it was the Jews of the Maghreb and their desired assimilation in order to elevate their lot from that of the colonized underclass to something resembling that of the French colonial class.

Again, this was no different from the dreaded mulatto mentality that once aspired for social status through its proximity to white paternal ancestry in the Americas—a point some had unsuccessfully attempted to exploit in their rejected bid to serve the Confederacy once Union soldiers had overrun Fort Sumter. Those who feel or view themselves closest to their oppressors are the ones who bear the brunt of such psychoses and neuroses with each reminder— *Step back; being half-white still makes you black!* So, the imposition of that *psychosis of deficiencies* and *inadequacies* was the same for disenfranchised Jews in Tunis or Tangiers as it was for blacks in Santiago Conakry, Kingston, Charleston, or New Orleans. Although denied, this is still pervasive in contemporary society, though most often visible among rich and elite blacks (same difference) and among those who aspire to black leadership, which means that in their search for assimilated approbation and acceptance, their loyalties can never ultimately be to the black community that elects them.

Rejection

On the individual level, the preponderance of rejection suffered—whether because of race, skin color gradient, class, sex, gender, ethnic origins, or religion, is generally painful, regardless of cause. When it's rejection by "the other"— that which is external to our identity-forming grouping—it's generally seen as discrimination. Depending on social levels, it may either cultivate the hated "self" that seeks renunciation through assimilation or further solidify the cherished "self" that seeks to retain and guard its identity at all cost.

But when it's rejection by our own kind, it's just seen as snobbery, prejudiced, classist, or elitist. If we're part of an oppressed group, we're likely to seek self-renunciation through assimilation as a way of overcoming but also as a means of inflicting sweet revenge. Many African Americans—rightfully or wrongly—silently view this to be the case with Supreme Court Justice Clarence Thomas. But no one has ever viewed Reverend Sharpton through this prism, which is natural as he has never held any positions of power.

Yet it's within this context that not being part of the black elite has given the Rev. the blues for most of his life. Money, power, and celebrity had pulled even to skin color gradient as the gold standard of the black bourgeoisie in America over time, and having none, except a tinge of color, had denied him the type of respectability he'd sought as a cure for his *psychosis of deficiency and inadequacy*. Straight out the gate in *Pharaoh*, Sharpton had told us that he was born into the African American gentry but then got booted out because of his father's weaknesses. Here, he seemingly shared much in common with the black kings and queens of Africa who'd precipitously fallen into slavery, yet still held on to fond memories of the pomp and pageantry of the good old days of royal life strutting along the Nile.

But nothing appeared further from the truth, as the crass, brusque preacher man has had nothing in resemblance to an heir of the genteel and pretentious bourgeois blackness in America. Sharpton had spent his entire early life, through the writing of *Al on America* at age fifty-eight, pouring scorn on the middle class and elite black establishment for supposedly rejecting him and kicking him out of the nobility. This fostered an identity developed almost entirely in response to social rejection. He'd had to define himself not only in relation to whites but also with respect to the type of African American he wasn't—middle-class or elite. As his alienation had roots in the elder Sharpton's abandonment and junior's need for corrective acceptance, the trunk and branches of a perpetually suffering succotash then flourished. From the need to organize protests to intimidate the faculty of his high school to kicking in the doors of the establishment in adulthood, the Rev. displayed the same impetus of many who'd led revolutions and counterinsurgencies in history—that burning desire to be accepted and to be contended with by the forces of the establishment they'd sought to dislodge and overthrow, as well as the desire to wreak havoc on their own that had rejected or failed to support them.

We saw this in the high-flying celebrity Sharpton of the Obama years, who seemed most at ease among those he'd once vilified—the moment he felt their acceptance. Once he believed he'd truly "arrived," like Haiti's Jean-Jacques Dessalines, whose first act after the revolution was to emulate Napoleon and name himself Emperor Jacques I, the Rev. was nothing short of imperious. He imposed himself as a kind of an administrative overseer and suppressor of black thought and freedom of speech by attempting to command obedience and to enforce proscription of black criticism of President Obama at each turn. For he and others he'd subordinated to the cause, the black presidency was more than an affirmation of racial pride; it was their opportunity to partake in the prestige and "privileges" enjoyed by white ruling classes for centuries. It was their turn, and we then saw eight years of manifestations born of that ingrained *psychosis of deficiency* and *inadequacy*. The Rev. could not see it but we could; deficiencies and inadequacies had branded him just as clearly as a tribe physically marks its own or as a rancher marks his cattle.

While white approbation was and remains atop the black middle-class' bucket list, for the Rev., having rich, powerful white friends was paramount, though it didn't come easy over the years. Kicking in doors and demanding a seat at the table under the guise of social and civil rights activism had made for a combination of public ridicule and the very derision and rejection he was battling in the first place. Many of his people—the middle-class black establishment—cringed at the cartoonish buffoonery he then regularly projected on to the nation via television. But the Rev. was living in a space where even nearing three hundred pounds, sporting processed hair, wearing a gaudy medallion, and bedecked in tight-fitting tracksuits, he couldn't understand why the media had ridiculed him or why even some African Americans he'd portended to represent had often scoffed at him. He was Fat Alfred with a bad attitude, regularly featured on the pages of either the *New York Post* or the *New York Daily News* competing with female patrons waiting to be coiffed in female hair salons in Harlem. Although he claimed to have reveled in the "buffoon-with-the-processed-hair" portrayals, telling us he'd even laughed at himself at times, it was clear that it had caused the Rev. much pain, so he then became the great cake walker; as they ridiculed him, he laughed at them.

He told us in *Stone* that he got television coverage because he was the ideal caricature of Tom Wolfe's Reverend Reginald Bacon in the flesh (*Bonfire of the Vanities*). He made excellent copy for comedic value on the evening news, and he relished that. He merely needed to be on site to be on television. To paraphrase writer Frantz Fanon, he was both cause and effect: he got attention because he was a buffoon, and he became an even bigger buffoon because it got him attention. At a certain point, though, many of those black elites soon realized the Rev.'s staying power, and they got behind him to do their own bidding. He'd given voice to that which the queasy black leadership was either unwilling to do or had chosen not to do—to ruffle feathers in response to racism. As he did this, he also charted his path to white acceptance through institutional emotional blackmail as a sort of civil rights hostage taker. He deployed this institutional emotional blackmail to near perfection against the Democratic Party from 2004 onward. But all along, he has never forgotten or forgiven the rejection he'd felt from middle-class and elite black America, and he was on mission to own them.

The result was a dual Sharpton narrative—that of the race-baiting demagogue held by his detractors and that of the savior of the downtrodden held by his admirers. Both served his interests quite well, depending on his objectives at particular times. But both were one dimensional, and each often missed the real Reverend Sharpton—the one with a desire for acceptance and praise-worthy approbation at any cost. This added to the complexity of the Sharpton phenomenon. Careful examination of his words has shown a man driven by a maladaptation that had likely taken hold in nursery and later, rejection suffered at the hands of his own. It is doubtful that he has ever known emotional well-being, the absence of which has led to a desperate need for attention, a yearning for white acceptance, and a demand for respectability from the black middle-class and elite—a respectability he ultimately found by hijacking its leadership.

Sharpton and the Black Elite

For at least three decades, the Rev. was like that poor kid who got kicked out of a fancy prep school after losing his scholarship for fighting, only to still hang outside the fences on weekends and taunt the rich kids—the elite and middle-class African Americans on the inside. Early on, no one had come in for more of his scorn and derision than the black elite—both individuals and institutions. Before joining and co-opting them, the Rev. had used *Pharaoh* to derisively lambast mainstream black politicians for serving themselves rather than their communities. He'd told us of a system of patronage, of overlooking infractions such as womanizing, and he'd assured us that he was out to change all that. He was the fearless kamikaze out to dive-bomb business as usual:

> So the establishment blacks saw me as a serious threat. The mere fact of my independence was a threat. In their hearts they could not disagree with me, they knew I was right on, but the fact they couldn't control my actions was a threat to them. I was altering the comfort level, showing their white allies how little power and influence they actually had…they are not looking at the fact that this beautiful young black man just got killed and the perpetrators might get away with it, and that I was trying to make sure people went to jail. They're wondering, "How does all this noise affect me?"[40]

He'd believed that the mainstream black politicians of the era couldn't have cared less about black men being killed off in the streets, as their only concern was what was in it for them. If voter suppression kept them in power, although Democrats, they were all for it:

---

40 Ibid., 112.

In many black communities when we start voter registration, I've had some of the local incumbents say, "Don't do that!" Only 4,000–5,000 people may vote in the primary, and those are the folks they are sure of. If we bring out 10,000 more people who may not like what's going on in their neighborhood, that incumbent may not win.[41]

To dethrone them, he'd needed to expose them as powerless to the white establishment and to the white masters who'd chosen them. There was little doubt that he was referring to, among others, New York's black political machine of David Dinkins, Basil Paterson, Ed Townes, Charlie Rangel, and others. The two oldest civil rights organizations in America—the NAACP and the National Urban League—didn't fare any better in *Pharaoh*. Sharpton said that if he'd contented himself with being "eloquent" with the failures of his elders, he would've achieved nothing in New York and *black lives* would continue not to have *mattered*. Again, these were the days before he'd bulldozed his way through the doors of each organization—the days before rising atop of the black establishment:

> I've had the opinion of saying, NAACP ain't done nothing, the Urban League ain't done nothing. Well, I've said all that, but when I got up and went to Howard Beach, something happened. Something none of us could have imagined. Three people went to jail for the racially-motivated killing of a black man. If I had contented myself with being eloquent with the failures of my elders, those three boys would have gone on walking around free after killing Michael Griffith. And more black kids would have been killed.[42]

To a certain extent, he was correct. Black America often views any demand for accountability from its politicians and institutions as manifestly poor manners, downright disrespectful, and the politicians and institutional forces know and exploit this mindset. Notwithstanding the historical legacies of the NAACP and Urban League, questioning their quotidian purpose or everyday relevance is

---

41 Sharpton with Hunter, *Al on America*, 123–24.

42 Al Sharpton and Walton, *Go and Tell Pharaoh*, 240.

viewed as almost anathema. For this reason, Sharpton's critique in *Pharaoh* had initially appeared an act of courage, but as it was only a preamble to getting a seat at the table, it was really an act of cowardice. He'd evoked a "Frazieresque" chord in his dismissals of the black bourgeois, but with a very different tone. Whereas the writer of the *Black Bourgeoisie*, E. Franklin Frazier, had laughed at the bourgeois class—even pitied it, Reverend Sharpton had menaced it for a gate pass. Back then he was trying to be among them while not of them; theirs was a front door to be kicked in and white acceptance, a back door to be knocked on. At one point, he was even confessional while in denial of the latter. "The goal of the average black—particularly a prominent black," he told us, "Is to be accepted by the white power structure and by white people."[43] Again, he was correct, but he'd failed to tell us that this was also a goal that burned like a furnace inside of Al Sharpton.

When that black family in northern New Jersey had faced a police brutality incident with their teenage son, they'd invited Reverend Jesse Jackson but had expressed a clear preference for Reverend Sharpton to yield the urge to cross either bridge or tunnel. They'd feared his presence would've upset their tranquility in suburbia. But the Rev. was having none of it, and he unleashed a tirade on the family, reminding them that they weren't even accepted guests but were indeed "housebreakers" in suburbia—mere interloping trespassers at risk of being tossed back into the projects by white folks at a moment's notice:

> Everyone forgets I spent the first ten years of my life in the Black bourgeoisie, and I know that attitude. All of those upper-middle-class blacks worry that they're two steps from being back in the projects. The black middle class doesn't make a claim on America. It's more like they are worried that they've gotten away with something. They're housebreakers, trespassing, and hope if no noise is made, no one will realize that they are there.[44]

---

43 Sharpton with Hunter, *Al on America*, 269.

44 Al Sharpton and Walton, *Go and Tell Pharaoh*, 168.

In menacing the black bourgeois elite and middle classes, he also reminded them of his usual claim that he used to be one of them, implying that they too might one day fall out of favor. He never missed an opportunity to remind them of their fear of a return to join the impoverished, essentially warning, *Without people like me, you all are just two clicks away from being tossed back into the projects where you came from.* From the beginning, the hurt, pain, and anger of black middle-class rejection had stung Sharpton, and *Pharaoh* was replete with as many bellicose opinions of that class of African Americans. Declarations of his bourgeois fellowship-before-peasantry have always accompanied his claim to perpetual affinity to the gentry. It was the light-skinned black who went around telling people, *I'm half Cherokee, half Choctaw,* half this, half that—half anything to make him or herself appear less African.

The treatment of his celebrity friends by white society had even further hardened his attitudes toward "uppity" blacks:

> I was there with James Brown on private jets, I've had lunch with Don King at the top of Rockefeller Center. I've seen the big money, about the biggest money that black folks get. But I've also stood with those two in court. I saw James Brown brought in wearing shackles, and I saw Don King treated like a purse-snatcher.[45]

But this was Reverend Sharpton arguing with Reverend Sharpton. In indicting the black middle class and elite, he'd told us that he was doing so only because even after his associations with numerous celebrities and big-moneyed players, he'd still felt rejected by this class. It was the resentment from exclusion that had produced the type of vocal condemnation, against which Oscar Wilde's Lady Bracknell had cautioned Algernon: "Never speak disrespectfully of society," she'd said. "Only people who can't get into it do that."[46] But *Pharaoh* was the Sharpton who couldn't stop speaking disrespectfully of his society because he'd found great difficulty "getting into it." As the elite black political class has always been a self-serving phenomenon of black life

---

45 Ibid., 169.

46 *Merlin Holland, The Importance of Being Earnest (Complete Works,* 2003, London), 409.

in America, the Reverend Sharpton of the '90s was merely the case of water seeking and finding open space—David seeking to join Goliath rather than to slay him.

What had initially seemed a shared mutual interest—the advancement of positions and status—then had many, like his old nemesis, Dr. Cornel West, coming to view him as a vehicle to advance their own interests. By the writing of 2002's *Al on America*, Sharpton's motives had changed, and that which he'd previously attacked, that of which he'd felt deprived yet entitled, was the thing he'd now craved the most—acceptance by the black political and social elite. It was the start of a disingenuous quid pro quo, and in no time, he was on his way to "returning." His once "ineloquence" quickly morphed into the eloquence of an NAACP and Urban League insider. By 2013's *Stone*, nearly two decades after writing that the NAACP and Urban league "ain't done nothing" for African Americans, the television star and "best friend" of the president of the United States was now at the epicenter of that very sociopolitical black bourgeoisie he'd previously condemned. He'd become its undisputed leader, a showstopper at Image Award ceremonies and the main speaker at the NAACP and the National Urban League conferences and gatherings. There he was, yanking around like a lap-dog, leaders like Urban League's Marc Morial, who'd all but subordinated his organization to Sharpton mania.

Surrogate Father

Biblical scholars are some of the best literary investigators because they seek to find the missing pieces—what should've been there based on what is there. By this standard, a first read of the Rev.'s hospital stay was like ruffling through a carton of Swiss cheese; it was riddled with holes. We could tell that much was missing and that yet other parts were invented, as they were clearly out of place.

In 1996's *Pharaoh* (five years after the incident), the Rev. wrote of his Brooklyn hospital room recovery from his 1991 stabbing by a deranged man. Immediately after surgery he'd received a slew of visitors, including pastors who were close friends and mentors, but he'd only had the urge to call Reverend

Jesse Jackson—an indication of the close, albeit strained bond between the two men at the time:

> Then everybody left, and I asked for a phone. I wanted to call Jesse Jackson. I don't even really know why, but for some reason I felt compelled to talk to him and tell him myself what had happened. We had not been close recently as we were when I was growing up, but he was still my hero, Adam [Clayton Powell] was dead, Jesse was the only minister whom I felt I could model myself on, look up to in that way...I called him at home in Washington and told him what had happened. I said, "There's still too much racism in this country and if I survive I hope I'm going to be even more serious now in the true King [Dr. Martin Luther] tradition of opposing it."[47]

In referencing the 1991 incident, Sharpton spoke of Congressman Adam Clayton Powell Jr., who'd been dead for nearly twenty years, as if he'd only recently passed—the extent to which *Pharaoh's* Sharpton was still in the tank for Clayton Powell Jr. But Jesse Jackson had become a surrogate father, his mentor, and idol. Jackson had shown the Rev. some measure of acceptance, which had made up for the rejection by Sharpton's own father and others in the black community.

Prodigal Father

Yet the pathos of acceptance and rejection was so intense in his life that at times it had brought the Rev. some level of confusion and hampered his ability to mature beyond the hurt of that fatherly rejection. The case of this single event—his hospital recovery room experience from that stabbing, for which he'd given us two different versions, was an example of this confusion. The importance here isn't that he'd given two versions but instead, his reasons for having given them.

While in that same hospital recovery room, the Rev. told of a message he'd received that his father, with whom there'd been no contact since childhood, or

---

47 Al Sharpton and Walton, *Go and Tell Pharaoh*, 179.

so he'd claimed, had called. We were then left to imagine the discussion with his father, as he had shown us nothing of it:

> About an hour after that a nurse came in and gave Kathy [wife] a note. She wouldn't show it to me, and I could tell she was weighing something in her mind. After what was probably a minute or two—it seemed a lot longer to me at the time—she came over to me and said, "This is a message from a man in Orlando, Florida, who wants to talk to you, he says he's your father." This was the first time I'd heard from my father since I was a kid, in family court. I tried to tell myself that it was probably a prank, but I told Kathy to get the phone and we'd see. She dialed the number, and I knew immediately that it was him. He had seen what happened on the national news and was concerned about my condition.[48]

Accordingly, the Rev. was surprised to hear from his father (that wasn't supposedly needed in his black family) after so many years of silence. He then went on to tell us of all the things he wanted to say to his father—of his fatherly needs as a child and teen that weren't met—but not of the things he'd actually said to his father:

> It was a strange situation for me, because there were all these things I had been waiting to say to him: "Where were you in my other crises, when I was getting arrested, when I was in jail, when I was on trial, where were you when I graduated from high school, when I needed somebody to tell me to stay in college?" But it seemed, suddenly, that none of that mattered. I just responded to his overture and returned the call.[49]

This was an early example of the rhetorical imitation and imagery not based on facts but so carefully crafted as to be convincing to the untrained eye. The Rev. had given no details of this conversation with his father, yet we were left convinced a conversation had indeed taken place. As Sharpton is a man of the

---

48 Ibid., 180.
49 Ibid.

cloth, the biblical comparison to our understanding of Saint Paul's meeting with Jesus was hard to miss. We were left convinced of a meeting in the flesh between Paul and his Savior, yet the evidence (time of existence of both men) suggests that this had never happened. So, like the Apostles, it could've been a Sharpton vision.

Unlike St. Paul, though, who'd told us a lot while showing us very little, even where the Rev. didn't intend to tell us anything in particular, he'd ended up showing us a lot. Initially, there was little reason to doubt a conversation had taken place, as for once, the Rev. could've found it too personal to share. But given his obsession, across his books, with disclosing the most mundane details of his father's departure and its impact on his life, any encounter with his father in adulthood—on the phone or in person—would've been a momentous occasion that would've stayed crystal clear in his mind. Additionally, in almost all other cases, including where he was clearly inventing stories of tangential encounters with others, the Rev. had gone out of his way to tell us details so in-depth to have even put words in other peoples' mouths at times.

Yet here he'd walked us slowly and painfully through the details of receiving a note that his father had called and of asking his wife to dial his father's number, "knowing immediately" that it was the elder Sharpton on the phone but said nothing of their discussion. He'd skillfully told us that his wife had dialed the phone for him to speak to his father and that he'd simply responded to his father's overture by calling him back. But he discussed the phone call by revealing not even a single line of dialogue between father and son.

Six years later, in the second phase of his public life, he wrote a new and improved version of Al Sharpton in 2002's *Al on America*. There, the Rev. recounted the details of the same recovery room stay, including the note that his father had called and the totality of the phone conversations he'd had while in the recovery room. This time, he confirmed that there was no discussion with the elder Sharpton, by pointedly telling us that he'd made only two phone calls—one to Reverend Jesse Jackson and the other to his mother. He'd rejected the overtures of his father and had refused to call him back:

A nurse brought me a note that said, "Your father called." I had not heard from my father since I was a kid, but I knew he had moved to somewhere in Florida. And the number on the note was a Florida number. I thought, "I've been indicted, been to jail, now he's calling? What am I going to call him for?" Kathy took the note and she didn't say anything. I asked her to find me a cell phone. She got a cell phone, thinking I was probably going to call my father. But I called Jesse. He was in Washington at the time, and when he picked up. I said, "Reverend, I don't know if you've heard, but I got stabbed today." The doctors came in later and said I shouldn't make any calls. That call to Jesse was the only call I made, except for one to my mother.[50]

The hospital room redux was almost cathartic, a correction the Rev. felt he'd had to make, a funeral procession he'd had to carry out. In his first book, he'd brought his father to life during his recovery room experience from a near-death injury. It was something that he wished had happened, a moment of cognizance, of being acknowledged by VIPs like the mayor, local and national politicians, and other dignitaries who'd come to pay their respects, yet unacknowledged by his own father. But he later grew uncomfortable with having dignified the prodigal dad under the circumstances. So, he killed off his earlier story of a rapprochement between father and son by writing a second version of events that essentially told us that there was no chance in hell that he would've spoken to that man.

The currency of emotional blackmail and the exploitation of pain is one thing, but the reality of the pain from parental rejection is an entirely different one. It was encouraging to see the Rev. come clean in the second version wherein he'd also affirmed Jesse Jackson as a replacement-surrogate father. But that didn't last for long, either. Only a few pages later in the same book, he then went after his new father, Jesse Jackson, with a vengeance. All in all, Alfred Sharpton Jr. was the boy who'd been ridding himself of daddies since he was ten. He was the irretrievably broken man who might have

---

50 Sharpton with Hunter, *Al on America*, 197.

indeed come to see no value in paternal relations because of the catastrophic suffering the loss of a father had wreaked on his own life.

Exploiting Dysfunctions

For most of us, family tragedies are sacred. We might reveal them for personal empowerment to avoid living with or being subdued by shame—for which we are the innocent victims. But to write three books hoisting the same childhood events over and over again as the driver of actions in adulthood soon appears disingenuous. The first time might be therapy, but the second and third are likely opportunistic.

There is little doubt that his family breakup had had a tremendous effect on the Rev., but as we read his books, we see that this wasn't an event that he'd held to any sacred standard. Though sometimes giving a slight nod to his mother in the numerous versions of his story, he generally cheapened what was supposedly a family tragedy by using his father's departure as a crutch, as a ploy for personal sympathy, as a weapon of manipulation and emotional blackmail of society at large—as an excuse for his own less than stellar adult behavior. The American public was his courtroom, and his defense was always the same: *Your Honor, it's not my fault. It's because I am from a broken home. When I was ten, my father ran away with my older sister, who was carrying his child.*

In one television interview, the Rev. as much as declared that the elder Sharpton's departure had made him the buffoon of the 1980s and 1990s—a presumptive quantum leap or cunning pretense, given that the millennium Al Sharpton was no less of a buffoon. He'd even used it as a defense in the 1980s-era Tawana Brawley hoax. Supposedly, he and his fellow knights in shining armor had been defending the chastity of a virgin maiden because of the way his father had abandoned his mother:

> And maybe we did bring a lot of that to the table in the Brawley matter. Maybe in my case it also had something to do with what happened between my father and my sister, all the emotions that were involved. Maybe the harder they attacked Tawana, the more I saw a vulnerable black woman, like my mother, that [sic] no one would fight for. At some point it stopped being about Tawana and started

being my defending my mother and all the black women no one would fight for. I was not going to run away from her like my father had run away from my mother, like so many other black men had run away.[51]

Whatever might have transpired at home with his father, rather than seeking to responsibly deal with his pain, the Rev. used it as "empowerment in victimization." At no point had he mentioned his younger sister as a victim or even his older half-sister who was manipulated into taking her stepfather as her lover. Even worse, the product of that union, Reverend Sharpton's half-sibling, of whose whereabouts he'd claimed total ignorance, was never mentioned as a victim of their collective father's incestuous duplicity. In his writings, it was all about Reverend Alfred Sharpton Jr., victim No. 1. It was his excuse for all occasions—a veritable gold mine.

But a close examination of this long drawn out epistle of paternal abandonment and lifelong despair was another Swiss cheese rummage. Something just didn't add up; there were too many holes. The departure of his father from home at age ten might have shattered the boy, but it's clear that other factors were at play as well, as his preaching had predated his father's leaving—a preaching he told us his father had opposed:

When my mother could no longer afford the house in Hollis, Queens, we were forced to move back to Brooklyn. She had to look for work, and while she did, we were on welfare. In the meantime, my father was in court trying to stop me from preaching. I don't know whether he did this for spite, or power, or my best interests but he was further harming our family.[52]

In the first instance, the father of a nine- or ten-year-old who goes to court to get an order to stop his child from preaching is really pleading with the court to force his wife to stop allowing their child to preach—pleading with the court to effectively affirm his rightful place as the father over his child. This would've come about only after lengthy disagreements between

---

51 Al Sharpton and Walton, *Go and Tell Pharaoh*, 136.

52 Ibid., 28.

Sharpton Sr. and his wife on the issue. More importantly, though, to have gone to court to stop what might be viewed by some as the exploitation of his child had shown some caring on the part of the elder Sharpton. But from the Rev.'s early accounts, we got a father who'd callously abandoned his wife and children.

That narrative of his father's abandonment with no news since he was a child was somewhat reaffirmed when Sharpton told us of attending his sister Cheryl's 1994 wedding. At the time of the nuptials, the forty-year-old Rev. said that it was the first time he'd seen his father *in many years*, not since he was ten, and the first time they were all (which could mean his half-sister) together in twenty-nine years:

> In March 1994, my sister Cheryl got married, and I flew to Atlanta to do the ceremony. My father was there. It was the first time I'd seen him in many years. He had another family—his new wife and kids were there with him—and my mother was there. Tina was there, too. It was the first time we were all together in the same place in twenty-nine years.[53]

Of the meeting with his father at the wedding, we'd gotten yet another version, almost verbatim of the hospital room conversation with the elder Sharpton, that had never happened:

> Many days sitting on airplanes, many long nights sitting in hotel rooms by myself, I had thought about the various ways I was going to curse out my father if I ever saw him again. But when I did see him, I didn't do anything but smile, because it didn't really matter anymore. I won [*sic*][54]

But the Rev. was also very clear when he'd said this, of his hospital stay three years before the wedding that, "This was the first time I'd heard from my father since I was a kid, in family court." Again, the family court was somewhere around age nine or ten, so he was somewhat consistent in his

53 Ibid., 267.
54 Al Sharpton and Walton, *Go and Tell Pharaoh*, 267.

narrative told in *Pharaoh*, in *Al on America*, and to anyone in the street who would listen to him tell the story for over two decades. He had not heard from his father since age ten when Sharpton Sr. had run off with the Rev.'s half-sister Tina.

It wasn't until 2013's *Stone* that the Rev. would finally come around to tell us that his father had later returned to take his sister Cheryl to live with him and his new wife after remarrying (not to the step-daughter Tina). The elder Sharpton had then partly raised his daughter Cheryl—the same Cheryl, whose wedding two decades before, the Rev. had described as having occasioned the presence of his family for the first time in twenty-nine years. So, even assuming that the old man had returned in the dead of night to sneak his daughter Cheryl away from her mother and brother, the Rev. had maintained close relationship and contact with Cheryl over the years. Therefore, he must have also had some contact with his father, with whom she was living, or at least have had news of him via her. This means that the entire narrative of paternal abandonment with no news since childhood rings fictional.

News of the wedding was at the end of *Pharaoh*, yet we would only hear of his father's return to take and raise Cheryl two books and seventeen years later in *Stone*. By then it had become exhausting to read about his years pondering what he would say to his father but hadn't. In fact, it was only in expressing his feeling of abandonment as the primary victim that he'd come around to tell us, in *Stone,* that his father had partly raised his sister:

> The abandonment was made worse by the fact that he had my sister, Cheryl, the first child he had with my mother, come live with him and his new wife for a while, leaving me behind in Brooklyn.[55]

As Cheryl had chosen to go live with their father rather than to stay with her mother and younger brother, she too could've been seen as having abandoned the family as well. Again, more importantly, a man who'd returned to take his daughter to live with him, though still a person stained by the sin of incest,

---

55 Al Sharpton with Chiles, *The Rejected Stone*, 17.

could hardly have been the heartless deadbeat dad who'd wholly abandoned his family—the one from whom there was no news since he'd absconded when his son was a mere ten-year-old. As we see above, that couldn't have been the case. Yet this is the story Reverend Sharpton had spent nearly three decades publicly exploiting for sympathy—the essence of societal emotional blackmail in victimhood.

Again, no one can deny the pain and devastation of such interfamilial degradations, especially for a boy who bore his father's full name and resemblance, as he'd told us. To have been rejected twice by his father—the initial absconding and then the return to take his sister and not him—must have been painful for the boy. But readers of the Rev.'s books could also see another side to the story. Although he'd never told us this and while he might still not be able to see things this way, he'd shown his readers that at a very early stage, he'd likely rejected his father in favor of others. This had come about when his mother had given him over to the de facto guardianship and leadership of the men in the church:

> I think in some ways my father resented Bishop Washington's influence on me. I think he may have felt I loved the bishop more than I loved him. There was always a tension there. All I knew was that I wanted to be like Bishop Washington, and though I loved my father, I never really wanted to be like him.[56]

The reduction of the father in the household was clear, which again, is an example of one integrative aspect of black familial life, earlier mentioned. A man who is head of his household, as the Rev. attests the elder Sharpton to have been, would not have had to go to court to get an order barring his young child from preaching and his wife from allowing it. A father in any sense of the word would've just ordered his son to do his homework and bar him from preaching again, under the penalty of being grounded. After doing that he would've laid down the rules to his wife and then marched down to the church to stop Bishop Washington from putting his boy on the soapbox—ever again.

---

56 Ibid., 21.

It's that simple—if we are to accept the Rev.'s version of things. No church in America could put a nine or ten-year-old child on the pulpit without some form of parental acquiescence and consent. None could do so in the face of a parental objection, even if only by one parent. It, therefore, stands to reason that his father had lost complete control of his home, of his family, and of any parental authority over his son—in this case to the influence of Bishop Washington and other ministers to whom the boy's mother had entrusted him. In the opening pages of *Stone*, the Rev. painted the picture for us:

> My mother recognized my yearning at an early age and did what she could to encourage it. When my family moved to a big house in Queens, she built me a little chapel in the basement, complete with three or four benches for pews and a little stage that was a pulpit. While the other kids in Hollis were outside playing punchball and stickball in the streets, I would go down to the basement and preach, lining up my sister's dolls on the pews to act as my congregation.[57]

His father might have been at his wit's end with a ten-year-old child who was beyond his paternal authority and a wife who'd facilitated it. No one can argue with Reverend Sharpton when he speaks of his dysfunctional childhood since even his recollection of the events is dysfunctional. His father was either not enough of a man in his home to exert sufficient control over the direction of his own child, or not allowed to be enough of a man to exert such influence and control. Either way, it chalked up to a situation that produced a broken child and later, an irretrievably broken man.

The multiple versions of the story told in his books suggest that long before his father had physically left the family unit, the young Sharpton had mentally left his father. The Rev.'s childhood adaption was typical of what Kardiner and Ovesey had described as the *Neurotic Elaboration*,[58] in which a cultivated "constellation of self-hatred" drives much self-contempt and contempt for those around us, thereby feeding an aspiration to be something

---

57 Al Sharpton with Chiles, *The Rejected Stone*, 12.
58 Kardiner and Ovesey, *The Mark of Oppression*, 295.

else. In Sharpton's case, that "something else" was being a child preacher, which had brought him a certain amount of prestige through adulation within his milieu among the black Holiness-Spiritualists sects.

Again, there is no forgiving the elder Sharpton's crimes against decency *a la* "Jim Trueblood," but it is hard to accept the Rev.'s version of the most crucial event he claimed to have shaped his life, without recognizing and questioning the inherent flaws in his telling of it. Maladaptation or some other kind of trauma had likely triggered varied neuroses since childhood. His years of preaching in front of multitudes, his great starvation for attention in adulthood, and his dogmatic personality, are likely due to other factors that predated his father's abandonment. Whatever might have happened in his home as a child, it didn't play out the way he'd told us; nor was his father's departure solely responsible for a lifelong existence in buffoonery.

In *Stone,* the Rev. told us that "greatness" was what he'd sought, while still blaming his father's departure somewhere around 1964 for the regrettable Reverend Al Sharpton Jr. some fifty years later. He was still nowhere near taking responsibility for his actions as an adult, which showed that he'd had much in common with his father and was more like Sharpton Sr. than he was willing to accept. By any criterion of responsibility—the foundation of greatness—Sharpton Jr., like the father he has condemned, is its antithesis.

Perpetual Infant

My college thesis for a psychology minor was on the theory of *transactional analysis*. It was that paper written the night before submission some two decades ago but still fresh in my mind. *Transactional analysis* was the brainchild of San Francisco psychologist Dr. Eric Berne, author of *Games People Play*. In a multistage polygon, Dr. Berne illustrated what he believed were the three ego states—Parent, Adult, and Child. Accordingly, the emotionally well-adjusted adult is expected to be within the Adult-to-Adult stage ("I'm ok; you're ok"). Varying other combinations come into play, based on stages of life, mental state, emotional maturity (well-being), adaptation, and so on:

- Parent-to-Parent; Parent-to-Adult; Parent-to-Child
- Adult-to-Parent; Adult-to-Adult; Adult-to-Child
- Child-to-Parent; Child-to-Adult; Child-to-Child

From his books, Reverend Sharpton appears to have never left the Child-to-Child stage ("I'm not ok; you're not ok"), an admittedly difficult task for African American men in general, in a society that excels at keeping them as pretentious little boys. In Sharpton, we've seen an exaggerated example of an emotionally immature man locked in a petty soul that reeks of a viscerally defensive and insecure mind—disposed to mean-spirited attacks on those he thought were not ok. At times, even the slightest sense of growth would've been a welcomed relief but that such sense of growth has never manifested.

In *Pharaoh*, the Rev. established a recurring pattern of belittling those he told us were mentors and idols, effectively elevating himself by reducing them, because he thought they weren't OK. But deep down he knew he wasn't either—always showing himself typical of many in the "I don't have it" class; whatever "it" may be, they stand ready to attack, reproach, take down, and pour scorn on those they perceive to have "it" in abundance.

His lack of formal education and status was always on display, often asserting, *You're not better than me because you're rich, privileged, or educated*. But this was precisely because he'd believed himself less than those who were rich, privileged, and educated, and he'd resented them for it. Uselessly making Dr. Cornel West his whipping boy quite early on had shown Sharpton's need to attack and deride the black educated class. Telling us of the lesson he'd supposedly learned from singer James Brown while about to preach at Harlem's Abyssinian Baptist Church and having to decide what kind of preaching to do while there was solely a hit-job on his sometimes friend and nemesis, Dr. Cornel West. The Rev. then stealthily eviscerated West as a man unwanted by a significant segment of his people—those darned Abyssinians up in Harlem: "That's what I realized at Abyssinian. If they wanted Cornel West, they would have asked him. They wanted Al Sharpton."[59]

---

59 Al Sharpton and Walton, *Go and Tell Pharaoh*, 78–79.

James Brown had shaped the Rev's decision to be authentic in preaching a whooping and hollering sermon at the Abyssinian Baptist Church, once he'd realized that the congregants had come to hear a genuine Pentecostal Preacher and not a cerebral intellectual like Dr. West. Reverend Sharpton could just as well have used the term "seminarian" to make the point that Abyssinian congregants weren't in church expecting to hear a Roman Catholic priest, but the child in him tended to name names in petty and vindictive ways. Professor West, although a theologian, wasn't known to America as a stump preacher, so Sharpton's reference to him out of the blue was sinister.

The perpetual child within him often asks, *Who do you think you are... talking to me like that?* In others, he often sees "children" like himself—to be admonished and rebuked: *Don't talk down to me; I ain't your boy. You ain't no better than me.* He rarely misses an opportunity to dignify the most mundane and irrelevant criticisms with his most visceral attacks. Self-modulation such as, *that's beneath me,* or, *I won't dignify that,* have never been a part of his makeup. He brings cannons to knife fights and has been in constant opposition to those he perceived as treating him like a child—even when he was indeed a child.

As an adult, he boasted of having insisted on signing his name as "the Reverend Alfred Charles Sharpton Jr." at age ten, which had shown the massive ego he'd had as a child. But to believe the telling of such a story was complimentary some fifty years later, showed that little had changed. The hubristic child was still the occupier of the adult body, so at near sixty, he remained proud of being an egotistical ten-year-old. Childish self-centeredness still drives a low tolerance for ambiguity that interprets differences of opinions as encroachments on his territory in strict black and white terms—to be attacked and discredited, as he would do in 2015 by lashing out and calling young activists, "ho[es]." For him, white opponents are driven by racism while black ones are Uncle Toms or sell-outs in the pockets of white racist masters. Reverend Sharpton seethes in resentment of anyone he perceives as having achieved a higher ground than he on the pyramid of tyranny; that is until he's welcomed into the club and given a feeling of acceptance. In *Stone*, he told us that while some people inherited wealth, he'd inherited dysfunction. And for this, he couldn't resist indicting the wealthy:

And those who inherit wealth should not act as if the wealth accrues some sort of merit on them, granting them a superiority over those whose beginnings were more humble. You shouldn't be humiliated if you're on the other side of the ledger, grappling with family dysfunction, because you had nothing to do with it.[60]

It was the child attacking other children. While he'd conveyed two messages, it was unlikely that he was aware of the second and more important one. He was too busy with behavioral control, telling others what they should and should not do, rather than focusing on what individuals in his position should do, which is to ignore the insecurities of those who abuse their good fortunes. But he feels disrespected and humiliated by those with benefits of which he's deprived—wealth, status, class, education, and prestige. This feeds a childish and almost thuggish combativeness at times:

> So put me next to a guy who had a daddy and a mommy and a trust fund to take care of his needs, and he's going to teach me about family values? Did his parents teach him more about family values than my single mother on welfare, getting down on her arthritic knees to scrub floors for me? I think not. I know more about family values than he does, any day of the week.[61]

The adult ego stage of Dr. Berne's transactional analysis recognizes others as adults, with conferred rights and obligations. Although sometimes appearing as if in the state of Adult-to-Child, whereby it would appear that he feels himself "ok" and others not so "ok," Reverend Sharpton has really been stuck in the Child-to-Child stage, whereby the inadequacies of a perpetual child leads a pretentious desire to always be rebuking others. Not only is he not "ok," but he has the need to view others as being "not ok" as well.

---

60 Al Sharpton with Chiles, *The Rejected Stone*, 13.
61 Ibid., 67.

Prodigious Infant

The way it is now, the asylums can hold the sane people, but if we
tried to shut up the insane we should run out of building materials.

—Mark Twain[62]

Writer H. L. Mencken once called the Pentecostals "palpable idiots," and
we might imagine the advent of the child preacher as among the factors that
had influenced his opinion. In the case of the Rev., the cult persona of the
"Wonderboy" preacher had its origins in a Pentecostal childhood. "I was ordained and licensed as a minister in the Pentecostal Church," he told us, "when
I was ten, shortly after my parents broke up."[63]

Figuratively speaking, the young Reverend Alfred Charles Sharpton Jr. was
on stage before he was off his tricycle. He was the black Marjoe Gortner, the
young Michael Jackson of the raucous Holiness-Spiritualists circles in Brooklyn
and beyond. But that was only his human side. Once the lightning and thunder
had ceased and the brimstone had no longer burned, we were able to count our
blessings for the budding messiah in our midst—equipped and ready to lead his
people out of the wilderness. *Pharaonic* Sharpton was Jesus and Moses wrapped
into one. First, we got a carefully developed picture of the child preacher of
extraordinary gifts and intelligence, after which we got the lawgiver yearning
for the "freedom of his people." In this, we saw the truths in the words of social
philosopher Eric Hoffer, who said, "That burning conviction that we have a holy

---

62 *Following the Equator - The Wit and Wisdom of Mark Twain,* 2.

63 Al Sharpton and Walton, *Go and Tell Pharaoh,* 32.

duty toward others is often a way of attaching our drowning selves to a passing raft."[64]

At Once Jesus...

Pharaoh had given us the distinct impression we'd had a living demigod on our hands—remarkably Christ-like in every way, especially as a youth. In recalling the images of the 1980s' Al Sharpton spray-painting Brooklyn crack houses shut, the picture of Jesus chasing the moneychangers out of the Temple was complete. Barring the absence of divine intervention, shining stars, visiting Magis, miraculous conception and birth to a virgin, or even an equivalent insecure Herodian leader in hot pursuit, Brooklyn's Wonderboy was the Jesus of our times—a black one at that, though more in line with the evangelist John's *tour de force*.

Our budding Lord and Savior had shown early spurts of genius since kindergarten: "Here we are, six, seven, eight years old," he'd told us, "And I'm their playmate, but I'm also the boy their parents went to hear preach on Sunday."[65] As he walked us through his storybook infancy, the parallels with the real Christ were unmistakable. At age four, when many children are learning to read by visual association and memory, the supremely gifted Reverend Alfred Charles Sharpton Jr. was busy trying to figure out how to serve his people through preaching—including to his classmates' parents.

At near sixty, he was still proudly constructing visuals of that childhood for us in 2013's *Stone*. He told us, "My preaching career started at the age of four, when Bishop Washington allowed me to stand on a box at the pulpit and sermonize to a congregation of nine hundred people on the anniversary of Junior Usher Board."[66] As earlier mentioned, whatever the reasons—maladaptation or other neuroses—it is clear that a particular kind of idiocy had taken hold from a very early age, likely spurred on by his environment. After all, who in their right mind, outside of the most backward parts of rural America, would sit in

---

64 Eric Hoffer, *The True Believer* (Harper Collins, New York, 1951), 14.

65 Al Sharpton and Walton, *Go and Tell Pharaoh,* 10.

66 Al Sharpton with Chiles, *The Rejected Stone,* 17.

a church and be enthralled by a four-year-old on a soapbox without calling the authorities to report child abuse?

And Moses Too...

Not to be outdone by the Nazarene, the Sharpton of *Pharaoh* and *Al on America* also had much in common with the Hebrew lawgiver. He'd opened *Pharaoh* with the following caption:

> Go down Moses;
> Down to Egyptland;
> Go and tell Pharaoh;
> Let my people go.

Part II of *Al on America* was entitled, "My People, My People." Throughout his books, he's often spoken with hubris and a sort of Mosaic temperance, especially when he spoke of "my people" and of his desired freedom for them. It was the writing of contemporary Negro Spirituals that mimicked the spirit of old Hebrew stories:

> My people, My people[67]...I want the freedom of my people, in matters large and small, and this is the next frontier...[68] Those people, blacks, are my people. I set out to serve them when I started preaching at the age of four, and that is all that I have ever wanted to do. Those people, the lower class, the lower part of the middle-income class, trust me. I was their child prodigy.[69]

Reverend Sharpton had written a book intended as a message to Pharaoh, not to any particular pharaoh but just to "Pharaoh." While even some Jews might have forgotten their time in Egypt, not so for the black preacher man from Brooklyn-Queens. So entwined was he in his Mosaic persona that seventeen years after writing his cryptic yet enjoyable missive to Pharaoh, he told us in

---

67 Al Sharpton and Walton, *Go and Tell Pharaoh*, vi.

68 Ibid., 266.

69 Ibid., 5.

Stone that, "For the first time in 5,000 years, there's no pharaoh in Egypt, Libya is changed, Syria is changed."[70]

Nitpicking details with the Rev. is a losing proposition, as he has perfected a life of carefully avoiding them. But it's not a stretch to ask where he'd been, given the last pharaoh was somewhere around 30 BCE—nearly three decades before the arrival of his Savior, Jesus Christ. How could this have missed the former Pentecostal and current Baptist minister extraordinaire? Did he actually believe that there was still an actual Pharaoh in millennium Egypt, thus an effort to write a real, albeit coded, message to him? Or maybe it was just a realization that his first book was a colossal waste of time—that he'd written a message to a phantom and not a real "living" Pharaoh. Who knows? When you're Moses, you're Moses—even if it's "Black Moses." *Pharaonic* obsessions then become hard to kill.

Tea with Widow Garvey

But in continuing with Jesus, such a prodigy was our young black Savior that as a ten-year-old traveling to Jamaica in the company of church elders, the Rev. remembered having read that Marcus Garvey was from Jamaica, and this spurred him into action. Needless to point out that he was reading about Marcus Garvey at the tender age of eight or nine, as opposed to mere mortals who had to wait for their high school senior year or even college-level black studies classes (then nonexistent in any case). While in a Jamaican hotel, he took it upon himself to look in the telephone book to find the number of Garvey's widow. He tracked her down and got her on the phone, whereby he explained to her that her late husband was his idol and got himself invited over to her house for tea and a nice conversation. Again, the Rev. was only ten years old:

> When I was ten, Bishop Washington took me with him on a Caribbean tour. There were about twelve of us from the church who went. I did most of the preaching. We went to Haiti, Jamaica, Barbados, Trinidad, Puerto Rico...When

---

70 Al Sharpton with Chiles, *The Rejected Stone*, 232.

we were in Jamaica, I remembered the book I had read about Marcus Garvey and remembered that he was from there, and decided to find his family. They were listed in the phone book! I called Mrs. Garvey and said that I was Reverend Alfred Sharpton, Jr. from New York in the United States and that I'd read a lot about her husband. She invited me over. I preached that night and the next morning I got up, got a cab—I was ten years old but the driver took me—and I went over to her house. 12 Mona Road.[71]

The picture was now of Jesus interrogating the High Priests in the Temple. The Wonderboy preacher was doing all the preaching in Jamaica and was now praying with and "interrogating" the wife of the Pan-African legend. We are required to imagine a child left on his own in a hotel room in a foreign land, with free access to the telephone and a telephone directory. Presumably, he also had a waiting taxi downstairs at his disposal, all while the adults were busy at the bar, in the pool, or out about town trying to find the tomb of George Liele (first ordained African American minister who'd fled to Jamaica during the Revolutionary War).

It was another fantastic story on so many levels that it was an obvious exaggeration or outright fabrication. I immediately saw the flaws in its construction of both physical and sociocultural attributes described, including the setup of homes in the area, the unlikelihood of a phone directory in a 1964 Jamaican hotel room, and the cultural behavior and attitudes of Jamaicans of a certain milieu around that time.

Upper Kingston was a very formal society in 1964 when the Rev. visited. Given her position, appointments and vetting would've been mandatory to meet with the widow of Jamaica's National Hero, Marcus Garvey. That Mrs. Garvey, then one of the more famous women in Jamaica, would've received an unknown and unaccompanied ten-year-old over for tea—just because he'd read a lot about her husband—is beyond belief. While the Rev. might have been accorded a level of respect and deference in America as a child preacher, seeking an unaccompanied audience with the widow Garvey in the upper echelons of 1964 Jamaica would've accorded him a "deference" given an impertinent child.

---

71 Al Sharpton and Walton, *Go and Tell Pharaoh*, 35.

He would've been laughed out of town followed by a phone call or letter to his parents, informing them to better "home train" their child to know his place in society and to show better manners.

Among other giveaways in this fantastic story was his description of 1960's Jamaica as if it were 1996 New York. He described a New York City house—in fact, a Brooklyn Brownstone with a door that opened onto the street:

> I knocked on the door, she looked out—she couldn't see me because I was too short and she came to the door three times before opening it—and she looked down and began laughing hysterically because she couldn't believe this little kid was the preacher who had called…She sat with me all day serving tea and talking, while I asked all kinds of questions about Garvey.[72]

Although a prolific description, it had nothing to do with a 1960's Mona Road home in Kingston, Jamaica—then with a big front yard that required maybe a good thirty seconds or more walk from the front entrance to what would've been a grilled-encased front porch with an iron gate. In the outer yard in between the two, a dog usually announced the presence of strangers at the front gate to the occupant of the house and all neighbors on the block. There was never an Upper Kingston home without a ferocious dog for protection against burglary and vagrancy, none with doors that opened to the street, and certainly none with a peephole through which to "look out," whereby a small boy might have been proximately invisible. I know all this because I was born at the University Hospital of the West Indies in Upper Kingston—right there in Mona.

In any case, the *rencontre* with the widow Garvey was one of the few stories in the Rev.'s first book that never made a repeat appearance in the second or third, which might be an indication that others might have also pointed out its palpable idiocy. That Reverend Sharpton had met the widow Garvey isn't in doubt. It is public knowledge and generally accepted fact. But it didn't happen as he'd told us and was likely as part of the contingent of religious leaders—former "Garveyites" paying homage to the wife of their hero. He might have also met Mrs. Garvey later as an adult.

---

72 Ibid.

Nonetheless, we couldn't have missed the Christ-like incarnation of the young prodigy in conference with very important adults. Nor could we have missed its comedic value. A ten-year-old in a hotel room had picked up the telephone book (which if existed, would've been available only to the roughly 46,000 elite island-wide customers and hotel front desk), called a prominent woman in the morning, and hopped into a taxi to be at her place for a cup of peppermint or ginger tea (Jamaican staples) in the afternoon. This story was dubious on many levels but most notably in this aspect: only the actual Nazarene did that sort of thing in those days.

Drinks with Adam Clayton Powell Jr.

At about the same time he was exploring a Jamaican phone directory in search of the widow Garvey's number, the young messiah was searching out local heroes in New York as well. He told us that it was through reading a book about Adam Clayton Powell Jr., also at age eight or nine, that he'd learned about Marcus Garvey, as Clayton Powell Jr. was a "Garveyite." The Rev. then convinced his older sister Cheryl to take him to Harlem to meet the congressman, who was also head of the Abyssinian Baptist Church:

> After service, I found my way to the pastor's office (when you'd been in as many churches as I had, you knew how to do that). In those days they had offices with doors where the top would swing open while the bottom stayed closed, and I can still see the church secretary leaning over the top and looking down at me, laughing and wondering what this little kid wanted. I said, "I'd like to meet Congressman [*sic*] Powell." She smirked and said, "Who should I say is calling?" "The Reverend Alfred Sharpton," I said. She said, "Reverend Alfred Sharpton?" I said yes. And she looked at me superciliously and walked away and didn't come back. After ten minutes I knocked and asked again…She disappeared into his office and immediately came back out with a sheepish confused look on her face. She waved to me and said, "Follow me."[73]

---

73 Ibid., 39.

Here, we got a repetition of the pint-sized genius who was too small to be seen by widow Garvey, who had to come to the door three times to see him. This time though, it was the "superciliously" smiling church secretary who'd had to lean over a counter to see him. Of that initial meeting, the Rev. painted a picture of his hero that would've been unflattering of a drunk, not to mention the national leader and scion of black New York politics and activism. The congressman-preacher had a reputation for women, and elsewhere in *Pharaoh*, Sharpton had even made admirable note of Clayton Powell Jr.'s masculine prowess—his gallivanting through Europe with two models, "one black and one white," in days when such conduct had still posed a danger for black men in many parts of America. Nonetheless, the Rev. chose the image of a half-naked man hugging two or three church grannies as a first impression of his hero to impart to his readers. For Sharpton, this was a rosy picture, as he was the one being recognized by the most famous black man in all of New York, who'd already known of him as the "Wonderboy" preacher:

> There was Adam Clayton standing in the middle of the floor with his pants on, no shirt, no T-shirt, bare-chested and his arm was around two or three older women—they looked like they were in their seventies or eighties. And he looked at me said very dramatically, "Here's the Wonder boy preacher from my friend FD Washington's church, Alfred Sharpton." I was in heaven. Adam Clayton Powell knew who I was. I said, "You know me?" And he said. "Of course. I listen to Bishop Washington's broadcast when I'm in town. Everybody knows you."[74]

It was the recurring pattern across his books to reduce others to elevate himself. The Rev. introduces us to the important people in his life—invariably national leaders or famous individuals—then uses his intimate knowledge of them to paint portraits that savage and reduce them in order to make himself appear rosy in the process. By fusing (*without integrity*) into their social orbit and high status in life, he elevated his own. By showing us their imperfections, he masked his own. Accordingly, the minister-congressman

---

74 Ibid.

invited the ten-year-old boy to Harlem's Red Rooster for a drink—oblivious to Sharpton's age or in total disregard for it:

> He [Powell] put his shirt and tie on and his jacket, then he looked at me and said, "Come on Reverend, let's go have a drink at the Red Rooster." "A drink?" I said, "I don't drink, I'm ten years old." He said, "A soda then." So we walked over to the bar and I sat there with Adam as he drank Scotch and held court. It was the most incredible exhibition of power that I've ever seen.[75]

The man-boy "bromance" soon intensified, and according to the Rev., the two would go on to develop a profound friendship that would see Sharpton become a fixture around the congressman:

> After that, every time he came to town I would try to attach myself to his entourage, and I was usually successful, hanging around with him after church or riding around the city in his car. He liked me, and I think he knew that all I wanted from him was to be around him—and since everybody else always had a request for something specific, that was easy for him, and even relaxing, because I would let him talk and blow off steam and was happy to listen.[76]

By all counts, it was a fruitful relationship in which the young Reverend was often the beneficiary of the great man's great wisdom:

> One day when we were riding, Powell turns to me and said, "Kid?" "Yes Sir?" He said, "Don't ever forget this: If you expose your own weaknesses, they can never use them against you. Cause can't nobody tell what everybody already knows. What might appear to be reckless behavior on my part is really defense. They can never threaten to expose me, because I expose myself."[77]

---

75 Ibid.

76 Ibid., 40.

77 Sharpton with Hunter, *Al on America*, 187.

Reporter David Frost had famously interviewed Adam Clayton Powell Jr. in the 1970s and this had left an indelible impression on the young Sharpton. The congressman had shown what he was made of, and the Rev., at the writing of *Pharaoh* in 1996, had also shown his continued adoration for Clayton Powell Jr.'s machismo:

> Adam just had his own style, his own way of doing things. I'll never forget the night he was on The David Frost Show. He was wearing a black turtleneck sweater and he had on this gold medallion and Coptic gold cross that Haile Selassie had given him. Frost's first question was, "Congressman, you know what's said about you, that you're arrogant, but how would Adam Powell describe Adam Powell?" And then Adam said, "I'm the only man in America that doesn't give a damn. I think that is why I liked him so much. He didn't give a damn, he couldn't be intimidated, not in Congress, not in New York, not on the street, not anywhere."[78]

As *Pharaoh* was the journey of the young messianic Reverend, we saw the ruler of Harlem, Adam Clayton Powell Jr.—then one of the most powerful black men in America—captivated by the ten-year-old. The Rev., in turn, deified Clayton Powell Jr. in *Pharaoh*, presenting him as his image of a man's man, a demigod in Harlem, a real black man, just oozing in testosterone. As time wore on, though, Clayton Powell Jr. would lose his luster as the hero of an Al Sharpton moving up the ladder (detailed in a later chapter). The "bromance" would give way to scorn and derision heaped upon the congressman, in Sharpton's deft decoupling from his former hero, in two successive books.

Adolescent Activist

As early as his freshman year at Tilden High School—the school we both attended a decade or so apart—the Rev. was more prone to courting strife than to seeking an education. This is not meant to diminish his role as a teen activist, as I came across a Tilden classmate of Sharpton, who told me that he and the Rev. had belonged to a school group called "The Forum" that was tasked with getting

---

78 Al Sharpton and Walton, *Go and Tell Pharaoh*, 40.

famous people to come talk to the student body. Sharpton was instrumental in getting Muhammad Ali, among others, to speak to the student group. But this former Tilden student also recalled that the Rev. had run a crooked raffle in school; Sharpton and two other guys who'd run the lottery had ended up winning all three prizes up for grab. That was the end of the Sharpton raffle at Tilden.

In my time at Tilden, some of my friends and I had thought that a few of those older white teachers might have been racists. At times, they'd seemed jumpy and somewhat afraid of us black kids. But it was only after reading *Pharaoh* that I would come to understand that they might have had good reasons to be fearful of some of us. The mystery of some of the haggard-looking, longer-term administrators and teachers was solved. Even more than ten years later, they'd still not fully recovered from the trauma of hurricane Sharpton; they were still worn out by the experience of the notorious teenage Reverend. It'd been a mere decade since they'd escaped near hell, so imagine welcoming the new classes each September since 1972, wondering which might hold the next "Reverend Alfred Charles Sharpton Jr."

Reverend Sharpton had boasted of that hell he'd inflicted by proudly showing us how he'd routinely emotionally blackmailed the entire school administration for almost nothing. Shutting down the school and interrupting the education of hundreds of students because he didn't like the meatloaf the cafeteria served was his way of "confronting the system":

> If we went down to the cafeteria at Tilden and we didn't like the food that day, we'd call a strike and close down the whole school. We hated the dress code— you couldn't wear jeans, you had to wear a shirt with a collar. We wanted to wear shorts, jeans, dashikis, kufis. We had strikes and demonstrations and we won. I was one of the ringleaders and it got so bad that the principal, Joseph Shapiro, would call my mother before school and ask "How's Alfred doing this morning? I need to know how many problems we're going to have at school today." I was learning to confront the system.[79]

---

79 Ibid., 51.

Recounting the zeal with which he'd set out to confront the system at such a young age had highlighted the sad insecurities and probable early traumas that had seen a young man more consumed with combativeness than with any zeal for an education. At an age when most boys were busy chasing girls, the youth, who was supposedly entrenched in the Word of Christ (an expert by high school), was embracing confrontation while thriving on trench warfare for no reason at all. His objective wasn't an education in the "ABCs" or the aesthetics of an enhanced intellect; neither was it manifestly charitable. The Christian preacher was happiest doing battle and imposing misery upon others. If the cafeteria food wasn't to his pleasing or if the school uniform didn't excite him, he declared war and shut down the entire school—sabotaging the education of the whole student body. It was the early perfection of confrontational blackmail.

This behavior would later propel him into leadership and national stardom, which is to say that there would be no Reverend Sharpton today at the forefront of race relations and atop black leadership, were it not for the amphitheater personality perfected as a teen that conditioned him to combative social blackmail. He's not only a product of his society but its indictment as well. Even as he'd boasted about terrorizing his high school, he'd failed to realize that the system that had conditioned a life spent in the embrace of reactive confrontation was the system that had also controlled that life in its totality.

College Dropout

The Rev. dropped out of Brooklyn College in his sophomore year because he was "too intelligent." He then spent an entire book insulting the black educated class (earlier pointed out), while showing he wasn't intelligent enough to even do that very effectively. Supposedly, he'd personally known all the people he was learning about in college and had become bored with the redundant education. "Much of what we studied I knew better than the teachers," he said. "Because I had been out there on the front lines doing it, and I knew personally many of the people we were talking about. This caused me to get bored, and I dropped out after two years."[80]

Beyond sympathizing with the curriculum at Brooklyn College in those days, we're left to imagine the level of devastation wreaked on the Rev. by such a restrictive degree program that had him studying Adam Clayton Powell Jr., Jesse Jackson, singer James Brown, and possibly a few others in a loop, ad infinitum. While he might have known those subjects by heart, it's clear, from his public comportment over the years that he was and remains deficient in other possible areas of valuable studies that he'd missed. But so caught up was he in his teen activism that it really is a surprise that he'd even made it out of high school. In fact, the dates of historical events for which he has stated an involvement would suggest that he didn't even graduate high school—if those involvements are correct. For example, he tells us of being a chief defender of Congressperson Shirley Chisholm against male religious and political leaders at a 1972 Gary, Indiana black political conference that had taken place when he was only a seventeen-year-old (discussed in a later chapter).

Additionally, a close look at the Rev. over the years has revealed somewhat of a functional illiterate. In his many years in the public domain, he has shown no capacity for learning—relying instead on trite platitudes and rhythmic generalities in his public discourse. In fact, even today, any pretense that Reverend Sharpton does anything beyond committing routine massacre and mutilation of the English language on his radio and television programs is the height of hypocrisy. In 2016, two decades after he'd told us this story in *Pharaoh*, a black media mogul openly accused the Rev. of illiteracy in a major lawsuit. Yet in 1996 Sharpton had given us his "brilliance" as the reason for having dropped out of college.

Many of us have known many people who dropped out of college for various reasons—financial problems, academic issues, family reasons, poor discipline, partying, stress, and so on. With Reverend Sharpton, though, things were different. He'd dropped out because he was a prodigy, a young genius who'd regularly rubbed shoulders with the subjects of his civics class. A college education in which he knew more than the teachers had bored the pants

---

80 Ibid., 64.

off him. While this might have appeared unprecedented as an explanation for dropping out of college, the Rev. might have been in "tradition," as he so often boasted.

In his epic midcentury book, *Black Bourgeoisie*, African American sociologist E. Franklin Frazier had shown us the emptiness imposed by racial oppression—an emptiness that drives a tendency to boast and to show off. Frazier cited an example of another such genius, profiled in the *Pittsburgh Courier*—then the nation's leading black newspaper. The *Courier's* May 22, 1954, Washington edition had touted the brilliance of a black man who was "too smart," so brilliant in his subject of study that no university in the land had a faculty with enough knowledge to instruct him for his Ph.D. studies.[81] This "brilliant" man might have indeed been the forerunner of Reverend Sharpton. Both were either the smartest people in the room or just traditional elements of the black bourgeois mindset that manifests emptiness bearing the *mark of the oppressed*—that same emptiness that inspires ostentatious boasting in a world of make-believe.

The Rev. then attempted to convince us of his profound regret for dropping out of college by telling us that he didn't need it, while showing us that he did—assuming he'd written the below himself:

> In 1975, I started running around the country trying to start up National Youth Movement chapters. This also hardened me against school, because I was telling myself that I didn't need school, I'm building a national organization, I know all these heavy hitters, what do I need a degree for? I'm saying this to make clear one of my profoundest regrets; I should have stayed.[82]

It isn't hard to imagine the potential for difference at a Brooklyn College with a curriculum that was tinged with a class or two in grammar in between those boring lectures on Adam Clayton Powell Jr. and Jesse Jackson. But being a dropout didn't affect the Rev.'s ability to be a critic of the education of African Americans. Not to be outdone on any issue, he'd taken a trip to Africa in the 1990s and returned with some critique of the black education

---

81 E. Franklin Frazier, *Black Bourgeoisie* (Free Press, 1957), 181.
82 Al Sharpton and Walton, *Go and Tell Pharaoh*, 65.

here in America that was as insightful as it was confusing. He'd believed this generation of African Americans was desirous of a "Garveyesque" move back to Africa, thereby meriting Booker T. Washington's industrial-type education:

> Too many young African-Americans are preparing themselves in ways that won't be necessary to African-Americans or Africans. They are not learning the tools and skills that will build anything, that will develop anything. Too many black students are studying what is essentially rhetoric—law, media, entertainment, music—when what we need are engineers and contractors. The last thing they need in Africa is a street-corner rhetorician.[83]

In other words, the last thing they needed in Africa was an entertainer or a rhetorician. The last thing they needed in Africa was an Al Sharpton.

---

83 Ibid., 250.

The "Anti-King"

If you pick up a starving dog and make him prosperous, he will not bite you. This is the principle difference between a dog and man.

—MARK TWAIN[84]

84 *Pudd'nhead Wilson - The Wit and Wisdom of Mark Twain, 4.*

*Reverend Al Sharpton greets Coretta Scott King during an event honoring the late
Reverend Dr. Martin Luther King Jr., on August 23, 2003, on the steps of the
Lincoln Memorial in Washington, DC, where Dr. King gave his "I Have a Dream"
speech forty years ago. (Photo by Paul J. Richards/AFP/Getty Images.)*

TO TELL MOST African Americans that the contemporary pretender to Dr. King's throne had started out by belittling Dr. King would be met by utter disbelief. But the nexus of naïveté, arrogance, hubris, and poor judgment had found comfort in megalomaniacal buffoonery when, as a forty-two-year-old, Reverend Sharpton had urged black politicians and activists to model themselves after, and to emulate Adam Clayton Powell Jr. but not Dr. Martin Luther King Jr.:

> Whenever you study a political leader, Mao or Castro or Churchill, you have to study them in the context of their environment and their times. Northern black politicians and activists should study Powell, because Martin Luther King is not really a model for them.[85]

In fact, some of the most irreverent sentiments conveyed in his books were his early attempts to belittle Dr. King, King's civil rights movement and the people around him. Without reservation, *Pharaoh's* Sharpton had taken great ease in launching reductive critiques of Dr. King and his legacy. The Rev. was so deep in the throes of idolatry for Adam Clayton Powell Jr. that he stood Dr. King and Clayton Powell Jr. side by side and made a strong case that the latter was the Babel Tower of the two. It was perplexing to see a black man in America writing a book noting unfavorable comparisons and even outright criticisms of the man regarded as a prophet by black America. But in addition to a youthful idolatry of Adam Clayton Powell Jr., it was also about the perverted notion of "greatness" Reverend Sharpton had chased around in his head. He's always believed himself capable of fully debunking Dr. King's supremacy at some point in the future, to claim the mantle of "great black leader."

---

85 Al Sharpton and Walton, *Go and Tell Pharaoh*, 41.

Civil Rights Usurpers—Arrivistes and Parvenus

Adam Clayton Powell Jr., who had ruled supreme over black New York City, had seen himself in rivalry with Dr. King. As Dr. King had sought to branch out of the South, Clayton Powell Jr. had once warned him to stay out of New York, even exploiting the homophobia of the era by threatening to publicly link Dr. King and his movement to unsung movement architect, the gay Bayard Rustin. Seemingly caught up in a time warp for some three decades, the then not so progressive Sharpton of 1996's *Pharaoh* was reflective of his idol in his sentiments. In paying the ultimate homage to Adam Clayton Powell Jr., he'd written a chapter telling us that Dr. King's work and legacy was nothing compared to Clayton Powell Jr.'s. According to Sharpton, Dr. King had operated in the simple context of a homogenous black-white environment in the South—an infinitely less intractable situation than the complex environment of mixed ethnicities that had faced Clayton Powell Jr. in New York. Dr. King was therefore not the universally accepted leader the world had come to know but was instead a marginal regional leader of a homogeneous Southern dynamic:

> King didn't operate in the northern urban context, King didn't have to deal with Caribbean blacks, West Africans, Latinos, twenty different white ethnic groups, all at each other's throats and all of them against African-Americans. In the South it was black and white. The North is much more complex.[86]

The Rev. then advised black activists and politicians outside of the South to avoid emulating Dr. King, because his greatness was supposedly a function of the simple environment in which he'd operated. There were no Africans, no Caribbeans, and no Puerto Ricans down South to offer enough of a challenge to Dr. King and the Southern civil rights groups, as there had been in Clayton Powell Jr.'s New York. But his efforts at belittling Dr. King had also shown Sharpton's ingrained demagoguery. Attempting to explain away the climactic Crown Heights riots that he'd stoked, he went out of his way to emphasize

---

86 Ibid., 42.

the differences he'd perceived between native and non-native blacks in Crown Heights—revealing the divisiveness at the core of his personality:

> Crown Heights has always been a strange piece of fabric of New York, populated as it is by a mixture of American and West Indian blacks (there is a difference) and a significant concentration of Jews.[87]

His attempt to point to differences among the Crown Heights residents had added no value to the sentence written, no value to the original point being made—his assertion of Dr. King's inferior challenges in the South. It was just to perpetuate divisions among people of color in New York City in support of his argument that foreign blacks, along with Latinos and ethnic whites, were all against African Americans.

At the writing of *Pharaoh* in 1996, the Rev. had already patented the exploitation of pain on the backs of black and brown New Yorkers of all stripes—including Caribbeans and Africans who were victims of racial injustice and the politics of race in the city. His predatory pasture had included names like Michael Griffith and Gavin Cato, among others, and would later include Abner Louima and Amadou Diallo—blacks of foreign origins whose mistreatment, abuse, and death had given life to Sharpton's business of activism. And it was precisely this that had led to his belief that he'd become even more powerful than Dr. King because his victims weren't solely native to Georgia, Alabama, Louisiana, Mississippi, or the Carolinas.

However, six years later, the Rev. changed tune in exchange for votes. In 2002's *Al on America*, he showed his Clayton Powell-like greatness by staking claim to leadership of that broader "black-brown coalition," of which he told us that no one (i.e., not even King) had ever previously done. He boasted that he could win the presidential election because he could get the votes of African Americans in Brooklyn, Manhattan, and Queens, and of Latinos in the Bronx, in addition to crossover whites and Jews throughout. This time around, though, the "inferior" Southern civil rights groups and the "simple" Dr. King—bereft of troublesome Africans, West Indians, and Latinos—were nowhere to be found

---

87 Ibid., 196.

in *Al on America*. In his rousing speech to the 2004 Democratic Convention, which would propel him into mainstream stardom, the Rev. told America that the black vote was soaked in the blood of martyrs, soaked in the blood of Goodman, Chaney, and Schwerner, soaked in the blood of four little girls in Birmingham.

But as he moved up the ladder, he became a late-stage convert to Dr. King's civil rights accomplishments, presumably having found either decency or an appreciation for the less complicated black-white situation of the South. Unsurprisingly, opportunism-in-leadership would also drive him to sound a different tone on black immigrants by the time we got to *Stone* a decade later in 2013. Times had changed:

> In the Brooklyn neighborhood where I grew up, I was surrounded by immigrants. Haitians, Jamaicans, Trinidadians, Dominicans, Nigerians, and Senegalese—you couldn't walk down the street without tripping over interesting folks. Like everybody else in America, these people were striving to work hard, send their children to the best schools possible, and trying to grab their little piece of that elusive American dream. So when the issue of immigration began to emerge as an explosive political football, my thoughts would drift back to the streets of Brooklyn. These were real people—people who were part of me. For me, it could never be them against us.[88]

But before his late-stage conversions, the New Yorker who would later build a career positing himself as a knight in the King's army, with claims to mantle and all, had, as a forty-two-year-old man in 1996, held Dr. King in very low regard. Holding flawed sentiments is one thing, but showing the poor judgment of articulating them in a book is quite another. Both King and Clayton Powell Jr. were leaders of their people and had operated in accordance with their respective circumstances and the challenges they'd faced. But history has never compared or elevated Clayton Powell Jr. to the level of Dr. King, so Reverend Sharpton's need to do both was vicious at best, sinister at worst.

---

88 Al Sharpton with Chiles, *The Rejected Stone*, 149–50.

As he climbed the ladder, the subject of Dr. King had grown a little tricky for the Rev. He'd started out by savaging the civil rights icon only to later find legitimacy by wrapping himself up in Kingly robes. Moving to dethrone Jesse Jackson, who'd assumed King's mantle to great personal success, the Rev. then did all in his power to portray himself as "in the tradition" of Dr. King—albeit an incarnation that had only come much later. But this was just the start of the irreconcilable dichotomies of *Pharaoh*.

Sharpton had written that he'd set out to serve his people through preaching in the church at the age of four and through activism at about four and a half. He was a "Garveyite" by age ten, having read all that he could have on Marcus Garvey—a man who was at his pinnacle in the 1920s and who'd died some fourteen years before Sharpton was even born in 1954 and therefore some twenty-eight years before Dr. King's death. Yet at almost fourteen years old when Dr. King had died, the prodigious teenager and young activist-preacher had felt no personal connection to Dr. King—the man he told us he'd once met with singer Mahalia Jackson, and whom he'd supposedly admired. But Dr. King's death had meant so little to the young Rev. that it had taken some explaining by his mother for him to have understood her tears:

> Then Dr. King was killed. We were watching television that Thursday night when it came across the screen that he had been shot in Memphis. My mother started crying. I didn't understand why she was so upset, crying like he was a member of our family. I'd met Dr. King and admired him, but I didn't feel the personal connection.[89]

He then went on to describe how Dr. King had become an influence on him after he'd seen the *Montgomery to Memphis* documentary on King's life. It was then that he claimed to have gone and requested that his church pastor make him the youth director of Dr. King's Southern Christian Leadership Conference's (SCLC) Operation Breadbasket. In other words, as a teenager, it had taken a documentary for the boy, who'd set out to serve his people since age four, to be inspired by the most important black leader in America:

---

89 Al Sharpton and Walton, *Go and Tell Pharaoh*, 44.

About six months after Martin Luther King's death, a film came out called King, A Filmed Record...Montgomery to Memphis. There was a song on the sound track by Nina Simone, the refrain of which was "What are you gonna do now that the king of love is dead?" I began to hear that song as a challenge. I felt guilty, like I had let Dr. King down, that I wasn't doing my part. So I went back to Operation Breadbasket and I asked Reverend Jones if I could continue a youth division, and he said he'd been hoping I would want to do that.[90]

But even this was hard to believe, as much of what the Rev. had said elsewhere in the same book was even more reductive of Dr. King. He'd seen Dr. King as a man chosen by the white establishment—at least preferentially, whereas his real hero, Adam Clayton Powell Jr., had been his own man—someone the establishment couldn't have controlled. The Rev. believed that Dr. King had become the heroic scion of civil rights only as a result of being a "safe" choice, as opposed to the rambunctious Clayton Powell Jr., who was torpedoed by the establishment and the media. Juxtaposed next to Clayton Powell Jr., the Dr. King he described in *Pharaoh,* even while softly refuting the notion of being "harmless," had stood deflated as indeed a harmless media-made effigy:

> The establishment didn't want blacks to emulate that independence [of Powell], that self-assurance, that arrogance. The media and the establishment could tolerate Martin Luther King, because he was "thoughtful" and "philosophical," and after they got through with him, they made him almost harmless, in their distortions...[91]

In 1996, the Rev. had still seen himself in unison of purpose with Adam Clayton Powell Jr. and not with Dr. King. That the media had regularly ridiculed him, had meant that he was in step with Clayton Powell Jr. and not with the media darling, Dr. King, and this had brought Sharpton much consolation. Elsewhere

---

90 Ibid., 47.
91 Ibid., 41.

he'd even inferred that the media didn't like him because he was no Dr. King, because he was instead, pure red-blooded Adam Clayton Powell Jr.

All the King's Men

Reverend Sharpton didn't just attempt to marginalize Dr. King, but he also went downstream after King's organization—the Southern Christian Leadership Conference (SCLC). He also tried to do the same to other civil rights organizations of the era as well, including the Student Nonviolent Coordinating Committee (SNCC) and the Congress of Racial Equality (CORE). However, it might have been personal with CORE, whose leader, Roy Innis, had famously tossed a then portly Sharpton from his chair for television viewers in 1988 after Sharpton had called him a sell-out.

Sharpton, whose National Action Network and its predecessor youth movement have achieved nothing on behalf of his people in nearly four decades, then attempted to downgrade the originality of the other civil rights organizations, including the NAACP—again in deference to Adam Clayton Powell Jr.'s accomplishments in the North. To him, Dr. King, his cohorts, and others were mere inferior carbon copies of Clayton Powell Jr.:

> Most young Americans, particularly whites, do not understand Powell's significance. Most of what SCLC [Dr. King's organization], SNCC, MFDP, CORE, NAACP, and the Freedom Riders did in the Civil Rights Movement, Powell did years before—boycotts, marches, sit-ins, and the like.[92]

Finally, in cynical defiance of reverence, Sharpton then presented the men around Dr. King as little more than insecure, ego-driven, petty bumbling idiots. He showed us, grown men, including civil rights leaders Hosea Williams and others, coming to blows in a petty dispute in New York. He carefully noted, almost sarcastically, that this was the supposed nonviolent organization led by Dr. King. By implication, this kind of pettiness and brute behavior was par for the course and the essence of King and his men—the heart of a movement the

---

92 Ibid.

world had come to revere. *Show me your friends, and I'll tell you who you are*, my grandmother used to say:

> I saw for the first time some of the personal tensions that would eventually un-dermine the Civil Rights Movement. Reverend Abernathy was there, along with Hosea Williams, and Williams says that he wants to know why the New York ministers aren't working with their "white allies" in the Village. Hosea disrupted the mass at Saint Patrick's Cathedral the week before and all the Catholic priests who had been coming to Breadbasket stopped. Another minister accused Hosea of disrupting the movement, and they actually came to blows. This was the non-violent SCLC, Martin Luther King's organization.[93]

The picture of internal pettiness was complete. Elders, like a pack of hyenas, had targeted the young Jesse Jackson for abuse because Jackson was getting more national attention than the rest. They'd even gone as far as to suspend Jackson from the SCLC for nothing but pure petty jealousy:

> The real fighting conflict was between Abernathy and Jesse. People were accus-ing Jesse of insubordination, and it slowly became clear there was going to be a split…When the breakup came and Jesse formed PUSH, I left [Breadbasket] as well and formed the "National Youth Movement." Abernathy was jealous of Jesse's star power and didn't want him around. They suspended him from SCLC for no reason. They worked at openly humiliating him. There is a lot of human drama that goes on behind closed doors in the ministry. Ego, envy, somebody's wife telling him, "Don't take that," or his children saying, "Why is he on the cover of Jet and not you, Daddy?"[94]

It is true that in the aftermath of Dr. King's death, frictions had emerged be-tween Reverends Jackson, Ralph Abernathy, and others, which had forced Jackson's departure from Operation Breadbasket somewhere around the end of 1971 to form his own organization. This had spelled doom for the Operation

---

93 Ibid., 59.
94 Ibid.

Breadbasket, and Sharpton stated that he (then a seventeen-year-old) had also left the organization around that time to form his own youth movement. But who needed to read such sordid details of civil rights leaders squabbling in a book about Reverend Sharpton's life? Surprisingly, though, only a year after he'd written the above in *Pharaoh,* this part of the story was turned upon its head by the Rev.'s own public action. Although having pilloried and laughed at the SCLC as being a knockoff of Adam Clayton Powell Jr.'s early achievements, in running for public cover a year later, Sharpton then declared himself a lifelong SCLC man.

During the 1997 New York City mayoral primary campaign, his primary opponent, Manhattan Borough President Ruth Messinger, had put the Rev. on the defensive by writing him a letter demanding that he denounce Nation of Islam leader Minister Louis Farrakhan for remarks she'd deemed anti-Semitic. Sharpton then postured his way to high umbrage by wrapping himself up in Dr. King's Southern Christian Leadership Council (SCLC)—the very group and people he'd depicted as bumbling fools with violent tempers only a year earlier. In his April 5, 1997, response, he put Ms. Messinger in her place with high indignation:

> I grew up in the civil rights' movement. At the age of 14, I was appointed Youth Director of the New York Chapter of the Southern Christian Leadership Conference, [founded by, the Rev. Dr. Martin Luther King, jr.], by the Rev. Jesse L. Jackson, (my lifetime mentor). Dr. King never personally denounced Malcolm X, Rev. Jesse Jackson never denounced the person of Minister Louis Farrakhan. I am in that tradition and spirit.[95]

In deflating Ruth Messinger's own posture, Sharpton had elevated himself to being youth director of the actual Southern Christian Leadership Conference (SCLC), while claiming himself a lifelong mentee of Reverend Jesse Jackson. Ms. Messinger's staffers had evidently failed to read *Pharaoh,* published the previous year.

---

95 Evan J. Mandery, *The Campaign Rudy Giuliani, Ruth Messinger, Al Sharpton, and the Race to Be Mayor of New York City* (Westview Press, 1999), 65.

The writing of *Pharaoh* was still in the *Jesse-the-surrogate-father* era and was most effusive in praise of Reverend Jackson. But as with Sharpton's descriptions of Adam Clayton Powell Jr., it was at times embarrassing to read his tales of Jackson as well. Describing Jesse's humiliation at the hands of Dr. King's men was deliberate—painting his mentor's early rise in the civil rights movement as that of a trampled-on doormat. He then went a little further, a little more evenhanded in his takedown of black leadership in general, indicting both Clayton Powell Jr. and Jackson—but not himself— for being petty:

> You've got to deal realistically with the personal insecurities and egos of everyone involved [in politics and activism]…I had seen it with Adam Clayton Powell and Jesse Jackson and others. I was expecting it. A lot of people act as if they have political differences, but it is not political at all, it's personal. It's envy, jealousy, it's a desire to be the one in the spotlight. We don't want to think that men and women who appear to be giants could be so petty, but they are.[96]

If the Rev. was present at a meeting of the civil rights heavyweights behaving poorly after Dr. King's death, he was a teenager living and bearing witness to history and its great men, which should've been sacred. Instead, he ran out and threw some of its most prominent names—Ralph Abernathy, Hosea Williams, and Jesse Jackson—right under the bus. As he'd never shown reverence for very much elsewhere in his book, one of his messages in *Pharaoh* was that the presumed pious men of the civil rights movement were essentially borderline thugs and by implication—that Dr. King might have likely shared their egotistical, brutish, and thuggish pettiness behind the scenes as well. Sharpton's message was loud and clear: *If Dr. King's organization was full of petty, violent, and vain men, then he might have been of the same cloth as well.*

At that time, Sharpton was speaking to African Americans uptown and in Brooklyn who might have remembered Clayton Powell Jr. and even to a few with fleeting memories of Garvey's glory. But later, when his mainstream

---

96 Al Sharpton and Walton, *Go and Tell Pharaoh*, 61–62.

ambitions took hold, the Rev. decided to remake himself into a King acolyte, opting for a full reincarnation in successive books. It was the morphing of that cobra into that entirely new species. All in all, the Sharpton of *Pharaoh* (1996) was actually against Dr. King before he was for him in later years.

God of the Metropolis

Modesty died when clothes were born.

—MARK TWAIN[97]

"AFTER US, THERE'LL be a catastrophe (*Après nous, le deluge*)" is a famous attribution to the great dame of the French gentry—that big-haired well-coiffed Marquise de Pompadour, famed mistress of King Louis XV and patron saint of the Al Sharpton hair-do. They were her words of comfort to her lover during the waning days of the Franco-Prussian Battle of Rossbach at the back-end of the Seven Years' War that had left France defeated and demoralized. This hubris wasn't exactly unusual or new in French Royal circles, as her lover's great-grandfather, the man who'd established France's absolute monarchy—King Louis XIV— had declared to Parisian parliamentarians a century earlier, in 1655, that, "The French State is me! (*L'État, c'est moi!*)"

Since then, both of the above sentiments have been attributed to many and have been heralded by even more. In black America today, there is never a lack of personalities across the spectrum who believe themselves to be both the barriers to "deluge" and the essence of the state of blackness. The behavioral controllers who promote simplicity and anti-intellectualism while attempting to suppress diversity in thought with threats of revoking the valued "black card," are examples of the latter. But among the black leadership—born of the black church and later perfected in politics—this wholesale "noble Frenchness" in mindset that sees itself as indispensable and indisputable, dominates.

---

97 *A Biography, Albert Bigelow Paine - The Wit and Wisdom of Mark Twain,* 18.

The preacher-politicians, by virtue of their church incubation with esoteric beliefs in divine ordination and so on, have always envisioned a deluge the moment they're no longer clutching a Bible on center stage. In recent decades, clutching the Bible has been accompanied by references to aspects of Dr. King's dream while leading protests or marches against racism. This has supposedly delayed the deluge and has made these activist-preacher-politicians, indispensable. However it's viewed, this mindset is still a product of in-church-acculturation or other religiously-indoctrinated hubris of the Black Gods of America.

In *Black Gods of the Metropolis,* writer Arthur Huff Fauset had profiled the inner city religious sects and the messiahs that had sprung up to serve the large migrating black population in the northern cities in the early to mid-twentieth century. They were the typical "movement-to-racket" messianic sects, and inherent to them was a certain paternal condescension used to indoctrinate followers. Control came through the typical means—brainwash and the removal of self-worth of the flock. A Cape Verdean, Marcelino Manuel da Graça, aka Bishop Emanuel "Daddy" Grace, of the United House of Prayer, was among the most noted and celebrated of the "gods." He indoctrinated his followers by "pointing out to them that when he took on earthly form, he chose to lead the Negroes, lowly in state though they are, rather than the members of some more privileged racial group."[98] Presumably, this "earthly form" was the process of immigrating to America.

Like Daddy Grace, Reverend Sharpton, a man perpetually convinced of his own indispensability and who has never been afraid of defending his turf, has always seen himself as both owner of the black condition and the barrier to its deluge. This, an ingrained belief formulated in a young life spent in the Holiness-Spiritualists sects. At heart, the Rev. has never seen himself as equal to ordinary blacks, and he's regularly taken umbrage in the absence of an accorded noblesse oblige. In any given moment of opposition, his innate response has been to attack and to condescend to black America—never hesitating to paint it as "needing him." Black America is Al Sharpton, and when he's gone, there'll be hell to pay. It was Daddy Grace over and over again. Grace had viewed his followers as "lowly negroes," and he'd often ranted against the "bourgeois negroes" who'd dared to question his jack-legged practices. Sharpton believed that he

---

98 Arthur Huff Fauset, *Black Gods of the Metropolis* (University of Pennsylvania Press, 1944), 23.

was the savior of the black race in New York and beyond and that solely he was responsible for advancements by African Americans.

This has seen him demean other African Americans with the same contempt and despotic paternalism of the dictatorial Daddy Grace. It's always been Sharpton's "despotism while saving us from tyranny." His assault on the middle-class and elite blacks was a page from Daddy Grace's book. Whether by telling a New Jersey family that they were trespassers in suburbia, by declaring black CEOs as tentative and powerless or by calling youth activists in Manhattan "ho[es] being pimped out," the Rev.'s megalomaniacal behavior has been consistent. It's deeply rooted in the repressive church milieu that conditioned him as a youth.

In *Stone*, the Rev. unknowingly showed his hand when he told a casual and tangential story of how singer James Brown had taken a half beat out of a church and changed musical history. Cathartically, it appeared innocuous, but it was a significant nod to Daddy Grace:

> James and I were driving his van, just the two of us, with him at the wheel—as a New Yorker, I've never learned to drive—down a dark street in the heart of Augusta's [Georgia] black community. Suddenly, James pulled the van over to the side of the road. He was staring across the street at a big church. I could see that it was the United House of Prayer for All People, the Augusta chapter of Daddy Grace's church. Daddy Grace was a charismatic black evangelist and one of the first black religious leaders to put a band in a church. "You hear that band?" James said to me, pointing up at the church, which was lit up like a Christmas tree and pulsing with the sound of a jamming band. I nodded. Smiling, James told me that he learned the beat he later made famous, the half-beat, from listening to the drummer in Daddy Grace's band. When James said, "I'm on the one!" that's what he was talking about. James took that half-beat out of the church and changed the course of music history.[99]

In his first two books, he told us that he'd modeled his life on Reverend Jesse Jackson's and Congressman Adam Clayton Powell Jr.'s. In the third, he claimed to have shaped it on Dr. King's. But he has never shown anything in

---

99 Al Sharpton with Chiles, *The Rejected Stone*, 81.

common with any of those men. His urge to tell his people that he was the leader who'd opened the way for them was just channeling his real hero and real role model—which was neither Jackson, Clayton Powell Jr, or King. As opposed to the paternal abandonment he often blames for the character of a buffoon, his personality was really shaped by the cult conditioning of his church and his admiration for one of its pioneers—Daddy Grace.

But there was yet another red flag raised across his books. The Holiness-Spiritualists sects to which Daddy Grace and others like Father Divine had given prominence had prohibited the processing ("perm" or straightening) of hair or had at least frowned upon it as taboo. In his books, the Rev. has had an obsessive desire to explain away the reasons for his processed hair, telling us, for example, that James Brown had asked him to do it. But to a nation accustomed to seeing him that way, his processed hair is hardly even noticed; no one really cared after a while. Yet he has continually written about it because, in addition to being an old mark of inferiority and self-renunciation among black men of his generation (outside of showbiz types), it also holds a stigma inherited from his church and from his real hero, Daddy Grace. It was that early church indoctrination that has compelled his need to justify crossing this taboo against processed hair.

With the Rev., hearing what he's told us has rarely ever matched what he's shown us. What he's shown us is that Daddy Grace—the charismatic midcentury cult leader of black America who was blindly adored by the flock he fleeced, was indeed the model for the Sharpton life.

The "Jack-leg Preacher"

The illiterate "jack-leg" country preachers are legendary in the annals of the black church. Today, they've come to be mostly associated with the Holiness and Spiritualists sects that form a large block of the Pentecostal denomination (H. L. Mencken's "palpable idiots") into which Reverend Sharpton came of age. These are the church folks who prostrate themselves, who speak in tongues, who leap, whoop, scream, and cry to music and tambourines while scaring themselves and the rest of us with hell, brimstone, fire, and the end-of-times apocalyptic rhetoric of the evangelist John's Revelations. For these reasons, black Lutherans, Methodists, Baptists, Episcopalians, and other seminarians often view them with derision as backward and *démodé*.

In his first book, the Rev. told us of his Holiness-Spiritualist upbringing under Bishop F. D. Washington (the man who'd put him on a soapbox before he was in kindergarten). As much as he'd regaled himself in stories of being a childhood Pentecostal preacher, Sharpton also readily conceded that the Methodists, Baptists, and other Seminarians had snubbed his Pentecostals, telling us, "The Methodists and Baptists looked down on Pentecostals. As ministers, we were considered to be jack-leg improvisers, while the elite were seminarians."[100] For him, this was yet another source of rejection by his own people. He's repeatedly told us that his sect was looked down on by seminarians like Reverend Jesse Jackson and others from the civil rights era, including Dr. King. So to flee the stigma of the jack-leg preacher, the Rev. then decided to become a Baptist. By the middle of *Al on America*, there was a picture of him and his family being baptized into the Baptist faith at Bethany Baptist Church; since then he has proudly referred to himself as a Baptist preacher.

He'd finally abandoned his jack-leg Pentecostal baggage, divorced himself from his past, and moved up the religious-social ladder to become an acceptable seminarian. But those ties had still bounded. Shedding his jack-leg baggage by becoming a Baptist seminarian had done little to lighten the ingrained Holiness-Spiritualists angst. Two decades later, in 2016, the Rev. was still echoing the same sentiments of rejection, telling writer James McBride, in McBride's book on singer James Brown, of how others, including Jesse Jackson and Dr. King, had thumbed their noses at his creed of Pentecostals.

Power Player, Fixer, "Godfather"

On his road to dominance, Reverend Sharpton had moved to spread his wings, real and imagined. To have claimed sole credit for securing the prosecution of racists who'd targeted African Americans in the 1980s and 1990s was nothing new, but in no time, he was also taking credit for every aspect of improvements and advancements in black lives as well—both social and economic. By the

---

100 Al Sharpton and Walton, *Go and Tell Pharaoh*, 49.

mid-1990s, he'd come to believe that he was either on his way to becoming the next Adam Clayton Powell Jr. or that he'd already become so. Black America was now Al Sharpton, and Al Sharpton was now black America (*L'État, c'est moi!*). Accordingly, those who'd encountered difficulties in business and economic participation in New York City were forced to call on him as a kind of fixer, godfather, or kingmaker, to take care of business.

For readers of his books, hearing the Rev. on New York City's leading black radio station, WBLS, is quite natural given his claim to having helped Percy Sutton establish WBLS's parent company—Inner City Broadcasting. As the Rev. told us,

> I wanted to help make black business powerful. So if we went to Macy's and picketed and got some contracts, or helped establish Inner City Broadcasting [the Percy Sutton company that owns Black station WBLS], well that is what we set out to do.[101]

For a generation, entrenched politicians and businessmen Percy Sutton and Basil Paterson (father of former governor) were at the nexus of New York City's black Democratic machine, along with Congressman Charlie Rangel, former mayor David Dinkins, and others. This meant that in their business dealings, these men were more likely to use Manhattan lawyers, business advisers, and political expediters, than a street activist from Brooklyn-Queens. But as with much that he's written about the famous, the Rev. had nothing to lose in writing these stories, because those knowing the truth were unlikely to waste time dignifying his claims, much less contradicting them. Here, he'd spoken of how he'd been "used," but notice that it wasn't he who'd felt used by Percy Sutton et al., but instead it was his youth movement that had received the criticisms:

> The National Youth Movement has received a lot of criticism over the years, including the charge that we were used by Percy Sutton and others to help their business activities or that we didn't sustain anything of permanence. I never had a problem with people "using" me, only with their misusing me. I think that the

---

101 Ibid., 61.

older black businessmen did gain some advantages—we helped them leverage contracts and such—and I think that some of them were cynical in that use. But my goal was to be used, to help expand black business, and that is what we did.[102]

The belief that he'd "arrived" had enabled him the duplicitous platform from which all natural-born *arrivistes* have traditionally been catapulted—the pretense of having the power to make things happen. His claim to helping to establish Inner City Broadcasting must have left members of the Sutton family and others choking with as much laughter as Congressman Charlie Rangel, on discovering that he'd arranged for Reverend Sharpton's inspection of American troops stationed in Kigali, Rwanda (a story we get to a little later).

Indictment

Whereas it had started in the church, the 1980s and 1990s had honed Sharpton's megalomaniacal persona, and much credit was due to former New York governor Mario Cuomo and state attorney general Robert Abrams. It was during Cuomo's tenure that the Rev. had led some of his most significant battles— sometimes even winning a few, including the fight for his freedom from imprisonment. It was never a straight trajectory up for the Rev., and a lesser soul might have buckled under the pressure. While defeating enemies that had included the governor, the attorney general, and the mayor of New York City, might have evoked a little hubris in the best of us, it had fomented outright megalomania in the man who was so conditioned by his church since before kindergarten.

Seeking to rid free space of Al Sharpton, the Democratic politicians ruling New York had gone after him with a vengeance to send him to prison. Like an awful spouse in a miserable divorce case, the state went over the top with a seventy-count criminal indictment. Among the charges were accusations that Sharpton had stolen $250,000 from his youth movement and that he'd raised money from fictitious organizations that he'd later used for personal expenses—a staple of many unprosecuted politicians.

---

102 Ibid.

To send a person away for a very long time, the authorities generally need only a single indictment for one solid count of criminal activity. So, a seventy-count indictment had amounted to throwing mud on a wall to see what would've stuck. Considering that the Rev. still owes the government millions in back taxes and penalties even today, it is likely that the prosecutors could've found a reasonably airtight single-count complaint with which to imprison him two decades ago, were they not so overzealous to be rid of him. But Attorney General Robert Abrams had opted instead for a nuclear option. It was a slam-dunk railroading of the Rev., and it failed miserably. The deliberateness of the efforts to destroy him had weighed heavily on the Rev., as it would've on anyone. Of their efforts, he was surprisingly candid in his assessment, echoing for the first time, some truth about the Brawley affair. "If they were fair," he told us, "They'd at least say, 'Sharpton was lying through his teeth about Tawana [Brawley], but what the state did was wrong as well.'"[103]

But Governor Mario Cuomo and A. G. Robert Abrams had yet to fully understand the force of nature that was hurricane Sharpton. The Rev. told us that Jack Newfield of the *Village Voice* had called him with the news that Abrams was about to indict him on more counts of tax fraud than he could possibly have committed:

> He [Newfield] said, "My sources in the Attorney General's office tell me it's going to be a tax indictment." I said, "Well, if it is, then I guess I'll join the black leader tax indictment Hall of Fame. Martin Luther King, Adam Clayton Powell, Marcus Garvey all had tax indictments. I guess I should be honored to have reached that level."[104]

Needless to point out that Sharpton had conflated the facts regarding some of the above-mentioned men. Nonetheless, in indicting him, little did Abrams and Cuomo realize that they were enabling and facilitating martyrdom through association. The indictments had propelled Sharpton spot onto his territory, right into his area of specialty—the cheapening of history, the

---

103 Ibid., 141.
104 Ibid., 144.

tarnishing of legacy, and the hilarious equivocations to prophets, deities, and demigods. Any occasion that had allowed Sharpton to equate himself to Clayton Powell Jr., Garvey, Dr. King, Gandhi, or Mandela was a good one, even if it had risked his freedom. He knew that he would've emerged a martyr for the downtrodden, stronger than ever—carrying the cross of Jesus if need be. In fact, on being indicted on seventy counts, Reverend Sharpton had morphed into Dr. King and Simon of Cyrene at once.

While leaving the courthouse in New York City, he felt they were trying to humiliate him by bringing him outside through the front doors, as bringing prisoners out through back doors was the norm. So, the Rev. brilliantly exploited the moment to his advantage, declaring, "I stepped through the door [of the courthouse] into the cameras with my handcuffed fists up and shouting, 'They did this to King! They did this to Powell! They did this to Garvey! This is my inauguration! I have arrived!'"[105] He'd used the opportunity to get the word out, to publicly elevate himself into good company, defiantly declaring to America that he'd "arrived."

Comparing himself to Dr. King would become the norm for the Rev. During the previously referenced 1997 New York City mayoral primary when rival candidate Eric Ruano-Melendez had accused him of being a divisive force in the city, Sharpton shot back, telling him that Dr. King was accused of the same before he was killed.[106] Ruano-Melendez then returned the fire, telling Sharpton that he was no Dr. King but was instead just a preacher without a church, to which the Rev. riposted, "So was Dr. King."[107]

The NY/Region section of the *New York Times* would publish the following headline on July 3, 1990: "After deliberating for less than six hours, a jury acquitted the Rev. Al Sharpton last night of all charges of fraud and larceny brought by the State Attorney General's office." Reverend Sharpton was a free man. But it was a bittersweet victory once he'd realized that martyrdom had been denied. There wasn't going to be a black-leader tax-prison Hall of Fame for him—at least not on that occasion.

---

105 Ibid., 146.

106 Evan J. Mandery, *The Campaign Rudy Giuliani, Ruth Messinger, Al Sharpton, and the Race to Be Mayor of New York City* (Westview Press, 1999), 249.

107 Ibid., 249–50.

"Good Friend" David Dinkins

Gratitude and treachery are merely the two
extremities of the same procession.

—MARK TWAIN[108]

*The African American Day Parade in Harlem on Adam Clayton Powell Blvd. from 111th St.
to 145th St. Former mayor David Dinkins greets Reverend Al Sharpton at the beginning
of the march. (Photo by Misha Erwitt/NY Daily News Archive via Getty Images.)*

108 *Pudd'nhead Wilson - The Wit and Wisdom of Mark Twain*, 17.

IN RECENT YEARS Reverend Sharpton has spoken fondly of his old friend David Dinkins, going as far as to post a picture of the former New York City mayor on social media in 2014 with the following caption: "Being interviewed with former NYC Mayor David Dinkins in his office at Columbia University. He has known me since I was 16 years old. I am now 60, and he is 88 years old." It was both a funny and sad moment for any reader of the Sharpton books, who would've been familiar with the many ways the Rev. had taken David Dinkins to the shed during Dinkins' tenure as New York City mayor. Experiencing the sixteen through sixty-year-old Sharpton is likely to have been no less than a monumental headache for the then eighty-eight-year-old David Dinkins. But as all politics have an element of show business, effusive smiles might just as easily convey favor as well as belying disfavor, betrayal, and treachery.

There were times when Reverend Sharpton's name-calling of David Dinkins was so routine and offensive that Sharpton attempted to ascribe it to others. He was angry with the old guard of black leadership he claimed had feared his independence—those whose failures he could not have been "eloquent" about. David Dinkins represented that old guard, and to undermine his black support in New York City, the Rev. had set out to discredit Dinkins as a sell-out among black New Yorkers. By the time Dave Dinkins had made history by becoming New York City's first black mayor, the upstart Sharpton had long been in his rearview mirror from Dinkins' days as Manhattan Borough president, which had seen the early phases of the Sharpton deceit and treachery against Dinkins.

Initiating Treachery

Having endured the political establishment's efforts to railroad him, the Rev. used *Pharaoh* as a vehicle to settle scores. Along with former governor Mario Cuomo, David Dinkins had come in for literary evisceration. Reverend Sharpton told us that Governor Mario Cuomo, a presumed friend of Mayor David Dinkins, had orchestrated his fellow Democrat Dinkins' 1993 defeat to Republican Rudolph Giuliani by commissioning and releasing a report that was critical of Dinkins' handling of Brooklyn's 1991 Crown Heights riots. These were riots in which Reverend Sharpton had been a major player—either as an inciter of violence or exhorter for justice, depending on whether the perspective was Jewish or black.

In blaming Cuomo for Dinkins' electoral loss, the Rev. told us that, "Cuomo iced him [Dinkins] by dropping the Crown Heights report in the middle of the campaign, roiling everything up again, and that was it. And it wasn't right."[109]

Maybe the white power structure did in fact "ice" Dinkins, but according to evidence later revealed in a book about that election, the Rev. had certainly "diced" the city's first black mayor. It's believed that he'd worked actively behind the scenes with Rudolph Giuliani's camp to oust his fellow African American, David Dinkins, from City Hall. It was never a secret that the Rev. was one of Dinkins' biggest detractors during that time—maybe with even more negative effects than Governor Cuomo's Crown Heights report, yet Sharpton wrote a book accusing the Italian-American governor of "icing" the African-American mayor. We then got the hilarious scene on election night when David Dinkins had lost the race. They'd all arrived at Dinkins' campaign headquarters for the results—the Reverends Sharpton and Jackson along with other dignitaries, including President Bill Clinton. But Governor Mario Cuomo was conspicuously absent and had instead sent an African American aide in his place. Sharpton was hopping mad at the governor's absence:

> This is important because Bill Clinton, the president of The United States, can take an entire evening for David Dinkins, but Mario Cuomo, the leader of the New York Democrats, can't come out to support his own mayor, a longtime loyal Democratic soldier...[110]

At some point, Cuomo's aide came over to ask Reverends Jackson and Sharpton if there was anything that they would've liked him to convey back to the governor. The Rev. gave us the gist of that conversation and the message he opted to send to the governor of the great state of New York:

> So Cuomo's aide looks at Jesse [Jackson] and says, "Is there anything you'd like me to tell the governor?" And Jesse said, "No, thank you." But I said "Yeah, you tell him to kiss my___, that he betrayed David Dinkins, and that he is a low-down good-for-nothing son of a bitch..." I went off. And through my tirade, I

---

109 Al Sharpton and Walton, *Go and Tell Pharaoh* (DoubleDay, 1996), 234.
110 Ibid.

could feel Jesse Jackson tugging at my sleeve, and saying, "High ground, high ground, high ground."[111]

But this was pure posture as the Rev. had apparently worked with Republican Rudolph Giuliani's camp to undermine Dave Dinkins in both the 1989 race that Dinkins had narrowly won and the 1993 race that he'd narrowly lost. Many had blamed Sharpton's involvement in the Crown Heights riots two years before for Dinkins' defeat. The riots had left many New Yorkers doubtful of Dinkins' abilities to manage the city. So, on that election night, Sharpton had gone to Dinkins' campaign headquarters to celebrate, not to support his fellow Democrat who'd just suffered an electoral defeat. Yet he'd found it convenient to blame Governor Mario Cuomo for Dinkins' loss.

In his 2000 book on the Giuliani mayoralty, *Rudy Giuliani: Emperor of the City*, local New York One cable TV reporter, Andrew Kirtzman, quoted African-American Republican and Giuliani campaign operative Arthur Bramwell as stating on the record that Reverend Sharpton had been working with the Republican Giuliani camp against David Dinkins all along. According to Kirtzman, Bramwell said that there was no question that Reverend Sharpton was anti-Dinkins. Arthur Bramwell was well placed to have known this, as he'd played the intermediary between the Giuliani camp and Sharpton.

Evan J. Mandery—a staffer on Ruth Messinger's 1997 primary campaign race—wrote of the length and depth of the relationship between Reverend Sharpton and Arthur Bramwell. Accordingly, after Sharpton had endorsed New York Republican Al D'Amato in the 1986 senatorial race, the senator secured a $500,000 grant from the Department of Housing to rehabilitate a building that ran a drug program sponsored by the Rev.'s National Youth Movement. The program was managed by the Youth Movement's then vice chair, Arthur Bramwell. It was from this program that accusations and criminal charges had emerged against Sharpton for defrauding the National Youth Movement of $250,000.[112] So, if Arthur Bramwell said the Rev. was working against Dinkins,

---

111 Ibid., 234–35.

112 Evan J. Mandery, *The Campaign Rudy Giuliani, Ruth Messinger, Al Sharpton, and the Race to Be Mayor of New York City* (Westview Press, 1999), 25.

it is because the Republican Arthur Bramwell, a long-time Sharpton confidant, was well-placed to know the details.

But differences in personalities and in approaches between the intransigent activist and the gentleman politician were also the cause of much of the problems between Reverend Sharpton and David Dinkins. In the mid-1980s, Dave Dinkins had City Hall in sight, and the Rev. had Al Sharpton in view. The two had clashed during that time when Dinkins, as the Manhattan borough president, had criticized Sharpton during the Tawana Brawley affair. A mutual distaste then fermented that would continue through Dinkins' years as mayor, which had seen the heights of the fractious relationship between the two.

Reverend Sharpton told us that during Nelson Mandela's first trip to America in the early 1990s, "I was excluded from those ceremonies because David Dinkins was angry with me over various things, and I was on trial for fraud."[113] We could only imagine Sharpton's anger and resentment toward Dinkins at being excluded from one of the biggest potential spotlights of the Sharpton life. But as Dave Dinkins had also represented that black middle-class and elite establishment that Sharpton had so passionately detested, the Rev. had made little effort to hide his disgust (earlier cited), while embellishing his Adam Clayton Powell Jr.'s *bona fides:*

> These world leaders [New York white politicians] had never been challenged until us. They had handpicked their opponents. They decided who the Left was, not the people...And the leaders, including the blacks, went along. They got a patronage job here, a neighborhood program there, a substance addiction or an illicit arrangement with a woman overlooked. Then here comes somebody [Sharpton] who says, "The hell with that, put me in jail," and alters the arrangements. Who wouldn't be mad?[114]

Sharpton had seen Dinkins as one of, or representative of, those docile black leaders, and he'd behaved quite like the petulant child during Dave Dinkins' mayoral tenure. It was low-level emotional blackmail, and when Dinkins didn't

---

113 Al Sharpton and Walton, *Go and Tell Pharaoh*, 252.
114 Ibid., 117.

play ball, the Rev. then went to great lengths to advance the idea in the black community that Dave Dinkins was an Uncle Tom.

The 1989 murder of Yusef Hawkins by a white mob in Bensonhurst, Brooklyn, had seen the reinvigoration of Reverend Sharpton (after the Brawley affair) back to the front and center of New York activism and anew in confrontation with Dave Dinkins—then still Manhattan borough president. Here the Rev. told us what he'd felt about Dinkins, albeit attributing the words to others. This had also shown Sharpton with a different objective from that of Reverend Jackson, who had wished to use the young man's murder to bolster Dinkins' electability. In two short paragraphs, David Dinkins was supposedly called an Uncle Tom at least three times:

> Then we heard that David Dinkins was on the way, and one of the cousins said, "That Uncle Tom. He's just coming out here after votes." About an hour later the doorbell rang [at the Hawkins household], and there he [Dinkins] was, looking me in the eye. I think he was surprised, and dismayed, because he had been so critical of me through the Brawley episode. He didn't want to deal with me...Dinkins came into the room and stood next to me, and said to everyone, "I'm here to give my condolences. I'm going to be the next mayor of New York, and when I am I promise this sort of thing will not happen." One of the younger cousins lit into him saying, "What the f--- do you mean, once you become mayor, who gives a f---, you Tom mother----. Who can help Yusuf now? What are you doing for us? At least Sharpton is talking about raising money for the funeral." The others jumped in calling him, "Uncle Tom" and accusing him of using them.[115]

Dinkins' tenure as mayor, starting in 1990, would later come to be defined by the Crown Heights riots—the fire that Sharpton hadn't started but had gleefully stoked. The Rev. had jumped into the thick of things, and this worsened the situation for Dave Dinkins, who many would later blame for mishandling the riots and the spiraling violence that ultimately led to the killing of rabbinical student Yankel Rosenbaum. While he'd expressed sorrow for the death of

---

115 Ibid., 159.

the innocent Rosenbaum, Reverend Sharpton told us that black residents of Crown Heights were so mistreated during the riots that he'd come to believe that Mayor Dinkins had "sold them out." In indicting Dinkins for the treatment of local black residents, the Rev. laid the betrayal directly at the mayor's feet:

> No one really took the black demands and concerns seriously during Crown Heights, and I felt that much of it was simply because there was no fear of organized black retaliation. The black polity was taken for granted, even by David Dinkins.[116]

As with the Yusef Hawkins reception, the Rev. continued to ridicule Dave Dinkins but again with attribution of sentiments to others. Either all of black Brooklyn had come to view the mayor as an Uncle Tom or *Uncle Tom* was a term that had rolled off the average Brooklynite's tongue as casually as a gulp of oxygen:

> We decided that Dinkins and I would meet at the funeral home and go from there to Restoration Plaza. Colin Moore, Alton Maddox, and two of the parents who had children in jail came along, and they suddenly lit into Dinkins—Uncle Tom this, Uncle Tom that—and Dinkins got mad and went off on them and it took a while to get everybody calmed down.[117]

Though Mayor Dinkins had been out of office for three years at the publishing of *Pharaoh*, the Rev.'s antipathy for him remained strong. In describing the scene on the streets in Crown Heights, Sharpton didn't hesitate to make himself the man of the people, while painting New York City's first black mayor as feeble and insincere. David Dinkins was a weakling of a figurehead that had needed Sharpton to play "good cop, bad cop" in the presence of his own white staffers. Dinkins couldn't have shown the whites in his administration that he was actually black on the inside. To illustrate, we were told of a gathering in a room—of the mayor and his deputy mayors and top police commanders and

---

116 Ibid., 209.
117 Ibid., 198.

Sharpton himself, along with some of the black parents whose children were arrested during the melee:

> I said, "You've got to release these kids. Nothing can happen until then." At one point I left the room to go to the men's room, and while I was in there someone came up behind me and said, "That's it, Al give 'em hell." It was Dave Dinkins. And I realized then that he was so tentative that he didn't want to offend his own administration, the people who he had appointed and could fire at will.[118]

Mayor Dinkins, like the feckless Pontius Pilate, was the man who couldn't get the job done, who didn't know what to do, who didn't have the heart to do anything. He was "tentative," not at all a leader with any legitimate authority or command to act from principles, conscience, or from his obligations to the residents of the city who'd voted him into office. Instead, David Dinkins had dreaded that his own white subordinates might have thought that he was on the side of the black folks in Brooklyn. Where Sharpton's former hero, Marcus Garvey, had once derided his nemesis W. E. B. Du Bois in direct terms, the David Dinkins the Rev. had portrayed was an indirect update of Garvey's Du Bois takedown— little more than a houseboy, little more than "a white man's nigger."

Finally, on that election night of Dinkins' loss to Rudolph Giuliani, the Rev. spoke of the sadness and the tears flowing in the room at Dinkins' campaign headquarters when the results had come in. NAACP's head Hazel Dukes supposedly cried like a baby or "like she'd just lost her closest relative."[119] But to Sharpton's surprise, the only person who wasn't upset at the loss was Dave Dinkins himself, who'd appeared relieved:

> People were wiping their eyes, sobbing, and I looked around the room and the only one not crying was David Dinkins. And I thought that, as disappointed as he was, he was relieved that the burden of governing the biggest city in the world was lifted from his shoulders.[120]

---

118 Ibid.
119 Ibid., 233.
120 Ibid.

It was another case where the Rev. couldn't have seen what he was telling us, even though we could see it clearly: Dave Dinkins had just received some good news—of a future free of the likes of the treacherous preacher from Brooklyn-Queens. What was there to cry about? The genteel man Sharpton had known since age sixteen had seen a welcomed future playing tennis as a better option.

A Call for Peace

It wasn't until the writing of 2002's *Al on America* that we would see the full extent of the Rev.'s treachery against David Dinkins. Sharpton's January 12, 1991, stabbing is well documented through the many versions he has written, based on his objectives at times of writing. In his first version of events during his recovery room stay, he'd exploited his own near-death experience just to discredit and embarrass David Dinkins, describing the following in *Pharaoh* (1996):

> I was just coming out of the anesthesia, semiconscious, and I sort of noticed four people standing in the room, and as my head cleared they gathered around the gurney and they all had masks on so I didn't know who they were. I didn't quite know what was going on, I didn't realize I was still in recovery and there was a danger of infection. One of the men with the masks reached for my hand and said, "Call for peace! Call for peace! Al, please call for peace!" As he kept talking I realized it was David Dinkins. And with him is Deputy Mayor Bill Lynch, Deputy Mayor Milton Mollen, and Police Commissioner Lee Brown... We'd had fallings-out and reconciliations down through the years, and there he was holding my hand and asking me to ask for nonviolence. I said, "What do you mean? I've never called for anything but nonviolence." He said, "There are people talking about burning down the city because of this." I still did not clearly know what had happened, just that I'd been stabbed and just had surgery. And that the first black mayor of the city is standing there holding my hand and saying, "Call for peace, buddy. Buddy, call for peace," over and over. So I said, "Of course I'm calling for peace!" Dinkins almost threw my hands back in my face and ran out the door, leaving Lee Brown and the two deputy mayors with me. I later found

out that he ran outside and told the assembled media, "I've just left Sharpton's bedside. He's calling for peace!"[121]

There was high drama in the room. Having come within inches of losing his life and still semiconscious after surgery, the Rev. had awoken to see that David Dinkins—the callous, calculating, self-serving politician, and spineless leader of the city of New York—had shown up to exploit his stabbing. Mayor Dinkins had hightailed into Sharpton's hospital room, barely saying hello, and while at the bedside of the groggy stabbing victim, Dinkins then took hold of his hands and demanded that the Rev. make a call for peace. Once Sharpton had agreed, the mayor quickly threw Sharpton's hands back in his face, after which Dinkins immediately ran outside to calm the anxious legions in Gotham by declaring to the waiting cameras that the oracle of Brooklyn had smoked the peace pipe. Dinkins had shown no concern for the Rev.'s health or conditions; there was no *Al, buddy, how are they treating you? How are you feeling? How's the food?* Instead, David Dinkins had merely shown up to extract a "call for peace" from the Rev.

The semiconscious Reverend Sharpton was shocked to see that the city's first black mayor had come to exploit the situation without expressing any interest in his condition. By all accounts, David Dinkins had behaved shamefully, except that it was all fiction—part of Sharpton's efforts to slander and malign David Dinkins, even after the mayor had long left office.

By 2002, however, the millennium Sharpton knew he'd have some repair to do to the damage done by his lies. He was then trying to go mainstream and needed friends and support. He couldn't have continued to antagonize New York City's Democrats, in particular, the black Democratic machine of Dave Dinkins, Percy Sutton, Basil Paterson, Charlie Rangel, and others—men who were intimate with Sharpton's past treachery against Dinkins. So, the Rev. tidily revised his *pharaonic* inventions that had slandered and mocked David Dinkins. Lo and behold, we got a new version of the same recovery room events that had nothing to do with the picture of the David Dinkins he'd previously painted for us in *Pharaoh*.

This time, in *Al on America*, there was no pretense of a fear of infection as the men had all taken off their masks to identify themselves. There were no

---

121 Ibid., 178.

demands for the Rev. to call for peace, no hands being thrown back in his face, and no David Dinkins immediately dashing outside the hospital to the waiting cameras to announce a Sharpton cry for peace without even checking on the Rev.'s health:

> I was in surgery for a while after the stabbing. When they finally brought me into the recovery room, I was lying there and looked up and saw David Dinkins. I had known David Dinkins since I was a kid…But around the Brawley case, we had gotten distant. He never told me directly that he disapproved of the way I handled the case; he just became distant. Then in 1992, when I ran for the Senate, he supported Bob Abrams against me…But he put our difference aside for a minute after I was stabbed in 1991. After surgery, they took me to recovery. I was really groggy, but I looked up and there were four guys standing around my bed with masks on. They took off the surgical masks and there was Dave Dinkins, Deputy Mayor Bill Lynch, Deputy Mayor Milton Mollen and Police Commissioner Lee Brown. "Oh, no!" I said. "I died and went to hell!" And we all had a good laugh. After Dinkins and the others left, they let Kathy [Mrs. Sharpton] in.[122]

A jovial visit that had seen them all in good spirits, cracking jokes, and sharing a good laugh on seeing the Rev.'s progress was more in line with the David Dinkins—gentleman above all—whom New York and the world had come to know. Outside of those who were present, it's hard to know what had really transpired in the Rev.'s hospital room during the visit by the mayor and his entourage. But like the different versions of the discussion with his father and other varying revisions to multiple stories told, one or both of those accounts was (were) fabricated, the former being likely.

Some two decades later, in 2013's *Stone*, the Rev. would finally give a nod to his treachery against David Dinkins over the years. Commenting on his new and improved self and his decision to "no longer make it personal," by choosing to forego name-calling a Sheriff in Sanford, Florida, during the protests in the aftermath of Trayvon Martin's death, the Rev. was almost confessional. "Hell," he said. "We used to call David Dinkins, who was New York's first black mayor,

---

122 Sharpton with Hunter, *Al on America*, 195.

names. What did that get us? Rudy Giuliani."[123] But even a Sharpton confession isn't without deceit, as he was partly responsible for "getting" Rudy Giuliani.

In a long life of treachery and deceit, no one was safe from the Rev.—not even New York City's first black mayor. Just as he'd pretended to be a Dinkins supporter on that losing election night in 1993, the same "anti-Dinkins" Reverend Sharpton from the 1990s and early 2000s was now touting the elder statesman as one of his oldest friends in 2014. However, the truth is that, as with his late-stage admiration for Dr. King, Reverend Sharpton was actually against David Dinkins before he was for him.

---

123 Al Sharpton with Chiles, *The Rejected Stone*, 118.

Godfather–James Brown

Man will do many things to get himself loved, he
will do all things to get himself envied.

—MARK TWAIN[124]

James Brown and civil rights activist Reverend Al Sharpton backstage at Madison Square
Garden on June 11, 1974, in New York City. (Photo by Waring Abbott/Getty Images.)

---

124 *Following the Equator - The Wit and Wisdom of Mark Twain*, 16.

THE REV.'S RELATIONSHIP with the godfather of soul, James Brown, is legendary, hence the reason for its introduction in an early chapter of this book. The world had seen that relationship right up to the end when a loyal Sharpton took charge of James Brown's funeral arrangements in 2006. The intricate relationship between the two men had served two purposes: James Brown had needed a son to mold, and Reverend Sharpton had needed a father to hold. Further, the Rev. had found a celebrity to whom he'd hitched his wagon. On the one hand, we got the feeling that Sharpton would've been nothing without Brown's fame and celebrity, off which to feed. But on the other, there is reason to believe that had there been no James Brown, the Rev. might have made much more of himself during the 1970s—a period in which he was mostly a James Brown gofer.

Luckily for us, though, the former was true, because, from this, we've gotten a treasure trove of valuable comedy—in particular, those famous Sharpton "lessons learned" from James Brown that have been proffered as evidence of time served.

At some point, the Rev. had become a protégé, groupie, consort, replacement of James's son Teddy, and all-around confidant to the soul singer. Yet in "admirably" writing of his relationship with Brown, Sharpton has often shown the tact and decorum of a James Brown menace or stalker rather than a protégé in admiration—just as he'd done with Adam Clayton Powell Jr. and Jesse Jackson. There were many points in his first two books where we could imagine Brown calling the Rev. on the phone to ask, *Damn, Rev.! Did you have to say all that?* Sharpton told us a lot more than we needed to have known about their relationship, but too little for us to make much sense of it. He described James Brown as the person with the greatest influence over him and the person most responsible for the man he is today. Yet his accounts of his experience with his hero were sometimes deliberately crude, crass, and contemptuous. It was indeed a Sharpton homage to James Brown by Reverend Al Sharpton.

Rumble in the Jungle

In casting doubt on his so-called lessons learned from James Brown, I opened this book with a segment on the contradicting versions of the Rev.'s tale of the two James Browns on the set of *The Blue Brothers* movie. This is because of the many such instances across Sharpton's books where he wasn't even sure of the lesson-learned to put forward—in a life supposedly shaped by lessons learned from James Brown.

In the *pharaonic* version of "Rumble," the Rev. had unnecessarily revealed the most intimate details of James Brown's dealings with cash, which had made Brown appear as diabolical as he was shrewd. When promoter Don King had offered Brown $100,000 to perform at the monumental *fight of all fights*—the 1974 matchup of Muhammad Ali and George Foreman in Kinshasa, Zaire (today's Democratic Republic of Congo), the godfather was incredulous. According to the Rev., Brown turned to him (Sharpton) and said, "Reverend, ain't no black folks got that kind of money."[125] But then they later met with Don King and apparently black folks did "got that kind of money," because James Brown and band, *sans* Sharpton, were soon on their way to the jungle to perform for the "Rumble." This was how the Rev. had recalled the day when he'd dropped Brown off at the airport in New York:

> The day James and the band are leaving we're riding to the airport, and halfway to Kennedy James says, "Reverend, where's the money?" I said I didn't have it, that I didn't think they could give it all to us at once. James said he wasn't leaving until he was paid. He made Don King's people come up with the money, a hundred thousand cash, and they did.[126]

He then told us that on Brown's return from Africa, he'd picked up Brown at the airport as well:

> The day of the fight, I get a call from James's secretary, saying, "Mr. Brown would like you to meet him at the airport." I couldn't believe it. The fight hadn't ended yet. But I went to meet James and asked him why he didn't stay and enjoy the fight and he laughed, "Reverend, how many times do I have to tell you that this is a business? I did my show, I made my money, I got things to do." And strangely enough, Mobutu put everybody connected with the show and the fight

---

125 Al Sharpton and Walton, *Go and Tell Pharaoh*, 69.

126 Ibid.

under house arrest afterward because of the high hotel bills, but James was here in the States, counting his money.[127]

History has recorded James Brown as a headliner at the multi-day concert event—then one of the biggest music festivals in the world, with stars like Hugh Masekela, Miriam Makeba, B. B. King, Bill Withers, the Spinners, Celia Cruz, and others. It was a well-covered event that had even spawned a documentary film some thirty-five years later. Needless to say, the facts are at odds with Reverend Sharpton's depiction.

In the version given in 1996's *Pharaoh*, he'd made it clear that he'd dropped James Brown off at JFK airport to fly to the fight and had picked up Brown at JFK airport on his return from the event. In 2013's *Stone* (seventeen years later), during a segment in which he'd again boasted of his friendship with Brown and of the celebrated life he'd experienced as a youthful player, the Rev. reiterated much the same thing (he was "there when he [Brown] left"):

> During the year and a half that I stayed with James, I was thrown smack into the middle of a teenager's dream: nights in Vegas, parties in Hollywood, shows in London. I was there when he left to perform before the 1974 Ali-Foreman fight, the famous "Rumble in the Jungle." I was nineteen, and I was a player at some of the most intoxicating cultural events of our time. Can you imagine?[128]

Rumble Redux

As sure as the *antistrophe* follows the *strophe*, as night follows day or the other way around, this story, as told in 1996's *Pharaoh* and in 2013's *Stone* (as shown above), would make yet another appearance in an entirely different form in the same book, *Stone*. To suit a different Sharpton objective, from one chapter to the next, the Rev. had two different celebrity affiliations about which to boast and ended up telling two different versions of the same story in the same book.

---

127 Ibid.

128 Al Sharpton with Chiles, *The Rejected Stone*, 77.

Here, he was consistent in showing us his celebrity affiliation but this time, with boxer Muhammad Ali. And this is where it had gotten really confusing:

> I knew some of the guys in the Nation of Islam and through them got to know Muhammad Ali. This was the mid-'70s, after he had regained his title in Zaire in 1974—a fight I had attended as part of James Brown's entourage. Whenever Ali came through New York, I would spend time with him.[129]

In this second version, he'd no longer taken Brown to the airport ("there when he left") for his trip to Africa, nor had he picked up Brown on his return from the African trip ("I went to meet James"). Instead, as a result of his friendship with Muhammad Ali, the then twenty-year-old Sharpton had traveled to Africa to attend the fight ("a fight I attended as part of James Brown's entourage").

In one swoop, the Rev. had erased over twenty-three hundred years of Aristotelian logic that has since guided Western thought development—in particular, the *Principle of Noncontradiction (PNC)*: "It is impossible for the same thing [Sharpton] at the same time [1974] both to be-in and not to be-in the same thing [Queens, NY/Kinshasa, Zaire] and in the same respect [physical form]."[130] But even if Aristotle hadn't laid it out so clearly for us, common sense stands to reason that no single individual can be in two different places at the same time—certainly not when sixty-four hundred miles separate both. Even the emergence of quantum physics, some twenty-two hundred years after Aristotle, can't reconcile model-dimensional realities that could place the same person in Queens and Kinshasa at the same time. So, what might have driven Reverend Sharpton to tell us that he was at sixty-four hundred miles away from home while he was really at home?

The first book was the autobiography of a rabble-rouser and the latter, the autobiography of an insider—a dispenser of advice on the path to American leadership and "adviser" to a president. It was the book by the Obama era oracle who'd moved from the "streets to the suites"—he who was finally savoring his turn in the VIP lounge, intoxicated enough to cobble together a slew of simplistic fabrications in a book and called them, *Life's Lessons for these Changing Times.*

---

129 Ibid., 113.

130 Aristotle, *Metaphysics-Book Gamma*, Penguin Books, (London, 2004) 88.

The newly minted *stone* was the mutation and maturation of that cobra into that new and enhanced hybrid form, but regardless of modification, the essential genetic makeup of a snake still leaves it a snake.

An upgrade in social status had still lacked the cultural mores, social conditioning, and systemic adaptation required to overcome the dictates of its primary genetic constitution. The Rev. was still fabricating, distorting, and confounding—even himself. His newfound condition had merely aggravated his insecurities and feelings of ineptitude, which then drove even more forcefulness and deliberateness to his fabrications. To show us a closeness to Muhammad Ali, he felt the need to show us his invitation to the fight and his presence at the 1974 boxing match as well.

In the first version, Sharpton had given us a very detailed description of the genius of James Brown. Brown was smart enough to perform, skip out on the fight, and return home, thereby also skipping out on former Zairian strongman Mobutu Sese Seko's house arrest of some of the entertainers for unpaid hotel bills. He'd made it back to New York in record time and Sharpton was there at JFK airport to pick up Brown. There was nothing complicated in understanding that version.

Although the Rev. had given a different set of details, the multi-week event was a festival, and the actual musical show had taken place weeks before the fight, due to a training injury suffered by George Foreman that had delayed the main event. The organizers of the concert had decided to allow the musical show to go on, even though the fight was delayed. James Brown, therefore, hadn't skipped out to return to America on the day of the fight (as told in *Pharaoh*), as both events were separated by several weeks.

But with the elevation of his social status during the Obama era, being a VIP in 2013 wasn't enough for the Rev. He had to scrub history to make himself a retroactive 1974 twenty-year-old VIP as well. So, in chapter 11 of *Stone*—"How to Be Great"—it was Sharpton's friendship and proximity to Muhammad Ali that was emphasized. In doing so, the Rev. nixed the previous version of being James Brown's taxi boy to and from JFK airport, and instead, he placed himself among the celebrities and dignitaries at the fight in Kinshasa.

In trying to reconcile the two versions, there was only one other possibility to contend with. Although a Christian preacher, Reverend Sharpton could've nonetheless walked the path charted by the pagan gods. For example, in his tale of Hercules' conception in *Amphytrion*, Roman playwright Plautus told us that once Jupiter had set his covetous eyes on Alcmena, wife of Theban military general Amphytrion, he'd disguised himself as her husband and stopped the constellations in their tracks—freezing time in order to indulge his nefarious desires with the man's wife. If Jupiter could've stopped time dead in its tracks for a carnal tryst, Reverend Sharpton might have reversed it in 1974—in order to be in both Zaire and New York at the same time—hence defeating the genius of Aristotle.

Processed Pompadour

February 26, 1992—Diana Brown, daughter of James Brown, James Brown, and Al Sharpton (L–R) at ribbon-cutting ceremony for Sharpton's Senate race. (Photo by Willie Anderson/NY Daily News Archive via Getty Images.)

As stated before, although popular among their parents' generation and considered acceptable for show-business types, processed hair was anathema to Reverend Sharpton's generation of conscious black men—those who'd come of age in 1960s-era black liberation movements. They'd seen it as a rejection of blackness—as a black man in the throes of deep inferiority complexes or as someone who was otherwise just "country." Additionally, as I've shown, it was also a prohibition of the Rev.'s formative creed—the Holiness-Spiritualists. We saw him struggle to justify his processed hair in the streets of New York, and this had shown yet another element of a life spent fighting rejection by his people:

> There was much tension, some of it legitimate, stemming from the anger coursing through the black community and the streets of Howard Beach, some of it ludicrous, such as the super militants who were shouting to reporters that I had forfeited my right to be an African-American leader because they didn't like my hair.[131]

The Rev. had needed a valid excuse—legitimization to avoid being laughed out of town (which had happened anyway)—and so he invented the novel idea that his trademark "do" was by special request to emulate and to honor his hero, Brown. It was command performance for James Brown. In *Pharaoh*, he'd told us it was the result of a request made by Brown, and in *Stone*, he explained that it was a form of validation he'd so desperately needed—that James Brown would've asked him to emulate him by processing his hair like his own. Brown had supposedly decided to make Sharpton over in his own image before a visit to the White House:

> In 1981 Ronald Reagan invites James to the White House to meet with George Bush, for Martin Luther King's birthday. He said he'd come, but he had to bring me. Before we go, he takes me to this lady in Georgia who does his hair and says, "I want you to do The Reverend's hair like mine, because when we go to the White House there's going to be a lot of press, and when people see him I want them to see me, like he is my son." I agreed, and she put the relaxer in my hair, then started rolling it. Halfway through, James says, "Reverend, I want you to make me one promise. I want you to wear your hair like that until you die." I said

---

131 Al Sharpton and Walton, *Go and Tell Pharaoh*, 108.

okay. Even when he was in jail and he'd call me, he'd say, "Rev, how's your hair?" And I'd say, "Just like you." People often say that wearing a process indicates self-hatred and imitates white people, but my hair has nothing to do with that, it is symbolic of my bond, very deep and intensely personal, with James Brown.[132]

This story is now part of the Al Sharpton-James Brown legend that the Rev. repeats on all occasions. In his bit-cameo appearance in comedian Chris Rock's 2009 satirical documentary, "Good Hair," Sharpton said that before the trip to Washington DC, Brown told him, "When we get to the White House, I want you to look like me because when people see you, I want them to see me—you're a reflection of me." It was indeed a sweet and heartwarming story of a surrogate father who'd commanded a "mini-me" to the delight of his surrogate son who then gladly acquiesced. Although it would appear reductive of a man to request or to insist that his protégé mimic his hairstyle as a sign of homage or reverence, feeling flattered, James Brown would've likely been OK with the story. But as touching a processed-hair tale of love and affection as it was, it was pure fiction.

The meeting at the White House with President Ronald Reagan and Vice President George Bush had actually taken place in January 1982. In the same book, *Pharaoh*, there is a picture of Reverend Sharpton and his fiancé Kathy, a former James Brown singer, at Caesar's Palace in Las Vegas in 1980—as he noted. In that picture, two years before the White House visit, the Rev.'s processed pompadour is way better than Kathy's. Possibilities of inebriation and wrong dates might be cited, but no man with an ounce of dignity forgets the year he took the woman he was about to marry to Caesar's Palace.

In his second book, *Al on America*, we got another hint that this story was fabricated when we learned that the elder Sharpton had processed his hair like James Brown as well. "The first time I set eyes on James Brown was when I was a little boy," Reverend Sharpton said. "My father was a fan of his. He used to wear his hair like James Brown, which made me want to do the same thing."[133] So this had created an early impression on the boy that

---

132 Ibid., 71–72.

133 Sharpton with Hunter, *Al on America*, 204.

prompted him to later emulate his father, who was of that generation where it was more common for black men of certain milieu to copy the aforementioned famed mistress of Louis XV—the Marquise de Pompadour.

But the ultimate proof that his hair-processing had predated any White House visit with James Brown comes in the form of a 1974 video online. From that era's black dance program "Soul Train," host Don Cornelius is seen introducing the then-teenaged Sharpton to present James Brown with a *Thank-You* plaque for his song "Payback." In that 1974 "Soul Train" appearance, the nineteen-year-old Rev. was sporting his well-processed pompadour. So, it's clear that his story of a James Brown homage for the benefit of President Ronald Reagan and Vice-President George Bush is completely fabricated. But once the Rev. had piggybacked a justification on one of the biggest names in show business, his processed hair was immediately indemnified. That James Brown had asked him to do it as a form of emulation had meant that from then on, Reverend Sharpton could've put a blowtorch to his entire scalp and he would've still been considered cool.

In the end, if Brown had indeed asked Sharpton to emulate him, the Rev. might have gotten off easy. Imagine the consequences had Brown been an orthodox Jew instead of just a Republican!

"Huggin' Up the Little Monkey Man"

If Ota Benga had had the talents of James Brown, how different might things have turned out for him? Mr. Benga, the Mbuti pygmy kidnapped in Africa and taken to America, was infamously encaged with an orangutan in a New York City zoo at the dawn of the twentieth century. It was an exhibition that fed the viewing public's appetite for *Social Darwinist* beliefs—the notion that Africans had evolved from primates and were therefore at home in close quarters with their cousins. For clarification, Mr. Darwin's position was that all human beings share a common progenitor with primates.

But so it was that Mr. Benga was viewed as the little *monkey man*. As he could neither sing nor dance the "Funky Chicken," he was denied the chance to overcome his adversities and had ended up meeting a different and rather tragic destiny. James Brown though, could sing and dance, so he became a superstar:

133

When the world looked at James Brown and was calling him a monkey, he looked in the mirror and saw a superstar. When the world was calling him a "nigga," he saw a strong black man. He could write, "Say it loud; I'm black and I'm proud!" after growing up in a place where blacks were forced to sit at the backs of buses, and where they hung signs "For Coloreds" to drink out of separate water fountains.[134]

To convey the adversities that the soul singer had had to overcome in life, the Rev. had felt it necessary to tell us that others used to call his idol James Brown, a monkey. Although Sharpton has often attributed words to others, we'd seen where they were sometimes his own words and thoughts and, in this case, his fixation on the word "monkey" appears to have been no different.

On the imperative need for us to support Africa, the Rev. had once said, "So I am not saying that we should fight for Africa because we're guilty or we owe them something; I'm saying that in order to get the monkey off our back we've got to get it off their back, because it's the same monkey."[135] On his reasons for not cooperating with authorities in the Tawana Brawley case, he'd asked, "Why should we trust the media, the institutions that have held us up to the world as monkeys for so many years?"[136]

Therefore, the need to tell us about the "world" calling James Brown a monkey is naturally suspect, given that "monkey" seemed more the mindset of Al Sharpton than of the world. In any case—true or false—it's hard to think that his idol, the proud James Brown, could've found this in any way, shape, or form, a respectful tribute.

"Small Man Indeed"

In a book about Reverend Sharpton, we heard tidbits of famous people with whom he'd been associated over the years—even of those with whom he'd had mere tangential connections. Once more, in what was more a reduction of James Brown

---

134 Ibid., 206.

135 Al Sharpton and Walton, *Go and Tell Pharaoh*, 247.

136 Ibid., 134.

than a tribute, the Rev. told of a visit to see Brown in prison, carefully pointing out that James' own children hadn't even gone to see their father. But he then spoke of Brown's looks relative to other famous black performers, and the parallels in sentiments toward the former *monkey man* was evident. Now, it was "many" who'd considered Brown "ugly," as opposed to the "world" calling him "monkey:"

> He was short, he was very dark, bowlegged; he didn't have a single Caucasian feature. Many considered him ugly. But he made it. He became successful because he worked hard..."Reverend, you know in the late nineteen sixties when I started there were all those pretty, yellow boys," he would say. "There was Smokey Robinson, Jackie Wilson, Sam Cooke. I had to beat them all. I had to figure out how to get past all of them."[137]

Again, it is unlikely that James Brown could've appreciated such personal details and awkward characterization being published in a book by his protégé. But Reverend Sharpton ruptures protocols of decency with the ease of an airfoil piercing airflow in open skies, and he'd felt it necessary to tell us that our imperfect celebrity idols were indeed flawed. Much like his revelation of internecine warfare among civil right leaders, writing gossipy and unflattering portrayals of celebrities or of the misfortunes of the famous people with whom he'd interacted was his way of reducing their social stature while he glowed like stardust. It was that *fusion without integrity* described by Erich Fromm.

Smokey Robinson, Sam Cooke, and Jackie Wilson are (were) legendary showbusiness names of the same stature as James Brown. If these were indeed the actual opinions of James Brown, they'd needed no disclosure in a book by Reverend Sharpton—about Reverend Sharpton. It is one thing to portray Brown as a man as small as he was short in a book written about James Brown but quite another in a book written about Reverend Al Sharpton. But the Rev. gaveth as he'd taketh, especially of those he'd deemed as his idols. As he'd sought their love, he ensured their denigration. Whether James Brown, Adam Clayton Powell Jr. or Jesse Jackson, Sharpton's mangled homages to the great men in his life had somehow always managed to be reductive of their stature while enhancing his own.

---

137 Sharpton with Hunter, *Al on America*, 207.

Breach of Decorum

NY Daily News Out. Reverend Al Sharpton stands next to the body of James Brown, which lies in repose during a viewing at the Apollo theater on December 28, 2006, in New York City. (Photo by Arnaldo Magnani/Getty Images.)

Democratic presidential candidate senator Barack Obama has a bite of fried chicken as he and the Reverend Al Sharpton have dinner at Sylvia's restaurant in Harlem. (Photo by Andrew Savulich/NY Daily News Archive via Getty Images.)

Decorum and tact—faculties of which the Rev. had long been dispossessed—had exited the pages of *Stone* the moment he'd painted us the picture of James Brown's funeral. It was distastefulness running its full course right up to the end. To show his importance to Brown's life and to the overall politics of the land, we got a picture of Sharpton standing as a palace or Swiss guard next to Brown's body lying in open casket (pp. 184–85). Its awkwardness was a reminder of the reason some cultures and religions prohibit such wanton exhibition of the dead without their permission. But none of that had mattered to the man who would've boiled the ocean in search of that one added photo op with a celebrity—even with a dead one.

The picture of the dead Brown faced one of the live, then-candidate Barack Obama biting into what appeared to have been a piece of fried chicken at Sylvia's Harlem restaurant during the 2008 presidential campaign. The purpose of this image is still a mystery. But as optical sensitivities were obliterated, the irony could hardly have been missed: one African American about to ascend the ladder of greatness was juxtaposed to another who'd just descended it. Somewhere in that juxtaposition was the convoluted optics of three black men—a buffoon, a presidential candidate, and a dead corpse.

Add the fried chicken to the mix, and the shock value was worthy of a VISA commercial—*Priceless!*

In his book, Reverend Sharpton had backed up his verbal vulgarity with an equal level of visual vulgarity that had merited a Joseph Welch to Joe McCarthy type rebuke: "Have you no sense of decency, sir? At long last, have you no sense left of decency?"

Surrogate Father–Jesse Jackson

Man is wolf to Man.

—THOMAS HOBBES[138]

Reverends Jesse Jackson and Al Sharpton shake hands during a protest outside the convention center on the third day of the Democratic National Convention, August 28, 1996, in Chicago, Illinois. (Photo by Jean-Marc Giboux/Liaison.)

REVEREND SHARPTON'S CHILDHOOD paternal dysfunctions are best seen through his relationship with Reverend Jesse Jackson. In Sharpton, Jackson had seen a

---

138 *De Cive* (London, Printed by J.C. for R. Royston, 1651) Introduction

good foot soldier; Sharpton, in turn, then set his eyes on being the next Jesse from a young age. At a certain point, the two had to contend with each other, given that they'd played in the same limited sandbox of civil rights activism and profiteering. But their smiles for the cameras in recent years mask deep, hard feelings and many petty betrayals. For Reverend Jackson, the irony is that Sharpton is the beast he'd created but couldn't control. The Obama era then saw the black Dr. Frankenstein all but neutralized by his own creation, left searching in earnest for even a modicum of redemption after relegation to the sidelines—having been trampled on by his very own monster.

Over the course of three books, we saw a back and forth between the two, from the view of Sharpton's rhetorical aims at the time of writing. One moment he spoke favorably of his mentor Jesse Jackson, while utterly destroying him the next. The Rev. detailed the treasured yearly Jackson-Sharpton family get-togethers but then pulled no punches in telling us that his sole ambition was to be the next Jesse Jackson—while Jackson is still alive. Reverend Jackson appeared at once to be Sharpton's mentor and tormentor—the model and the obstacle to its replication—in Sharpton's objective of capturing the mantle of black leadership, worn by Jackson to great success for some four decades.

We saw the slope of admiration ascend the highest peaks only to plunge. In going after Jackson, the Rev. masked neither motives nor methods but did so in such a way as to conceal the full extent of his machinations. However, the second-rate forger he is, Sharpton often painted the most detailed aspects of his experiences and events—those he wanted us to see—yet did it so clumsily that we immediately recognized it as fake, as complete fabrications to mask the truth.

By the time we got to 2013's *Stone*, Sharpton was firmly in control of the agenda, licking his chops about being the "main civil rights guy" in the country, sanctioned by presidential imperātum. Here he wasted little time on pleasantries toward Jesse Jackson. Jesse Jackson's daughter had sat at the wedding of the Obamas two decades before and is also godmother to one of the First daughters—an indication of closeness between the Jacksons and the pre-famous Obamas. Yet it was Sharpton, not Jackson, who was now being invited to watch the Super Bowl at the White House with the First Family. In a split-second, Jesse Jackson was vanquished in favor of Sharpton during Obama's reign.

Early Meeting

The national director of Operation Breadbasket in the late 1960s was the brash young medallion-wearing brother with an afro. As Reverend Sharpton initially told us, Reverend Jesse Jackson, "Didn't really look at me, he actually kind of looked past me."[139] During a later rally and ribbon-cutting ceremony, the dignitaries had included famed gospel singer Mahalia Jackson, with whom then child preacher Sharpton claimed to have toured. After Mahalia Jackson approached the "Wonderboy" grinning and pointing, warmly saying, "There's my little boy preacher,"[140] the Rev. was then allowed to speak. Once Jesse Jackson had seen the recognition given Sharpton by the other Jackson, Jesse then acknowledged the young Rev., breaking the ice between them.

The relationship then solidified with Operation Breadbasket's New York boycott of A&P supermarket. Its tough-guy president, William J. Kane, had refused to meet with black leaders mounting the protest, and the Rev. described their decision to "occupy" A&P's Manhattan corporate headquarters on Lexington Avenue. Although an underage minor at the time, he was in the thick of things:

> A white guard, part of A&P's security force, came over to me at about midnight and said, "Aren't you gonna go home, kid?" And I said, "No, I'm going to stick it out." He said, "Have you had anything to eat?" I said I hadn't. He said, "Don't you want something?" I said, "I can't leave the ministers…" The Reverend Jones's [leader of the operation] brother, who was a lawyer, came and said there was a danger of Reverend Jones being charged with contributing to the delinquency of a minor if I was taken into custody. So they decided I wouldn't be arrested and the white guard pulled me over to stand by him.[141]

The young Rev. wasn't under arrest, but he'd wanted to stay and ended up staying with the preachers in jail that night. As if sleeping over at his friend Leon's house, he then just called his mother and casually told her that he was going to sleep in jail for the night, although not under arrest. That night, the jail area had

---

139 Al Sharpton and Walton, *Go and Tell Pharaoh*, 48.

140 Ibid.

141 Ibid., 57.

apparently turned into a church hall, with the Operation's secretary given free rein to move in and out of the cell area:

> They put all thirty-two preachers in jail, where they had to spend the night, and though I wasn't "in jail," I wanted to stay there with them. So I called my mother and told her where I was, and lay down on the floor and went to sleep. The secretary of Breadbasket had come to the jail to help out, and about two o'clock in the morning, the phone rings and the secretary comes into the holding cell and says, "Reverend Sharpton, someone wants to talk to you." I got up and answered the phone, and a voice said, "Young buck, give me a report, tell me what happened." I said, "Who is this?" He said, "This is Reverend Jackson." I jumped for joy. I said, "Jesse?" This was the first time he had called me, [sic] I couldn't believe Jesse Jackson wanted to talk to me. I felt like I had arrived. I told him what had happened and he said, "Can you get the youth together for tomorrow and some of the preachers?" "I'm flying in tomorrow, and we're going back to A&P."[142]

It was *Fantasy Island,* with Jackson as Mr. Roarke and Sharpton, his Tattoo in tow. To believe any of this requires a presumption that in those days, New York City jails were kind of like fancy public toilets in high-end department stores with baby changing areas. In this case, a space for the under-aged left overnight while not under arrest—those who'd preferred to remain in solidarity with the adults under arrest. In any case, that was the beginning of the impressionable youth's relationship with the suave and brilliant strategist and tactician Jesse Jackson. Reverend Sharpton was left in awe:

> This is when I began to understand that Jesse was a very sharp strategist. With Reverend Jones and the others in jail he felt it was imperative that we send a second wave, and that he get arrested. We went back to 420 Lexington...Jesse took us back to the elevators, we sat down inside of them, and after a while the police started arresting everyone, including Jesse...His plan had worked. It went out

---

142 Ibid., 58.

over all the wires, all the news, that Jesse Jackson had been arrested. That finally got A&P to negotiate.[143]

Over the years, the Sharpton tactics that had started in the Tilden High School cafeteria were then perfected under Jackson's tutelage in the A&P takedown. The formula was simple and straightforward: cause commotion, cause maximum shame and embarrassment, but most importantly, be sure to get on television while getting arrested. Jesse Jackson's early advice to the young Rev. was, "All you got to do is choose your targets and kick ass."[144]

The A&P story had presented yet another view of young Jesus, the Wonderboy among his elders. Arresting and locking up thirty-two ministers meant that they had to have been taken to some kind of central booking area with enough space to accommodate them. As a youth among adults being arrested, the Rev. would've certainly been released to the custody of his mother or other adult concerns, to juvenile detention, or to Child Protective Services. A teenager allowed to sleep on the floor outside of a jail cell, awaiting his comrades in arms under arrest rings fictional. So does the idea of a secretary being allowed to walk into a New York City jail in the wee hours of the morning to "help out" or to wake up the Rev. to take a telephone call—either from inside the holding cell or from outside on the floor where he slept. Somewhere in the archives of time and space lies the true story of the preacher-men's early relationship, but it's unlikely to have been as was told by Reverend Sharpton.

African Safari

Later, the two men took a trip together to Africa, with Sharpton as the likely invitee of Jackson. But Reverend Sharpton then did a remarkable thing; he wrote Reverend Jackson entirely out of the trip—never once mentioning his mentor while giving the distinct impression that it was solely his trip, his exclusive story, as he'd told it in *Pharaoh*:

---

143 Ibid.
144 Ibid., 48.

I became increasingly upset by what was going on in the central African country of Rwanda and in the refugee camps in Zaire. In August I decided to go over there and see what the African-American community could do to help alleviate the suffering, and it was one of the most moving and horrifying experiences of my life...I saw little kids die.[145]

Yet again, it was the second-rate forger at work, and he'd failed miserably at his painting. It soon became clear that another son of Africa had been leading him around, as Sharpton's own statement had hinted of other nonlocals on the trip as well. "Us" being warned was a clear reference to other foreigners, as locals wouldn't have been "risking infection" by touching their own:

I went to the orphans' camp, over 3,000 orphans, and they warned us very strictly not to touch the kids because of the risk of infection, but I just couldn't help it. I just kept picking up and holding them, I had to.[146]

They then passed through Zaire and Rwanda and made a visit to Gorée Island off the coast of Senegal. Gorée is well preserved, and the most famous of the original points of departure of slaves then headed for the dreaded *Middle Passage* on the transatlantic journey to the Americas. Today, it's a tearjerker, an emotional experience for visitors from the global African diaspora—kind of like the black equivalent of Jews visiting Auschwitz, Buchenwald, or even the Holocaust Memorial Museum in Washington DC. People of different shades and skin tones, of different cultures, and speaking different languages with varying accents and dialects, have echoed the same sentiments of the Gorée experience—more touching than any family reunion, funeral, wedding, or baptism they'd ever experienced. For African Americans, Afro-Latina(o)s, and Afro-Caribbeans, a visit to Gorée Island is the ultimate sharing of brotherly and sisterly love with people they've never met, but with whom they share the

---

145 Ibid., 246.
146 Ibid.

common bond and experience of being descendants of slaves who might have started their journey there.

The careful reader of Sharpton's books had known that Sharpton and Jackson were at Gorée Island even before reading the chapter, as a picture at an earlier point in the book had hinted of the location. While the details of his African adventure start on page 246 of *Pharaoh*, there is a set of pictures of the Rev. among African children well displayed on the unnumbered pages between 212 and 213. Although there is none with both men together in the first few pages, on the 5th page of those photographs, there is a small dark headshot of the two men taken in a room with French inscriptions, "Slavery at Maurice island [Mauritius]," etched on the wall in fine scripts. Sharpton's own caption noted, "Jesse and I visited a former slave camp in Senegal," and this was an initial indication that both men were likely together at Gorée Island, or in the least, that both were traveling together in Africa. So, there was an early expectation to read about it, which made the omission of Jackson all the more obvious.

But even in describing this shared experience, the Rev. went to great lengths to write pages upon pages of his African expedition while omitting his traveling partner Jackson from the journey. Sharpton didn't see it fit to share the pages of his book with his mentor. It was a sign of the shallow kinship he'd felt for Jesse Jackson even as he'd earlier boasted of their closeness. Earlier, he'd lavished glowing admiration for his surrogate father and had included, in the same pages of the same book, a picture of the two with their children at their annual Christmas get-together in Jackson's Chicago home. Again, we might recall that a year after publishing *Pharaoh*, the Rev. had shamed New York City mayoral candidate Ruth Messinger into silence by telling her that Jackson was his lifetime mentor. Yet with near diabolical pettiness only a year earlier, the Rev. had told us of a solo visit that he'd made to Gorée Island, never once mentioning his traveling partner, Jesse Jackson:

> I remember a trip I took to Gorée Island in Senegal, where the slaves actually shipped from during the Middle Passage. I think the absolutely most emotional experience of my life was going to that village in the slave quarters, looking in

the little rooms where everyone was kept all crouched together, and looking through the door they call the Door of No Return...[147]

Even assuming that bad blood had emerged between the two by the time he'd written *Pharaoh* in 1996, the emotions of such a shared experience by the race leaders should've transcended pettiness. While we were still many years away from his putsch to dethrone Jesse, it's clear that the Rev. had already started to eye his target.

He would finally make mention of Reverend Jackson on the trip but in a context that made his wider omission even worse. He claimed that there was a poster of "Jesse Jackson for President" on a wall—also noted in the caption of the two in the earlier mentioned picture. But this was likely another invention, as Gorée Island is about the history of the slave passage and not a "Where Are They Now" museum. Though I wouldn't be surprised if there are now posters of Africa's favorite son, Barack Obama, all over the place.

In any case, assuming this to have been true, it would've been a moment made even more poignant, guaranteed to bring his traveling partner, Reverend Jackson, to tears. Yet the Rev. had made no mention of Jackson's presence, even while he'd sought to exploit Jackson's fame and stature:

> When we came out of that building, there were some African kids running around and playing, and inside of one of the houses there was a poster of "Jesse Jackson for President." As much as I had supported Jesse, and for as long, I had not understood until then what that means, that he ran for president of the United States, because those people there on Gorée can look out the Door of No Return and realize how far those slaves have come.[148]

He then went on to detail other parts of the trip for us, including his arrival in a shell-shocked and deserted Kigali, Rwanda's capital city, which had forced him and "his party" to head for the airport—then under the control of

---

147 Ibid., 248–49.
148 Ibid.

the US military. Again, no mention was made of Reverend Jackson among his party. But this was where the story had gotten really good. According to the Rev., while in Kigali, the commander of the American troops had accepted him as a visiting dignitary and had given him a chance to review the troops:

> The commander of those troops let my party in and had me review the troops, because Charles Rangel and others had sent word ahead that I was to be treated as a dignitary. I deeply enjoyed reviewing the troops, as most of them were young black men from the United States.[149]

What appears to have been an arrival by land from Zaire through war-torn Rwanda then gave way to an impromptu affair of state, with the appropriate improvised stagecraft deployed for the visiting dignitary and his party at the airport. Such a review of American troops there in the middle of Africa wasn't at all difficult to envision:

> Rev: *No Justice!*
> Black soldiers: *No Peace!*
> Commander: *At Ease Soldiers!*

At times, reading a Sharpton book does the strangest things to the mind. I had an epiphany at that point: it was the deep drawl of Meryl Streep, as Danish Baroness Karen Blixen, going off in my head, ever so slowly saying, *I once had a farm in Africa! I once had a farm in Africa!*

It's hard to believe that I was the only one to see the humor in this. Congressman Charlie Rangel, for example, must have chuckled himself into a near coma. But all in all, this was Sharpton's solo trip to Africa. He'd told us the story in the first-person singular—removing any chance of being over-shadowed by his idol, Reverend Jesse Jackson. This wasn't Jesse Jackson's moment to be shared, not his for the spotlight of an African odyssey. It was Reverend Sharpton's, and the black Odysseus had needed no sidekick to contend with.

---

149 Ibid., 251.

Safari Redux

Jesse Jackson must have fumed on reading Sharpton's description of his Africa trip, possibly angry enough to have called out the Rev. after the mid-1990s publication of *Pharaoh*. So, six years later, in 2002's *Al on America*, Sharpton rewrote this story of the African trip, telling what appears to be the more likely version of events. There was no surprise here; Jesse Jackson had gotten the David Dinkins' treatment and, as expected, it was a 180-degree turnaround:

> In 1994, I went to Senegal to the African, African-American Summit. On the second night of the conference, Rev Jesse Jackson brought my wife and me to [Gorée] Island, the primary place where slaves were held before being shepherded into slavery. Reverend Jackson had been there before. But it was my first experience and one I will never forget.[150]

It wasn't just the misrepresentation of facts, but as if driven by a serial compulsion, the Rev. had extended such great efforts at imparting such profound details, all while indulging in pure pettiness. As if possessed by uncontrollable urges or combustible desires, he concocted stories for an America that cared so little about what he has had to say, that in his near two decades of writing, it has hardly taken notice of his nonsense—certainly not enough to have called him out as a buffoon. The ancient Greeks called it *pathos*—a deleterious deficit of attention that drives the need to appeal to the emotions of others. Abraham Kardiner and Lionel Ovesey just called it a *mark of the oppressed*.

Dialogue Attributions

The Jackson omission in Sharpton's account of his African adventures was only part of the comedy. We've already seen Sharpton present his own thoughts while attributing them to others in his efforts to paint David Dinkins as an Uncle Tom. Later, we'll see "others" styling Jesse Jackson as a sell-out. But we know these others are just stand-ins for the Rev.'s own thoughts and opinions because he tends to give us variants elsewhere in the same chapter, in the same

---

150 Sharpton with Hunter, *Al on America*, 79.

book, or across his books, in his own voice. As he often writes like a deaf man listening—clueless how his words resonate, how his phrases intertwine, or how his dialogues reverberate—at times, it has been more than just being tone deaf but more like being completely brain dead.

In one of the more embarrassing-to-read stories in *Pharaoh,* we got a dialogue laced with trite stereotypes of impoverished Africans Rev. had met while on his trip. But he couldn't have seen the transparency of his effort to simplify Africans and so he'd put the most awful words in the mouth of an African youth. It was a heartless affront to decency, maybe even a case of literary child abuse. Firstly, no one across the different countries and cultures of the continent referred to blacks from America as "African Americans" back in the 1990s—a time when Jesse Jackson's name-change of the race hadn't even caught on in America. For Africans, African Americans were just "Americans" or "black-Americans." Yet among refugees in a camp, Sharpton claimed to have had this awkward conversation with a nineteen-year-old Rwandan student:

> One of the students, about nineteen years old, looked me right in the eye and said, "You're from America?" I nodded. He said, "African-American, the most educated and powerful Africans in the world. Why don't you act like it?" So I asked him what he would like for me to tell African-Americans when I got back home, what could American blacks do for Africans? I expected him to say, "Send money, send medical supplies, send engineers," but what he said was, "Tell them the first thing they can do for us is to tell the rest of the world the truth. If the truth is told around the world of how Europeans stole the resource of Africa and expropriated African labor to build these empires, the acknowledgment of the truth will begin the process of healing that is needed in Africa."[151]

It was beyond literary child abuse—more appropriately, literary waterboarding or in the least, "enhanced" verbiage. African Americans are often incensed when whites simplify Africa and blacks in general, so such portrayals, from a grown man with claims to being a race leader in America, might infuriate many.

---

151 Al Sharpton and Walton, *Go and Tell Pharaoh,* 248.

Those who've never known hunger know not the value of food, at least not to the same degree as the starving. "The poor on the borderline of starvation live purposeful lives. To be engaged in a desperate struggle for food and shelter is to be wholly free from a sense of futility. The goals are concrete and immediate. Every meal is a fulfillment; to go to sleep on a full stomach is a triumph."[152] An impoverished student in a refugee camp of a war-torn African nation was therefore likely to have thought of little beyond food and security—that which is essential to his or her survival, per Abraham Maslow's physiological needs.

Yet in a refugee camp there in the hinterlands of Africa, Reverend Sharpton just happened to have stumbled onto a young W. E. B. Du Bois or a young Walter Rodney, who'd exhorted him to go spread the word about European exploitation, and by implication, its underdevelopment of Africa. But the Rev. didn't stop there; we then got a saccharine-infused story of an elderly man in Goma that inspired as much giddiness as it did a sort of macabre sadness. It was storytelling that was at once a diabetic and diarrheic:

> Something that was deeply touching happened to me in Zaire, when I was asked to preach, with a French interpreter, at a church in Goma. There's a custom in Zaire that after church, even though they're very poor, the head minister has the visiting minister and any other clergyman present at the service to his house... There was an old minister there who didn't speak a word of English, and he asked me through an interpreter, "Are you from America?" I said yes. Then he said, "I heard that long ago they took some Africans to America, and I always wondered what became of them." That shook me. It was a hard thing to think about because I thought, "Yes, they carried us off four hundred years ago, and what did become of us?" I couldn't really say.[153]

Imagine that—an old African who'd heard of some Africans being taken "long ago" was wondering what had become of them, as if it were the eighteenth or nineteenth century and he was just emerging from the jungle. There is no doubt that certain rural parts of Africa, as in America, are still awaiting

---

152 Eric Hoffer, *The True Believer* (Harper Collins, New York, 1951), 27-8.
153 Ibid., 247–48.

the arrival of the twentieth century, not to mention the twenty-first today. But Goma, although nearly a thousand miles away from Kinshasa, is nonetheless part of the former-Zaire, of whose capital city the Rev. had so carefully written of visiting, in his varying versions of the Ali-Foreman "Rumble in the Jungle." With the passage of two decades since the fight, someone in Goma must have heard that the Africans taken to America a long time ago had long returned to mount that spectacular combat in Kinshasa.

Additionally, we're told that this was a minister, and not a remote tribal leader, who was wondering via a French interpreter on the fate of the slaves. So, it begs to question how the old preacher had come to receive his French tongue and Christian faith in the first place, without knowledge of some of those slaves—then living in France, in Europe, and in the Americas. Someone must have at least told him that James Baldwin and Richard Wright had long made their way to Paris—France then still his "mother country."

As it's useless to indict the Rev. for distastefulness, the reader just sighs and wonders, *Did he really believe Africans to be that simple?* But there might yet have been another explanation: Africans are geniuses at pretending to be silly and simple as a way of laughing at the ridiculous and simple-minded. Much like the slaves who'd once delighted in the cake walks while laughing at their masters, on realizing that he was in the presence of an imbecile, the old minister in Goma might just have played up the moment for all it was worth.

Prodigal Brother-Kenny

A truth is not hard to kill...a lie told well is immortal.

—MARK TWAIN[154]

THAT THE MAN who'd been in service to his people since age four had forgotten to serve and save his own sibling had portended a complete disaster for a black America in which he'd anointed himself its leader. How could a future black America be accounted for if the Rev. couldn't have even accounted for his own long-lost brother?

In one of the final stages of his first quarter performance, Reverend Sharpton told of attending the October 1995 Million Man March in Washington, DC, wondering what might have become of his long-lost brother. The youngest Sharpton was a boy, a little brother-nephew named Kenny:

> Black men are often castigated or ridiculed or dismissed, and there were one
> million of us together in honor and fellowship. Looking out over all those men
> assembled together peacefully and joyously, I couldn't help being profoundly
> moved, and as I was being introduced before I spoke, I couldn't help thinking
> about my brother Kenny, and how there was a need for some forms of atone-
> ment in our community. Had Kenny chosen the street life, and had he landed in
> prison, because of the emotional pain and estrangement he felt after he learned
> of the circumstances of his birth? That was still running through my mind as I
> talked about living up to obligations, family renewal and unity, and being open to

---

154 "Advice to Youth" (speech) - *The Wit and Wisdom of Mark Twain,* 35.

what we as black men needed to do to prepare ourselves, our children, and our communities for the future.[155]

After incessantly reading of the incestuous family shame that had engulfed the Sharpton family, it was natural to have expected an update in later books, in particular, on the whereabouts of his young sibling—the product of Sharpton Sr.'s affair with his stepdaughter. We've seen the devastating impact this has had on the Rev., so as the direct issue of the dysfunctional events, it must have been doubly difficult for the youngest Sharpton later on in life. Left to his own devices, he might have run off to become a mercenary, to foment revolutions in Africa or in Latin America, or maybe even to join the French Foreign Legion, where no questions are asked on entry. But as this was an American story as opposed to say, a French one, some kind of happy ending was expected, which was a good enough excuse to follow the Sharpton books over the years.

Whether at a wedding, a baptism, or even a funeral, we'd expected an update via some form of a family reunion or gathering with some members issuing apologies to recipients who then doled out certificates of forgiveness. And we did see this reunion, though without being told of it directly. So, we were left to assume that some apologies might have been made even in the absence of forgiveness. After all, incest and betrayal are hard to forgive.

But the Rev.'s *pharaonic* declarations of concerns for his long-lost brother, while at the Million Man March, was astounding. Public figures in America aren't very difficult to find. Whether in politics, sports, entertainment, or even in winning the lottery, the moment that most people achieve fame—as opposed to infamy *à la* "O.J."—they're likely to have a flurry of distant relatives emerge from the woodworks just to "see how they're doing," to rekindle old familial ties that never really existed.

Since the late 1980s, there was hardly a soul in metropolitan America who didn't know of, or who might not have heard of Brooklyn's own beguiled. It is, therefore, a safe bet to believe that had the Rev.'s brother been cooped up in a cave in Tora Bora or laid out on the white sands of Bora Bora, by 1995, little Kenny would undoubtedly have gotten the news that his famous relative

---

155 Al Sharpton and Walton, *Go and Tell Pharaoh*, 260.

had made something of himself in New York. Even if Kenny weren't naturally disposed to looking up his brother, he would still likely try to reach out to his famous uncle out of reverence. If incarcerated, he would be even more likely to make contact, looking for help with bail, bond, lawyers, legal fees, and so on.

On one level, connections lost between the Rev. and his brother from physical separation would've been compensated for on another level by genetics. A quick round of Biology 101 shows the profound connection that exists between Reverend Sharpton and his brother—a link that would've spurred an even stronger impetus for the two men to know of each other's whereabouts—had Kenny been genuinely unaccounted for, as the Rev. had told us.

A statistical probability tree might be more illustrative, but an imaginary ladder will work just as well for this limited purpose. If we think of the Sharpton family's genetic hierarchy as a ladder, we have the following:

- The Sharpton parents are on top, the third level.
- Reverend Sharpton and his half-sister (Kenny's mother) are on the next level down, the second level. Each received one set of twenty-three chromosomes from their mother in common, thereby inheriting and directly sharing common maternal genetic traits with each other. Reverend Sharpton received his other set of twenty-three from his father—Alfred Sharpton Sr.—while his half-sister received her other set of twenty-three from her father (unknown male).
- On that second level where we find the Rev. and his half-sister, we also find one-half of Kenny, based on his set of twenty-three chromosomes received from Alfred Sharpton Sr.—the father he shares with Reverend Sharpton. This means that Kenny and the Rev. directly share many of the same inherited traits from their father in common.
- We find the second chromosomal half of Kenny on the next level down: the first level based on the set of twenty-three that he received from his mother, the Rev.'s half-sister—thereby also sharing this set of common traits with the Rev., albeit indirectly.

So as a full person, little Kenny dangles between the second and first levels of the ladder. His second level chromosomal half, received from his father, is inherited genetic programming directly shared with the Rev. His third level chromosomal half, received from his mother, is inherited genetic programming indirectly shared with the Rev. In a nutshell, given the shared maternal and paternally inherited biological coding, which adds up to a very deep connection between Kenny and the Rev., on the physical, spiritual, and behavioral level, the brothers/uncle-nephew likely share more in common with each other than does Reverend Sharpton with his own two daughters—to whom he's given only one set of twenty-three chromosomes. Indeed, as an organ donor, Kenny is likely a better match for the Rev. than Sharpton's own daughters.

Yet at the Million Man March in October 1995, the Rev. said he'd looked out on the oceans of men in the nation's capital and could not have helped thinking about what might have become of his little brother. Unsurprisingly, the truth would reveal itself all of seven pages later in the same book, when Sharpton unknowingly showed us something new. We recall here his sister Cheryl's March 1994 wedding—a wedding that was the sort of family reunion to be anticipated:

> In March 1994, my sister Cheryl got married, and I flew to Atlanta to do the ceremony. My father was there. It was the first time I'd seen him in many years. He had another family—his new wife and kids were there with him—and my mother was there. Tina was there, too. It was the first time we were all together in the same place in twenty-nine years.[156]

When people show up at a wedding, it generally means that they're invited and that there is still an all-around familial rapport, even tangentially. It's an indication of open lines of communication and contact. Usually, the first thing that happens on seeing family is to catch up on what has been going on in their lives. People share news of other family members, hear of health, children, love, marriage, relationships, jobs, death, and so on—good news, bad news, gossip, secrets, taboos, and all. It's safe to assume that everyone at the wedding would've been apprised of poor little Kenny's condition and whereabouts,

---

156 Ibid., 267.

as both of his parents were present. Additionally, were his whereabouts really unknown during the wedding, it would've likely been part of the wedding story told by Reverend Sharpton in *Pharaoh*, as in, *It was a beautiful wedding, except that we were all wondering about Kenny. Nobody had any news of him.*

So here again, it's difficult to believe that while Reverend Sharpton was at the Million Man March a year and a half after his sister's wedding, he'd had no knowledge of the whereabouts of his brother, born to his father and his other sister, both of whom were present. Yet there he was standing on that platform in Washington DC feigning celestially pious concerns for his long-lost brother as if the boy had disappeared at sea back in the 1970s.

Like many other things he's written about, the sole purpose of the Kenny story was the Sharpton need for sympathy, his overwhelming capacity for public emotional blackmail—a self-centeredness driven by an absence of empathy. It was still all about the Rev.—victim No. 1 of his father's treachery. He'd never mentioned nor spoken of his sister Tina nor of Kenny as a victim, so in posturing on about his brother, Reverend Sharpton had proven himself the worst messenger for his message. Whatever had become of Kenny was well known to him before taking that stage at the Million Man March. Had the Rev. not known the whereabouts of his only brother, it was because he'd had no interest in knowing it.

End Act I

Act 11: Turbine Megalomaniac

At 50 a man can be an ass without being an optimist
but not an optimist without being an ass.

—MARK TWAIN[157]

Reverend Al Sharpton and Majorie Fields Harris attend Friends of the High Line
Fifth Annual Summer Benefit at Cipriani Wall Street on July 13, 2005, in New
York City. (Photo by Joe Schildhorn/Patrick McMullan via Getty Images.)

---

157 *More Maxims of Mark-The Wit and Wisdom of Mark Twain*, 29.

THE EVE OF the new millennium was the start of the second act of the Sharpton public life. He was at an inflection point and had needed a new projectile to change course and ditch the old ragamuffin buffoon America had come to know and loathe. The piston engine of the 1980s through '90s barnstormer was no longer enough. For his desired launch into the stratosphere, he'd needed turbine thrust. The greener pastures he'd sought had meant cultivating new respectability to go mainstream and become a national figure, which had also meant being accepted by those who counted (white America) and by those who were needed (black elites). The Rev. had come to realize that revolution wasn't his to foment in America, so he decided to embrace the system and to make it work for him, and work for him, it did.

But there were the usual challenges in the mainstreaming of a rabble-rouser, namely, a necessary reincarnation into something new and hybrid by putting the old Reverend Al through a meat grinder. This had meant burying the dead boy (Adam Clayton Powell Jr.) and hiding the live girl (Jesse Jackson) lying in his bed. He'd become contemptuous of both, but the live one had merited special attention, as it was standing in his way of "greatness."

In a system where power is derived from the ability to deliver votes—real or perceived—Sharpton then took his phony electoral "issues" campaigns to the national stage. He'd been practicing phantom runs for public office in New York for over a decade, and feeling that newfound turbine propulsion, he ran for president in 2004. Though having no aspirations for elected office, he'd needed a national profile to catapult him to take the black leadership from Jesse Jackson. Jackson's run for president in 1984 and 1988 had cemented his position as black leader, and as in all aspects of the Sharpton project to become the next Jackson, mimicry was his first refuge.

Like any successful launch of a new projectile, it was all about an effective launching pad, and the Rev. had needed to develop a new base while expanding the old one. This had required pivoting to constituents he'd once scorned and even vilified—Jews, Latinos, non-native blacks, mainstream black middle-class and its elite, and the full embrace of Dr. King this time around. Many among the black elites then foolishly joined his campaigns with high hopes. But Sharpton simply used and laughed them out of town the moment he'd no longer needed them.

Of real importance, though, was his need to woo the white establishment and its power brokers—at once both the easiest and the most challenging group to court because both had long since figured him out. Even in viewing him as a demagogue, they'd never doubted his aspirations for their approbation and acceptance, as they'd always known him to be on sale at bargain-basement prices. As a financial instrument, he was an unrated noninvestment-grade junk bond in search of investors—willingly and therefore easily controlled by others, so that part might have been appealing.

Al on America was the firing of that new propulsion. Although the invention of stories had continued, his rhetorical jujitsu was intensified. He'd had a new audience to convince and needed to have been convincing. So, the crowning of Reverend Al Sharpton as an exemplar—the most brilliant, the most moral, the most intuitive, one of America's foremost intellectual black minds—was completed. He was on his way to becoming *the most interesting man in black America.*

Channeling Dr. King, the Rev. had seen himself as a transformative leader—a thermostat that changed the temperature rather than one that merely measured it: "Dr. King once said that there are two types of people: There are those who are thermometers. A thermometer records the temperature. And there are those who are thermostats; they change the temperature. A true leader is a thermostat because they change the temperature."[158] But on the top shelf of his jailhouse library, Winston Churchill, the cigar-chomping imperialist who'd once declared his aversion to "preside over the liquidation of His Majesty's Empire," had also peeked out at Sharpton. As he told us, "Dr. King was a thermostat. Nelson Mandela was a thermostat. Gandhi was a thermostat. These were all great leaders. So was Churchill. I read everything I could get my hands on about Churchill."[159]

Right out the gate, 9/11 had given him a pretext for getting his millennial ducks in order. So, he took a sympathy trip to Israel to gain some "street cred" in lower Manhattan and in Brooklyn and arrogated himself into a protest all the way in Vieques, off Puerto Rico, to burnish it in the Bronx. In no time, the Rev. was eminently qualified—at once an expert while arrogantly ignorant

---

158 Sharpton with Hunter, *Al on America*, xv.
159 Ibid.

of everything and eminently knowledgeable of almost nothing. Throughout it all, his conduct reflected his education—heavy in form and light in substance. Linguistically, *form* was one-third simplistic, generic, and emotional, while *substance*, two-thirds hot air and low in density.

At times, as during his attacks on African American decadence, we got glimpses of common sense, but being Reverend Sharpton, he often drowned out the substance of potentially good arguments with platitudinous gibberish. All in all, millennium Al was the start of *faking it till he made it*. His manifesto, *Al on America,* is best summed up by the words to an old Tom Waits song, "Lie to Me."

Dawn of Decadence

Although the work of the self-professed intellect, his millennial manifesto was neither Newtonian in its *Principias* nor Malthusian in its *Principles*. And although the Rev. had told us that Bayard Rustin, the architect of the March on Washington, was the one who'd given him the seed money to start his first youth movement, his manifesto was in no way "Rustinian" in its momentous blueprint. Instead, *Al on America* was pure comedy—an update of Jules Verne's fictional Phileas Fogg but without his manservant, "Passepartout." It was *Eighty Days from Sea to Shining Sea,* with an amazing Reverend Sharpton accomplishing the most amazing feats, yet still incapable of articulating policies or engaging political discussions beyond the simplistic. It was also another round of blame ascribed to the elder Sharpton's abandonment, for junior's character as a buffoon.

Al on America was the introduction of a candidate—albeit a "Manchurianish" one—and for a moment, it had appeared as if the Rev. had actually turned a corner and had somewhat matured. In his attempt at transformation, he did have his moments in that two-thirds corridor, where he'd shown us a somewhat different Al Sharpton—often marveling us with candid introspection on black America. But as it was a book and not a pamphlet, to our delight (or dismay), he'd kept on writing. We were then forced to read extensive fluff, useless preambles, and to bear witness to a showman's whimsical exhibition. As there wasn't enough substance to fill some 270 pages, new versions of old stories were invented, which not only gave rise to much fiction in the second book, but also validated the first as having been equally fictitious. Heroic *pharaonic* stories—Howard Beach, Bensonhurst, Yusuf Hawkins, Bernard Getz, and the stabbing of Al Sharpton—were all regurgitated.

Among the reasons the Rev. had given America to vote for him were his ability to identify with those who were struggling to put food on the table—having once been on welfare, his capacity to discuss difficult issues such as the death penalty—having once seen a man put to death, his credentialed foreign-policy expertise—having twice been to Israel and once or twice to Africa, and his ability to get the Latino votes—having once protested on Vieques, Puerto Rico. Where none of that worked, he then asked America to vote for him out of pity—because his father had run off with his sister, abandoning the family unit and destroying his middle-class bourgeois life in Queens.

Where he showed some level of courage by introspectively speaking "directly" to African Americans, it was by way of conservative black and opaquely white racist talking points—in a book aimed at a white audience where he knew it was safe to make critical observations of black America, given the likelihood of only a few black readers of a Sharpton book. While his reincarnation had come with ten and twenty-point plans for his 2004 presidential run, most of the first three-quarters of *Al on America* had done little to convince anyone that the Rev. could've been a leader, much less the one he'd aspired to be. Instead, it ended up reaffirming the notions of an ignoramus inherently bereft of minimum standards of decency—an attack dog still on the hunt.

Toward the end of the book, there was one segment—"Is Black America Worthy?"—that was well worth reading. It was the only chapter in which the Rev. wasn't praising himself while belittling others. Instead, he told us the theme of "worthiness" had come out of a 2002 program in Philadelphia, hosted by television personality Tavis Smiley, during which Baptist scion Dr. Gardner Taylor had asked the question, "Are we worthy of the legacy we inherited?" It was here that the Rev. then dispensed the type of cultural critique more akin to conservative talking points, revealing his somewhat contrarian nature, while proving that all politics isn't just local but is indeed racial—especially when practiced by a black man.

Otherwise, *Al on America* was still Reverend Sharpton versus Reverend Sharpton. In one moment, he advocated tutelage and proscription (prohibition of thought and actions imposed upon black America) and in the next, he criticized black America's culture of tutelage and proscription that he'd in large part perfected and expanded. The first Al Sharpton amplified and reaffirmed stereotypes of inferiority complexes and simplemindedness by demanding that minority parents with children in school be given a reason by school boards to be involved in their children's education. Accordingly, love, responsibility, and parental duty of care be damned. It was beyond their natural faculties:

> Certainly, parental participation in the elections of local school boards has been very low. But I don't see that as apathy or the parents' not caring, as much as that the boards have not given them a reason to vote and be involved.[160]

But as a man who is consistently inconsistent, the second Al Sharpton then reversed his tone in the same book and later affirmed that racism should not be used as an excuse for parental neglect. "Racism doesn't explain why parents don't vote in the school board elections or why they don't check their children's homework every night,"[161] he said.

As if a shout-out to white folk, his tone then ventured into the very "Sister Souljah" territory for which he'd earlier excoriated and condemned President Bill Clinton. This is the so-called race card drawn by white politicians when convenient since time immemorial, but so named after President Bill Clinton, who, as an honored guest of Reverend Jesse Jackson, had famously sent up a "dog whistle" to white America by hoisting a little-known rapper's comments to fifteen minutes of fame by suggesting that they were representative of the black community:

> Bill Clinton used that opportunity to place race politics by criticizing Sister Souljah at the Rainbow Coalition Conference...Clinton accepted Jesse's invitation and hospitality at the conference, then embarrassed Jesse in Jesse's own

---

160 Ibid., 138.
161 Ibid., 264.

house…It was the old southern race code of "I'm in charge of my niggers, things are in control around me."[162]

But the Rev. was reaching out to white America by claiming to take on the new *black dilemma* while indicting others (and unknowingly himself) in the black leadership by pointing out that in many ways the black community they'd collectively shaped, had become its own worst enemy:

> We have to be just as vocal about those who use racism as an excuse for failure as we are about the individuals and system that use racism to knock us down. We must take responsibility for ourselves. In a lot of ways, we have become our own worst enemy. We don't even support one another in business, but we want to complain about how we don't get the same opportunities and we don't get the same consideration in business.[163]

Elsewhere he'd shown the emerging confidence of a black leader ready for the climb to higher ground, but the issue of trust had still lingered. As usual, even though Sharpton hadn't seen it while writing it, the reader could still see the need for a parachute. But it was in these rare moments that the Rev. had managed to surprise us in *Al on America*:

> Black folks must begin to pick ourselves up by our bootstraps and take responsibility for ourselves. Yes, there is racism. But racism doesn't make parents not apply pressure to our children to do better in school…So even if the system isn't getting the job done, that's no excuse for us not to get the job done, too. When did failure and decadence become black culture?[164]

Such observations didn't negate the presence and harsh realities of racism but precisely the opposite; they'd recognized them and argued the need to be better equipped to deal with them. It's a fallacy that plagues black thought

---

162 Al Sharpton and Walton, *Go and Tell Pharaoh*, 210.

163 Sharpton with Hunter, *Al on America*, 266.

164 Ibid., 264–65.

in America—that continued weakness is the first refuge from the perils of racism—when millions of years of evolution have taught us that adaptation and variation are the keys to strength and survival:

> The first thing black America must do is stop making excuses for why we aren't where we need to be and find a way to get where we must go. Those people who built our legacy didn't make excuses. They made a way out of no way. They didn't just sit around complaining about the white man; they fought the system that oppressed us. They didn't cry about racism; they marched, they died, they wrote, and they sang about overcoming it.[165] Yes, racism in America may have knocked us down, but we are responsible for making sure we get back up. Racism is an overused excuse. White people and racism are not the reason why far too many blacks stay home on election day.[166]

Although a man discredited today for other reasons, comedian Bill Cosby was earlier pilloried for expressing much the same sentiments Reverend Sharpton had expressed in 2002. Admittedly somewhat patrician in tone and approach, which many had found condescending, Mr. "Pound Cake" was nonetheless attacked for blaming the victims of racism and not the system and for "airing dirty laundry" that was already airborne. But again, the Rev. had expressed much the same sentiments only a few years earlier but to no consternation or condemnation by the black media—which had either shown a level of connivance in black America or had proven that his people neither read nor cared about what the Rev. has had to say:

> Racism doesn't make men father children then walk away from the responsibility of raising them. According to recent reports, 70 percent of all black babies born in our country today are born out of wedlock. Racism may have provided despair, poverty, lack of education, and conditions for that statistic, but racism

---

165 Ibid., 261–62.
166 Ibid., 262.

certainly did not make these fathers turn their backs on their own children. No, it takes something more to walk away from a child.[167]

One person who didn't care about Sharpton's 2002 comments was 2013's Reverend Sharpton himself, who then took great umbrage at the notion that single parentage was a problem in black America (earlier mentioned) because as the issue of a single-parent household, he said he'd turned out just fine. Likewise, his mentor Jesse Jackson had also ignored or disregarded Sharpton's comments in *Al on America*. Some five years later, Jackson would threaten then-candidate Barack Obama with neutering for echoing similar sentiments of responsibility but had never sought to geld his protégé back in 2002 for conveying much the same—then stated in even more indignant tones:

When did failure and decadence become black culture and success and excellence be equated only with white culture? That mentality must stop. There are children all over the country, black children, who fear being ostracized by their friends and even family for doing well in the classroom.[168]

While a message of responsibility in the face of decadence is one thing, the invocation of stereotypes is quite another. Some elements of truth do underlie the deterioration innate to many parts of the increasingly permanent black underclass, and this has given rise to continued political maligning on both sides of the aisle. But the decadence that the Rev. had criticized while speaking to his intended white audience in *Al on America* is the same decadence for which he was in favor, the same decadence he'd preached and perfected over the years, and the same decadence that he would return to embrace and to re-advocate in time. So as usual, it was confusing to follow him on both sides of the issues. But as with others in black leadership, Sharpton had always found it easier to blame societal racism without apportioning any internal responsibilities, as this would've forced him to actually do some work to fix things within his reach. It would've forced him to bring solutions to the table—something for which he

---

167 Ibid., 265.
168 Ibid.

has never been conditioned. For him and others, blaming the system—rightfully or wrongfully—is their way of washing their hands of needed work to be done.

In their dated mindsets, it suffices to just march, protest, blame, and complain, in attempts to shame a mostly indifferent white America, exhausted by black claims. But in complaining, they also belittle and stunt black America's abilities to reach its full potential; they negate the long history of struggles, hard work, and communal/self-reliance. As products of "The Great Society," they've conditioned the masses to fight retroactive battles of respectability and to revel in bourgeois and pretentious moral indignation—at the cost of improving their material conditions in order to face the future. The black America on whose behalf they advocate is without agency or natural faculties, or so they believe. Therefore, indignant condemnation feels better than the awful task of improving internal conditions.

Had the Rev. emphasized this message in his stump speeches, he might have found enough credibility to court that wider white audience willing to buy it. More importantly, though, he might have truly been the transformative "thermostat" he'd aspired to be by leveling with his followers. By "leveling" I mean to make it clear that even in the race-free world of their utopian dreams, challenging issues would still remain. In a society founded on economic determinism, *equality* can exist only in the imagination without the foundations for economic thriving, as it is the economic condition and not pretentious moral supremacy that ultimately determines the human condition in America. The modern American is the economic man or woman. But can anyone imagine such a stump speech by Reverend Sharpton or others in black leadership in America?

Given his history, the Rev. would've been booted off the stage by black folks for hypocrisy if he were ever to be forthright, as his ascendancy has been in the leadership of lies and subterfuge. So, on the other hand, it was no surprise to see a hypocrite exposing his own hypocrisy and that of the black chattering class—all for the benefit of his desired white readers and the few well-heeled blacks he was then attempting to cultivate. Like the white politicians he'd derided over the years, the Rev. was just pandering to white America with *Al on America*. His manifesto wasn't meant as a discussion to be had within his own community. Pure and simple, it was an exercise in connivance and hypocrisy.

Hubris, Arrogance, and Ignorance

Hailing an emerging generation of black CEOs, which by all standards was a significant accomplishment for these men and for the black community, *Newsweek* magazine had the temerity to place three of America's leading black CEOs on its cover in 2002—lauding them as the new "black power." Reverend Sharpton was seething red. He'd thought very little of these titans of business—American Express CEO Kenneth Chenault, former AOL-Time Warner CEO Richard Parsons, and former Merrill Lynch CEO Stanley O'Neal—and had interpreted the coverage as an affront to his supremacy. He, therefore, reacted with an unhinged tirade that was pure jealousy and petty envy. Telling us that these men didn't own those businesses because whites had chosen them, Sharpton made the case that they'd owed their positions to him. He was the real "black power" deserving of coverage. How dare *Newsweek*—to have called these men powerful?

In his black world, it was blasphemy to pay homage to African Americans who were neither athletes nor entertainers, not preachers behind pulpits nor activists in the streets. The article was never an attack on the civil rights movement but just a recognition of a few black leaders who were corporate pioneers. But the budding race leader wasn't having any of that, so he took the time to launch a mean-spirited, petty, and vitriolic tirade against the magazine and the men, in a vain attempt to demean the accomplishments of the latter:

> There was a cover of Newsweek in January, 2002 that featured American Express CEO Ken Chenault, Merrill Lynch President Stan O'Neal, and Dick Parsons, CEO of AOL Time Warner, with the headline "The New Black Power." What black power do they represent? If their predominantly white board of directors decided tomorrow to replace any of them, Chenault, O'Neal, and Parsons would be unemployed. None of them are accountable to black people; they were not chosen by black people.[169]

In other words, the CEOs were trespassers in the boardrooms and offices—subject to being tossed out at will by white board of directors (by the way,

---

169 Ibid., 188.

sharing something in common with white CEOs as well). But the truth is that black pioneers in industry have paved the way for widespread black employment and advancement outside of politics and civil service and beyond the realm of local functionaries. African Americans who succeed in corporate America do so on their own merits.

Booker T. Washington had once suggested that the vote was useless without industrial independence—his people couldn't eat the vote. In other words, having the vote was useless if they were dependent and impoverished, economically excluded and unable to acquire wealth in a capitalistic society. The last time I checked, Washington was still being pilloried by a bourgeois black America for those thoughts. Nonetheless, many had heeded the call, and much of the economic inclusion since then has been the result of early black pioneers in business, including some of the first black women to hold secretarial and support positions, or even the famous ones who'd made a fortune selling hair and beauty products to their people. In fact, the black church itself was once a great incubator for entrepreneurship.

Early "Don't Buy Where You Can't Work," and "Spend Your Money Where You Can Work" campaigns in cities like Chicago, New York, and Philadelphia did open the door for limited employment in local businesses. Dr. King had even adopted earlier efforts in Philadelphia into his Operation Breadbasket, in his efforts to nationalize boycotts and force local businesses to hire African Americans who patronized their businesses. It was King's attempt at developing that economic foundation. But on the whole, private sector jobs have never been mandated by civil rights activism, as even affirmative action programs have been limited to government jobs or to contractors doing business with local, state, and federal agencies. No government agency or civil rights activist has ever told a private enterprise to hire a black director here or a black vice president there.

So, taking umbrage at the spotlight shone on others or claiming that private sector African-American executives had owed their positions to him and others like him, was supreme arrogance compounded by willful ignorance. A belief that black power lies only in the hands of those who march and protest had completed the hijacking of black history, primarily by the "diversity hostage taker" known more for corporate shakedowns than for diversity undertakings:

They are there because we fought to get the corporate world open. Because of those efforts, we now have black CEOs. Rather than say they're the new black power—to suggest that they are an alternative to civil right leaders—understand that they need the "real black power," just as much as the rest of us.[170]

To contrast accomplishments, in less than fifteen years at center stage, Dr. King had changed America, leaving both Civil and Voting Rights Acts codified as laws of the land. But in over forty years on the scene, Reverend Sharpton can hardly point to any tangible achievements on behalf of his people. At least, before attempting to codify ignorance with the suggestion of teaching *ebonics* in schools, his mentor, Jesse Jackson, had led a movement that encouraged an entire generation to believe in itself and to resist its continued oppression. Additionally, Jackson is also the sophisticated statesman that Sharpton has never been.

Although the Rev. had laid claim to singularly changing the landscape in New York City for African Americans, there were thousands of other black, Puerto Rican, and white activists in the trenches as well. Brooklyn, Harlem, and the Bronx were always hotbeds of militancy and black nationalism. The Rev. was just the most boisterous and ballyhooed, in part because of his boisterous physical presence and ballyhooed made for TV personality. But his life in activism is still without a single tangible Sharpton-inspired legislative promulgation on behalf of his people. And that's where it really counts. In other words, he really has nothing to show for his long history of marches and protests.

A decade later, as the ultimate insider during the Obama years, the Rev. had the president of the United States an US attorney general visiting his Harlem compound to pay homage. Yet he was unable to get federal civil rights indictments against those responsible for the deaths of Trayvon Martin, Michael Brown, and Eric Garner—among the many celebrated cases he'd championed by the time of writing 2013's *Stone* to tout himself as the top black leader in the land. But in his mind, he was the power in black America in 2002. He then went on to tell us how he'd viewed himself vis-à-vis the black community as if he were a special prosecutor or a federal magistrate capable of dispensing justice:

---

170 Ibid., 188.

It is an insult to say to the black community that they are the new black power. Are they now suggesting that if someone shoots Mrs. Diallo's son, they should call Dick Parsons? Are they now suggesting that if there is another Abner Louima case, they should now go see Ken Chenault?[171]

In that fractured logic of a livelihood gained in the world of race and racial persecution, "black power" means leading protests and marches—after the fact. It had never occurred to the Rev. that having power means not having to perpetually march and protest oppression. Had his black power indeed existed, it would've been preventative in nature and not reactive. Society would not have given Sharpton the space to thrive on the continued abuse and suffering of the wider black masses, as equal protection under the law and other constitutional guarantees would've been inherent for his people. Had he any real power, Reverend Sharpton would've never had to protest a second or a third case of police brutality because agents of law enforcement and elsewhere would have long gotten the message that *all lives matter*—including *black lives*.

Power is at once economic, social, and political—none of which the Rev. has ever possessed, therefore never having served any relevant purpose akin to a CEO, with the ability to hire tens of thousands off the unemployment line. Ken Chenault, Dick Parsons, Stan O'Neal, and others have created well-paying jobs for multitudes. Including his own, Reverend Sharpton, on the other hand, is unlikely to have created two well-paying jobs in his lifetime that weren't subsidized by corporate and political welfare or by fee-based activism. Even under his construct of "black power," it is clear that this was more realizable with African Americans in CEO chairs and in boardrooms than with those leading ersatz protests and commemorative marches.

What *Newsweek* magazine had rightfully deemed "black power," were individuals who'd had a seat at the table through which they could've hired tens of thousands of African Americans, directed millions of advertising dollars to black media outlets, steered millions of contracts to minority vendors, or even have mandated certain affirmative programs with third-party vendors and

---

171 Ibid., 189

contractors. They were leaders who'd created jobs, opportunities, economic participation, thereby enabling wealth creation in the black community.

The Rev. had used the same old argument in his attempt to delegitimize the black CEOs as he'd done earlier in delegitimizing black politicians—that they weren't chosen by their people. Yet a decade later, he would reach the pinnacle without ever being chosen by his people. He'd run several election campaigns without ever winning a single primary, even in places like South Carolina with majority black Democratic primary voters. As writer Juan Williams pointed out, the Rev's 2004 presidential campaign had garnered fewer delegates to the Democratic convention than Shirley Chisholm's largely symbolic, yet historic 1972 run. And as earlier mentioned, Sharpton's path to the stratosphere—his job at MSNBC—was neither ordained nor commanded by his people. Yet in 2002, he'd derided Messrs. Chenault, Parsons, and O'Neil, as illegitimate because African Americans didn't place them in their jobs at American Express, AOL Time Warner, or Merrill Lynch.

Across the board, the Rev. had shown and would continue to show himself and his cohorts as the very essence of powerlessness, the very essence of continued black weakness in America—if for no other reason than for having recognized him as a leader.

Endnote:

Disclosure: I started my career in the 1990s at the American Express company working under Kenneth Chenault.

Middle East Expert

Concerning the difference between man and the jackass: some observers hold that there isn't any. But this wrongs the jackass.

—MARK TWAIN[172]

Israeli chief rabbi Meir Lau (L) speaks with controversial activist Reverend Al Sharpton at a meeting on October 30, 2001, in Jerusalem. Sharpton, who is visiting Israel and the Palestinian Authority, declared that he is not anti-Semitic and has always dealt "fairly and squarely" with the Jewish community in his hometown of New York. (Photo by David Silverman/Getty Images.)

172 *Notebook - The Wit and Wisdom of Mark Twain,* 4.

OF REVEREND SHARPTON's many well-crafted pieces of fiction, his accounts of his trips to Israel and his protest on Vieques in Puerto Rico merit particular attention for compounded ignorance and an amplified imbecility. These, along with a twenty-four-hour mystery trip to Cuba, a bizarre story of taking a plane to the jungles of Sudan, where he hid in bushes to watch a slave-trading operation, and his visit to South Africa as an observer to the election of Nelson Mandela, were all cobbled together as part of his foreign-policy credentials touted in 2002's *Al on America.*

The first Israeli trip was a late 1990s twenty-four-hour adventure when Sharpton, then like the James Brown he has written about, was as unapologetically black as he was proud of it. The second trip, though, was in the era of the "mutated" millennial Al—now a black man modulated by his mainstream ambitions and in an intensified search for white acceptance, who would tell CNN's Bob Novak two years later that,

> I'm not running an African-American campaign. We're running a broad-based campaign that includes African-Americans and Latinos and gays and lesbians and laborers and others.

To that end, seeking to step up his game and to go mainstream in New York politics, the Rev. moved to court Jewish support and to mend fences in the Jewish community after a long and decidedly anti-Semitic past. So this time, he took Jewish attorney and friend Sanford Rubenstein with him on his trip to Israel and left black nationalism behind him back in Brooklyn where it had belonged. But in spite of pretenses of being an international savant ready to tackle foreign policy on day one of his presidency, those trips hadn't much enhanced the Rev.'s knowledge of the world. As he would later, in 2013's *Stone*, bemoan the loss of a pharaoh in Egypt for the first time in five thousand years, it showed that the then unrepentant novice was a complete neophyte back in 2001, and so it was that his account of that second Israeli trip was equally neophytic.

The Rev. had blundered his way into a conflict that was incomprehensible to him before his trip to Israel and would remain so long after. While in no way condoning the regional violence, he'd nonetheless shown little understanding of the dynamics of the region while revealing that he'd lacked both judgment and credibility to speak on the issue of Middle East peace. Failing to understand critical elements of the ethnoreligious quagmire of the region, he'd judged the situation by our standards (*death as the ultimate sacrifice*), telling us that "individual terrorists were willing to make the ultimate sacrifice—with their lives—to spread their evil and make their point."[173]

That religious indoctrination manufactures kamikazes who believe in martyrdom and paradise in the afterlife and therefore see no "sacrifices" in death, was lost on Reverend Sharpton. Their franchise is death for that which we deem worthy of living—values, ideologies, and beliefs. That there are no reincarnated witnesses to validate or invalidate beliefs in afterlife paradise, brainwashed killers are conditioned to gladly chose "paradise," which constitutes no "sacrifices" at all in their view. The Rev. had completely missed this point.

But his ignorance knows no bounds, and on an issue near and dear to his heart—that of sacred religious sites being exposed to violence—the Rev., in a veiled yet comical attack on then-President George W. Bush, proposed a novel solution. He wanted the American president to convene a global summit to declare that sacred places were indeed "sacred." To this end, Sharpton told us that, "If I were President, I would have convened world leaders to say that certain places—like the birthplace of Jesus, the Western or Wailing Wall, and Mecca—are sacred."[174] This time we could imagine the grimaces on the faces of both Israelis and Palestinians at such a summit, and even the horror on the faces of the guardians of Holy Mecca and Medina—the Saudis.

After a trip in which he'd familiarized himself with the issues and the players and had overheard all that he'd needed to hear of garlic and the male virility from Palestine Liberation Organization chairman Yasser Arafat, Sharpton then focused his ire on President George W. Bush for his failure to bring peace to the region. Among his suggestions to the leader of the Christian world was that the president convenes a peace summit to negotiate peace between Jews and Arabs at, of all places, the Church of the Nativity—birthplace of Christ

---

173 Sharpton with Hunter, *Al on America*, xiii.
174 Ibid., 54.

and symbol of an ancient Christendom that had triumphed over, and later per-secuted the Jews:

> If I were president I would have gone there myself—not sent one of my minions—and tried to negotiate a stalemate at the Church of the Nativity. But this president did neither, yet he poses as one who is so committed to Christianity.[175]

It was hard to tell whether or not this was a completed thought, as the Baptist preacher had given no indication as to whether or not full Jewish conversion to Christianity would've been a prerequisite for attendance at such a summit. He also seemed to believe that regional peace was to be for the benefit of Christian or-thodoxy rather than for the benefit of Israelis and Palestinians. Either way, it was the type of arrogance, insensitivity, and ignorance of history that has traditionally wreaked havoc on global politics by empowered ignoramuses. In a period when the Muslim world was incensed by what some had viewed as a Christian crusade against Islam, Reverend Sharpton had chosen to evoke the battle at Jaffa between England's King Richard I ("Richard the Lionheart") and Sultan Saladin. This bat-tle was the result of the Lionheart's own commitment to Christendom. This time, though, rather than a showdown at Jaffa, it was to be peace summit at the Church of the Nativity where Jews would now have a seat at the table, so it was OK.

For Sharpton, the need for a secure and peaceful future for the Jewish and Arab populations was not the real issue. Instead, it was President George W. Bush's lack of commitment to the Christian world. Other than that, it was yet another brilliant idea from the Christian preacher then seeking to be the next leader of the free world and in particular, the next leader of the Christian world.

Fast forward ten years, and we would find the same intractable situation befuddling President Barack Obama as it had for several presidents predating George W. Bush. Yet in 2013's *Stone*, the Rev. would espouse an entirely differ-ent tone. He then wrote glowingly of President Obama's accomplishments in the realm—implying but explicitly omitting the subject of Middle East peace:

---

175 Ibid.

That is the challenge of our age, whether we're talking about domestic fights in the US Congress, religious conflicts in the United States and abroad, or civil and human rights movements across the globe: how to deal with the extremists and zealots. It has certainly been a hallmark of President Obama's time in office.[176]

Dealing with Senate majority leader Mitch McConnell and House Speaker John Boehner was now in the same class as taking on HAMAS, the Muslim Brotherhood, Hezbollah, ISIS, al-Qaeda, the KKK, local white extremists, and other domestic terrorists. Accordingly, President Barack Obama, whose legislative agenda was thwarted by the Republican Congress, had performed exceedingly well on each of these fronts. They were the hallmarks of his time in office.

An Israeli Foe

Recounting his journey, in 2002's *Al on America,* to becoming a late-stage supporter of Israel and his recollection of his Israeli trip the previous year (2001) can only be fully appreciated by first taking a retroactive look at Reverend Sharpton's first visit a decade before. Then, he was seeking neither friendship with the Jews nor with the Jewish state. 1996's *Pharaoh* had told of his first Israeli trip (1991)—in hot pursuit of a bandit. The Rev. and his sidekick, attorney Alton H. Maddox, had gone there in 1991 on a mission to serve a subpoena to Yosef Lifsh—the result of a lawsuit filed in New York. Mr. Lifsh, the Jewish driver involved in the Crown Heights vehicular accident that had triggered the riots, had fled to Israel on his release without charges in New York. Sharpton had described a trip that was as whimsical as it was laced with anti-Semitic stereotypes. It is unimaginable that there was a single Israeli or Jew on the planet who wouldn't have taken offense:

> When the suit [on behalf of the Cato family] was heard the judge asked about the defendant. We said we thought he was in Israel. The judge then said we had to make an attempt to serve Lifsh and be able to prove that attempt before Lifsh could be held in default. "No problem," I said, "we're going to Israel." People

---

176 Al Sharpton with Chiles, *The Rejected Stone,* 231–32.

thought I was bluffing, even when we made our reservations and paid for the tickets. But there we were, Maddox and me, flying El-Al to Tel Aviv on the weekend of Yom Kippur. We're on the official Israeli airline going over there to pursue and serve a Hasidic Jew and everybody on the plane knows it. The Jewish community views Crown Heights as an assault along the lines of Kristallnacht, and they're looking at us like we're monsters.[177]

After attributing Jewish views of the Crown Heights riots to those of Kristallnacht—Night of Broken Glasses, during which German Nazis had torched synagogues, vandalized Jewish homes, schools, and businesses, and had killed close to one hundred Jews—the Rev. was surprised at being accused of grandstanding. But if that weren't enough, he then went "Shakespeare" on us by showing us a real-life Shylock in Israel, offering to pay him money to get out of the country:

So we fly ten hours to Israel, not even talking, just sitting there. We land in Tel Aviv, go through customs, and when we come out, it seems like the entire Israeli press corps is there. Flashbulbs are going off like firecrackers, and then out of nowhere this man, long-bearded, comes up to me, holds a two-inch wad of hundred-dollar bills in my face and says, "I'll pay you whatever you want to get out of our country."[178]

He also showed us a Jewish woman who, during the holiest period on the Jewish Calendar, had approached him with nothing but evil in her heart, telling him to go to hell. Beyond the conveyance of this being representative of Israelis, we also felt the pain such un-Christian behavior had caused the Christian minister. In any case, the picture was clear—Israel was *hell* and *hell* was Israel:

Then a woman—and mind you, this is Yom Kippur, the high holy days, Jews from all over the world are flying in for the day of atonement to cleanse their sins—runs up to me and yells, "Go to hell, Sharpton, go to hell." And with my

---

177 Al Sharpton and Walton, *Go and Tell Pharaoh*, 199.
178 Ibid., 199–200.

Brooklyn smart-mouth I say, "I am in hell." Of course the headlines in America the next day, on Yom Kippur, "SHARPTON SAYS ISRAEL IS HELL." It was like Howard Beach or Bensonhurst all over again, and that was hell to me.'[179]

As the story continued, it wasn't hard to recognize the local hero of that entire twenty-four-hour visit. It was the lone Arab cab driver who was the only person with a heart in all of Israel during that period of high atonement to have acknowledged the presence of the two black men from New York. It was as if the Israeli taxi drivers entering the airport for pickups were all pre-warned: *Do not pick up the two Schwartzas waiting at the taxi stand or you'll be arrested*:

> Finally, we get out to the curb and tried to get a cab. We had decided we were going to the American Embassy. We know we couldn't find Yosef Lifsh, he's somewhere out there in Israel, but the entire country is about to shut down for the holiday, and we need to see the consul to enlist his help. Our plan was to serve the embassy, which can, in legal matters, be his proxy, and then leave. But no cab would drive us. The Israelis just sat there, and when we'd say, "Taxi?" they would act like they didn't hear us. So we stepped out into the street, and we saw an Arab cabdriver and asked him if he would take us and he said yes...[180]

But it was serious business. The Rev. had spent $8,000 in plane fares and was able to obtain receipts of the delivered subpoena from the American Embassy in Tel Aviv to present to the New York court, in the Cato family's wrongful death lawsuit (family of the two young victims, whose injuries and death had precipitated the riots). Sharpton and Maddox then returned to New York almost as fast as they'd left:

> We had a very nice meeting at the embassy, [*sic*] we served them, and they said they would serve Lifsh if they could find him. They gave us a receipt, then we had coffee and headed back to the airport.[181]

179 Ibid.
180 Ibid.
181 Ibid.

Given the tone and substance of Sharpton's 1996 account of the 1991 trip, it was all the more surprising to read his about-face desire to return to Israel as a peacemaker six years later. Few people of sound mind would've wanted to return to "hell," even fewer African Americans—to any place that reminded them of Bensonhurst where local residents had fed them watermelons while yelling, "Niggers go home."

An Israeli Friend

Yet a trip back to Israel appeared inevitable in the new millennium. After his daughter's schoolmate had lost his mother in the 9/11 attacks, the issue of terrorism was brought home to the Sharpton family. We were told that this had inspired some sympathy for the Jewish state and in 2001, the Rev. convened a meeting of Jewish leaders in New York and sought their advice and help for a new trip to Israel:

> After September 11, I started thinking, "Now I understand what people go through in Israel and parts of the Middle East." They go through this every day. Maybe it's time for me to take a leap and identify with the victims of terrorism—not deal with foreign policy, but deal with the concerns of everyday people, like the everyday people who are dealing with it now in America...[182]

It was hard to miss Sharpton's assurance to us that his interest was "not to deal with foreign policy"—as if he were a State Department envoy and not just a professional marcher from Brooklyn. But he was moved to understand what was going on in the Middle East after the 9/11 attacks, so he called up some of his powerful Jewish friends for help. In *Al on America* he'd listed them as a Rabbi friend, members of the World Jewish Congress, and members of the Conference of Presidents of Major Jewish Organizations:

> So I called this rabbi and told him that I wanted to meet with some Israeli victims of terrorism because I want to know how they cope, how they deal.

---

182 Sharpton with Hunter, *Al on America*, 42.

He said the only way to do that is to go to Israel [a seemingly surprising suggestion] and he said it wasn't safe over there. I said, "No, now is the time to go."[183]

Many years later, in *Stone*, we were shown Sharpton, the insider with influential friends. Then the Rev. said that the trip was organized by his friend, Mortimer Zuckerman, publisher of the *New York Daily News* (previous target of a Sharpton picket and protest who'd laughed Sharpton out of the *Daily News*' office):

> After the events of September 11, 2001, I called Mort Zuckerman, the owner and publisher of US News and World Report and the New York Daily News, who at the time was chairman of the Conference of Presidents of Major American Jewish Organizations. I told him I wanted to go to Israel. Because I was a controversial figure in some Jewish circles, I thought it would be a powerful message if I went there to make a statement about how the world must stand together against terrorism, extremism, and the shedding of innocent blood. Zuckerman thought it was a great idea, and he arranged a formal invitation to me from the government of Israel.[184]

In a stunning turnaround from a decade earlier when there had been no interest in even staying a full day for a little sightseeing at some of the holiest places in Christendom, the Rev. decided to return to Israel, this time, "prepared to make sacrifices—even the ultimate sacrifice." We could've envisioned his detractors' disappointment that his preparations were for nothing:

> I think it would be a more important statement to go during a time of danger and meet with people. I mean, would there ever be a "safe" time to go? I knew it was dangerous for me to go to Israel, but it was more dangerous for me not to go. How can I preach unity, how can I be for justice and understanding and healing, if I am not willing to make sacrifices—even the ultimate sacrifice—to see those

---

183 Ibid., 43.
184 Al Sharpton with Chiles, *The Rejected Stone*, 226–27.

things through? How can I be a leader if I am not willing to go on the front lines and fight these battles?[185]

Up to that point, Reverend Sharpton was known as a "Jew-baiter" and an inciter of anti-Semitism in New York City, since the days of the Crown Heights riots and Freddie's Fashion Mart tragedy in Harlem. So, knowing his intended audience, he did attempt to address his issues with the Jewish community head-on in *Al on America*, but by obfuscating and going on the offensive. He challenged anyone who would accuse him of anti-Semitism during his 2004 election campaign to cool it because his statements in the past were nothing compared to those of former president Richard Nixon's anti-Semitic discussions of thirty years earlier with super evangelist Billy Graham:

> In 1972, Graham told Nixon in the Oval Office after a prayer breakfast that Jews had too much power and that "this stranglehold has got to be broken or the country's going down the drain." Graham also said that [sic] "they [the Jews are] the ones putting out the pornographic stuff..." Nixon is also heard referring to Jews as "kikes." This was the president of the United States and one of the most revered religious and spiritual leaders in this nation having a discussion about how Jews were taking over and running the country and how to stop them from controlling the media. And they call me an anti-Semite?! Jesse Jackson referred to New York as "hymietown" more than twenty years ago and he's still trying to live that down. And Billy Graham gets a free pass? I dare somebody to bring anti-Semitism into the presidential race of 2004.[186]

As usual, the Rev. had gone on the offensive to avoid being on the defensive; it was classic Sharpton—to be first on the attack, the first to make others the punch line, lest he is made the punching bag. But as a deflective strategy, it couldn't have been very effective, as few people in America—especially those seeking to become president—would've ever resorted to self-benchmarking

---

185 Sharpton with Hunter, *Al on America*, 43.
186 Ibid., 221–22.

against Richard Nixon as a way of ameliorating their public image and making themselves more acceptable. This is what I meant by merely lowering the bar to allow an easy walkover—codifying contemptible conduct (See "Departure Point").

Nonetheless, Reverend Sharpton had now become a lover and friend of Israel—well prepared to die over there for the cause of world Jewry and for Israel's very existence. In a "Sharptonesque" way, the mendacities of madmen are often to be accommodated. He'd needed the help of the American Jewish community, and they accommodated his move from rabble-rousing race-baiter to a mainstream friend of the Jewish people. The Rev. had needed "props" for his political campaigns in New York, and Israel needs and deserves friends, not enemies.

Meeting Arafat

Former Israeli prime minister Ehud Barak, whom he'd met on the plane, had suggested that the Rev. meet with the Palestinians and make an appeal for peace:

> On the plane ride over, the former prime minister of Israel, Ehud Barak, was on board, and we had an opportunity to talk. He said it would be important for me not only to learn about terrorism from the Israeli side, but he asked if I would meet with the Palestinians and appeal for peace.[187]

This time around, according to *Al on America*, the Israelis were quite welcoming. There was no "long-bearded" man handing the black man a wad of cash to leave his country, no atoning sinner sending Sharpton to hell. Instead, the Rev. had met with Foreign Minister Shimon Peres and was given an escort to meet with Palestine Liberation Organization chairman Yasser Arafat:

> When we arrived in Israel and met with Shimon Peres, he also suggested that we meet with Arafat. "You must meet with him and urge them to stop the violence and the terrorism." I told him that I heard Arafat would be out of town. But Peres

---

187 Ibid., 44.

said, "He's not expected to leave until tomorrow. Perhaps you can meet with him before he leaves." We were able to get in contact with Arafat's people and schedule a meeting for noon that day. I left Peres's office and was escorted in a van by his people to the Gaza Strip.[188]

Security was tight as his heavily armored escort detail snaked its way through what was the real *hell* to reach Arafat's compound:

> Driving through the Gaza Strip—before Israel bombed Arafat's compound—it already looked like a war zone. For about two miles, from the Israeli checkpoint to Arafat's compound, we drove through utter squalor. The area was full of bombed out buildings—shells of buildings…We had come to the region with armed security around our vehicle with sirens blaring, but these guys were clearly military.[189]

The immediacy of the events was notable; the Rev. had landed in Israel and was almost immediately commandeered by Shimon Peres to go see Arafat—that very day. Sharpton didn't tell us how he'd heard Arafat would've been out of town, but as a true man of God, the presumption of omniscience was left to us. We then witnessed the entire stagecraft of his meeting with Chairman Arafat—television cameras, coordinated handshakes, Arafat's denunciation of terrorism and of Osama bin Laden, and the exchange of gifts:

> They come in, boom, boom, boom, with the cameras, and then Arafat makes a very shrewd political move…After they take their pictures, everybody's thrown out and we begin finally to talk. We talk about terrorism and what happened on September 11, and immediately Arafat denounces Osama bin Laden. "Bin Laden does not represent Islam!" he said. [190]

---

188 Ibid.
189 Ibid., 44–45.
190 Ibid., 46.

But it wouldn't have been a visit to the old country without gaining a bit of ancient wisdom, and we saw a long-protracted conversation between Arafat and Sharpton's traveling partner, New York attorney Sanford Rubenstein, on the qualities of garlic:

> So I'm sitting at the table across from Arafat, and Sanford Rubenstein, one of my attorneys as well as Abner Louima's attorney, who accompanied us on this trip, was sitting next to Arafat. For the first five minutes of the meal, Rubenstein and Arafat were talking about what garlic does to middle-aged men and how it keeps them healthy and virile. Nobody would believe that this Jewish lawyer from Brooklyn is sitting there talking with Arafat about the beneficial properties of garlic while I'm trying to deal with terrorism.[191]

The Rev. was bemused. He was all about business, yet while he was there "trying to talk terrorism," these two men were discussing how to butter their bread—discussing the benefits of garlic as an aphrodisiac and as the answer to middle-age male virility.

Israeli Redux

Unsurprisingly, in his last book, 2013's *Stone*, we would get a different variation of the same Israeli trip. The immediacy of being commandeered to go see Arafat the moment Sharpton had landed was gone. This time, the Rev. had spent many days touring, seeing the famous sites and monuments, and meeting with Ethiopian Jews, among many other activities. Only then, and after much cajoling by Shimon Peres and the Israeli community, did he actually yield and visit Arafat's compound:

> I saw all the important sites while I was there—the Holy Land, Calvary where Jesus was crucified, the Wailing Wall, the Holocaust Museum. I met with some of the Ethiopian Jews living there. I also met with many families who had lost

---

191 Ibid., 47.

family members to terrorism…[192] But while I toured the country, I kept hearing the same message from various Israeli leaders: I needed to go over to the Palestinian side and also talk to them about fighting terrorism. But I was nervous about that, given the sensitivity of the American Jewish community and knee-jerk tendency of the American media to stir up controversy. I remembered all the trouble Jesse Jackson got in back in '79 when he hugged Yasser Arafat. In the middle of our meeting with Shimon Peres—I was traveling with a mixed delegation of blacks and Jews—Peres implored me to meet with the Palestinians.[193]

He did meet Ehud Barak on the plane ride over (in first class), but Barak had never implored him to go speak to the Palestinians as in the first version. Instead, what we got was a corny joke about terrorists getting two birds—Sharpton and Barak—with one stone, also a likely invention, as he, Sharpton, was hardly a "bird" on the radar of any terrorist group:

> On the ten-hour flight to Israel, I saw that I was sitting in first class with Ehud Barak, who had just stepped down from his post as prime minister after losing to Ariel Sharon. I went over to speak to him. Barak said to me with a laugh, "You know, I was thinking with me and you on the same flight, if the terrorists knew we were here together—boom!" The whole rest of the flight, I would jump every time the plane hit a bump, thinking to myself, Why did he have to joke like that?[194]

But on entering Israel the second time, it was a slapstick farce worthy of Sam Peckinpah's efforts to bring back the *head of Alfredo Garcia*. This time around, Sharpton's former Arab taxi driver appears to have been radicalized into a merciless kamikaze, as the now sinister Arabs seemed to have known Sharpton was in town—this time to be "nice" to the Jews. So, they decided to give him a firsthand demonstration of their craft. One of the first things that the Rev.

---

192 Al Sharpton with Chiles, *The Rejected Stone*, 228.

193 Ibid.

194 Ibid., 227.

witnessed while making his way from the airport to the King David Hotel was an exploding car:

> After I had landed and we were on our way to the King David Hotel, a car blew up about a half a mile in front of us. That was normal life for them; it didn't even seem to be that big a deal, which really exemplified for me the purpose of my visit.[195]

As with his trip to Africa, where he'd "reviewed" American troops in Kigali, Reverend Sharpton also conducted some American diplomacy as well—with the acquiescence of Secretary of State Colin Powell—in spite of his original desire to not deal with foreign policy. But as he was credentialed via the Israelis, it was OK:

> "You should denounce bin Laden [*sic*] and terrorism from the Arab side. You should go to Palestine," he said. "The right wing in America would distort it if I went over there," I said. "They would say I'm united with the Palestinians." But Peres dismissed my concerns. "We will tell them we invited you." I still wasn't sure, but then he said, "It's all arranged. You're meeting at one o'clock with Yasser Arafat." "Huh? How am I doing that?" "We've arranged it," he repeated. "We've already informed your State Department and Secretary Colin Powell."[196]

It is believable that the Rev. had met with Shimon Peres and others, including the PLO chairman, Yasser Arafat. We can also feel some level of confidence that Chairman Arafat and Sanford Rubenstein had indeed exhausted much time elucidating the aphrodisiacal benefits of cooking with garlic, as this was consistent in both stories. Though some years later, we would discover that the Rev. might have served himself well to have partaken of those garlic discussions rather than just "trying to talk terrorism" with Arafat. In an ironic twist of life imitating art, or maybe fiction in this case, on January 2015, Mortimer Zuckerman's *New*

---

195 Ibid., 228.
196 Ibid.

York Daily News reported on a New York City police investigation of allegations against Sanford Rubenstein—of which Rubenstein was later cleared. Among the contents found by the investigating authorities was a prescription for Viagra in the name of Reverend Al Sharpton. The Internet lit up:

No Viagra, No Peace!

All in all, the new millennium had seen a converted Reverend Sharpton as a friend of Israel, and that was indeed a good thing.

Perfecting Treachery

Virtue has never been as respectable as money.

—MARK TWAIN[197]

Democratic activist Reverend Al Sharpton, followed by demonstrators out of the Palm Beach County Emergency Operations Center in West Palm Beach, Florida, November 26, 2000, where the canvassing board was continuing a manual recount of ballots after the Florida State Supreme Court mandated accepting hand-counted ballots for certification by November 26, 2000, at 5:00 p.m. EST (2200 GMT). (Photo by Rhona Wise/AFP/Getty Images.)

FOR A GENERATION, there has been no greater "misleader" than the Reverend Al Sharpton. While not the only one, and in many ways simply building on the foundation laid by others, the Rev. has nonetheless put the business of exploiting

197 *The Innocents Abroad - The Wit and Wisdom of Mark Twain*, 10.

his people's suffering on steroids, as writer Juan Williams once inferred. From any number of the activities cited here, Sharpton has shown a callous propensity for making money and for milking prestige out of his so-called "issues" activism.

In 2004, though, the Rev. took treachery to a different level by emotionally blackmailing the entire Democratic Party. He mounted a mole candidacy as the Republican-financed-Democrat that then forced the big hug of recognition and preeminence he'd long sought from the Democrats. Although we know him as a Democratic activist-politician, the opportunistically nonaligned Reverend Sharpton ran a presidential campaign that was silently financed and managed by the visceral Republican strategist, Roger Stone—allowing himself to be a Republican pawn in an effort undertaken solely to weaken the eventual Democratic nominee. But if you ask Reverend Sharpton, he'll tell you that it was an "issues" campaign, which then means that they must have been "issues" on which the Republicans were in agreement with Democrats.

While electoral politics is known to be treacherous, in that 2004 election campaign cycle, the embarrassed Democrats had to contend with a candidate who was a known mole in their midst, right there on the stage with the other major candidates during the primary debates. They never publicly attacked the Rev. on the issue as he wasn't a serious threat. They also feared alienating black voters. Additionally, they knew that he was just trying to amplify his vote-bartering operation in order to trade with bigger bargaining chips for endorsement. The bemused Republicans, on the other hand, knew that they were holding the leash to a wounded dog, but they certainly wanted no public association with the Rev., so they, likewise, made no issue of his treachery.

It was then that *Time* columnist Joe Klein had called the Rev. a "criminal buffoon" and a "waste of time." But the criminal buffoon appeared to have wasted little time in pulling it off quite well. His bold-faced treachery was likely the reason the Democrats had then decided to co-opt and "contain" him in the aftermath of the 2004 election. Knowing him to have been a wild card, in addition to a potential perpetual mole from one day to the next, they'd had the choice of either co-opting him or contending with him nipping at their heels, so they chose the former.

For the Rev., the benefits were clear: his actions would certainly elevate his profile and empower his bargaining position with the Democratic National

Committee and with front-runner John Kerry. Running for president is the equivalent of being an Oscar-nominated actor; the end result is higher prestige and a higher earning potential all around. In Sharpton's politics, the endorsement is a cash cow. After having perfected the practice in local New York City politics, running in the big league had then meant bigger ransoms.

We'd gotten a sample of this from mayoral candidate Ruth Messinger's former campaign research director, Evan J. Mandery. In his book, *The Campaign— Rudy Giuliani, Ruth Messinger, Al Sharpton, and the Race to Be Mayor of New York City, Mandery, spoke* of the Rev.'s cash demands for endorsing fellow Democrat, Messinger in the 1997 mayoral election against Rudolph Giuliani:

> Behind the scenes, Sharpton's people have opened negotiations with our political department about a possible endorsement. They want money, which is no surprise. What is a surprise is the amount they are demanding…they're talking about hundreds of thousands of dollars. We're telling them that we don't have that kind of money, which is really a polite way of saying we have the money but choose to spend it on television ads.[198]

It was lucrative work for those who could've gotten it, and the Rev., who had been practicing the craft for years in New York, would go on to perfect it into an art. This has since sent his stock shooting into the stratosphere as a Democratic insider, at least as the Democrats' overt mouthpiece.

Vulture

During the 2008 economic meltdown, there was hardly a television appearance by the Rev. in which he didn't decry the predatory lending practices on the vicious Wall Street. Yet on Malcolm X, Marcus Garvey, and Martin Luther King Jr. boulevards across America, he was guilty of even worse. The story of the Rev. and "Loan Max," cited by writer Juan Williams and elsewhere in the public space, was the nexus of the heartless meeting the callous—in the same body.

---

198 Evan J. Mandery, *The Campaign Rudy Giuliani, Ruth Messinger, Al Sharpton, and the Race to Be Mayor of New York City* (Westview Press, 1999), 293.

According to Williams, Loan Max was a predatory finance company, effectively a legal loan-sharking operation that charged what amounted to usury rates of interest that topped 300 percent. It took the titles to its borrowers' cars and other personal assets as collateral, which it then often sold off, as most borrowers were bound to default at those levels of interest. People who have to borrow at 300-percent interest rates are generally the types who are incapable of repaying even at normal annual percentage rates (APRs), below 20-percent for the average credit card. Loan Max, therefore, made a windfall from its high-interest rates as well as from the value it received from the sale of pledged collateral. This devastated many of the poor black and brown families on which the company preyed—the very downtrodden at the core of what the Rev. often claim as *his people*:

> Those people, blacks, are my people. I set out to serve them…and that's all I've ever wanted to do. Those people, the lower class, the lower part of the middle-income class, trust me. I was their child prodigy, those working class black folks, the maids and janitors, cooks and doormen…[199]

Loan Max knew of the trust and confidence his people placed in the Rev., so it hired him as a pitchman to advertise its business to them. Sharpton appeared in ads targeting poor African Americans with bad credit, selling them high-interest predatory loans and other services. With him as the face of business, Loan Max legitimized itself to its targeted clientele.

Though desirous of freedom for his people, their bondage had worked out pretty well for Sharpton over the years. On the one hand, he repeatedly reduced the value of their votes by trading them for cash endorsements, while on the other, for a fee, he eagerly returned many to economic servitude through predatory financing schemes that had fleeced them outright. The freedom Sharpton had therefore envisioned for his people in the next frontier appeared to have been anything but free.

---

199 Al Sharpton and Walton, *Go and Tell Pharaoh*, 5.

Rent-a-Demonstration

The barnstorming days of the early Sharpton years were the days of the chump change hustler. Big money would later come from endorsements and corporate shakedowns. In *Pharaoh,* he'd made a distorted comparison between the aims of his National Youth Movement and those of the SCLC's Operation Breadbasket, telling us,

> We were going to go after major corporations with young people and get economic concessions. We were going to go after thousands of new voters, particularly young people...[200]

While Operation Breadbasket was about economic empowerment through direct action against businesses that had refused to hire African Americans or those that weren't "net-positive" participants in the black communities in which they operated, the Rev.'s movement was solely about economic concessions that were net-positive to Al Sharpton. Companies targeted for protests and demonstrations just had to make donations to his National Youth Movement or its successor, the National Action Network, in order to enjoy a level of indemnification from the nuisance of a Sharpton action. Others placed him on illusory advisory boards for a fee, to the same effects—the Rev. would spare them any protests or public attacks that could've resulted in embarrassment or negative press coverage.

In a November 21, 2014, *Salon* article, "Al Sharpton's Latest 'Hustle': New Lessons, New Reports of Troubling Finances," former *New York Daily News* columnist Jim Sleeper recounted the comical attempt by Reverend Sharpton to shake down *Daily News* Publisher Mortimer Zuckerman back in the 1990s:

> When I was writing about Sharpton as a columnist for the New York Daily News in the mid-1990s, Mortimer Zuckerman, the paper's publisher, had a meeting with Sharpton that encapsulated a lot of what I'd learned about him. Sharpton had been out in front of the Daily News for two days with his megaphone and his sad stragglers, chanting about racism, and now it was time for the ritual

---

200 Ibid., 60.

extortion meeting, at which the beleaguered CEO learns what it will take to get rid of the annoyance. Zuckerman, along with a black News executive assistant and some editors, had a sit-down with Sharpton and other frozen-in-time protesters. More instructive than the substance of the negotiation was the way the meeting ended.

"I'd like to ask that we all hold hands, close our eyes, and pray," said Sharpton, careening gently into a holy roll. Imagine Mort Zuckerman and eight or 10 others sitting in a circle with Sharpton, hands joined, heads bowed. "Oh Lord," Sharpton intoned, "we pray that you will help your servant Mortimer Zuckerman to create a more diverse, inclusionary Daily News. Amen."

"Excuse me, Reverend Sharpton," Zuckerman said as all present opened their eyes; "I'd like to address a few words to the Lord, too, if I may." So all held hands and closed eyes again. "Oh Lord," Zuckerman prayed, "we ask that you will protect and prosper our honored guests, and that you will help them to understand that, with your guidance, I, as the proprietor of the Daily News, I will do with it what I think best. Amen."

As they opened their eyes again, Sharpton raised an eyebrow at Zuckerman and, with a mischievous, connoisseur's smile, stage-whispered, "Nice!"

This has been Sharpton's modus operandi—routinely selling threats of boycott and protests as both product and service. The playbook was consistent: turn up the heat by threatening to boycott or protest to get a buyout or a payoff (except in the case of the brilliant Mortimer Zuckerman and a few others). Striking a deal then saved the Rev. from having to pretend to stage a phony march while protecting the companies from having to implement real diversity and equality in its employment practices.

Let's say that the ACME Company wants its management ranks to remain all white and male and its employee workforce mostly white. For a fee, ACME's crafty CEO and its board of directors will either make a donation to the Rev.'s movements or put him on a "board" or "advisory committee" that never meets—for a lesser fee but with added prestige for him. This solves ACME's problem, absolves it of any diversity obligations, of any pressure to bring black, brown, or female executives into its boardroom, and in some cases, of any requirement to be socially responsible or legally compliant.

It will generally start off as a corporate "Mexican standoff." Initially rebuffed, the Rev. will huff and bluff and threaten to stage marches and protests while the company executives have a brandy, share a good laugh, and pretend to take him seriously—while ignoring him. Sooner or later, though, the executives will come to realize the potential inconvenience of having a number of smelly and displeasing street people—the "sad stragglers" Jim Sleeper described—taken from local shelters to march in front of television cameras outside their company's main entrance. After some posturing back and forth, a decision will then be made to donate to the race leader's organization in order to be rid of him. The Rev. then laughs all the way to the bank while the corporate leaders go back to their brandy and laughter—affirmed in their preconceived notion of black leadership as a complete fraud.

In fairness, Reverend Sharpton was just emulating his former mentor Jesse Jackson. Companies like Anheuser Bush, accused of racial discrimination and disenfranchisement in its network of distributors, had reportedly made significant donations to Jackson's organization under threats of protests. Juan Williams reminded us that in the 1980s, Reverend Jackson had led a boycott of Budweiser with the slogan "Bud's a Dud." The end result was that he'd secured a multimillion-dollar beer distribution operation for two of his sons.[201] Settling up with men like Jackson and Sharpton was the quickest way for these companies to outsource their ethical obligations and social responsibilities. In doing so, they also escaped potential public-relations blowback, while the underlying issues of racist and sexist hiring and promotion practices remained intact.

Juan Williams had cited another such example of the Rev.'s "corporate action," which was also covered by the *Wall Street Journal*. Detroit-based Adell Broadcasting Corporation, a white-owned company, had wanted to force cable company Charter Communications, another white-owned company, to carry its programming. Unable to reach a deal, Adell brought out the Tommy Gun by hiring Reverend Sharpton to stage a "civil rights" protest against Charter Communications.[202] Unless we are to accept that white-owned Adell was denied a deal with Charter because of Adell's white ownership and

---

201 Juan Williams, *Enough* (Crown Publishers, New York, 2006), 51.
202 Ibid., 53.

management structure, in which case the Rev. would've merited much ku-dos for opposing white-on-white discrimination, this had had nothing to do with civil rights or diversity causes. Yet in the bartering of services, the Rev. took Adell Broadcasting's money and staged a protest in front of Charter Communications' office. Quoting the *Wall Street Journal,* Juan Williams said this:

> Sharpton got out of a limousine in March, 2002, to lead three busloads of protest marchers in chants of "No Justice, No Peace!" outside of Charter's headquarters near St. Louis. One of the protest organizers working with Sharpton said he got people to join the protest by pulling them out of home-less shelters, giving them a meal and fifty dollars. He told the Journal that, "I like to refer to it as a 'Rent-a-Demonstration.'"[203]

In those days, the Rev.'s shakedown fee was a mere $10,000 and the cost of his "militant activists" taken from homeless shelters, a mere $50 and a meal. It was a runaway boondoggle for Sharpton. But again, let's not begrudge him, as he'd merely followed the Jesse Jackson playbook. In an exaggerated example of how these men had perfected the corporate shakedown under the guise of civil rights activism, Williams had noted that the same company, Adell Broadcasting Corporation, had also paid Jesse Jackson to pressure Charter into coming to the table. When asked about it, Jackson said,

> It is not unusual for the people we help to help the organization [Rainbow Coalition/Operation PUSH, National Action Network, etc.]. That does not affect our integrity at all. It's the way we survive.[204]

For his part, by recruiting protesters out of homeless shelters to stage paid-for-protests, the Rev. had indeed become Jesse Jackson on steroids. It was the way they "survived." Jackson had indeed created a monster even Dr. Frankenstein might have envied.

---

203 Ibid., 54.
204 Ibid.

"A Black Pawn Accepting Cash"

More than a decade later, and we would find Reverend Sharpton—the inside man—being exposed for his hypocrisy. In 2016, black entertainer and media mogul Byron Allen, his Entertainment Studios Network, and the National Association of African American Owned Media (NAAAOM) launched a $10-billion lawsuit against the very same Charter Communications, against whom the Rev. had "demonstrated" for unfair practices on behalf of Adell Broadcasting Corporation. In doing so, Mr. Allen resorted to the use of section 1981 of the Reconstruction-Era Civil Rights Act (CRA) of 1866 to charge Charter with discrimination in its cable business practices. In combination with the Fourteenth Amendment, 1866's CRA section 1981 was Congress' effort to extend constitutional protections to minority businesses by protecting the rights of the then freedmen to conduct business in the face of black codes that were erected by whites to disenfranchise black enterprises during Reconstruction.

The crux of Mr. Allen's case was that black-owned media receives almost nothing (less than $10 million) of the $70 billion spent per year by the cable industry in licensing cable networks. It accused Charter's executives of racial bias in their decision-making and accused the company of excluding black-owned media companies from contracts with channel carriers, which gave rise to the appearance of modern-day black codes in the industry. Although the lawsuit has survived Charter's initial request for a summary judgment dismissal by the federal court, the outcome remains unpredictable. But notably, this time there were no demonstrations or condemnation of the industry practices by Reverend Sharpton—then an industry figure with his own television show. It was quite the contrary, as neither Byron Allen nor any other black media concerns had employed him. Sharpton had found a new and more lucrative way to survive. The irony, though, was that in the process, Mr. Allen had also directly accused the race leader of being a "pawn" used to further discrimination against minorities in the industry.

Allen's lawsuit against Charter communications wasn't his first try at the issue. In a now-dismissed 2014 $20-billion lawsuit (under appeal as of this writing) against Comcast (parent company of Sharpton's employer, MSNBC), Allen had also gone directly after the Rev.—then accusing him and other institutional black figures of accepting large cash donations to "whitewash Comcast's discriminatory business practices." In addition to highlighting Rev.'s educational and intellectual deficiencies, Mr. Allen then referred to him as, "nothing more than a black pawn in a very sophisticated white economic chess game." The tables were turned on the Rev.

When Hollywood was accused of racism, for snubbing minority actors in 2016, Sharpton then accused Cheryl Boone Isaacs—the black president of the Academy of Motion Picture Arts and Sciences—of much the same. He called her, "nothing but a pawn, and the black face of Hollywood's system and culture that is racist, sexist and lacks true diversity." Byron Allen had given it to Reverend Sharpton as good as the Rev. was used to giving it to others.

Puppet Master Roger Stone

Roger Stone, pictured at his office in Fort Lauderdale, Florida, is a veteran Republican political operative with a reputed skill for dirty tricks. (Carl Juste/Miami Herald/MCT via Getty Images.)

As earlier mentioned, millennium Al had set out to reinvent himself, primarily by running for unattainably high elective offices. But lacking the funds, this wasn't an easy task, so on cue, he just as quickly availed himself for sale, not only to high-bidding cash holders but also to a low-bidding credit-card holder. Entered Roger Stone—long-time Republican operative and agent provocateur, Nixon-era "dirty tricks" veteran, Donald Trump confidant of over four decades, and current figure in the "Guccifer 2.0/Julian Assange/WikiLeaks" affair and the wider investigation into suspected Russian hacking to influence the 2016 American presidential election. In a modern-day version of a dirty-tricks operation, the Republican Stone had financed and managed "Democrat" Al Sharpton's 2004 Democratic primary campaign for president—a cynical effort to weaken the eventual Democratic nominee. Stone and the Republicans had found in the Rev. a perfect pawn to be used.

There is a picture of Roger Stone on the internet posing as James Bond, British super spy 007, and to say the least, Stone has been no less than the 007 of Republican politics for decades. Flamboyant, colorful, hilariously entertaining, liberal ("libertine") in his private life, and viscerally conservative in his politics, Stone has left more political careers in the graveyard than Ian Fleming could ever dream of writing about. One writer called him a political assassin. Long before being embroiled in the quagmire of suspicions and investigations emerging from the 2016 presidential election, Roger Stone was a legend in the underbelly of Republican politics. He spearheaded the street forces in the effort to block the recount of African American and Jewish votes in Miami's Dade County during the Bush versus Gore election 2000 farce. By all appearances, it was a "tumultuous" experience as chronicled with high umbrage and much posture by Reverend Sharpton in a chapter of 2002's *Al on America,* "Voting and Campaign Reform:"

> Our reports showed that tens of thousands of votes—primarily in black and Jewish areas were not accounted for properly. I got out of the car and there were about forty or fifty Republicans waiting for me. They went crazy and started heckling me. I couldn't believe it. I said to them, "You guys call yourselves patriots but have the audacity to be out here trying to stop counting the votes of the people?"[205]

---

205 Sharpton with Hunter, *Al on America,* 119.

In another chapter in the same book, the Rev. had given us a civil rights soliloquy, detailing his response to those Republican hecklers in Miami during that Bush versus Gore 2000 election recount:

> I'll never forget that morning in West Palm Beach. While I was outside the voting center interviewing upset and disenfranchised voters, one of the hecklers yelled out, "Al, why don't you just get over it?" "Get over it?" I said. "It might be easy for you to get over it because all you had to do was turn eighteen to be able to vote...My mother could not vote until she was well into her forties. And I will die fighting before I just "get over it" and allow it to go back to the days of Jim Crow. Get over it?[206]

Roger Stone was the organizer of those Republican hecklers Sharpton had so vividly described in his 2002 book. To secure the Republican victory, party leaders had tasked Stone with disenfranchising those very voters the Rev. had interviewed and on whose behalf, he'd supposedly intervened. As the consummate civil rights leader, an affronted Sharpton had spoken of remembering the martyrs who'd died for the cause and of his resolve to press on with the business of the recount:

> I can't, especially when I think of how those poor girls were killed in that church in Birmingham one Sunday morning during Sunday school...When I think of Medgar Evers who was in his thirties, with three kids in the house, and who got out of his car one night and, in his own driveway in Mississippi, got his brains blown out because he was leading a voter rights' campaign...When I think of how two Jews and a black man—Andy Goodman, Michael Schwerner, and James Chaney—left the Northeast in June 1964, to make sure that I would have the right to vote, and never returned home, I'm never going to get over that.[207]

They were the same emotional talking points he'd put to use throughout the 2004 election cycle. But ever seeking to elevate himself and to challenge Dr.

---

206 Ibid., 119–20.
207 Ibid., 120.

King's supremacy, the Rev. had again taken great care to tell us that certain things that he'd done in Florida, were the "first ever" done (i.e., not even Dr. King had ever done them):

> I had to do something. In Florida, we retained attorney Jesse McCrary, the first
> black to be secretary of state of Florida. We filed the first ever voter rights' lawsuit
> in that state...Nationally, we cannot wait until 2004 to have a repeat of 2000.[208]

But he didn't wait for a repeat of minority voter disenfranchisement in 2004. Instead, he undertook his own efforts to ensure it with genuinely an undisputed "first ever" act—he would run for president in modern times as a candidate for a major political party while being financed and managed by the opposition. It's not hard to see that while he was telling us in 2002 of his deeply emotional 2000 experience in Florida, he was likely, at the same time, cultivating a relationship with the source of that profoundly emotional experience—Roger Stone. But as earlier pointed out, the Rev. could also have known Roger Stone through local New York City interactions, given Stone's long friendship with the likes of Donald Trump, a longtime friend, and likely Sharpton benefactor, courtesy of their mutual friend, boxing promoter Don King.

But the first hint of suspicion had come from the Rev. himself. He was careful to write an entire epistle on the Florida experience with as much granular and over the top details, but without any mention by name, of the leader of those hecklers—the leader of the effort to block the recount. There were hecklers, anti-democrats, fascists, and racists, in Sharpton's account but no Roger Stone. So, there must have been a good reason to have hidden Stone's involvement, likely because while posturing, the Rev. had already cultivated or was in the process of cultivating a benefactor.

Within two years at most of the Florida events, Sharpton would collaborate with the very man who'd taken credit for organizing those "get-over-it" hecklers who'd succeeded in stalling the ballot counts—the result of which was the defeat of Sharpton's supposed valiant effort and of his party in a very consequential election. In spite of the memories of Medgar Evers, the Sixteenth

---

208 Ibid., 119–21.

Street Baptist Church bombing victims, Andy Goodman, Michael Schwerner, and James Chaney, or of his mother's inability to vote until well into her forties, the Rev. appeared to have "gotten over it," all in no time. Whatever lawyer he might have hired in Florida and for whatever purposes, none of that had mattered in the end, as he'd later availed himself as a pawn to the man who had hindered the recounts that had damaged Democrat Al Gore's chances.

As a cunning Republican operative, Roger Stone was undoubtedly seeking to damage Democrat John Kerry's chances in 2004 as well. That the Bush-Cheney team had tapped Stone to undermine the 2000 Florida recounts was a testimony to his effectiveness as a party operative. The Rev.'s involvement with the Nixon-era veteran of dirty tricks was itself a dirty trick. What value could there have been for the opposition in supporting a third-tier candidate in a political nomination process but as a tool of sabotage? Roger Stone had seen an opportunity in Reverend Sharpton, and he took it. Journalist Juan Williams, who'd included this piece of Sharpton treachery in a segment of his book, *Enough...*, had this to say:

> Sharpton did take the Jackson model of modern black politics to a new low, however. To finance his failing campaign, he reportedly took $200,000 from a Republican political strategist known for playing dirty politics.[209]

> The only time Stone [ever] showed an interest in Black politics was when he joined the effort to block a recount of Black and Jewish votes in Miami-Dade County to protect candidate George W. Bush's presidential victory in the 2000 election.[210]

Roger Stone and the Republican Party had wanted a weakened and beaten up Democratic nominee against whom to run in the general election, and they handed Sharpton a Billy club. According to the *Village Voice's Wayne* Barrett, in addition to putting one of his lieutenants, Charles Halloran, in charge of running Sharpton's campaign, Stone had also placed another five or six of his aides from previous campaigns to take control of the entire campaign operations.

---

209 Juan Williams, *Enough* (Crown Publishers, New York, 2006), 52.
210 Ibid., 52.

This had made it a de facto Roger Stone campaign—managed, financed, and operated by Stone, but with Reverend Sharpton as the figurehead candidate.

Stone was also instrumental in putting together the Rev.'s application for federal matching funds and had generated contributions for the Rev. in some states where Sharpton had little or no support. In some cases, these contributions were from family members and political allies of Stone—conservative types who abhorred everything Reverend Sharpton represented politically. But they were in perfect synch with Stone's objective of weakening Democratic nominee John Kerry, and so they contributed to financing the original black Trojan Horse. Roger Stone reportedly later bragged of loaning money to Sharpton's National Action Network (NAN) and of even allowing the Rev. to use his credit card to cover thousands in NAN costs—neither of which the Rev. could've legally done for his campaign under existing campaign finance laws.

Of the events, *Atlantic Monthly* writer Mark Bowden had said, "There could only be one plausible reason for Stone's helping Sharpton, and that was to undermine the mainstream appeal of the Democratic Party by forcing whoever became the frontrunner to deal with Sharpton's ostentatiously leftist agenda."[211] But this was being kind or maybe somewhat naïve to believe that the Rev.'s "ostentatiously leftist agenda" was the real driver of his behavior. The campaign that ended up catapulting the Rev. to the podium among the national Democratic candidates during the primary debates and as a speaker at the Democratic Convention had little to do with bringing his "issues" campaign to the forefront, as he often claims. It had more to do with the Rev.'s naked ambition, infused with treachery.

For Reverend Sharpton—the poster boy of contemporary racial racketeering—waging a campaign solely to deplete primary votes from the eventual Democratic nominee, John Kerry, would empower his bargaining position with the Democrats for endorsements, for cash, and for respectability. This was Sharpton at his best; he'd reached the big leagues, and thanks to Republican efforts, the ugly frog had found a way of being kissed into a princely welcome among the Democrats.

In 2004, the Rev.'s die-hard Democratic supporters—the little old women and elderly men, of whom he has often spoken, the hotel workers,

---

211 Ibid.

the secretaries, the mail carriers, and the maids who voted for him in election after election—were all duped, just as much as elite black supporters like Dr. Cornel West and others who'd shamelessly jumped onto the "scampaign" bandwagon, as writer Norman Kelley had called it.

Although widely written about, no one—black or white—had really cared that the Rev. had lived up to the widely stereotyped expectations of the inept, mediocre, and corrupt black leader. Who would've really cared that he'd lived up to what was expected of Al Sharpton? Had such a betrayal been pulled off by a white political candidate, he or she would've long been driven out of town in shame *a la* Democrat John Edwards—that year's Democratic vice-presidential candidate who was later discarded by the establishment on revelations that he'd cheated on his terminally ill wife. But a prevailing double standard of reserved mediocrity for black leadership often means that expectations are so low that running a mole candidacy wasn't even a blip on the radar for Sharpton's white handlers. It certainly didn't register among his constituents and his champions in the black media and black politics—many of whom were seduced by the same ill-gotten gravy train that had transported the Rev.—couldn't have cared less.

It's the contemporary form of nineteenth-century colonial practices under which the Europeans had installed weaklings and puppets that served to continue the exploitation and oppression of the indigenous. Indeed, no one has ever elected the Rev., and his ascension and empowerment atop black leadership were precisely because he's a morally impaired weakling, precisely because he's controllable and is ultimately for (on) perpetual sale. No one knew this better than "High Commissioner" Roger Stone. But on the other hand, there was also "China Town's" Noah Cross, who'd famously told us, "'Course I'm respectable. I'm old. Politicians, ugly buildings, and whores all get respectable if they last long enough."

Democratic Subterfuge

Reminding us of the Rev.'s "bombastic, self-righteous condemnation" of Green Party candidate Ralph Nader, after Nader had entered yet another presidential race in 2004, writer Norman Kelley had coined the term "Scampaign 2004" to describe Reverend Sharpton's own effort that year. Many had blamed Ralph

Nader's third-party run for Democrat Al Gore's defeat to Republican George W. Bush in Florida in 2000, but not the Sharpton of 2002. In *Al on America,* the Rev. was unapologetically effusive in his opinion of Nader's 2000 bid—squarely blaming the Democrats—not Ralph Nader, for Al Gore's defeat:

> Ralph Nader ran for the Green Party in 2000. He got three million votes. There are some who will argue that he cost the Democrats the White House. I don't blame Nader for running; I blame the Democratic Party. Obviously, there were three million people who Al Gore and Company did not represent.[212]

He didn't see Nader as an "egomaniac" or as a "Bush contract" then, but all of that changed less than two years later when it was the Rev.'s turn to play the spoiler. He'd now come to view Ralph Nader's latest attempt as a cynical ploy, and Nader, as an agent of the Republicans. Sharpton declared,

> The only reason he is running is either he's an egomaniac or as a Bush contract. What's the point? This is not 2000 when progressives were locked out. I'm going on a national crusade to stop Nader. This is only going to help Bush.[213]

So, in his power-hungry zeal in the 2004 cycle, there had stood Dr. Faustus bombastically condemning another for having made a Faustian Bargain. The master of hypocrisy is a master at projecting as well, so barely two years after absolving Ralph Nader of blame, the Rev. then switched tone to call Nader a "Bush contract." In Nader's campaign, Sharpton had found the perfect model for a shakedown but had wanted to own that space for himself in 2004. Writer Norman Kelley had noticed it as well, describing the Rev.'s comments as "eerie" and "unreal," given that by then it had been revealed that Sharpton was the real "Bush contract."

As pointed out, although reported in a few newspapers, the story had had little appeal to the powers that be and the mainstream media, which had accorded the Rev., all the legitimacy of a legitimate candidate, had largely ignored it. As

---

212 Sharpton with Hunter, *Al on America,* 23.

213 Norman Kelley, *The Head Negro in Charge Syndrome* (Nation Books, 2004), 193.

opposition research is at the heart of all major political campaigns, the special-ists know everything there is to be known, so both Democrats and Republicans had known the full details of Sharpton's treachery all along. As previously men-tioned, there were full-length exposures by the *Village Voice's* Wayne Barrett, who'd detailed Roger Stone's financing and staffing of the Sharpton campaign. As early as February 4 through 10, 2004, in a series of articles entitled "Sleeping with the GOP," followed by another, between February 11 and 17, under the banner, "Sharpton's Cynical Campaign Choice," Wayne Barrett had exposed the Rev.'s 2004 presidential campaign for the treacherous fraud that it was.

Where Reverend Sharpton has often dismissed the "paternalism" of the *Village Voice*, other outlets, including the *Atlantic Monthly* and the *New York Times*, had also covered the issue. It was a public secret known to all—the Democratic Party honchos, black media & leadership, Republicans, and the mainstream media—except to the public, for whom it had remained largely unknown and for whom it would likely have been met with utter disbelief in any case.

But this was no surprise to those who'd followed the Democrats' *L'Enfant terrible* over the years, as he'd been very candid in his previous assessment of the Democratic Party and was very overt in his dealing with it. In spite of current pretenses, there was never any love lost between the Democratic Party and Reverend Sharpton. From his days of being "for" David Dinkins while work-ing to undermine him, the Rev. was in his element—having spent two decades running for office as a perfectly nonaligned opportunist for sale to the highest bidder. Sharpton has never hidden his intentions.

In 1996's *Pharaoh*, he'd done his best take on words once uttered by the likes of Henry Kissinger and France's General Charles de Gaulle, among many, to express this nonalignment while outlining his guiding philosophy. He'd learned the cardinal rule—"Interests" was the governing principle of politics:

> As the old political saw goes, "No permanent friends, no permanent enemies, only permanent interests." That's how everybody else in the country plays the political game and how blacks are going to have to learn to play it.[214]

---

214 Al Sharpton and Walton, *Go and Tell Pharaoh*, 244.

Expanding on the "kingmaker" earlier described, in 1986, the Rev. had endorsed conservative Republican Al D'Amato over fellow Democrat Mark Green in New York's US Senate race. D'Amato, who would later anger Sharpton by voting against the 1990 civil rights bill, had nonetheless secured him a nice government grant in the interim as a *thank-you.*

In 1992, he'd turned New York's US Senate primary on its face when he entered the primary against Democratic state attorney general Robert Abrams, who at that time was prosecuting him on tax evasion charges. The election was in November 1992, and the Rev. was due to show up in court for trial the following January. Many had blamed him for depressing Abrams' black support and his narrow defeat by Sharpton's old friend, Republican Al D'Amato.

After working behind the scenes to undermine Mayor David Dinkins in 1993, the Rev. then worked hard to publicly blame Mario Cuomo and Democratic establishment for having mistreated David Dinkins because he was black. We recall his assertion that Mario Cuomo had "iced" Dinkins. In 1994, Sharpton then cornered the Democrats by "primarying" established Democrat and elder statesman, US Senator Daniel Patrick Moynihan for his US Senate seat, or probably for having written that 1965 report, "The Negro Family," that the Rev. had so hated. The Democratic party could have ill afforded to alienate black voters—many of whom had believed Sharpton and had held the party responsible for not doing enough to support African American Dinkins the previous year. The Democrats then had to kowtow and do business with the Rev. in that election as well.

That same year, it was an open secret that the Rev. had supported Republican George Pataki in New York's gubernatorial race against Democrat, Governor Mario Cuomo. After Pataki's victory, it is said that Sharpton was among the first people invited to the governor's mansion. In both the 1992 state attorney general and the 1994 gubernatorial race, the Rev. had crossed his party to take revenge on fellow Democrats he'd seen as his persecutors—Robert Abrams and Mario Cuomo.

As earlier stated, in 1998 Sharpton was back to endorsing Democrat Mark Green in the Democratic primary for Al D'Amato's US Senate seat, on the pretext that Green had integrity and was consistent on issues affecting the working-class. Mark Green lost the primary to Rep. Charles Schumer, who then courted the Rev.

As the kingmaker in the earlier cited 2001 mayoral race, Sharpton and Green were back at it again with the Rev. ultimately supporting Green's primary opponent, Fernando Ferrer. Even after Ferrer had lost to Green in the Democratic primary, the Rev. still refused all party calls for him to back his "fellow Democrat," Green. This was the race in which Jonathan Capehart, then working for Republican-"Independent" Michael Bloomberg, had played active go-between for Sharpton and Bloomberg—an indication of how easily Reverend Sharpton works both sides of the fence. Michael Bloomberg had gone on to defeat Democrat Mark Green in that race. Hence Sharpton became the self-declared "kingmaker."

So, nothing about his 2004 presidential run was surprising to a political establishment well familiar with the Rev. Before being a beneficiary of the setup, he was a strident critic of the Democratic Party and the "controlled" black leaders within it. We recall here, his candor about voter suppression by Democratic incumbents to keep their seats:

> In many black communities when we start voter registration, I've had some of the local incumbents say, "Don't do that!" Only 4,000–5,000 people may vote in the primary, and those are the folks they are sure of. If we bring out 10,000 more people who may not like what's going on in their neighborhood, that incumbent may not win.[215]

He was never hesitant in ridiculing the Democrats, either. When his 1997 New York City Democratic mayoral primary challenger Eric Ruano-Melendez had accused him of breaching the separation of church and state in violation of the Constitution and of belonging to organizations seeking to overthrow the country, the Rev. shot back, asking Ruano-Melendez, "Like the Democratic Party?"[216] In 2002's *Al on America*, he essentially described the Democratic Party as the plantation to which he was unceremoniously aligned, yet ceremoniously affixed:

---

215 Sharpton with Hunter, *Al on America*, 123–24.

216 Evan J. Mandery, *The Campaign Rudy Giuliani, Ruth Messinger, Al Sharpton, and the Race to Be Mayor of New York City* (Westview Press, 1999), 249.

The Democratic Party acts like we are their mistress that they have to hide, like we're some political scarlet whore rather than their respected partner. Either we're going to have a healthy marriage or we're getting a divorce and marrying someone who will respect us. We will no longer allow ourselves to be screwed by the Democrats.[217]

It was the political version of former Alabama governor "Big Jim" Folsom's insight on southern segregation—that whites (men) worked themselves up into a frenzy over segregation during the day but work themselves up with equal frenzy, integrating (with black women) during the night.

But Reverend Sharpton had become tired of being the nighttime bedmate in an unholy union with the Democrats. In 2003, he echoed as much in describing his nonaligned history, stating publicly that, "I'm not gonna be a battered wife for the Democratic Party." Around that time, he was in full campaign mode and just couldn't resist attacking his party. Under the title, "Al vs the Dems: Presidential Candidate Sharpton Goes After His Party," writer Thulani Davis quoted the king of the photo op at Sylvia's Harlem restaurant, as telling the *Village Voice* in 2003 (February 26 to March 4) that the Democrats had taken advantage of the black community, because black folk had allowed them to. Norman Kelley quoted the Rev. as echoing the same thing around that time as well:

I don't blame the candidates; I blame that on us. We need to stop allowing our communities to be photo ops for Democrats who won't address our issues. For a party that gets 92 percent of our vote, I mean, this is ridiculous. They should be dealing with these issues across the board.[218]

Four months later at the NAACP's July 2003 conference, the year before the presidential elections, the Rev. reiterated the same message, this time reminding the Democratic Party of his willingness to make its segregationist past an issue if the party had failed to accommodate him. The NAACP, which had long allowed itself to become the "DUF" (designated ugly friend) of the Democratic Party, had attacked President George W. Bush and three other lower tier

---

217 Sharpton with Hunter, *Al on America*, 177.
218 Norman Kelley, *The Head Negro in Charge Syndrome* (Nation Books, 2004), 191.

Democratic candidates for their absence from its conference. Under the headline, "No-Show Equals No Vote, Irate NAACP. Hosts Say," the *New York Times* reported on July 15, 2003, that the Rev. had brought down the house with his attacks on the Democratic Party:

> But it was Mr. Sharpton who brought the crowd to its feet. Mr. Sharpton compared the Democratic Party to the late Lester Maddox, the former governor of Georgia who in the 1960's chased black patrons from his restaurant with an ax handle. "Anytime we can give a party 92 percent of our vote and have to still beg some people to come talk to us, there is still an ax-handle mentality among some in the Democratic Party," he said, raising an ax handle. "I want to stop people from wanting our vote but not wanting to be seen with us in public, treating us like we are some political mistresses."

For good measure, Reverend Sharpton had amplified his words with much stagecraft by appearing on stage at the NAACP event wielding an actual ax handle—an appearance for which he'd received thunderous applause and standing ovations by the hall of mostly black Democrats. Most were oblivious to the Democrat's Republican-financed campaign in that election cycle. Yet again, he'd made fools of them all.

But the Rev. was on a mission, and that year, he told CNN's *Crossfire* that many Democrats were "elephants" in "donkey jackets." Arguing that Democrats had morphed into "Republican-lite" on issues like health care, war, and taxes, he told host Bob Novak that he believed that the Democratic party had moved far to the right, that the party had a "bunch of elephants running around in donkey clothes."

By all means, his so-called issues campaign was a push to emotionally blackmail the Democratic Party by being its embarrassment—his preferred currency of trading. But of greater importance is that it had spoken to the level of connivance and decadence in a black America where the Rev. would later be allowed to hijack its leadership and have all its essential institutional elements fall in line behind him with no resistance. As went Reverend Sharpton, so did the National Urban League, the NAACP, and many others.

"Scampaign"[219] *2004*

(L–R) Democratic presidential candidates Reverend Al Sharpton, Representative Richard Gephardt, retired general Wesley Clark, Senator Joseph Lieberman, Senator John Edwards, Representative Dennis Kucinich, former governor Howard Dean, former senator Carol Moseley Braun, and Senator John Kerry take to the stage prior to the start of the Detroit Democratic presidential candidate debate at the Fox Theater, October 26, 2003, in Detroit, Michigan. Sponsored by Fox News Channel and the Congressional Black Caucus Institute, it is the fifth Democratic candidate debate to take place in seven weeks. (Photo by Bill Pugliano/Getty Images.)

Blackmail is the oldest and most effective tool in an arsenal of weapons for any given battle. While primitive in form, it remains effective in substance, especially when deployed by someone well-schooled in its usage since high school.

At the 2004 Democratic convention, there was intrigue in Boston. For over a year, the Rev.'s journey to the podium was mired in terse emotional blackmail and public recriminations, leveled at his party. Rather than asking for a seat at the table, he'd demanded one and had ended up getting it, though only after much haranguing. To get his prime-time speaking slot, he stared down party

---

219 Writer Norman Kelley's description of Reverend Sharpton's 2004 presidential campaign; *The Head Negro in Charge Syndrome* (Nation Books, 2004).

honchos and announced that he would either speak from the podium inside the convention hall or from a stage outside in the parking lot. Again, it was the tactic perfected over several decades since his A&P Supermarket days with Jesse Jackson—bring the target to its knees through maximum embarrassment in front of the television cameras.

The Kerry campaign, party leaders, and the Democratic National Committee bigwigs must have shuddered to think of the possibilities of the Sharpton spectacle to unfold outside of their convention. Who would the network and cable stations have cut to—the polished prime-time speakers coronating Boston's Brahmin, John Kerry, on the inside or the raucous hillbilly circus anointing Brooklyn's beguiled, Al Sharpton, on the outside? They were all aware of his ax-handle performance at the NAACP the previous year, and they'd also known that Republican masters were pulling the strings of the puppet in their midst. But the thought of Reverend Sharpton in front of news cameras in the parking lot outside the convention, wielding the Lester Maddox ax-handle while reminding America not only of Maddox's but also of the Democrats' not-so-distant Jim Crow and segregationist past, must have brought on panic.

While an eloquent young black politician from Chicago wooed the crowd on the inside with stories of nominee John Kerry's heroic past on a riverboat, an ineloquent black bloviator from Brooklyn would've been on the outside reminding America of "Pitchfork" Ben Tillman, James K. Vardaman, Citizens Councils, all-white juries, "little man's demagogue" George Wallace, axe-wielding Lester Maddox, and the like. If he were angry enough, Sharpton might have even reminded America and accused the Democrats of Sam Hose's lynching. Party officials must have imagined the post-convention headlines:

Sharpton Reminds Crowd of:
Segregate Us Now!
Segregate Us Tomorrow!
Segregate Us Forever!

The Democratic National Committee caved and gave the Rev. the speaking slot he'd demanded. So, in casting their votes for him, his supporters had unknowingly supported the Rev.'s lone quest for respectability—his desire for rehabilitation from political "scarlet whore" to a pampered mistress. But he'd achieved that "respectability" by being the quintessential political scarlet whore if there is such a thing. By mounting a nefarious campaign with Republican money and management, the Rev. didn't just reduce the value of the votes he'd received in the primaries, he'd obliterated it. While believing they were voting for "issues," his voters had ended up voting solely for advancing Reverend Sharpton's ambition. The Rev. had surpassed all the transgressions for which he'd previously attacked others, showing the currency of blackmail and its potential to embarrass, to be as good as gold, still the best weapon in any arsenal. More importantly, though, he'd once more proven Hoffer's point—the "cause-movement" had degenerated into a full-blown racket.

Nearly a dozen years later, we would get a sense of the Democratic Party's fear of Reverend Sharpton from the Rev. himself. In 2013's *Stone,* he recalled the 2008 campaign where then-candidate Barack Obama had sought his support by begging the Rev. not to do anything that might have hurt him, even if Sharpton wasn't going to support him. This was likely a factor in Obama's elevation of the Rev. by courting him in the years since, in spite of the risks of tarnish by association. Though I've explored another reason (later chapter), what better way is there to control your loose cannon than to control its fuse?

In the end, the ironies of Reverend Sharpton, John Kerry, and Barack Obama—three leading personalities from that 2004 Democratic Convention—can't be overlooked. Reverend Sharpton had gotten his podium time at a convention for an election that Kerry had lost—the same convention that had introduced Barack Obama to America. Barack Obama later became president, with John Kerry shaping and articulating his second-term foreign policies while for his part, Reverend Sharpton has laid claims to advising President Obama on domestic ones.

Destroying Idols

And Idols are created in order to be destroyed.

—James Baldwin

The Reverend Jesse Jackson (left) and the Reverend Al Sharpton confer as they visit the scene where Sean Bell was killed in Jamaica, Queens. Bell, twenty-three, who was supposed to marry the mother of his two children on Saturday, November 25, was shot in the neck and killed at about 4:00 a.m. that same morning when five plainclothes police officers opened fire on his vehicle outside the Kalua strip club on Ninety-Fourth St., where he had been celebrating his bachelor party. (Photo by Michael Albans/NY Daily News Archive via Getty Images.)

FOR READERS OF the Sharpton books who've also studied black history, the problematic surrogate father-son relationship of Reverends Jesse Jackson and Al Sharpton might be reminiscent of that of writers Richard Wright's and James Baldwin's in many aspects. The exception is that where Baldwin had admitted the possibility of subconsciously setting out to undermine his mentor Wright, dethroning Jesse Jackson was the all-encompassing conscious objective of Reverend Sharpton from day one, and he later admitted as much.

A generation ago, Richard Wright and his protégé James Baldwin had endured an equally problematic surrogate father-son relationship in Paris. By his own account, Baldwin had seen Wright, the established writer and his sponsor to France and its intellectual circles, as the king to be dethroned. Testimonies from others in their circle, including Chester Himes, revealed a terse relationship of heated arguments between the two men. In Baldwin's spring 1949 essay, "Everybody's Protest Novel," he'd taken direct aim at Wright's famous book, *Native Son,* belittling his mentor's work as "protest literature." His critique, published in *Zero Magazine* in France, had appeared in an article right after a short story written by Wright. A furious Richard Wright then confronted James Baldwin and accused him of betrayal. Not only had Wright recommended him for the fellowship that had brought Baldwin to Paris but in his effort to open doors for his protégé, Wright had also introduced Baldwin to Zero's editor. It was indeed, "Betrayal 101." Of the events, Baldwin would later write, in *Nobody Knows* (p. 157):

> I had mentioned Richard's Native Son…and Richard thought that I was trying to destroy his novel and his reputation…I was wrong to have hurt him. He saw clearly enough, far more clearly than I had dared to allow myself to see, what I had done: I had used his work as a kind of springboard into my own…For me, he had been an idol. And Idols are created in order to be destroyed[220]

---

220 Michel Fabre, *From Harlem to Paris: Black American Writers in France, 1840–1980* (University of Illinois Press, 1991), 198.

As they are men of different literary mindsets, we could never get Reverend Sharpton to be as candid as James Baldwin. But across his books, Sharpton's treatment of Jesse Jackson was even worse than Baldwin's treatment of Wright. Although consistent with the treatment given to all his so-called idols like Adam Clayton Powell Jr., David Dinkins, and Dr. King, Reverend Jesse Jackson stands out as "Exhibit No. 1" in Sharpton's perfection of treachery. While neither man would publicly admit his true sentiments for the other, based on the Rev.'s treatment of Jackson in his books, it's hard to conclude anything but a mutual loathing. Where he'd courted the affection of others while degrading them, Sharpton had sought Jackson's mentorship while knifing him in the back. As Jackson was mentoring him, he was envying Jackson.

In *Pharaoh*, Adam Clayton Powell Jr. was gold dust, all but deified before later being disavowed and eviscerated in successive books. The young Sharpton was so fascinated by Marcus Garvey that he'd claimed to have visited Garvey's widow in Jamaica on his own as a ten-year-old, only to later hide those early Garvey admirations. David Dinkins, who was later lauded as an idol since age sixteen, was castigated and ridiculed in the first Sharpton books while the Rev. had worked to undermine him in real life. James Brown was a little different. He too was a surrogate father, a mentor, and an idol to the end, but in a successive book, Sharpton reduced Brown to little more than a peasant—revealing intimate and embarrassing details that effectively painted the godfather as a country bumpkin at heart.

The two exceptions to this pattern were Dr. King and Nelson Mandela. As shown, the Rev. had first rejected and belittled Dr. King, only to later embrace him as a requirement to climbing the activism and political ladder. Nelson Mandela, claimed as a hero in Sharpton's later book, was in the present too large a celebrated global figure for the preacher from Brooklyn to belittle. Additionally, any association with Mandela could've only elevated the Rev.'s prestige as the South African icon had moved closer to global canonization straight through to his death.

For Reverend Jesse Jackson, though, it was different. In him, Sharpton had seen his Pompeii to be confronted head-on, which he did both in his book and behind the scenes. On his way up the ladder of activism and fame and with aspirations of moving into the mainstream of politics and the power structure, the

Rev. needed to have crossed his Rubicon by defeating his former mentor, who was then a formidable stumbling block to Sharpton's ambitions. Once he'd felt capable of flying solo, he then jettisoned Jackson like overweight cargo—aggravated by the fact that Jesse was alive for his own funeral.

We'd seen some of his early pettiness towards his mentor when the Rev. had omitted any mention of Jesse Jackson on their African trip in his first book, even though it was an African tour in which he was a guest of Jackson's. We then got a taste of Sharpton's viciousness towards Jackson during a June 18, 2001, jailhouse interview when he was asked if the Tawana Brawley affair had damaged his chances at high political office. "I think the Brawley case pales in comparison," he said to Fox News. "Did I take the blood of the guy I loved and put it on my shirt?" This was a reference to the long-running rumor that an ambitious Jesse Jackson has smeared the blood of a dead or dying Dr. King on his clothes to enhance his own prestige as the inheritor of the flame.

So, while pocketed during much of the 1980s and 1990s, the 2000s had seen Sharpton's handheld garrote moving ever closer to Jackson's neck, right up to the point where the old man stumbled and fell on his own sword, which then made it easy for Sharpton to finish the job. The Rev. then just reached for his pocket tool and twisted away at his former mentor's neck.

Presidential Protestor

The Rev.'s assault on Reverend Jackson had taken shape with a Sharpton edict that was as illustrious as it was ironic; at least it would turn out to be quite ironic. It was as if it were a premonition, a foretelling, or advice to the future president Barack Obama:

> My criticism of guys like Jesse is that you can't be in and out. If you decide to go in, stay in and let those who are still out do our jobs. But don't go in and run …If I win the next race…I will be president. That's what I'll be. I will give up my other job. I'm not going to try to be the president and the protestor of the president. [221]

---

221 Sharpton with Hunter, *Al on America*, 201–2.

This was purely an attack on Jesse Jackson in 2002. A little later, I get to the hypocrisy of the Sharpton who would be a doormat for the Obama administration while taking the civil rights movement hostage. But for now, let's look at how the future would ridicule the Rev.'s own demagoguery against his former mentor.

As an African American and as president, Mr. Obama would be hard-pressed not to march, even ceremoniously to commemorate the big-ticket items like Selma or the March on Washington—hard pressed not to protest himself as president. Had the president read *Al on America*, it might have made for some very awkward discussions with the likes of Congressman John Lewis, who was beaten up on the Edmund Pettus bridge while participating in the 1965 Selma to Montgomery march. It would've been tough for Mr. Obama to explain his administration's reluctance to overtly support commemorative protests, as he would've been protesting himself.

But back then, in his attack on his former mentor Jesse Jackson, by painting Jackson as somehow being inside the Clinton Administration, that was exactly what the Rev. had suggested the president not do. It was Sharpton's effort at bullying Jackson into relinquishing the profitable pastures of protesting to him, accompanied by far-fetched comparisons to Dr. King's "outsider" relationship with President Lyndon B. Johnson, among other condemnations of his former mentor (next segment).

Yet in 2013, Reverend Sharpton led a slew of TV-chasing celebrities, public personalities, and political leaders, in an ersatz commemoration of the fiftieth anniversary of the March on Washington—a mythical event that might have best been left untouched. The irony of the black president speaking at the event wasn't lost on two fronts. First, Mr. Obama was now representing an element of Dr. King's unimagined dream; he was the president of the United States, sitting atop the system and the power structure that Dr. King had protested. Second, the commemorative protest was led by Reverend Sharpton, the man who, in an attempt to undermine his former mentor Jesse Jackson a decade earlier, had warned that the president should never be a protestor of himself. Although the participants wouldn't have seen the irony of the situation, the Rev., one of the event's chief organizers, or at least one of its key front persons, should've recalled his long-erected prohibition.

While in 2002 an African American sitting in the White House might have seemed unimaginable, it was nonetheless a reality in 2013. But in typical Sharpton versus Sharpton fashion, the Rev's long-forgotten edict was most notably forgotten or ignored by Reverend Sharpton himself. There he was, leading President Barack Obama in the protest of President Barack Obama.

Jettisoning Jesse Jackson

Reverend Al Sharpton (L) and Reverend Jesse Jackson walk down the steps of the US Supreme Court on October 10, 2012, in Washington, DC. The high court heard oral arguments on Fisher v. University of Texas *at Austin and was tasked with ruling on whether the university's consideration of race in admissions is constitutional. (Photo by Mark Wilson/Getty Images.)*

A deliberate kneecapping and scalping of his former mentor had accompanied the Rev.'s move toward independence and mainstream statesmanship. It was a determined effort to destroy this idol that was "created to be destroyed." In *Al on America*, the Rev. finally showed us his lifelong dream, and it wasn't to be Adam Clayton Powell Jr., as readers of his first book had been led to believe. Becoming the next Jesse Jackson was a paramount ambition the moment Jackson had chosen to mentor him on his way up. Sharpton then mimicked

Jackson to great success, and in his efforts to depose and dispense with his mentor, he eventually deployed Jackson's own tactics against him.

Early in *Al on America*, the Rev. had told us of his ambition to replace Jesse Jackson's Rainbow Coalition: "My movement," he said, "is the next generation of the Rainbow Coalition."[222] The boasting of the close relationship we'd gotten in *Pharaoh*—that of the Jackson-Sharpton annual family get-togethers and the daily phone calls between the two men during a six- or seven-year period—then gave way to open attack on Jackson in *Al on America*. Supposedly, it was because of Jackson's closeness to President Bill Clinton and the Clinton administration.

Then, the Rev. accused Jesse Jackson of trying to have his cake and eat it too, giving Jesse the option of continuing to be Bill Clinton's social adjutant, on the condition Jackson relinquished the reins of the profitable business of activism to him:

> There's no one I know who has a more brilliant, fertile mind [than Jesse Jackson]. He is hardworking. I learned about the value of getting up early every morning from Jesse. And he is very, very committed. But I began to question the direction that commitment was taking in the late 1990s. Jesse had developed a closeness to Bill Clinton. And I felt his relationship with Clinton and the White House was getting in the way as an activist. I felt that if he was going to represent the civil rights cause, the human rights' cause, Jesse had to choose between whether he was going to be part of the structure or challenge the structure. Dr. King, as close as he was to Lyndon Johnson, came out vocally against the war in Vietnam. He never took a presidential appointment. He challenged the system."[223]…If I don't win…and if I decide to advise the president, whoever [sic] the president is, then I'm not going to lead the Movement. I cannot tell the Movement, "Now wait a minute, I'm wearing this hat at eleven, but at twelve, I'm the leader of the Movement." Either you are or you are not…Jesse ran as an outsider. But when he became an insider, that's what he needed to focus on…I

---

222 Ibid., 18.
223 Ibid., 197.

take nothing away from him for that. But say that's what you're doing. The Bible says, "No Man can serve two masters."[224]

But unlike Sharpton, who would later make a living as President Barack Obama's lackey and an adjunct of his administration's communication directorate, Jesse Jackson was never a nightly television spin-doctor for Bill Clinton during the Clinton years. Fast forward a few years, and it was the Rev. who was now being accused of an even worse betrayal of his people. In a February 8, 2010, interview, television host Tavis Smiley told the *New York Times* that it was difficult for Sharpton to be the "water carrier" for the White House and at the same time, trying to be the titular head for Black America. It was the same accusations Sharpton had leveled against Jackson—sanctioned by biblical edict against serving two masters.

In fact, in 2002, the Rev. had spent the entire last quarter of *Al on America* attacking his former mentor for conduct that he (Sharpton) would amplify to the *n*th degree a decade later:

> There is nothing wrong with working from within the system. There is a legitimate role for that. You had Whitney Young and others who were close to the system. But you can't be Dr. King and Whitney Young at the same time. You need both, but you can't be both. And where I started having levels of tactical discomfort with Jesse was over this issue. You can't be the insider on Wall Street and challenge Wall Street. You can't advise the president and be the insider to the White House and challenge the president.[225] While Jesse was inside the White House with Clinton, I was outside calling for economic accountability on Wall Street. I was outside, calling Clinton's hand on welfare reform and the onerous crime bill. Jesse was virtually silent on those issues. He was an insider. After seven years of us being close again, we started to split.[226]

---

224 Ibid., 201–2.
225 Ibid., 197–98.
226 Ibid.

Sharpton's pretext for the split between Jackson and him was that Jackson had become a sell-out. With nails all over his mentor's coffin, the Rev. then just hammered away, even searching the past for symbolism to declare his former idol and mentor a "vagabond" and a "nomad":

> When I spoke at the Million Man March [1995], I said, "We all come from different houses but we're all on the same block." There's the NAACP house, those who fight on the inside along with the system...There's the Urban League, which deals with the corporate inside...There are those who fight from the outside using nonviolent protest—the civil rights' house. But you cannot live in all houses—you start looking like a vagabond, a nomad, or a homeless person...Jesse wouldn't stay in his house.[227]

As total ruination of Jackson's reputation and credibility was the objective from the start, the Rev. suggested that Jesse Jackson—then leader of black America—was a white supremacist's dream (even worse than a sell-out). In doing so, he'd left little doubt that he'd also believed former president Bill Clinton a white supremacist as well:

> A white supremacist must always feel that you submit to him, which is why, while I respect and admire Rev Jackson, I psychologically could not deal with his conceding or deferring to the White House. Somewhere along the line, we need to define ourselves for ourselves.[228]

Reverend Sharpton's first line of attack against black enemies—foreign or domestic—had always been to suggest that they're Uncle Toms or sell-outs to white racists. These old criticisms of Bill Clinton had rung fresh to me during the 2016 election cycle, because as the other half of the former First Couple, Sharpton's candidate, Hillary Clinton, had to have been seen as a white supremacist (or former) as well. In any case, the change in mindset over the years was remarkable. The man who'd attacked Jesse Jackson for his closeness to President Bill Clinton

---

227 Ibid., 200.
228 Ibid., 269.

would later spend eight years conceding, deferring, and being a doormat of the Obama administration. Maybe the Rev. had come to believe that with a black man in the Oval Office, absent the risk of pliancy to white supremacists (or to biracial ones), there had no longer existed a need for "self-definitions," thus enabling full service to two masters—contrary to his Bible.

In any case, by this point, the Rev. had started to parade around Jackson's carcass, announcing through a bullhorn that he was now the new sheriff in town—the new and improved Jesse Jackson, who was neither an Uncle Tom nor a sell-out. In the event vagabond, nomad, or white supremacist deferent hadn't fully captured the essence of Jesse Jackson, the Rev. then moved downstream to pile on even more. This time, he advanced the notion of "Jesse the usurper" who'd never even had the support of those around Dr. King in the first place. As evidence, Sharpton reminded us that King's widow, Coretta Scott-King, had withheld her support from Jackson in the past:

> My only comfort was history. I remembered that Jesse had to deal with many around Dr. King, like Andy Young and Mrs. King, who wouldn't support him when he ran for president. They wouldn't support him in some boycotts. I thought, "Maybe I'm going through the same thing with him that he went through with others." But I would have thought that he might not want to do that to the next generation.[229]

When all else fails, Reverend Sharpton will always invoke the name of Dr. King in going for the kill, showing no hesitation in disparaging or cheapening King's name for selfish and sinister purposes. But he'd learned the lesson from Jesse Jackson of at least pretending to "take the high road," and as a man of God, he then went as far as to bless the dead, or near dead, by making a public homage to his mentor, or sort of. "I am grateful for my recent experience with Jesse," he said. "It forced me to grow in many areas and take stock of where I am and where I am going."[230] It was a Baptist benediction or otherwise, the beautiful

---

229 Ibid., 199.
230 Ibid.

woman dumping the lovesick guy with those dreaded words: *Goodbye lover; it was nice knowing you.* It was then that we'd realized that Jesse Jackson was toasted.

The Rev. was going where Jackson had neither been nor could ever go. But if writing a book overtly disavowing his mentor in such a forceful manner wasn't enough, Sharpton took great pleasure in reminding America of Jackson's lapse in judgment behind that hot microphone at Fox television studio, where the Chicagoan was not very nice to his fellow Chicagoan, Barack Obama. If that still wasn't enough, the Rev. then descended even further into the gutter. He reminded America that as Jesse was hunkered down on bended knees spoon-feeding President Bill Clinton the Lord's Prayer in the White House, during Clinton's "Jimmy Swaggart moment," Jackson too had sinned by siring a child out of wedlock with an assistant. "Contrary to popular belief," Sharpton said, "We [Jackson and he] didn't split over his scandal with Karen Stafford and the baby he had out of wedlock. We divided over philosophy."[231] It was over. Reverend Jackson was *done for*—vanquished from relevance, as dead as a doornail. Reverend Sharpton was now undisputedly, the new sheriff in town.

This needless evisceration of Jackson in his books is what I mean by knee-capping and scalping. There was never any "popular belief" that the Rev. and his former mentor had parted ways over the latter's affair with a woman. America had neither known nor cared about Jesse Jackson and Al Sharpton's relationship or the women with whom they were involved. Besides, the Rev.'s purity on the issue of relations with staffers was as doubtful as Jackson's. In any case, the rupture between the two was only discerned from Sharpton's written and public takedown of Jackson—in Sharpton's deft effort to decouple and destroy his former idol.

Modern-Day Gelding of a "Negro"

Finally, the Sharpton-Jackson saga climaxed with hilarity in 2008, when a funny thing had happened on the way to the general elections that year. After much effort over the years to undermine and bring down Jesse Jackson, Reverend Sharpton then received some help from the most unlikely of

---

231 Ibid., 198.

sources—from Jesse Jackson himself, who had finally yielded and severely wounded himself in the process.

On a bright and sunny day, Jesse Jackson had woken up, put on his clothes, and hightailed over to a Fox television station to shoot himself in the foot and possibly elsewhere as well. He'd found the sweet spot Sharpton had been aiming at for some time, and in a heartbeat, *boom!* It was over. The moment of Jesse Jackson's fancy funeral was at hand.

Candidate Obama had given a speech extolling the need for responsible behavior among young black men. As previously noted, he'd echoed much the same sentiments the Rev. had written a few years back in 2002's *Al on America.* Yet Jesse Jackson, who had then ignored Reverend Sharpton's comments, nonetheless took great exception and umbrage to Mr. Obama's remarks and off a deep end he went, in a full rage.

Jackson was so thin-skinned and insecure about any critique of the culture he'd perfected—one in which introspection was neither encouraged nor tolerated—that he could've hardly watched himself being eclipsed by the telegenic Mr. Obama and his seemingly new age of black leadership. Obama had nothing in common with Jackson's form of preachy tutelage, indoctrinated reverence, indoctrinated victimization, and pretentious morally assuasive indignation. He became furious at candidate Obama, and ignoring his own earlier advice to the Rev., he opted to "take the low ground"—brilliantly venting that fury, unknowingly, straight into a hot microphone in the Fox TV studio. The Christian Reverend had famously yet unceremoniously voiced a desire to cut off candidate Obama's "nuts."

Of course, this was just posturing from Jackson, who in an instant was witnessing the obliteration of his legacy. But it was nonetheless a vivid reminder that "black-on-black" violence was a real phenomenon, especially at the leadership level. Not only had Jesse Jackson expressed his surgical mindset but, in an instant, he'd also brought the "half-black" presidential candidate right back into full-blown "negritude," by referring to him as the *n*-word—that non-romantic form of black expression, according to professor Dr. Michael Eric Dyson (explained later). The circumstances were as ironic as the incident was comical. Here was the epicenter of conservative America being audience to one black man desirous of gelding another. The liberal Democrat Jackson had finally given Fox's conservative Republican audience an issue on which they could've all agreed—someone needed to have cut off (or "cut out") Barack Obama's nuts.

Unsurprisingly, public opinion rallied to he who was in ascendance and under threat of being de-seeded, while resoundingly rejecting the other—the harbinger late-stage surgical desires in his descent. But such was the grotesque response by the shrinking leader of black America—particularly hypocritical, given that candidate Obama's sentiments had mirrored those of Reverend Sharpton's only a few years earlier, then free of any ensuing menace to the Rev.'s valuables by his former mentor Jesse Jackson.

With this act of ignominy, Jesse Jackson had commenced his own political *seppuku*—sealing his fate in his protégé's long battle to dethrone him. The Rev., the ultimate beneficiary, grasped the opportunity. In addition to public comments in media appearances, he would revive the issue by giving us wall-to-wall coverage of Jackson's *faux pas* five years later in 2013's *Stone*:

> "I wanna cut his nuts off," Jesse added… I went on Anderson Cooper's show that night and defended Obama again. I said I loved Reverend Jackson, that he had mentored me and I had learned a great deal from him, but I didn't agree with him…As I left CNN after doing Cooper's show and got into the car to go to Fox to do Sean Hannity's show, I talked to Reverend Jackson. Let's just say he was less than happy with my position. After we hung up, I got a call from a friend at Fox…"Before you get out there too far defending Jesse, you should know we have not released the full tape," he said. "What are you talking about?" "Jesse also used the n-word," he said. "You know the n-word that y'all said we should bury?"…I felt a sinking feeling in my stomach. Jesse had used the n-word in reference to Obama? That was an entirely different matter…The incident certainly didn't help Reverend Jackson's relationship with the Obama camp. Senator Obama saw that not only did I understand what he strategically had to do for his candidacy, but I was also fighting with people I had decades of history with, on his behalf.[232]

---

232 Al Sharpton with Chiles, *The Rejected Stone*, 185-6.

The Rev. then publicly eulogized Jesse Jackson's leadership in 2013. Speaking to the *New York Times* on February 24, Sharpton lobbed Jackson a backhanded slap and a fastball at the same time: "He ended up fighting the people he helped make way for," he told writers, Jodi Kantor and Monica Davey, referring to Jackson. In the end, James Baldwin's words had lasted the test of time. Jesse Jackson's dethronement and demise were complete. A new prince had been crowned and with his coronation, he'd shown yet again that idols were indeed created in order to be destroyed.

The Flight of a Trotskyist

As I read three Sharpton books on his treatment of another of his idols—Harlem congressman Adam Clayton Powell Jr.—I'd recalled a recurring joke of French politics for a generation of its politicians. On acceding to high political offices, it used to be a common thing in France for young Trotskyists to attempt a rewrite of history—to make a clean scrubbing of their past, thereby erasing any trace of youthful admiration for, or allegiance to the architect of the Bolshevik Revolution, Leon Trotsky. Invariably, they would fail miserably, as writings from their young Trotskyists' university days tended to resurface. Were these politicians the beneficiaries of the same conditions as the Rev., whose writings are rarely read by anyone, much less scrutinized (your writer, an exception), they would've been home free by just updating their manifestos. Previous theses would never be examined, thereby leaving few or no contradictions to answer for. But the French were neither as lucky nor as gifted as Sharpton, who moved seamlessly from one existence to the next, in complete denial of the former and with no one to say, *Wait a minute here! Let me get this straight!*

As the Rev. pivoted mainstream in his second act, not only had he busied himself preparing the town square for Jesse Jackson's demise, but he'd also used *Al on America* to distance himself from his controversial mentor Adam Clayton Powell Jr. We saw the start of a soft self-exoneration for having once admired the congressman, which started with an indictment of the congressman for being immoral—apparently a typical and, therefore, exculpatory trait for preachers in Sharpton's world:

Adam Clayton Powell Jr. had power. He always did it his way. And while some people said it was his downfall, I always admired that about him. I don't justify any of the things Powell did. And I don't judge him, either. I know a lot of preachers who are immoral.[233]

By the time we got to intermission in his third act in *Stone*, Adam Clayton Powell Jr. had become a youthful indiscretion to be hidden, a disassociation to be made with fierce urgency—much as Trotsky had become for some of the middle-aged *députés* in France's *Assemblée Nationale*. Reverend Sharpton had had a "Trotsky problem" in Obama-world, which wasn't a good thing. The Obama era was essentially a Dr. King revival. There was considerable choreography and much stagecraft expended in presenting the president as the culmination of Dr. King's dream. In this presentation, there was no space for variations to include rabble-rousers like Adam Clayton Powell Jr.—known for being passionate and charismatic but also for being among the most controversial figures of his time, who was eventually being driven out of office under a cloud. The Obama aura was one that courted little or no public controversy—the antithesis of Clayton Powell Jr.'s existence.

Adam Clayton Powell Jr. was a "Garveyite"—an admirer of Marcus Garvey—and that was certainly no path to impressing President Barack Obama. Recalling the Reverend Sharpton who'd told us that he'd stepped out of a New York City courthouse door for the waiting cameras with his handcuffed fists up and shouting, "They did this to King! They did this to Powell! They did this to Garvey! This is my inauguration! I have arrived," a simple regression shows the other problem for the former Clayton Powell Jr.-Garvey groupie turned Obama acolyte.

Although both Clayton Powell Jr. and former president Barack Obama are of mixed racial backgrounds, the white side of the family had accepted and raised Mr. Obama while the "mulatto" Clayton Powell Jr. had known white rejection and racism all his life as a black man, raised by black folk. The result was two very different men of different eras—the pro-Garvey Clayton Powell Jr. and the anti-Garvey Obama. Even though never publicly

233 Ibid., 187.

admitted, over the course of eight years in office, President Obama, son of a white mother, had steadfastly refused to issue a pardon to the anti-miscegenist Marcus Garvey, even though history had shown Garvey to have suffered a miscarriage of justice.

So, on all sides, the Rev. was hemmed in by a past in opposition to his present self. Were the First Family to know of his once fanatical adulation for Clayton Powell Jr. (and Marcus Garvey) or that he'd once cautioned aspirants against using Dr. King as a model for activism—suggesting instead that they emulate Adam Clayton Powell Jr.—that would've posed a risk for Sharpton, possibly even jeopardizing his White House gate pass. So, in 2013's *Stone*, we were given a different rendition of the Al Sharpton-Adam Clayton Powell Jr. story. This time around, we saw the Rev. visiting the Abyssinian Baptist Church to meet the congressman but gone was much of the previous hype— given way to an Adam Clayton Powell who was now just the kind of preacher the "innocent" mind of the young Sharpton had wanted to be:

> I would go up to see him at the Abyssinian on Sundays, entranced by his electrifying sermons. I would hang out after church and find a way to attach myself to his entourage. This was the kind of preacher I wanted to be.[234]

The Rev. had entitled the chapter, "Learning from Flawed Leaders." It was stealth effort at disassociation from Adam Clayton Powell Jr., by declaring that he'd now understood Clayton Powell Jr. to be flawed, but carefully communicating that in knowing the "bad" Clayton Powell Jr., he'd learned what not to be in life. This had all the hallmarks of the cynical church upbringing, which even I had known of first-hand. As a child of about seven- or eight-years-old, whenever I'd attended a funeral, I could always tell when the church had considered the dead a rotten sinner and not a saint. At some point during the funeral service, there would either be the singing of a hymn or words from the minister to the effect that, *If I should die and my soul shall be lost; it's nobody's fault but mine.* It was the church's way of washing its hands of the sinful soul. Reverend Sharpton's style was to speak of learning from flawed leaders.

---

234 Al Sharpton with Chiles, *The Rejected Stone*, 26.

But full-on disavowal of his former idol was still a little trickier than with others like Jesse Jackson. The name Adam Clayton Powell Jr. had still carried much weight uptown (New York City) in both black and brown communities that formed the core of the Rev.'s political support. Additionally, he'd been so overt and fierce in his admiration for, and deification of, Clayton Powell Jr. over the years that it was a little more difficult for Sharpton to have then just stood up and said, *I knew Adam Clayton Powell Jr., but Adam Clayton Powell Jr. was no hero of mine!* However, although it wasn't easy, neither was it impossible, as the Rev. had already laid the foundation for some distance in 2002's *Al on America* by indicting the congressman for not having been a "true leader":

> Adam Clayton Powell did not care about being accepted by society...Adam Clayton Powell taught me this valuable lesson first. You cannot be a true leader if you don't care about what people think or say about you. Powell was on the David Frost Show once...David Frost asked Powell, "Reverend Powell, you have been a member of Congress for over twenty years and you pastor one of the largest congregations in the world, yet you have been married four times; you drink liquor publicly; you have girlfriends, you have been indicted for tax evasion and sued. How do you rationalize all of this?" Powell looked at him and with a smirk said, "Don't be jealous baby. Don't be jealous."[235]

Those were fighting words. Knowing the mindset of the "leader"-obsessed Sharpton, nothing could've been a cheaper shot at Clayton Powell Jr.'s image. When the Rev. had deemed another as less than a true leader, it was near time to pack it in, close up shop, and go home—even if that shop had been closed for over four decades.

In 2013's *Stone* (Obama era), Sharpton finally decided to deal with his Trotsky problem head-on with a full-blown self-exculpation, explaining that he was an impressionable fourteen-year-old who didn't know better. He then blamed Adam Clayton Powell Jr. for shaping the less than stellar persona of the barnstorming "uncaring, I'm going to be me" 1980s-era Al Sharpton.

---

235 Sharpton with Hunter, *Al on America*, 186.

Accordingly, it was no longer the elder Sharpton's abandonment that had created the buffoon, but instead, it was Clayton Powell Jr.'s infectious bravado that had inspired Top-Ten hits like the Tawana Brawley hoax. From there, the Rev. then slugged it out with his former idol, landing his biggest blows below the belt:

> I was amazed, exhilarated. Can you imagine the impact of that kind of bravado on an impressionable fourteen-year-old boy? I yearned to get to the point where I could be so bold and uncaring about what people thought. And when I was early in my career, during the Bernard Goetz, Howard Beach, and Tawana Brawley years, that's exactly how I was. My mind-set was, *I'm going to do me, I'm gonna be me. I don't care what anybody thinks.*[236]

Nothing had changed in the philosophy, ideologies, or behavior of the long dead Clayton Powell Jr. in the intervening years. It wasn't as if the congressman had been discovered in the interim to have been a Russian spy or a pedophile or anything unknown at the time of his death. But much had changed in the Rev.'s aspirations, circumstances, and social status. And he'd written accordingly. We then watched as Sharpton led an expansive *auto-da-fé* and pulled out the garrote he'd long affixed to Jesse Jackson's neck, this time twisting and turning about the neck of yet another idol—Adam Clayton Powell Jr.

At age forty-two, his Clayton Powell Jr. hagiography (*Pharaoh*) had lauded his hero for just about everything under the sun, including Clayton Powell Jr.'s bravado in not giving a damn, during that interview with television host David Frost:

> Adam said, "I'm the only man in America that doesn't give a damn." I think that's why I liked him so much. He didn't give a damn, he couldn't be intimidated, not in Congress, not in New York, not in the street, not anywhere.[237]

---

236 Al Sharpton with Chiles, *The Rejected Stone*, 27.
237 Al Sharpton and Walton, *Go and Tell Pharaoh*, 40.

But in an exculpatory move, the late-blooming scruples-filled Rev. had found Jesus and was now condemning his former demigod for those very same comments made to David Frost—this time, indicting Clayton Powell Jr. for having a "flawed mindset" in not having given a damn. If we're to believe the Rev., he'd only started the maturation process after the age of forty-two—somewhere between 1996 and 2013:

> But one day, as I started to mature, I realized that Adam's mind-set was flawed. That [Powell's response to David Frost, of not giving a damn] was not leadership reflected in that way of thinking; it was selfishness...If they [people] are going to invest their faith and their hopes and their ambitions in you, then they have the right to expect that you are going to be the kind of leader who does care what people think...After going through the Adam period...I eventually saw a transformation in my thinking. I started to realize that you need to give a damn...With all due respect to one of my early idols, they have the right to expect you to give a damn.[238]

For many people, the experience, as a ten-year-old, of being taken around New York City by a local legend would've occasioned a lifetime of reverence. But not for the Rev. *Stone* was written to impress the nation's First Reader and many others in that circle so there could've been no hedging with his looming Clayton Powell Jr. problem. In Sharpton's new position of near-respectable statesman, he'd felt the need to be resolute in his disassociation of his former hero, so he claimed to have traversed a so-called "Adam period." As he'd done to Jesse Jackson, obliteration and complete destruction of the man who'd once meant so much to him was now his sole objective. We then saw a complete denunciation of Clayton Powell Jr. in a tone that screamed, *Damn you Adam! Damn you!* But that was just a warm-up.

In their efforts at self-exculpation, the French politicians didn't go after Leon Trotsky or his reputation. They merely tried to hide their own Trotskyism and youthful admiration and affiliations. But the Rev. wasn't schooled in gentility, so he'd dispensed with pleasantries and went directly for overkill, or we might say, "the re-kill." In what might be a case of a literary archeological expedition,

---

238 Al Sharpton with Chiles, *The Rejected Stone*, 27–28.

the newly minted *stone* then stood at the tomb of a man who'd been dead for over four decades and did a complete unearthing of his bones—just to show that he and Clayton Powell Jr. were made of different stuff. The extraordinary efforts spent in distancing himself from the congressman were near sociopathic. It wasn't just the mere scrubbing of Leon Trotsky from old campus newspaper archives, but more like going down to Mexico and personally dealing the blunt blow to his head. It was Brutus on a mission to take down his dear Caesar, though Sharpton's Caesar was the ghost of a man who'd been dead for forty-one years.

While in the hospital after his 1991 stabbing (1996's *Pharaoh*), he was still in Adam-land. "Adam was dead," he said. "Jesse was the only minister whom I felt I could model myself on, look up to in that way."[239] In other words, even then, Jesse Jackson was only the replacement, a second-choice surrogate father instead of Clayton Powell Jr.—then still dearly held in high esteem by the forty-two-year-old Sharpton. Six years later, even in telling us of his 2000 trip to Cuba two years before, (2002's *Al on America*), the Rev. was still wrapped up in the masculine shawl of Clayton Powell Jr., proudly telling us of staying at the same hotel that had once lodged his idol:

> We landed [in Cuba]. We checked into the Hotel Nacional, a very old elegant Caribbean-style hotel—very regal. And it happened to be the same hotel Adam Clayton Powell Jr. stayed in when he travelled there. So I was really excited.[240]

But by 2013, even peripheral associations with Adam Clayton Powell Jr. had bothered Sharpton, and so his *Stone*-age mutation included a composite disrobing in which he retroactively absconded from Clayton Powell Jr.'s Cuban abode and told us he'd now stayed in a different hotel:

> I got on a plane with three others from my group and we landed in Havana, where they immediately took us to the Hotel Presidente and put us up in very nice suites. Right away, I put in a request to meet with President Fidel Castro.[241]

---

239 Al Sharpton and Walton, *Go and Tell Pharaoh*, 179.

240 Sharpton with Hunter, *Al on America*, 66.

241 Al Sharpton with Chiles, *The Rejected Stone*, 220.

The two hotels are as different as the Plaza Hotel and the Waldorf-Astoria in New York City. Both are premiere lodging experiences (Cuban style), but the locations are entirely different with entirely incompatible scenery and feeling. Hotel Presidente is in the middle of Havana by Revolution Square/Plaza while Hotel Nacional is almost off the water. No one confuses a stay at the Waldorf-Astoria with a stay the Plaza Hotel; neither could anyone have confused Havana's Hotel Nacional with Hotel Presidente. An alternative view might be that the Rev. had lied in *Al on America* to embellish his closeness to Adam Clayton Powell Jr., in which case it had shown his continued fidelity to his hero even then. But in either case, his evocation and revocation of the congressman in this regard highlights the deliberate effort to convey different messages at different times to different audiences. Here, he needed to make it clear to President Obama—who, like most Americans, was unlikely to read a Sharpton book in any case—that Adam Clayton Powell Jr. was no hero of his. If Clayton Powell Jr. was the type to have stayed at the Waldorf-Astoria, Sharpton was the type to be found at the Plaza.

But the Rev. still wasn't satisfied with his hit-job on his former idol, so he then went directly after the four-times-married Clayton Powell Jr. for his biggest known weakness—his philandering:

> If you are a father, do you love your wife and children and family life enough to summon the discipline to turn away from the pretty girl in accounting with the come-hither smile? Is a half an hour with her in a stairwell or a hotel somewhere spectacular enough for you to throw away all that happiness and possibly wreck your children in the process?[242]

Without the need to mention him by name, as it is public knowledge that Adam Clayton Powell Jr. had kept a place in Bimini, Bahamas, Sharpton then continued to troll his former idol with evisceration:

> Yeah, that young lady looks great, but is she worth it? Is it worth you not being able to have the moral authority to stand up and raise issues? What's more

---

242 Ibid., 27–28.

important to you, a weekend in Bimini with a young woman or standing up and changing the course of history?[243]

At the writing of 1996's *Pharaoh,* Congressman Adam Clayton Powell Jr. had been dead some twenty-four years (1972), with enough time for history to have evaluated him. Yet the Rev. was still effusive in his adoration at that time. But the changes in Sharpton's circumstances by 2013 had rendered Clayton Powell Jr. a Trotskyist albatross to be removed from the neck by any means necessary. So, by the end of 2013's *Stone,* the Rev. had torn the man who'd given him such notable life lessons as, "Knowing when to hit it and when to quit it," into more pieces than the Levite had done to his wife (concubine) in Gibeah. There was little left of the dead man's dignity, little dignity left of the dead man—he who was a stranger to neither women nor liquor. Sharpton declared, "If I'm oppressed and I need you to be the one to bring my message," Sharpton said, of Clayton Powell Jr., "I don't need for you to be distracted by whom you are going to bed with, being intoxicated in public, not giving a damn."[244]

Even Brutus was somewhat kinder to his charge: he'd at least stopped the bloodletting once Caesar was dead. The Rev. though, as vain as he's insecure, had gone out and unearthed the dead Adam Clayton Powell Jr. and bled him dry one last time for good measure anew. This wasn't just the case of an idol that was created to be destroyed. It was Reverend Sharpton finally taking the flight of the Trotskyists—finally taken care of his Trotsky problem.

---

243 Ibid., 78.
244 Ibid., 28.

The Interloper

The East Wind, an interloper in the dominions of Westerly
weather, is an impassive-faced tyrant with a sharp
poniard held behind his back for a treacherous stab.

—JOSEPH CONRAD[245]

*Portrait of American religious leader and civil rights activist Reverend Al Sharpton as he stands in
the hallway of the Brooklyn House of Detention. (Photo by New York Times Co./Getty Images.)*

---

245 *The Mirror of the Sea: Memories & Impressions* (repr. Sarup & Sons, New Delhi, 204), 74.

A KENNEDY, A protest in Puerto Rico, an interloper, and a stolen diary had all rounded out the second act of the Sharpton chronicles with a bang. The conclusion of *Al on America* had kept us hanging, although not longing for that next big installment, which would arrive over a decade later in 2013. In between that time, there was a lot to observe and even more of the Sharpton condition to affirm. For a member of America's most famous family, though, Robert Kennedy Jr. didn't have to wait for affirmation of anything Sharpton, as he'd long concluded that the Rev. was the "stench" that had stained black America forever.

Protest in Vieques

In *Al on America,* the Rev. had told us that in 2001 he'd heard of a protest in Vieques, Puerto Rico, where there was an effort underway to stop the US government from using the small island off Puerto Rico's mainland as a testing site for bombs and missiles. Once he'd learned that others, including Robert Kennedy Jr., were taking part in the efforts, he joined the action at the request of some local New York City politicians:

> I got involved with Vieques when some prominent Latino politicians from New York asked me to get involved. They felt my involvement would bring more light and attention to what was going on in Vieques.[246]

A few state-level Latino politicians from New York City, whose support he was courting in his effort to pick up some Latino votes for his black-brown coalition, were involved. The Rev. then flew to Puerto Rico and joined others in cutting through the barbed wire and breaching the security perimeters to enter the grounds. As he'd wished, he was promptly arrested in Vieques, gaining the maximum publicity he'd needed to pick up those Latino fans in the Bronx:

> I was compelled to stand with them [the Latino community in protesting American government bombings on Vieques, Puerto Rico]. My move also

---

246 Sharpton with Hunter, *Al on America*, 62.

strengthened a black/Latino coalition that went beyond politics and resonated on a street level. That had never been seen in this country before.[247]

The Rev. had taken the initiative for the sake of the black-brown coalition, which he told us was a first in American history—yet another sign that even in 2002, he was still of a mindset that he would or could become "greater" than Dr. King. Dr. King had never put together any such raucous diverse coalition outside of the homogenous South. In any case, on returning to the island for court sometime later, a federal judge in Puerto Rico, unmoved by public reaction or political correctness, gave the Rev. the attention he'd sought. By Sharpton's own account, he was given "three whole months" of custodial care, which he went on to describe as a harrowing ordeal, "one of the biggest sacrifices I have ever made in terms of time." Elsewhere he described it as a whole "quarter of a year":

> For a quarter of a year, I was forced to reflect on what I was truly about…This is where I decided that I had to change. I had to move beyond my own interests and the interest of my people. I had to work for the interests of all people and to recognize that all people are my people, too…[248]

His description of what were only a few days spent in a Puerto Rican jail before being transferred back to New York had ended up sounding more like a twenty-year stint in Alcatraz. Apparently measuring his time spent in months hadn't fully conveyed enough of a halt in the movements of the constellations during his lockup, so across his books, he then "common-sized" (equivalent mathematical baseline) the time, which then gave us, "a quarter of a year." In 2013's *Stone*, it was back to time spent in days; in referring to the period spent by himself, after his colleagues had been released, he'd told us, "However, an amazing thing happened during those fifty days in that federal jail. In a sense, I had a fifty-day-long meeting with Al Sharpton."[249]

---

247 Ibid., xiii.

248 Ibid., xiiv.

249 Al Sharpton with Chiles, *The Rejected Stone*, 160.

Where the former Saul had found his meaning of life on the Road to Damascus, the Rev. had first found his in a hospital recovery room in Brooklyn after being stabbed in 1991 (*Pharaoh*). Seventeen years later, though (*Stone*), it was in a jail cell in Vieques, Puerto Rico. This time, he'd also learned that he'd had to move beyond his own interest and the interests of his people, having discovered that "all people"—presumably Puerto Ricans—"are my people too." But it was a discovery he could've easily well made by hopping on a northbound D train at 125th Street in Harlem to the Bronx or maybe just by walking a little south and east to 116th Street and 3rd Avenue in East Harlem. In any case, the Rev. was now strutting in the big leagues with his name attached to a Kennedy in a protest, and from this, we experienced a form of *ironic rebound* that was hard to overcome:

> In that jail, locked away alone in a cell smaller than a bathroom, I had one of the most important meetings of my adult life. I had a meeting with Al Sharpton.[250]

Ironic Rebound, a theory in self-destructive behavior, tells us to embrace the image of that white bear on the mountaintop. Otherwise, it'll never leave the mind; it'll consume us. In other words, embracing rather than ignoring things that beset the mind—whether they are positive or negative—is the only way to clear our minds. So, as he'd weighed in at nearly three hundred pounds in those days, the Rev. wasn't just staying in that jail cell "smaller than a bathroom" but was rather wedged in it. Even with the best of mind control, it was difficult not to imagine the varying difficulties of that cell experience, so we were obliged to imagine and embrace them. As the usual fire starter serving up his own oxygen, not only is Sharpton the actor playing the buffoon on stage, but he's also one who often insists on doubling as script-writer of his own sketches as well.

Of this great "coming to Jesus" moment in the cell (for trespassing on government property in Puerto Rico), the Rev. told of being chained and handcuffed and then being put on a military barge headed back to the mainland to serve his time. "I found myself chained to the bowels of a barge," he said, "as

---

250 Sharpton with Hunter, *Al on America*, xiiv.

if it was 1801 instead of 2001 and I was traveling the Middle Passage."[251] For the man who'd been to Gorée Island in Senegal and who'd written of seeing the *Door of No Return* for slaves being taken through to the Middle Passage, he nonetheless painted this silly contrivance, evoking a grotesque comparison to that which should be sacrosanct for him. Again, were a white person to make such a comparison, the race leader would've fiercely lambasted him or her as a racist for cheapening his ancestors' horrific experience. But such is Sharpton's buffoonery that even while buried knee deep in the grotesque, he often amounts to little more than a roving comedy sketch anyway.

As earlier stated, the Rev. has always believed he was entitled to, and was deserving of due deference in treatment—a kind of *noblesse oblige*. So, while *Stone* was a book about leadership in which he spoke of sacrifices, he nonetheless cried like a baby for a ninety-day stretch in jail—something a great many black teenagers in New York City will regrettably experience before their eighteenth birthday. In fact, in some cases, he'd sounded more like a disaffected preppie from a Connecticut suburb than an adult black man from urban Brooklyn-Queens.

On further reading, we then discovered that he was indeed accorded that *noblesse oblige* throughout the process. At first, he'd given us the feeling that he'd spent his time in maximum security lockdown under harsh Alcatraz-like conditions. But in a later section where he boasted about his VIP status in New York's political scene, he revealed that his jail time was spent in the lap of luxury. So luxurious was his incarceration that he spent it being a nuisance to jail officials in Brooklyn—all a result of his political connections to Senators Charles Schumer and Hillary Clinton, Congressman Charlie Rangel, and others who'd intervened to get him transferred from Puerto Rico and "deposited" in Brooklyn:

> When we were deposited in the federal facility, the New York Senators, Chuck Schumer and Hillary Clinton, called to check on us. After two days, Schumer and Clinton arranged for us to be transferred to the federal jail in Brooklyn. They couldn't do anything to reduce our time, but they could have us moved to a more convenient location.[252]

---

251 Al Sharpton with Chiles, *The Rejected Stone*, 154.
252 Ibid., 158.

After only two days, he was back in his home borough where, according to him, he and his three codefendants—Assemblyman Jose Rivera, Bronx Democratic Party chairman Roberto Ramirez, and City Councilman Adolfo Carrion ("The Vieques Four")—"would be doing their hard time":

> We had to keep those shackles on all the way to Kennedy Airport. When we landed, I looked out the window and saw twelve government cars on the tarmac. Twelve cars! Like they were bringing in John Gotti or something. They carted us to the Brooklyn House of Detention, where we would be doing hard time.[253]

But this "hard time" was really being pampered in a wing of the Brooklyn Detention Center, where the Rev. watched the television of his choice and slept in any cell of his choice. They were the only ones being housed on that wing of the jail, because, according to him, as VIPs, the city couldn't have risked anything happening to them in the main inmate population. This was quite believable, as he'd previously sued New York City for failing to protect him during his 1991 stabbing. Anyway, the Puerto Rican judge had given Sharpton a "measured" sentence, because while his codefendants had been given only a month, the Rev. had gotten three, so he'd had the entire wing to himself for the remaining two months—that "fifty-days-long" meeting with himself. So bored was he just sitting around, eating, and watching television, that he came up with the idea of fasting to break the monotony and to keep attention on himself:

> So there we were, four men in a ward that was large enough for ninety. We could sleep in whatever cell we wanted, could watch a bunch of different TVs. One of the most dramatic things I came up with to break the tedium was a fast. Nothing steals away the boredom like the growl of an empty stomach. It was a classic political-prisoner tactic, used by everybody from Gandhi to Nelson Mandela to Martin Luther King Jr. We would get a visit from the doctor twice a day, taking our blood, checking and double-checking that we weren't getting sick. They could not have us getting sick in their custody. When the doctor would come, I'd say, "Here comes Dracula to take my blood." That was our little joke.[254]

---

253 Ibid., 159.

254 Ibid., 160.

In other words, his solemn meeting with himself was likely a decision-making meeting— deciding which television set to watch on any given day or which shows to watch at any particular hour of the day. But he also did a lot of reading while sitting in his jail cell doing his hard time for the Vieques protest. As repositioning himself as a King disciple was a big part of his attempts at mainstreaming in *Al on America*—written a year after Vieques, we'd found him reading up on Dr. King. Everyone who reads Dr. King also reads Gandhi, so the Rev. was also in step there as well. As he was gearing up to lead the free world, it had also made sense that he'd read up on Winston Churchill, so there was no surprise there either—apart from implications of the impressive library at the Brooklyn Detention Center's VIP wing. It appears that administrators were serious about making intellectuals out of their charges on release.

> I spent much of my time reading and studying those who came before me. I reread Long Walk to Freedom, the autobiography of Nelson Mandela...I read about Mahatma Gandhi...I reread the autobiography of Dr. Martin Luther King Jr., who helped me define and identify the character of a true leader...I read everything I could get my hands on about Churchill. I would consider his policies imperialistic. But he was a great leader.[255]

However, more than a dozen years later when he became a "presidential advisor" and an intellectual guru who was disseminating leadership principles, the Rev. then had to act as if he'd at least read the part. So, except for books by or on Nelson Mandela, who was mentioned in both accounts, Sharpton's reading list during the same jail stint had significantly evolved from *Al on America* to *Stone*. Though not naming the books, in 2013's *Stone*, he name-dropped the great thinkers he'd read:

> I did a lot of reading, devouring books by serious thinkers such as Paul Tillich, Arnold Toynbee, Reinhold Niebuhr, Nelson Mandela. It became clear to me that serious movements inevitably always must broaden.[256]

---

255 Al Sharpton with Karen Hunter, introduction to *Al on America* (Dafina Books/Kensington, 2002), xv.
256 Al Sharpton with Chiles, *The Rejected Stone*, 162.

The Kennedy Diary

As much of the self-promoting hype written about Vieques over two books was unsurprisingly inconsistent, I'd decided to check to see how this had been reported in the media at the time. In seeking to cross-reference some of the contradictions, I was aiming to see if the Rev. had issued any public retractions or correction for any aspect of the stories he'd written. Vieques was a well-documented event with the involvement of other big names, in addition to Robert Kennedy Jr.'s, which made public corroboration or refutation relatively easy. It was here that a diary not meant for public consumption had ended up providing much clarification.

In a breach of his privacy, Robert Kennedy Jr.'s diary was stolen and its contents published in a New York City newspaper. Its revelations, though, did clarify many aspects of Sharpton's differing accounts of the protest. As it turned out, Mr. Kennedy Jr. and labor leader Dennis Rivera were the first on the island. Neither had pulled any strings or used any connections to get transferred back stateside; both had chosen to serve their jail sentences locally in Guaynabo, outside of San Juan, as their purpose was to draw global attention to the cause and not to themselves.

Environmental lawyer Robert Kennedy Jr. had taken his punishment like a person of honor by marching into court to tell the judge that since he'd followed his conscience, he would gladly accept the sentence of the court and serve his time with peace of mind. But for the Rev., it was the opposite; his purpose was to draw global attention to Al Sharpton, and through his written accounts, we saw the usual histrionics of a petulant child at play. He couldn't stop talking about the round-the-clock efforts of famed Harvard law professor Charles Ogletree and other prominent legal minds to get his sentence reduced, while at the same time, in the "Sharptonesque" contradiction, he managed to declare a "resolve" to serve his time:

> In the meantime, a slew of lawyers, such as Harvard Law School professor Charles Ogletree, were running around to the appellate courts, trying to get our sentences reduced or thrown out. But I was resolved that we should do the time.[257]

---

257 Ibid., 159.

But there was another surprise to Reverend Sharpton's story as well. His account of protest was yet another occasion for him to remove the "Jackson" shadow from the Sharpton experience. The fear of being overshadowed by Jesse Jackson that had led him to write Jackson out of their African trip the first time around had also driven him to give two accounts over a thirteen-year span, of the well-publicized Vieques protest, without ever mentioning the participation of another key member of the Jackson family. He'd told us of Robert Kennedy Jr. and the Latino politicians; but he'd never mentioned the involvement of Mrs. Jacqueline Jackson, wife of Reverend Jesse Jackson and the woman who'd once welcomed the Sharpton family into her home for the Christmas holidays over many years. Mrs. Jackson was among those arrested and charged with trespassing for protesting at Vieques, and she'd ended up serving a ten-day sentence. In 2002's *Al on America*, the Rev. had made the point that the Vieques protest was a man's affair:

> If Dennis Rivera, Robert Kennedy Jr., Adolpho Carrion, Jose Rivera, Roberto Ramirez, and I had not done what we did, it would not have been a national issue and Bush [*sic*] would not have been forced into a position to respond.[258]

In 2013's *Stone*, he gave us extensive details of those involved, once more describing an adventure that was the work of the crucial all-male six-some: Sharpton, Robert Kennedy Jr., and local New York Latino politicians Adolfo Carrion, Jose Riviera, Robert Ramirez, and labor leader Denis Rivera. He also told us that, "There were at least 100 other defendants there, all of them Vieques protestors."[259] But out of a fear of sharing the stage with, or being overshadowed by, the Jackson name, the Rev. had written two books with dedicated chapters on Vieques, naming names but never once naming Jacqueline Jackson. Reverend Jesse Jackson had also made a late stop in Vieques to soak up some of the press coverage that his wife had merited, but Sharpton had made no mention of that either.

---

258 Sharpton with Hunter, *Al on America*, 64.

259 Al Sharpton with Chiles, *The Rejected Stone*, 155.

For Sharpton, being a VIP had meant being treated as such—even in jail, and there was this tangentially funny part of Robert Kennedy Jr.'s diary that was corroborative of what the Rev. himself had actually written. Kennedy had noted that in her visit to see him in Vieques, Senator Hillary Clinton "spoke of her recent visit to Sharpton in a Brooklyn cell block where he was alone with four television sets." Hillary Clinton told Kennedy Jr. that Sharpton had griped about being strip-searched and that he also "went off on Jesse" [Jackson]. From the Rev., we got this:

> What started out for me as one of the low points of my career, with shackles and strip searches and long lonely nights in an empty ward, in the end turned out to be one of the most important periods of my life.[260]…We could sleep in whatever cell we wanted, could watch a bunch of different TVs.[261]

Among the diary's gossipy revelations were Kennedy's opinions of certain known personalities—noted some twelve years earlier. As we read his view of black leadership, we were back once more, facing an *ironic rebound*. A white bear had appeared on a mountainside, and we were obliged to embrace it; attempting to ignore it was futile. Robert Kennedy Jr. had had a mouthful to say of both Reverends Jackson and Sharpton—opinions that reinforced public perception of the two as racketeers of black America. He'd described Reverend Jackson as having "a desperate and destructive addiction to publicity," citing Jesse's behavior at labor leader Cesar Chavez's 1993 funeral. Apparently, Jackson had pushed "Cesar's friends and family out of the way to make himself lead pall bearer" for the cameras, which had led Kennedy to note, "I feel dirty around him, and I feel like I'm being used. I feel like with Jesse, it's all about Jesse."

But it was Reverend Sharpton who'd come in for much chastisement and ridicule. According to the *New York Post*, which had published excerpts of the diary, Robert Kennedy Jr. had called the Rev. a buffoon who'd never escaped the "stench" of his advocacy for Tawana Brawley. His observations had also put the Rev. into perspective as the so-called leader of black America:

---

260 Ibid., 163.
261 Ibid., 160.

> Sharpton has done more damage to the black cause than George Wallace [Mr.
> "segregation forever" former Alabama Governor]. He has suffocated the de-
> cent black leaders in New York. His transparent venal blackmail and extortion
> schemes taint all black leadership.

The revelations had forced Mr. Kennedy to issue the following damage-control
apology in the aftermath:

> Nothing in that diary was ever meant for publication. I have nothing but respect
> for…Rev Sharpton and Jesse Jackson, all of whom have distinguished themselves
> as extraordinary national leaders over the past decade.

His statement was understandable, as personal opinions not meant for public consumption were leaked—something we all dread, and for which we
would've all been furious. But in spite of its means of sourcing, we still
couldn't ignore the information or fail to accept the obvious: notwithstanding
Kennedy's standard form-apology, his criticisms of the Reverends Sharpton
and Jackson were just the long-held opinions of the thinking, yet silent public. Although these were the private muses of one man to his diary, they were
and still are opinions and beliefs undoubtedly shared by most Americans—
black and white—including those who court Sharpton on television, those
who've continually imposed his presence on our consciousness, those considered friends and foe alike of the black community, and correspondingly, those
most likely to legislate in its favor or against it.

Robert Kennedy Jr., the author of a book on legendary Civil War-era African
American hero, Robert Smalls (*The Boat Thief*), is, without doubt, a friend of
black America. If these were the observations of a friend, it isn't hard to imagine
the opinion held by party operatives and the power handlers of Sharpton. It isn't
hard to believe that this is also the opinion of the mainstream politicians and
business people who dole out money to Sharpton's phony movements and organizations in exchange for his vote-brokering come election time or in exchange
for buying out real diversity concerns in corporate America. It is this maligned
opinion that had seen Roger Stone so easily co-opt Reverend Sharpton in his
subterfuge against the Democrats.

With each television or newspaper interview, with each of the Rev.'s appearances as a host, guest, or contributor, we get an exercise in the underlying connivance of the mainstream establishment that accredits him while comically hoisting him to white America as black America's leader. There isn't a single television personality over the age of forty who doesn't know the full history of Sharpton, not a single one who hasn't long formed an opinion of him as a charlatan-simpleton—a sentiment that no doubt colors black America with the "stench" of Reverend Sharpton and others like him.

End Act II

Act III: Jet-Propelled Buffoon

There is no character, howsoever good and fine, but it can
be destroyed by ridicule, howsoever poor and witless.

—Mark Twain[262]

*Civil rights activist Al Sharpton walks out of the West Wing after he and a group of civil
rights leaders met on the Voting Rights Act with US president Barack Obama, Former
Attorney General Eric Holder, and Former Labor Secretary Tom Perez on July 29, 2013,
at the White House in Washington. (Photo by Mandel Ngan/AFP/Getty Images.)*

---

262 *Pudd'nhead Wilson - The Wit and Wisdom of Mark Twain*, 17.

THE REJECTED STONE was the third act culmination in which the Sharpton machine, having been newly equipped with jet-propulsion in the aftermath of the 2008 presidential elections, was now a vehicle attempting to reach the stratosphere. But as it was still guided by the same old, tired, and worn late-century instruments and tracking radials, it wobbled as it climbed. Although we were surprised at its progress so far, we'd still envisioned its eventual plummet. The only question was, When?

The Dualist Theater

To effectively treat their patients, psychotherapists first try to figure out the drivers of the patients' behavior. They seek to isolate contributing factors that might include those due to what biologist Richard Dawkins might call smart memes—non-genetic cultural transmissions through imitation—or others due to what that the rest of us might just call dumb genes—genetic transmissions. The challenge is then to understand what exactly are the drivers of neurosis and where do they actually reside. Are they intangible memes etched and replicated in our minds or are they tangible genetic imbalances and faulty modulations of the brain, commonly regarded as neurological disorders?

Enters cognitive philosopher Daniel Dennett, who has spent a lifetime attempting to demystify "consciousness." In his exploration (efforts to either affirm or refute) of French philosopher René Descartes' "dualism"—the belief that the mind and brain are two distinct entities—Dr. Dennett coined the term "Cartesian theater" to describe the imaginary staging area of the brain that would be necessary for dualism to be a valid concept. This is a triage theater where sensory data/signals would supposedly be processed, directed, projected, and commanded for decision-making and actions. It's an imaginary area according to Dr. Dennett, as he isn't a believer dualism.

But there are times when even the humanities or the social sciences are unable to adequately provide the explanations we seek. This is precisely the case with the Sharpton manifestations that have left us often confused for over three decades: Are they the result of a single dual-entity or of two distinct entities (mind and brain) regulated in (by) such a triage area?

Seen through his books, his manifestations do appear to thrive in a kind of "dualist theater" but one in which single substances often branch off into opposing and contradictory forces while competing for the attention and to the benefit of a uniquely all controlling host entity (area)—the Sharpton ego. In this sense, deciphering his manifestations by reading his books has been like a vast hybrid study of philosophy, psychiatry, and biology at the same time. At times, we're sitting in that staging area—given a first-hand and up-close view, watching the traverse of a billion neurons, each in a duality of purpose, excel at mayhem, mischief, and a kind madness comprehensible only to the host entity. Yet at other times, we're sitting in somewhat of a real theater, watching an actor on stage performing for an audience of one—himself (either mind or brain), simultaneously sitting in the box seat of the audience, effusively cheering on the guy onstage, as one (both) exudes a potent sphere of energy felt only by the other (himself). It is our introduction to *the most interesting man in black America*.

The Most Interesting Man in Black America

We were at his reincarnation, which saw attending politicians, social dignitaries, and celebrities alike praise his presence while humbled by it. The clergy in attendance blessed it. He'd failed to pay the government its taxes, but as he was guided by higher authority, the government was more than willing, in fact, honored to forgive his civic obligation. We were bearing witness to *the most interesting man in black America*, and we supplicated the gods for the opportunity. We too were humbled in his presence, but most importantly, we were grateful for the chance to see his denial of continuance to his old form; his mutation from one phenotype into a new and improved hybrid type had just been completed.

It was a reincarnation as a television effigy, a cable network personality, and an intellectual guru—to match new circumstances as an inside the Beltway man. And though from the very start, we were watching Sisyphus being overwhelmed by the very boulder he'd lifted onto his head, we were happy to be part of the audience, because, in reality, we'd known that it was a point of departure to some high-octane level buffoonery.

Through plots and subplots, we followed, as the once *rejected stone* regaled himself in exaggerated self-importance as a leader on the world stage, while eviscerating good taste in near masochistic delusions of aspirations to greatness. "I don't think in any way that I've achieved greatness, but I have to be honest and admit that greatness is what I seek," he said, to the effusive cheer of his other half sitting in the audience. Accordingly, in the pursuit thereof, he was even "eating for greatness." On hearing of this ultimate ambition in seeking greatness, a reasoned mind in the audience whispered a question to the man sitting next to her. *In which part of the developing world?* She asked.

But it was the plausible deniability that harkened back to the Tawana Brawley affair. *The most interesting man in black America* was always the last to know—the last to know that the Brawley story of rape was a hoax and now last to know that great individuals, unlike wealthy ones, didn't speak of being great or of their aspirations to greatness, as history has traditionally been the sole author of greatness—Winston Churchill notwithstanding. On the upside, though, from a slow read of his words, it was clear that the future—even in the developing world—would have little to fear, as "greatness" to be realized anywhere on planet earth by *the most interesting man in black America,* was a near cosmic impossibility.

Among his other moments of profundity was this lesson on leadership— "If you want to lead, you must decide where you're going," to which he then asked, "Do you have the character to get to your destination?" We could feel a river running through it though not through him, as it was clear that even a horse-driven carriage was likely to get us there faster than the "character" he'd described.

Next up was his mental rejection of the dreaded middle-age lust for "arm candies" in one moment, only to give us the gory details of dating his trophy girlfriend, born around the time he'd already celebrated his twenty-fifth birthday. Then came his new status as power-player. The man who'd had once taken "hobos" out of a homeless shelter to stage a rent-a-protest, was now impressing us with his great friendship with, and his role as advisor to a president of the United States. We got play-by-play replays of dinner at the White House and of watching the Super Bowl with the regal First Family, inclusive of descriptions of the spectacularly wonderful First Lady and the beautiful First Children. But then just as quickly, to advance a belief that two-parent black families—like that of Sasha and Malia Obama's—have neither existed nor been of any importance in black America, he dashed out of dinner and football with the First Family to go all the way back to slavery for evidence in its support. In no time, he was a smash hit—the toast of the town to deadbeat dads all over black America. But that was just hors-d'oeuvres while we'd waited for the main course.

We'd seen the mutation, though we were still unsure of the constitution of the new form. He then clarified this for us by telling us that he'd matured—now a new man accepted into the gentry, a squire of the highest caliber. Like Weldon Johnson's fictional *Ex-Colored Man,* he'd "passed," though regrettably for black America, not from the black to the white race but gleefully for him, from peasantry to the gentry among which he thought he'd rightfully belonged all along.

But being *the most interesting man in black America,* and now its preeminent black leader was about his desire to fly first class, his mandate to eat in fancy restaurants—Harlem's Sylvia's Restaurant for political photo ops notwithstanding. It was about his need to be looked upon with respect by the black elite, having felt some level of acceptance by white America. Now a high-colored aristocrat, the likes of the men at the golden era of nineteenth-century blackness, he was the Pinckney Benton Pinchback (governor), the John Mercer Langston, the Henry Highland Garnet (advisors to powerful men like Presidents Hayes and Garfield) of contemporary times. As he regaled himself in his newfound nobility, both his halves—the man on stage and the one in the audience—were relishing their turn in the sun. For those who'd missed the hors-d'oeuvres, he re-emphasized that he'd now had "social stature" in society.

The most interesting man in black America then declared that he wasn't a "self-interested hustler" by showing us that he was indeed. He spoke of the person he used to be and of the one he'd become while showing us the one he really was—which was mutually exclusive to both. There were the many quantum leaps that had presumed a present that was different from the past, a today that was different from yesterday. But as we watched, we noticed that mutation hadn't changed a thing:

I can talk in a personal way about vanity because I went through it myself, when my vanity outran my sanity, that period of wanting to be in the newspaper, rather than being more concerned about what I'm saying and whether I'm using it for good.[263]

In his book tour, which had included a visit with the queen of the *mea culpa*, Oprah Winfrey, he'd proclaimed that he was no longer a buffoon and had presented *Stone* as a sort of *autobiography of an ex-buffoon*—presumably a retired one. But in doing so, he defeated his very purpose, because accordingly, all those buffoonish things he'd done over the years were solely the result of pain from paternal abandonment. It was his father's fault—the same "pre-mutation" condition he'd used as an excuse since time immemorial.

Yet in a heartbeat, the new aristocrat was still more likely to run out and affirm long-held views of him as a peasant racketeer than he was to affirm any decorum of newfound nobility. Like the roughneck street thug invited to the swanky upscale party on the rich side of town, who then runs out to brag about every cute girl he'd kissed, *the most interesting man in black America* loudly declared that he'd finally "arrived," that he'd come full circle. Showing his first-class lifestyle, he effectively told us, *It's my time now!*

He was the nightmare of Abraham Maslow's imagination—a figure at the pinnacle of delusions of grandeur, wallowing like a hog in a trough of self-actualization and importance between New York and Washington, DC. Like the hated Paris of Jean Cocteau that couldn't stop speaking of herself, the mimetic actor on stage, inventing and reinventing along the way, couldn't spare a moment to talk about anything other than himself—*the most interesting man in black America*. As he showered himself with accolades, they were simultaneously absorbed by the other half of his duality, sitting right there in the audience.

He was the muse who'd seen his own likeness in the image of a painting and was hypnotized, the misogynist whose books had conveniently lacked space for mentioning the women in his life—his mother, his wife, his daughters, his sister, or even his half-sister Tina, who was the carnal victim of his lecherous father.

---

263 Ibid., 46.

Pharaoh had taken us through the pitiful displays of turd in all his grandiosity—the Christ-like ingenuity, the Mosaic grandeur, and the Pauline fearlessness as a guerrilla fighter for his people. *Al on America* was a whimsical exhibition of a showman with mainstream ambitions for black leadership and white love in which he'd extolled his qualifications for high office—none of which were particularly high. But having found a new body, form, and status by the writing of *Stone,* he'd changed his tune. "If I had gone to Congress," he said, "I don't know if we would have been able to pass racial-profiling laws."[264] The audience noted the hilarity in substance and form, and this time, the whispering woman in the audience found the courage to bravely yell out the question on everyone's mind: *When did Reverend Sharpton get a racial-profiling law passed? On which planet?*

As the man onstage mused on, we couldn't help the mental comparison to the notorious imbecilic show-offs over time. He'd brought to mind that other charlatan of contemporary times—she who'd seen Russia from her Alaskan back porch while hunting a moose but had mistaken it for an early return of Halley's Comet. Nor did the historians in the audience fail to notice the similarities to that other famed charlatan of antiquity: Lucian of Samosata's "Peregrinus"— the second-century Christian cynic and multi-life charlatan from Parium who'd exploited Christian gullibility and conned his way atop the church in Palestine until he was discovered and kicked out. Subsequently conning his way across the Mediterranean, he'd then met his just end atop a pyre outside the Olympiad in Greece—accidentally by his own hands while in the commission of yet another trickery. As we all laughed and silently ridiculed the man on stage, like those who'd cheered Peregrinus on to his death, our guy on stage intensified his performance, but for the sole benefit of his counterpart sitting among us in the audience. It was a mutual admiration to the complete exclusion of all others, absent any force in nature to say, *Man, you're delusional!*

By the end of dinner, we'd experienced enough pomp and glory to convince us to either canonize *the most interesting man in black America* or to shoot him out of a cannon. It was then that the psychiatrists among us in the audience began to explain it all as havoc resulting from single substances having gone haywire.

---

264 Ibid., 13.

We'd been in the presence of the Narcissus of our time, watching him hover over a pool of water as he took sweet comfort in telling his reflection, *I, and only I, will be the truly great black leader of all times!*

By the end of dinner, we were all humbled by the experience, still honored by his presence.

The Rejected Stone

The Rejected Stone was a culminating affirmation—the "dénouement" of a buffoon. Nearly five decades in the public eye had neither slowed nor changed any aspect of a fundamentally flawed and opportunistic personality, and it showed in this 2013 literary iteration. The simplicity and pettiness of the previous two books continued, but this was buffoonery's ground zero. Yet, the Rev. did his best to convince us that he was a changed man—no longer a buffoon.

Acceptance and dominance long in the craving were affirmed without shame or reservation. The Rev. revealed his life-long mission of social climbing and his desire to be accepted by those who counted—white America. He also showed his need to be respected and admired by those who'd once shunned and ridiculed him—black America, presumably for being bloviating, tacky, thuggish, ostentatious, demagogic, a bully, a charlatan, or possibly for all of the above in no particular order. He was now convinced that he'd finally achieved both. So he told us not to begrudge him his first-class flights, his White House gate pass, his television show, or for having "social stature" because he'd earned them without having preplanned them:

> I think people sense that drive and purpose in me, which is why they don't be-grudge me the first-class flights and the fancy hotels to which I now have access...Having a turbulent flight to Cleveland in first class isn't a bad day for me...When I was protesting in Howard Beach or Bensonhurst or Vieques, I did not say, "I want to do this so that one day, I'll have access to the president of the United States and go to the White House and the inauguration and have my own MSNBC show and have social stature."[265]

---

265 Ibid., 167–68.

At best, the book was a silly contrivance in an attempt to convince us that he wasn't the Reverend Reginald Bacon of Tom Wolfe's *Bonfire of the Vanities,* by showing us that he was indeed the Reverend Reginald Bacon of black America. At worst, he convinced us that he was a cheap imitation of 1970s-era television character George Jefferson. He'd moved on up to the "deeluxe" apartment in the sky and was now the beneficiary of all associated accoutrements. But who but a buffoon would write a book to tell the world that he or she was now in possession of "social stature"?

Though claiming to have retired his buffoonery, there was little that was autobiographical or "ex" about a book of continued inventions in which we were given much the same. Barring physical appearance, right through the last word on the last page of *Stone*, it was a mystery to find any discernible changes from the days when the Rev. had called New York governor Mario Cuomo a "low-down good-for-nothing son of a bitch" in print. He was still a man beholden to personal grudges, even for things that had occurred many decades in the past. His enemies were to be neither forgiven nor forgotten, except by satisfying the core requirement of extending the hand of acceptance that he'd sought from corners that were white, rich, famous, or influential. The difference here was that among the famous and influential were now many of the black faces that had once shunned him, which signaled coming full circle to the respectability and dominance he'd always craved and exacting a kind of show-off revenge, which said, *Look at me now!*

Stone was a book on "paths to leadership," in which the Rev. delineated, "23 Life Lessons for These Changing Times." While few would've expected lessons that echoed, say a Jack Welsh or Warren Buffet in an Al Sharpton book, even fewer would've expected to read twenty-three platitudes and generalities likely to have been found in fake fortune cookies dispensed in a fake Chinese restaurant somewhere in the Rev.'s former Brownsville, Brooklyn neighborhood. At age fifty-nine and after a long life in the church, in activism, and in politics, his leadership advice was more akin to a small-time trickster taking a stab at that which he knew least—how to fly straight.

The question was still the same: Was he a perverse creature or just a practical joker? Pick either or choose both! Either way, *The Rejected Stone* was the same old Reverend Sharpton. The new aristocrat and *most interesting man in black America* was the same old buffoon.

Inaugural Day

"Greatness" was affirmed by invitation to President Obama's second inaugural. The Rev. was riddled with emotions as he walked to the Capitol Building and joined luminaries, celebrities, and the president's close friends and family members. As he stepped out on to the open inaugural stage and saw himself on the big screen, he thought of his mother who'd died the previous year and of childhood friends who might have been in prison, on drugs, or dead. It was a somber moment:

> A Black man, a friend of mine, was being sworn in as president of the United States. And a Puerto Rican woman was swearing in the vice president [sic]. As America changed, grew more tolerant and more accepting, it allowed people like me to change tactics. I no longer had to be as confrontational to get an audience. I no longer had to be as radical to make the authorities pay attention. The country grew and, in the process, allowed me to grow.[266]

The days of *L'Enfant terrible* were supposedly behind him, and with the changes underway in the country, he believed he'd no longer needed to be confrontational to get an audience. Yet even during such a moment, the Rev. showed that he was still quite *terrible*—by receding to gloat and boast:

> I wondered if any of those kids who had laughed at me, the boy preacher, were watching me now…I thought about all my critics through the years: those racists who threw watermelons at me when I marched through Bensonhurst, those in the media and beyond who ridiculed me when I defended Tawana Brawley.[267]

At the inaugural of his "friend" for the highest office in the land, Sharpton still took the time to think about the media that had ridiculed him over Tawana Brawley—as if an official invitation had somehow validated or negated the impact of his hoax of the century. There he was, bearing witness to the long march from slavery to the second inaugural of a black man as president—the historic

---

266 Ibid., 5.
267 Ibid., 2.

affirmation and confirmation that the first election (2008) wasn't a fluke. Yet at such a monumental occasion, the man who'd boasted of spending a lifetime in the fight for his people's freedom could but sit there and think about the children who'd laughed at him while they were all children and about the racists who'd thrown watermelons at him in adulthood.

He was in a beautiful lush forest counting every ugly tree he'd met along his path, failing to realize that children laugh and pick on each other, precisely because they're children and that adult racists indulge in racism, precisely because they're cultivated racists. On such a day, neither should've mattered as neither had prevailed. So instead of standing tall in victory, he sullied the moment by sinking deep into the gutter. A year after the inaugural, a further lack of etiquette would then oblige him to write and tell us all about it.

There was an instructive moment when he told us of his ordained path to the White House ceremonies that day, which reflected a genuine belief that it was biblically charted for him to have made his way back into white acceptance and the black bourgeoisie—the Obama presidency. As he sat on the platform among those representing American power, he didn't find his presence on the stage at all unbelievable. In a prodigal sort of way, the *rejected stone* was finally home in the edifice built by slaves, the structure that had housed forty-three previous white occupants:

> I believed what the Bible said, that the rejected stones would become the cornerstones of a new world order. Race and class and gender bias and homophobia were all on their deathbed, on the verge of being swept into the dustbins of history.[268]

Fast-forward to the 2017 melee of Confederate adoration by the extreme right and in an apparent rebuke of his dustbin beliefs four years before, we found Sharpton telling PBS's Charlie Rose that it's time for the federal government to cease maintaining the Jefferson Memorial in Washington DC with taxpayer funds, because Thomas Jefferson had owned slaves. Apparently, the brooms had been worn out in their dustbin duties, or the sweeping itself had turned out to

---

268 Ibid., 6.

be slower than he'd envisioned, so he was back to fighting the retroactive war of respectability. But even then, as if foretelling his own attempt at sugarcoating, on the very next page of the book, the Rev. showed that the dustbins of history had posed no threat to his livelihood because they'd either been filled up too fast and with many leftovers or hadn't been filled quite quickly enough. He was still having to march and protest:

> The America I faced in the 1980s wearing my jogging suit was not the same place as the America I speak to now, yet I still find myself leading marches to protest outrages such as the shooting death of Trayvon Martin or the widespread attempts to roll back voting rights.[269]

The human condition is such that given enough time and space, most of us will eventually reveal our own image of ourselves (occurrence). So, on page seven of *Stone*, the Rev. encouraged us to read through his journey to understand that he wasn't the self-interested hustler or the troublemaker often depicted over the years:

> As you read through the following pages and get a sense of my journey and the lessons I've learned, I believe you will come to understand why I've not been unsettled or slowed down by the attempts over the years to paint me with a broad brush as some kind of troublemaker or self-interested hustler.[270]

This was where the image of 1980s-era Sharpton walking around with his FBI-issued electronic surveillance briefcase had come to mind. Even worse, though, the two hundred and fifty-four pages that followed would also show the affirmative journey of a dedicated trouble making self-interested hustler—highlighting the dissonance that underpins the egos of turds and buffoons.

He then went on to give us a glimpse of his capacity for brutal honesty as well, but from the usual perspective that is positive for the Rev. and negative for others.

---

269 Ibid., 7.
270 Ibid.

Here it was the revelation of the so-called velvet ministry of the black church, of which he's eminently qualified to speak, having been a minister since age four:

> The hypocrisy of the black church on this issue [homosexuality] is absolutely breathtaking to me. As I said before, anyone who has spent more than five minutes in a typical black church knows how huge a presence gays are, particularly in the music ministry.[271]

In his effort to court the (mostly) white LGBTQ community, the man who once styled former New York City mayor Ed Koch as a "punk faggot," threw his black church under the bus—outing a significant segment of his flock so that he could hoist himself as a beacon of progressiveness. Luckily, as black congregants across the land were as unlikely as anyone else to read an Al Sharpton book, the Sunday morning choir band likely continued to sing, clap, and entertain as usual—neither unsettled nor interrupted by the Rev.'s attempt to paint it with a broad brush.

In Midst of Legends

As he sat there at the inaugural, among the famous and powerful, the Rev. realized that he was in the midst of legends, even naming names that many might not see as quite legendary:

> I looked around the congregation and saw the secretary of defense, the secretary of state, people who controlled the military-industrial complex. Sitting among them were people like me and Martin Luther King III, people who had come out of the freedom movement:[272]

Unless perpetual internecine warfare and litigious public battles among themselves and with King luminaries like Harry Belafonte and Andrew Young had constituted the new "freedom movement," the King children, although a symbol

---

271 Ibid., 57.
272 Ibid., 3.

of past greatness, can hardly be considered contemporary "freedom fighters." But as the Rev. continued to elaborate, we realized that he was really talking about Al Sharpton. Martin Luther King III was never investigated, indicted, nor charged with fraud; nor was he ever involved in or chastised by the media for the type of race-baiting and strife inducements that had produced the Tawana Brawley affair, stoked the Crown Heights riots, or incited murder at Freddie's Fashion Mart. Once more, we were seeing the usual usurpation of black legacy and an effort to piggyback on the King name to legitimize Sharpton:

> Although we were not veterans of wars, we were veterans of battles. We were scarred not by warfare but from the handcuffs and the media attacks, the false investigations, and the merciless and reckless allegations.[273]

But the inaugural experience was a high mountain train ride that was bound to jump tracks soon or later, and this happened when the Rev. met the late Nobel Laureate, Elie Wiesel. Things then went from farce to insult to severe injury in no time:

> As we left the church, I stopped and met Elie Wiesel, the Nobel laureate who had survived the Holocaust camps in Nazi Germany. I thought about how there currently were and had been battles fought all over the world for human rights, whether against the Nazis, against apartheid, against slavery and segregation, against Northern racists. And I knew that while it was impressive to meet the heads of state and commerce, the freedom fighters like Wiesel and Martin III and others who joined that morning were the people I most admired.[274]

Again, Reverend Sharpton could've hardly spoken of anyone but Al Sharpton, even if it meant demeaning a Holocaust survivor. The northern racists were Sharpton's persecutors—those white racists, but for whose persecution, he would've long achieved "greatness" and been a made-man of the establishment. This included former New York governor Mario Cuomo, former state attorney

---

273 Ibid.
274 Ibid., 3–4.

general Robert Abrams, former New York City mayor Ed Koch, and others. The people of Bensonhurst and Howard Beach, some of whom had "kindly" offered him watermelon and the n-word, and the New York press corps that regularly ridiculed him had rounded out that group. To Sharpton, they'd all presumably shared much in common with Hitler's Nazi machine, hence his basis for equivocation to, and for his great admiration for the Holocaust survivor, Elie Wiesel.

It's hard to believe the Rev. had ever even known of or thought of Elie Wiesel before that day, not to mention having had the Nobel laureate as someone he'd "most admired." Wiesel had never figured into any of his books, even after the Rev. had returned from his love-fest in Israel the second time. The expert in false equivalences had failed to realize that Elie Wiesel didn't just face a human rights' battle in Europe but was instead the victim of a totalitarian-commanded antisemitism that had sought to exterminate his people from the face of the earth:

> Because I knew that, like me, they had had periods in their lives when they were
> not exactly warmly embraced in the corridors of power, when they might have
> even been considered pariahs. They were there because someone had recognized
> the value in their struggles.[275]

In other words, being shunned by the New York establishment for over two decades of mischief and chicanery had somehow placed the Rev. in the same boat as Elie Wiesel, who along with European Jewry was once considered a "pariah" and "unwelcomed" in European halls of power. Where Al Sharpton exists, arrogance and ignorance manifest in abundance.

Infallible Tax Dodger

The book on leadership showed a "leader" who had yet to grasp the most fundamental concepts of leading, such as being fallible—accepting that he'd often

---

275 Ibid., 4.

been wrong on many issues, such as the Brawley affair, or that paying taxes is a principal obligation of the citizenry, himself included.

But the Baptist preacher was of a level of infallibility rivaling that of a Holy Roman Bishop—no less than that of early church leader, Irenaeus of Lyon, or that of the Bishop of Rome in later times, Pope Pius IX. Though having pleaded guilty to failing to file tax returns back in the early 1990s, a decade earlier in *Al on America,* the Rev. had still obfuscated about his failure to pay his taxes—essentially in both tone and substance, rejecting any notion of civic citizenry. Back then, illogic and false equivocation had amounted to a belief that it was OK to dodge taxes because corrupt corporate entities were doing the same:

> I've been accused of not paying enough taxes. I know I have paid more taxes than Enron, and Enron employees probably paid more taxes than Enron, too.[276]

In 2013's *Stone,* we got much the same, but this time, in his attempt to delegitimize the friendly Obama administration's authority to tax and levy him, the Rev. evaded the actual matter of his taxes owed and instead chose to tie any recognition of his tax obligations to a biblical edict:

> The government came along and accused me of unpaid taxes in amounts that exceeded a million dollars. Even if you didn't do anything wrong, you can't say, "To hell with them!" and walk away. The Bible tells us to avoid even the appearance of wrong, so even if you didn't do the things you are being accused of, it becomes a huge distraction.[277]

Sharpton didn't believe he'd done anything wrong by not paying his taxes over the years, nor had he even recognized the government's claim for back taxes as legitimate. But just because the Bible advises to "avoid even the appearance of wrong," he had to deal with his tax situation to avoid it becoming a "distraction." Absent was any notion that the buck had stopped with him. Although it

---

276 Sharpton with Hunter, *Al on America,* 108.
277 Al Sharpton with Chiles, *The Rejected Stone,* 78.

was a book on "leadership," *Stone* was just another book on buffoonery. In fact, it was the original *biography of a buffoon*—portrait of an Al Sharpton still on active duty in the service of buffoonery, bereft of the slightest grasp of the "leadership" to which he'd long been a pretender.

The Obama Era

Don't part with your illusions. When they are gone
you may still exist, but you have ceased to live.

—MARK TWAIN[278]

*Former US president Barack Obama (second, R) holds a meeting with African American civil
rights leaders in the Roosevelt Room of the White House, February 18, 2014. Flanking
Obama are former Attorney General Eric Holder (L) and senior advisor Valerie Jarrett (R)
with Reverend Al Sharpton (L), president of National Action Network also attending. Obama
discussed how the administration could continue to further partner with the groups on issues
such as criminal justice reform, income inequality, and the Affordable Care Act. (Photo by
Mike Theiler/White House Pool (ISP Pool Images)/Corbis/VCG via Getty Images.)*

278 Pudd'nhead Wilson - The Wit and Wisdom of Mark Twain, 34.

SOME OF US often naïvely wish that people who run for public offices would do so by telling us the truth—that in a democracy with checks and balances, they can't single-handedly effectuate the changes they often promise in order to be elected. This is because their effectiveness is a function of their legislative acumen and leadership abilities—that rare ability to cajole, to convince, to make deals and trade-offs, and to be able to influence friends and opponents alike.

In its purest form, government in every society since time immemorial has been in the service of particular classes of people—invariably the ruling classes of the aristocratic nobility, the feudal-landed, the wealthy-plutocratic, the military-elite (junta), autocrats, kleptocrats, the bourgeois, and so forth. The "Third Estate" in France had revolted and abolished "privilege" only to put the revolution in the hands of the emerging bourgeoisie. In America, where we speak somewhat pretentiously of "democracy," it is still a government in service of a particular class—the empowered capitalists who govern with acquiescence in the name of the majority.

Those of us who recall our intro-to-philosophy college class on Jean-Jacques Rousseau's political writings, in particular, *The Social Contract*, will have known that governance in our type of democracy governs for what Rousseau had termed the "sovereign," meaning the majority—in our case, the white majority. In the same sense, ignoring pompous scholarly analyses, at the heart of "utilitarian" principles of men like Jeremy Bentham and later John Stuart Mill that influenced early American development, were frameworks for governing for the happiness of, and for the benefit ("greatest amount of good") of the majority.

So even setting race aside for a moment, democracy is still a system in which power and influence are derived by tending primarily to the economic interests and social well-being of the majority. In America's emotionally charged hyper-capitalistic democracy, money co-opts the malleable majority across the spectrum—Bubba and Becky, the so-called low information average white voters, while race isolates and separates the malleable minority—the all-inclusive black and brown voters of all stripes. There is, of course, the somewhat trite "coalition," language thrown about by the Democrats and the Left. But that only serves the minority interests and well-being where coalition partners wield actual power in governments—as the Liberal Democrats once did in the United Kingdom, the Green Party across Europe, or other leftist or rightist parties in southern Europe, such as Italy's Northern League of the 1990s.

But in the two-party system of America, black America is often the purchased "coal" in that Democratic coalition's fire, whereby it has to sit down and toe the line, not of its own interest but of the interests of the wider Democratic party ideology. This wider party ideology still tends to reflect the interests of the majority and other empowered minorities of the coalition—among which black America generally does not figure.

President Bill Clinton's 1994 Crime Bill, for example, was a legislative bull-dozer that tore through the heart and soul of black America. It codified inequal-ity in the legal treatment of black defendants, in particular, drug users—by exaggerating the penalties for drug-related crimes most endemic to the black community. Unlike today's drug epidemic affecting white America, which is viewed with sympathy as a health epidemic, back then black America's drug epidemic was criminalized as a near national security threat. The 1994 Crime Bill—by a Democratic administration with the full support of mainstream black legislators—inflated the definition of "criminal activities" and imposed exces-sive sentences for even minor drug use, such as for Marijuana, which is now legal in many states. Circumstances were such that enforcement of the law in certain areas became exercises in race-profiling, which meant carting off black youths to prison by the busload. The result has been the permanent exclusion of millions of African Americans from the economic system, from productive life, and from society at large in favor of penal institutions.

The 1994 Crime Bill was effectively a dragnet for many whose main crime was in being black and poor. It was the Democrats' effort to mollify the white majority's concern about spiraling drug use and crime. But it was to the detri-ment of large swaths of black America where families were torn apart—the result of which is a number of today's young adults having endured depraved upbringings in the system, bereft of fathers and even of mothers and of any sem-blance of normalcy since birth. Had a Republican president signed that Crime Bill, black Democrats in politics would've never yielded in their condemna-tion—the same way they've never yielded in condemning President Ronald Reagan for policies they'd deemed adverse to the black community in the 1980s.

Yet one by one, black elected officials all rushed to support Secretary Hillary Clinton in her primary battle against Senator Bernie Sanders in the 2016 election cycle. Even in the aftermath of her electoral defeat, Congressman John Lewis' birthday wishes to Mrs. Clinton addressed her as "Madame President." This loyalty of the black leadership to Clintons and the Democratic party highlights not only the anemic position of being a member of a coalition that works primarily for the interests of others and often to the exclusion of your own. It also highlights the effectiveness of coalitions at getting the least influential members to surrender loyalties to constituents in favor of the coalitions. For black America, it's been a near-totalitarian political experience—even with one of its own at the top.

Put another way, the so-called coalition hasn't worked out too well for black America for this reason but principally for another as well: Why would any person or institution extend valuable or meaningful resources and political capital on a product that's easily and cheaply acquired on the open market? In this sense, but for the fact that they were preambles to entry and to perfecting a racket, Reverend Sharpton's *pharaonic* arguments that the black vote was taken for granted by the Democrats were indeed valid.

So, ignoring the flowery rhetoric of dreams and the morally assuasive indignation and condemnations alike, power in American is still derived the way it has always been—by co-opting and serving the malleable majority while dividing and isolating the even more malleable minorities. The latter is generally bereft of the requisites of participation—numbers or wealth in order to wield influence. This doesn't mean that Americans stop believing in Emma Lazarus' "The New Colossus" or that we cease to embrace the aspirational King Dream. It just means that we must also face the realities of our conditions within the contexts of our existence.

As such, a few of us had held no illusions of President Barack Obama's abilities to transform black America in spite of that flowery rhetoric about "Change You Can Believe In" along with other extensive campaign stagecraft executed to convince black America that Dr. King's dream had finally been realized. On the other hand, though, even more of us were yet quite surprised at how little the president had tried.

African-American "Black" Exceptionalism

From one end of big city America to the other, there are columns of inner-city reservations inhabited by African Americans trapped and mired in multi-generational despair. We find the same, although in different forms in rural America. The black poverty rate of 25.8 percent in 2009 had climbed to 27.2 percent five years later, according to the Pew Research Center. The US Census Bureau showed that it had dropped to at 24.1 percent in 2015, but that had still left it at a level of more than twice that of the 11.6 percent for whites. Across all other major categories and indices—from earnings (median income), wealth, and education gap to crime rate disparities—the differences between black and white America remains staggering. These are just the facts; there's no suggestion that the issues weren't inherited or that they'd resulted from the president's tenure in office.

Yet a black America that had looked to the black president for specific help needed not only didn't get it but also didn't even hear the president articulate its concerns. Like the phantom David Dinkins first described by the Rev., it appeared as if Mr. Obama was afraid to remind America that he was black by showing that he'd had the interests of the black community at heart. This, by the way, isn't mutually exclusive to the interests of white America and others but just needs to be included.

As stated above, limited expectations had accompanied reasoned minds, but there's no denying that regardless of the spirited defenses and excuses offered by his supporters, President Obama had failed to explicitly articulate or address some of the key issues facing black America. This validated the theory Rousseau and other since then that government, especially in a democracy, is a servant of "interests"—of the economically empowered, of the majority, or of both.

Columbia University professor Fredrick C Harris termed the lack of presidential attention to the needs of black America during the Obama years as "African-American exceptionalism." Quite unlike "American exceptionalism" that deems America the greatest country on earth, or "French exceptionalism" that deems the French the most culturally sophisticated in the world, or even "British exceptionalism" that deems the Brits as supreme specimens and the great civilizers of earth, "African-American exceptionalism" in the Obama-era meant that blacks had willingly settled for almost nothing in exchange for the "race pride" that came with seeing a black face and a black family in the Oval Office. In other words, in its failure to hold its leaders and the black president tangibly accountable to it, black exceptionalism deems black America as anything but "exceptional."

In exchange for vicarious affirmations of racial pride, the black community that voted for the president in the highest proportions of all his constituent coalition ended up getting the least. And it was mostly OK with that—satisfied with symbolism but almost nothing tangible. Yet it remains in the continued deification of President Barack Obama up to the present. If you ask most African Americans what had the president done for the black community, the answer will invariably be that he'd passed "ObamaCare"—echoing the conservative belief that African Americans are the primary numerical or per capita beneficiaries of the Affordable Care Act. But what good is health insurance when your community is bereft of education, jobs, or adequate housing and is preyed upon by the repugnant agents of decadence, such as ignorance, violence, and crime?

In critiquing the lack of specific initiatives directed at black America in the era of the black president, Professor Harris said the following:

> As the argument goes, a focus on local activism will create change from the bottom up, allowing issues to move their way to national politics and, as a consequence, set the national agenda around community-focused issues. While activism should be encouraged at all levels of government, asking blacks to pursue such a narrow strategy amounts to what I would describe as African-American exceptionalism. That is to say, every other issue constituency within the political system can be encouraged to present their policy objectives—especially constituents that are part of the president's electoral coalition—directly to the president, except black voters.[279]

---

279 Fredrick C. Harris, *The Price of a Ticket: Barack Obama and the Rise and Decline of Black Politics* (Oxford University Press, 2012), xi–xii.

Put another way, unfulfilled demands and expectations of government were immediately suspended or deferred during President Obama's eight-year reign, during which deft connivance had seen the black elite, led by Reverend Sharpton and supported by the black media and political leaders, collude to suppress any such demands and expectations of the black president. For example, most African Americans have ignored the irony that the worst gutting of voting rights (Voting Rights Act-Section Four's preclearance provision) in a generation had occurred under President Obama's nose. Yet there was no valiant presidential push for new legislation to correct this; nor was there any overt pushing of the issue on the president or any lobbying of the Congress from Reverend Sharpton and other African-American politicians around the president. But in a few years when its disenfranchising effects will kick in to threaten their livelihoods, the responsibility and blame will be squarely parked at the feet of Republicans and others in power. The loudest voices of condemnation will be coming from black elected officials and their surrogates—all of whom had connived in silence during President Obama's tenure.

They will say that they would've never succeeded with the Republican-controlled Congress. But how would they know if they hadn't even tried, beyond lip service? Congressman John Lewis once led a sit-in to protest inaction on a gun-control bill, so why couldn't he have moved with the same valiance to restore protection of voting rights in the Southern states? Were this an issue that might affect his "safe seat" on the other hand, he and others in the same situation, would have likely led indignant in-Congress sit-ins on a weekly basis.

Brilliance and Cynicism

Were black America a Catholic population, there would be a clamoring today by some 90-percent of populous for Rome to start President Obama's beatification preparation tomorrow. This points to the essence of democracy in black America—it's largely a dictatorship modulated by the reelection of ineffective incumbents each election cycle, again, in exchange for a sense of racial pride. It's an arrested dictatorship well accepted by its people, and in this sense, the notion of democracy held by others must be admitted as a principal casualty of oppression for the oppressed. In this, we find brilliance and cynicism in black leadership at all levels—whether it be voter suppression for incumbents to win primary elections or even at the national level where a president might have elevated a flawed leader solely for comparative purposes.

In revisiting the "Marable irony," Reverend Sharpton's ascendancy under President Barack Obama might have just been a function of timing and a coincidence of events to the desired effect of controlling the fuse of a loose cannon. Or it could've been the result of well-placed cynicism and brilliance at play— the former, an agent acting on behalf of the latter.

President Barack Obama could've used his platform to catapult the next generation of black brilliance—a new generation of clean, educated, intelligent, and morally untainted black leaders—into the stratosphere as his lasting legacy. But instead, he embraced the Rev., even during a second term when he had no longer needed him. The president effectively swapped the dinosaur, Jesse Jackson, for the scoundrel Al Sharpton. This might have told us much about Mr. Obama that many would prefer to ignore—that he was just another politician, as cynical as he was brilliant.

The man who'd orchestrated the most effective political campaign of the modern era couldn't have failed to see that however dignified he might have been as president, with Reverend Sharpton at the podium of black leadership, the latter would've suffered immensely. How could Mr. Obama not have seen the inevitable "stench" to engulf black leadership with the visible ascendancy of a man as tainted as the Rev.? Here it's difficult to miss Mr. Obama's apparent indifference toward the notion of black leadership in general—beyond its utility to him as he'd climbed the political ladder and later when as president, he cultivated its subordination and servility to his administration for the duration of his tenure.

The president had reinforced upon black America the image it has long held of itself—inferior, cartoonish, and less than equal. Little appeared to have changed in the politics of the black vote since the nineteenth century. We'd seen yet another not so subtle affirmation of a belief in black America's deserved and therefore reserved second and third-class status in society during the Obama era. The difference was that it was now a black man atop the system, working on behalf of the Democrats to co-opt the "preacher-for-sale" and dispatching him and others to ensure black America's obedience and prolonged "wait."

In any case, Mr. Obama's legitimization and empowerment of the Rev. was black America's equivalent of the empowered extremes in the Middle East—those that have long captivated and taken their people hostage to mediocrity while thwarting possibilities of peace and prosperous futures. The exception here was that in captivating and taking black America hostage to his subterfuge and mediocrity, the Rev. was sanctioned by the most popular black man in America and the most powerful man and institution in the world—the president and the presidency of the United States. Add the Democratic Party apparatus to the mix and Sharpton's ennoblement and enablement was complete. Nationwide exposure on MSNBC then brought him full circle with near-stratospheric legitimization and imposition. But as in those parts of the world controlled by despots and demagogues, recent past and history, in general, have shown that a people led by the morally bankrupt, condemns itself, or is otherwise condemned to moral bankruptcy. And this is a history that the brilliant Mr. Obama knows all too well.

On the one hand, the Sharpton ascendancy might be viewed as a crude joke with cynicism leading the laughter, but on the other, it might also be seen as even diabolical when considered that the president might have sanctioned and elevated the flawed preacher precisely for comparative purposes. If Mr. Obama had seen it fit to occupy the space of the "dignified black man" solely by himself, such a dignity could only be further comparatively enhanced with the Rev. prominently placed in the public sphere. Where President Obama already stood tall in the eyes of many (Adonis for the Nubians across the land), when placed next to the (then) pudgy and (since) diminutive yet perpetually whimsical Rev., the president became a demigod. It was the type of stagecraft that would've invariably induced a figurative comparison to further elevate the already distinguished Mr. Obama on any given day. The sight and disposition of the often-reviled Reverend Sharpton might have then also served as a tacit reminder to white America of the type of black man the president was not—the type he could've been but had chosen not to be, the type they'd neither elected nor gotten as their president.

271

In addition to making history all around, President Obama's election had served two other principal purposes. It was black America's vicarious moment of transcendent assimilation, and it was liberal white America's moment of ultimate comfort and security—to feel good about itself and to feel further secured in pursuit of its *manifest destiny* of dominance, wealth, power, and happiness. His election was liberal America's ultimate outsourcing of its guilt because although it had elected a black man, it hadn't changed any fundamental aspect of its attitude and disposition toward racism or black oppression in America.

We never saw any decrease in racism across the liberal spectrum. But well-positioned blacks could then hardly complain. African Americans had no easier time functioning in places like New York or Massachusetts after Obama was president. Indeed, luminary bourgeois Henry Louis "Skip" Gates, a big man on campus at Harvard, was "shown his place" when he was arrested on his own property, at his front door, by a society that had still deemed him "suspicious" in Cambridge. It was, of course, an issue of "law & order" and not of race, because they'd elected a black a president and had dispatched enough silly black faces to the podium to spread the message of a "post-racial" America. So how could anyone have accused liberal America of racism in those days after it had just elected a black man as president?

So, the elevation of the boisterous Reverend Sharpton might have been the president's own reminder to the Democrats and Liberals that there was still blood in the streets and that he was the only real estate in town to be purchased. As he provided instant mollification, he might have also been ensuring his legacy as the "exceptional one." With Sharpton having his square of land in the town center, liberal white America could but move closer to Obama deification, much as black America had already done. It was the ultimate good-cop versus bad-cop optics—an earthly beatification through comparative indignation.

Contemporary Overseer

With the election of America's first black president, many African Americans had rightfully felt a genuine change on the horizon. But this wasn't to be. The black Brahmins sitting atop a presidium encircling the president immediately set out to co-opt his relationship with black America. Like a Praetorian guard, the Rev. had tasked himself to lead the charge. Soon after the 2008 elections, he took responsibility for providing "cover" for Mr. Obama—effectively "bogarting" the ultimate symbol of black bourgeois arrival to the absolute economic, political, and social detriment of the larger black community. The moment Sharpton and other black elites had tasted a little of the prestige of power via White House invitations, they, along with the black media, commenced their conniving to enable their own narrow self-interests and the elevation of their own social statures by abrogating presidential accountability to the wider black community. President Barack Obama was *their* president, not the (black) peoples'. It was an orchestrated "black exceptionalism" on steroids.

Their objective was straightforward—the imposition of a feudal-type gag order on African Americans to ensure little or no vocal criticisms of the president's focus or lack thereof on the issues affecting the black community. As the principal architect of the effort, the Rev., at once Pit Bull and Rottweiler, then ring-fenced the president by constructing a sort of *Maginot Line* that separated Mr. Obama from the broader concerns of his race. During the eight years of Obama's presidency, Sharpton took it upon himself to lead a vehement embargo on the free speech of black America. The preoccupation was with "protecting the president"—from black folks who might grumble. Aspirations were to be immediately deferred or sacrificed, but as there was history in the making with a black face in the White House, it was mostly OK with black folk.

While the rest of America had elected and had gotten a president who was African American, Reverend Sharpton and others informed black America that it had elected and had gotten Kim Jong–*Something*. No interrogation of the president's commitment to black America was to be tolerated, lest it will be viewed as a sell-out of the race by "self-hating" blacks. Grumbles of displeasure with the president's lack of direct initiatives or questions as to the return on investment on the black vote were soundly rejected as traitorous. The dictum was equally straightforward: *Sit your behind down and shut up!* The movement for equality had passed its active phase into the mature stage of holding power. Its leaders, therefore, moved to command the absolute obedience of the masses. It was a page taken directly from Eric Hoffer's *The True Believer*.

With 2013's *Stone*, Sharpton, the self-proclaimed "new man," then showed himself to be the same old vituperative vicar bearing much vengeance. The anachronistic mindset was still at work. As to any efforts at presidential accountability, Sharpton was outright dismissive:

> I've heard a scholar criticize [Obama] by saying he doesn't understand the legacy of Dr. King and Ella Baker. When I heard that, I thought, He's not trying to be Dr. King and Ella Baker. He's trying to be John Kennedy and Lyndon Johnson. Civil rights leaders like me, we're trying to be Dr. King and Ella Baker. Once you understand that distinction, you have a much clearer picture of Barack Obama and his relationship to the black community. He wasn't trying to be Booker T. Washington; he was trying to be George Washington.[280]

The scholar was likely professor Cornel West. Sharpton, who, on his return from Africa many years before, had previously advocated an industrial education for African Americans. Now he was telling the black community to understand that the black president wasn't trying to be like the black "Washington" who was responsible for pumping millions of northern philanthropic dollars into needed industrial education of emancipated blacks but was instead trying to be like that other "Washington"—the white Founding Father.

Needless to say, any comparison of contemporary presidents to George Washington is abject buffoonery, but Sharpton *a la* Daddy Grace or Father Divine had again remerged to denigrate and educate the "po' lowly negroes" with the nerves to question President Barack Obama's commitment. According to the Rev., they'd failed to understand the black man in the White House and his purpose. It was a new day in America but the same old one for black America. The empowered class of African Americans was still silencing the masses—this time by the perfection and imposition of the ultimate Trojan horse.

As has been the relationship between elected black politicians and their constituent, "black exceptionalism" had mandated the visceral obedience of the black masses to the black president. Awash in sentimental pride, the black man or woman would've been crazy to not have fallen in line—especially when the

---

280 Al Sharpton with Chiles, *The Rejected Stone*, 194.

choice was the white Democrat or the white "racist" Republican Congress. The latter has long served and governed to the exclusion of black interests—quite possibly because it hasn't gotten the black vote in a while, so it's a vicious cycle that nonetheless hems in the black voter. As the numerous elected black leaders who serve and govern to the tune of their own interests and to the exclusion of black interests at large is never a factor of consideration, it all added up to a kind of conniving depredation. In exchange for silencing the wider black community, the Rev. and others got their bread well-buttered in that their thriving business—grassroots activism, television jobs, and so on, had remained untouched and made even more lucrative. As they ascribed blame to the Republican congressional opposition, black America got much inspiring rhetoric but almost nothing in terms of specific initiatives.

As it stood by and watched significant executive orders peeled off for others, such as Latinos, gays, and women, black America got hardly anything of significance. It got the pardoning and commuting of a few unjustly harsh prison sentences of men convicted of drugs and other offenses, and for that, its adoration of President Obama skyrocketed—an example of the low standards of expectation, notwithstanding the happiness of the released and their families. Elsewhere, there were the bourgeois accoutrements and empty ostentation of "the most beautiful First Family," "the classiest president ever"—as if anyone had been around since 1789. "President Obama is so dignified" soon became the calling card of vicarious black pride in its misplaced priorities and rejection of utility. Dignity, class, or beauty has never translated into economic revival or improved social conditions of any people in modern societies. Instead, they were replicated memes of a well-orchestrated vicarious mirage by overnight illusionists—Reverend Sharpton, the coterie of black political leadership, and the black media.

In 2012, *Newsweek* magazine called Mr. Obama "The First Gay President." His labor secretary (and current DNC Chair) Tom Perez once told Politico.com that, "When I reflect on the breadth and depth of what he has done for Latinos, it really makes him, in my mind, and in the minds of so many others, the first Latino president." Enrique Peña Nieto must have been jealous.

While African Americans had in large part agreed that the president's executive orders for others were the right thing to have done, many had still wondered why was there nothing major for black America. When would President Obama be the "First Black President" as well? Besides, executive orders—real or symbolic—require no congressional approval. In the meantime, the Rev. posited himself as a domestic policy advisor to the president on anything from the Trayvon Martin murder case in Florida to health care legislation—for which he claimed to have supposedly been attacked by the Left, "for being too close to the president." Yet as he bragged of his proximity to President Obama, Sharpton had failed to register his own declaration of uselessness:

> If I'm attacked from the left—people saying, "You're too close to Obama, you're becoming a part of the system"—my response will be, "OK, got it. But I need to get this Trayvon Martin case in court." Or, "OK, I heard you but I need to help the President with health care."[281]

The Trayvon Martin court case in Florida had come about from social media-driven public outrage, not from Reverend Sharpton. As there were no federal charges brought against Martin's killer, a reasonable conclusion is that the Rev. was of no importance in the process at the federal level. He'd had zero influence within the White House, zero influence within a Justice Department led by an attorney general who'd once been a visiting supplicant to his Harlem compound.

As for "helping the president with health care" and other legislative issues for which he's asserted an important role, the Rev. has never been capable of organizing or mustering anything resembling a lobbying effort to deliver any legislative votes for passage of anything in Congress. This, because outside of a possible few "friends" within the Congressional Black Caucus who seek his endorsement come election time and avoid him the remaining eighteen to twenty months, he has forever been toxic on Capitol Hill. He's even attested to delivering petitions to Washington for investigations—none of which have ever been acted upon. But in telling us of those delivered petitions, he was satisfied in highlighting his importance.

---

281 Ibid., 120.

We then got bullying and the dispensing of near Mafiosi-type intimidation, in which Sharpton shamelessly further insulted the intelligence of African Americans:

> When I hear people in the black community take umbrage at the notion that he's not the President of black America but the President of all America, I feel insulted because it feels to me as if we're saying that this black man should be loyal just to us, rather than giving him space to run the world.[282]

Here, the Rev. established a standard of exclusionary conflation that was pure hypocrisy. In the same way that young activists are often forced to point out that *black lives matter* doesn't mean that *other lives do not*, black need for presidential accountability during the Obama years didn't mean an expectation that the president shouldn't have been president of all of America or been allowed the "space to run the world." And Sharpton understood this perfectly. Black critics of the president had never suggested that President Barack Obama not be president of all America, nor had they ever attempted to infringe on his "space to run the world." A few had just suggested that he be president of black America *too*. But Reverend Sharpton still wasn't buying the arguments of those in the black community who'd criticized the president:

> I kept hearing…He did stuff for Latinos, such as protection for the children of some undocumented immigrants; he did stuff for gays, such as stopping "Don't Ask, Don't Tell," and supporting same-sex marriage; he did stuff for women, such as the Lilly Ledbetter Fair Pay Act, which helps women seek equal pay.[283]

In typical Sharpton fashion, he'd mangled his position so much that he ended up supporting his opponents':

> But my response was, yeah, and the women's groups brought him Lilly Ledbetter, gay groups fought for same-sex marriage, Latino groups brought him the DREAM Act

---

282 Ibid., 194.
283 Ibid., 198–99.

and immigration reform, and I even led a march with them in Arizona. He didn't just sit down on his own and just pull this stuff from his imagination. They all brought these issues to him. So what the black activists are saying is, because he's black, they want him to write the black agenda and bring it to himself? And then if I meet with him and talk about a Black agenda, I'm too close, and I'm a sellout?[284]

No one had accused Sharpton of being a sell-out for meeting and discussing the "black agenda" with the president; they'd accused him of being a sell-out for meeting and discussing the Sharpton agenda with the president. Yet in the midst of this, he never missed the chance to extol his bona fides to the fast-growing Latino community. In telling us that Latinos were the ones who'd brought the president the DREAM Act, he made the unremarkable comment that "I even led a march with them in Arizona." In both tone and substance, the race leader was proud to tout his actions on behalf of those who might have voluntarily crossed the border in the last two or three decades. Yet punted on any obligation to act on behalf of those who were kidnapped, stolen, and brought here against their will between the second decade of the seventeenth century and the first of the nineteenth.

It was yet another revelatory moment. The man who'd claimed service to his people since age four had shown himself bereft of emotional intelligence and self-awareness by proudly, yet shamelessly, listing a slew of deliveries by the black president to various constituencies without being able to list a single item specifically aimed at his own community. Sharpton had shown power being wielded by other major constituent groups in the Obama coalition but none by his own, especially after repeatedly presenting the president as his "good friend." Was America to accept that Dr. King's people had no longer DREAMED? Where was their ACT?

Nonetheless, this had unsurprisingly contradicted his previous position where he'd shown that there was a black "leadership" charged with bringing issues of black America to the president, and it was in fact leaders of the NAACP, the Urban League, and the Reverend Sharpton, among others. On the previous page of the same book he'd told us that he'd indeed gotten together with the

284 Ibid.

heads of those organizations to craft a "black agenda" to bring to the president in his second term (the famous, *wait until his second term!*):

> After Obama's re-election, I got together with other black leaders such as Ben Jealous of the NAACP and Marc Morial of the National Urban League to craft a Black agenda to bring to the President. I think it is something that we should have done earlier, during his first term.[285]

Again, this was classic Sharpton buffoonery. On the one hand, he laid claim to having actually crafted a "black agenda" with the NAACP and Urban League honchos to give to the president—earlier implying having discussed this agenda with the president but telling us nothing of its contents or of whatever became of it. Yet, on the other, he then blamed so-called black activists for failing to craft an agenda as gays, Latinos, and women had done.

In March 2010, speaking of a February meeting with the president, the Rev. told the *Grio* that, "To meet about black unemployment is a black agenda unless you feel the black unemployed don't count. You can't get a blacker agenda to me." Whatever that "black agenda" might have been, specific policy initiatives were never publicly revealed nor acted on. In that same March 2010 interview with the *Grio*, National Urban League boss Marc Morial was on the defensive, echoing Sharpton in refuting any criticism of the president:

> [It's] a difference between being in the press box, being in the fancy suites at a football game and being down on the field. And I think where I am, where Rev. Sharpton is, is down on the field helping to move the ball forward [for African-Americans]."

For his part, Mr. Morial would later feign a resolve to push the president harder. In 2011 he too was among the collective of other black leaders who'd demanded and received a meeting with the president at the White House, where they presented a policy wish list of teen summer jobs programs, job training programs, and job placement programs to spur economic development and reinvigorate

---

285 Ibid., 198.

the black community. Then, Mr. Morial told us that he'd attended the meeting to tell the president that, "There is so much more that needs to be done." Of the president, Morial then claimed, "He heard us, listened and acted." President Obama had supposedly included five of their provisions in his overall jobs program to Congress, where it all stalled.

If there had indeed been a goalpost, neither Sharpton nor Morial had moved the ball an inch closer. Yet as the self-proclaimed black leader, the Rev. used his book to absolve himself of any responsibility for the absence of specific presidential initiatives from the African American in the Oval office aimed at black America. Instead, Sharpton blamed so-called black activists, whose job it was (not his) for bringing issues facing black America to the president's desk—as Latinos, gays, and women had done. Read another way, black activists were lazy while hard-working white women, gays, and Latinos had done the necessary legwork to get their agenda actioned.

Reverend Sharpton's sentiments encapsulated the black leadership's bankrupt mindset and highlighted its ineffectiveness. By this reasoning, if it had wanted President Obama to show it some love, black America should've made and delivered its own list of concerns to the black man from Chicago with a television in the White House. Why would there have been a need to tell the former community organizer Obama anything about the issues facing black America? Unless of course, as his Republican detractors and others have alleged, he's not "of black America."

As this was in a Sharpton book that proffered his leadership ideas, it was natural that the Rev. had failed to adequately interrogate himself on the role he'd actually played in that dynamic. As an "insider," he'd made no effort to mask his abject uselessness—his utter waste of time and space he'd occupied.

Twenty-First-Century Demagogue

Inherent in the long history of racism in America is the racist and derogatory portrayals of African Americans in newspapers and other media. With their so-called Negro dialect, nineteenth-century writers, such as Thomas Nelson Page, William P. Calhoun, Thomas Dixon, and Henry Stillwell-Edwards, had given rise to popular stereotypes that had become household. Prominent black writer and lawyer of the era, Charles Waddell Chesnutt, had taken exception to these portrayals, explaining that,

> The fact is, of course, that there is no such thing as a Negro dialect; that what we call by that name is an attempt to express, with such a degree of phonetic correctness as to suggest the sound, English pronounced as an ignorant old southern Negro would be supposed to speak it.[286]

These portrayals—staple of mainstream newspapers and magazines for a long time, were described by *Negro* intellectual Rayford Logan as invariably that of the noble savage or the sad mulatto. One such example was a Henry Stillwell-Edward's character, Isam. Isam often went fishing when told to pay his poll tax. One day, his former master had tried encouraging him to pay it so that he could vote, by scholarly telling him, "Isam, you have a voice in the management of this great nation and the development of your own race. What could be better than that?" Isam responded as any noble savage or sad mulatto would. It was simple enough, "Yas suh," he said. "Fried catfish!"[287]

In the twenty-first century, Reverend Sharpton wasn't beyond evoking nineteenth-century racial stereotypes to discredit his own community. He'd still viewed black America as a community of Isams, wherein issues always come down to frying catfish or fish frying of any kind. To him, those in the black community who might've been upset at being ignored by the democratic process had to have been contemporary Isams with fried fish on the brain; any discord had to have had something to do with a fish fry. Accordingly, the Rev. was so upset at the muted mumbles of black discontent with their circumstances under President Obama that he took a stereotypical cannon from the nineteenth century and fired it straight into the twenty-first:

> I think a lot of the criticism was coming from a place of insecurity, almost like the nervous high school kid who likes the pretty girl but isn't sure if he's good enough for her, so instead of asking her out, he's going to wait for her to call him

---

286 Rayford Logan, *The Betrayal of the Negro* (Da Capo Press, 1954), 240.
287 Ibid., 377.

to prove she really likes him...Sometimes the tone of the Obama criticisms felt as if critics were saying "He didn't come by my fish fry, so I'm going to attack him."[288]

With an infinite capacity to insult, this was the level of debasement the black leader had accorded his community in 2013. Yet it was but one example of his genuine belief that President Barack Obama was the Robert Mugabe or the Yoweri Museveni of black America, or at least he and others would've liked the president to have been as such. But the Rev. didn't stop there. In an almost confessional reproach, he then projected his own specialty onto others by decrying Obama's black critics as having been bought and paid for. "Come on," he said. "Are you kidding me? Just tell the truth...Say you don't agree with him or you don't like him or some Republican gave you some money to attack him.[289]

Given his own conduct over the years, it was natural that Sharpton would've seen others from his own perspective. The motives that he ascribed to others were the ones to which he subscribed. He'd certainly gotten paid to launch protests, to level criticisms, and even to mount a mole presidential campaign. So why would those Obama critics be any different?

The Long Wait

There is a hope that acts as an explosive, and a hope that disciplines and infuses patience. The difference is between the immediate hope and the distant hope. A rising mass movement preaches immediate hope. It is intent on stirring its followers to action, and it is the around-the-corner brand of hope that prompts people to act. Later, as the movement comes into possession of power, the emphasis is shifted to the distant hope—the dream and the vision...it prizes obedience and patience.[290]

---

288 Al Sharpton with Chiles, *The Rejected Stone*, 198–99.
289 Ibid., 201.
290 Eric Hoffer, *The True Believer* (Harper Collins, New York, 1951), 30.

Writer James Baldwin once echoed black America's frustration when he told us of his impatience and bewilderedness at the perpetual expectation that African Americans should *"wait"*—wait for things to change, wait for equality, wait for dignity, wait for their human rights to be respected, and for their civil rights to be protected and enforced. Baldwin had then asked, "Why should I wait any longer?"

The often-overlooked part of Baldwin's frustration is that those who'd always counseled him to wait were the well-placed self-serving blacks whose job it was to calm the nerves of an anxious white America fearful of threats and disruptions to its way of life by black demands for equality and even for justice. It's an even bet that Baldwin's frustration was aggravated by knowing that the protracted *wait* for black America was perfected as art by its own agents. The black preachers who were dispatched in the aftermath of Emancipation to get new landowners to sign away their land for life as sharecroppers on the very land they'd inherited, weren't just the messengers of the *wait* of a free people but were instead its choreographers and orchestrators as well.

And so it was interesting yet unsurprising to see the Rev. and other black surrogates master the handling of black impatience during President Obama's first term. At each turn, they provided the answer to Baldwin's question by telling black America that, *the president's hands are tied. Just wait for his second term.* A confused black America then quickly accepted its place in the catacombs of the protracted *wait* by reminding itself that it had elected a president whose survival to a second term—paramount to his legacy—had primarily depended on doing nothing for it in the first place. Again, "black exceptionalism" mandated the prioritization of the black presidential legacy over the well-being of the black community.

Yet by President Obama's second term, the Rev. and his cohorts then moved to Plan B—they perfected the blaming of the intransigent Republican opposition in Congress for Mr. Obama's continued inaction on black America's behalf. But while ascribing blame to Republicans for blocking the president's legislative agenda was valid, the real damage was already done by a first-term failure to act when President Obama had had both houses of Congress for two years. *To wit*—he'd delivered the Lilly Ledbetter Fair Pay Act within a few weeks of being sworn in.

The Rev and his cohorts were like the bookies who'd talked their clients into pre-betting on a horse running in the Saturday afternoon derby knowing full well that the same horse would've first been racing in that Saturday morning's steeplechase as well. When the horse limps in dead last in the afternoon derby, the bookies all of a sudden remember the early morning steeplechase; it's the reason their clients have lost money. The horse was beaten up, almost crippled before the derby gates had even flung open. *What happened?* Asked the stunned clients. *That darned steeplechase,* one of the bookies responded as he shook his head.

That the Republican opposition had blocked the Obama agenda or opposed any initiatives intended for black America was unremarkable for anyone with a brain. What else could've been expected? The black leadership has not worked to cultivate a single friend among the majority Republican congressional opposition over the years, and black America has voted Democratic for the last fifty years or more. That "modulated" black dictatorship to which I made earlier reference isn't only encouraged by black leadership but is sustained and maintained by black America's refusal to accept the realities of the two-party democracy in America: you feast when your party has power and see famine when it doesn't. In the case of black America, though, there's an exception; it experiences a retrograde famine even when its party—the Democratic party—is in power.

So, congressional Republican intransigence should've long been baked into the price of the black presidential stock in the first place and was therefore not a valid fallback excuse in President Obama's second term. Why would the opposition Republicans support or deliver agendas for those who don't vote for them? Black Republicans are taken care of individually or as small groups. "Interests" is not only the governing principle of nations, but it's also the governing impetus of power and therefore of politics as well. To pretentiously believe otherwise is fanciful and ineffective.

But this goes to the heart of another aspect of men like Reverend Sharpton and the coterie of black leadership in America. They constitute a magisterium that thrives on moral indignation in a society that mandates material practicality. They often feel little obligation to do hard work on behalf of their people as long as they remain steadfastly indignant of their people's condition—steadfastly indignant about that which they do little to ameliorate in the first place.

For Sharpton and others, White House access had translated to corporate board appointments, university jobs, elevation as "public intellectuals," political consultancies, television appearances as hosts, contributors, commentators, and the like. So while the president had single-handedly enhanced their own positions, enhancing the condition of the masses in any significant way had required congressional legislation, above and beyond executive orders, which wasn't in the cards in any case. Yet even after a first midterm electoral washout for Mr. Obama's party in Congress, the conniving black cognoscenti continued to tell black America to wait, as it continued to rack up its White House invitations, its interviews, and its "selfies" with the president and First Lady.

What then could the "bottom-up" activism of Reverend Sharpton and the black intelligentsia have produced for the black community, without any legislative influence in Congress? The answer is nothing. Their uselessness combined with the futility in banking black America's fortunes on one party in a two-party democracy (being the "coal" in that one-party coalition), was on full display during the Obama years. Again, that one-party Democratic coalition has been to their benefit, although to the detriment of the people they claim to represent. There's no suggestion that black America should run out and start voting Republican, but it should definitely run out and force both parties to compete for its vote.

So, with so-called leadership based on the "emotional" and valuing the intangible, it sufficed to simply make noise, to posture indignation at the racist "others." Influencing legislative promulgation, on the other hand, requires rational and tangible hard work and the heavy lifting that neither Sharpton nor his cohorts were willing to undertake, which is unsurprising. Who in their right mind could be expected to work at destroying their own livelihood?

Professor Harris, who's no doubt a James Baldwin fan, had also noted the following:

> This exceptionalism is grounded in the false—and disingenuous—idea that just because the president "happens to be black" that black voters and other advocates of racial equality should not expect the president to respond to policy issues aimed directly at addressing the persistence of racial inequality. Those supporting the idea of black exceptionalism are asking black voters and black political elites to suspend their rights as citizens.[291]

---

291 Fredrick C. Harris, *The Price of a Ticket* (Oxford University Press, 2012), xi–xii.

Although the truth, in theory, it's a theory that assumes *a priori*, a genuine concern for the black community by its advocates like the Rev. and others who'd thrived during the Obama era. But it's hard to assume any such genuine concern, given that the business of activism requires that massive disfavored underclass for which to "advocate." From Sharpton's own words in *Stone*, it was clear that the black political elite was primarily responsible for orchestrating the "black exceptionalism" during that time. They'd ensured that the president didn't address specific policy concerns and that where any such policy concerns were delivered to him, they were understood to be mere window dressing in the first place. Sharpton, the man schooled in emotional hostage-taking by ensuring public embarrassment for the cameras since high school, had ensured that no lobbying efforts or grassroots public pressure was brought to bear on *his* president or his administration. Instead, he seemed to have spent his time in an admiration society, later tell us in his book about the "wonderfulness" of the Obama administration and of the people in it, including presidential assistant Valerie Jarrett, who'd treated him so well.

So, while a magazine like *Rolling Stone* had hailed Mr. Obama as one of the greatest presidents ever, black America was not allowed to question the meaning of "greatest" as this was viewed as traitorous. It was not allowed to question the high unemployment rates among black males, not allowed to inquire if President Barack Obama had maintained George W. Bush's level of commitment to fighting AIDS in Africa, and so on. Instead, the black community was still being asked to "wait"—this time by the Rev. and others who'd merely continued a long history of African-American betrayal at the hands of the empowered among them.

False Equivalences and Reduction of a President

To fully appreciate the hypocrisy of Sharpton and other black surrogates during the Obama presidency, it's worth taking a look at their pre- and post-election behavior. During the 2008 election campaign, the Rev. and others were all over television parroting the white progressive talking points given to them. The long primary battle between Senators Obama and Clinton was good for Mr. Obama, they said because it would've made him a better general election candidate and a better president. But once Mr. Obama became president, this same group saw things differently—as far as black America was concerned. Like a new convert to a religion (the black insider class), the Rev. was as zealous as he was fanatical in his assumed role as chief defender of the president. He gleefully led the chocolate Mafia's unleash of a campaign to nuzzle black America and to relinquish black folks of their rights as equal participants in the democracy.

Straight out the gate, Sharpton had established a dialectic of false equivalences by declaring that he would never say anything that could've harmed President Obama. Early on in his radio show, he effectively threatened to go after African Americans who would dare to criticize President Obama. Looking back at his own conduct, in *Stone*, the Rev. claimed that it would take scholars years to figure out if his interactions with the first African American head of state had been appropriate, as he'd had to grapple with the question of, "How do you hold him accountable without undermining him at the same time?"[292] But if he were genuinely unsure of how to hold the president accountable, why had he worked so hard at suppressing the rights and abilities of others to do so by mandating such obedience from black America?

By his logic, white criticism had made Mr. Obama a better candidate and a better president, but black criticism would've undermined and harmed him by playing into the hands of his enemies. Presumably, asking for direct actions targeting youth unemployment, education, and training programs, or empowerment zones with tax incentives for business to invest on Martin Luther King Jr. boulevard, and the like, had equated to calling the president a socialist or a Muslim—his enemies' preferred nouns of choice. To Reverend Sharpton and others, for African Americans to have questioned the net-positive or -negative impact of the Obama presidency was a surefire sign of traitorous self-haters.

But the truth is that there were two parallel tracks on which we had mutually exclusive trains. An honest questioning of the president's policies, or lack thereof, toward black America, didn't negate the fact that the president had had real enemies in Congress whose top priority, beyond their initial indifference to black issues, was to deny the first black president any significant policy success

---

292 Al Sharpton with Chiles, *The Rejected Stone*, 195.

or legacy. Indeed, the senior senator from Kentucky, Mitch McConnell, had told us as much before the ink had even dried on the voting ballots. Why, therefore, conflate the two? Why equate black demands for accountability with aiding President Obama's enemies—people who'd needed no aid in their enmity of the president under any circumstances?

As many African Americans had already known of Sharpton's sentiments and treatment of those he'd deemed Uncle Toms, with a few exceptions on the Left, most of the black community just followed suit by sitting down and shutting up. (Black conservatives herein excluded, as they earn their livelihood mimicking Sharpton-type demagoguery on the right, in their critique of Democrats and of Mr. Obama—fairly unfairly). No one had wanted the Rev. out there calling them an Uncle Tom in the pockets of racist supremacists, so the silent plurality stayed silent.

Unsurprisingly, it worked like a charm. Sharpton's sentiments soon became widely accepted and deeply ingrained in the conscious of the masses, whose sense of nothingness was often deferred by projecting themselves into importance and relevance vis-à-vis the "classy" African American First Family in the White House. It was a brilliant strategy; the Rev. and others had succeeded in convincing much of the black community to affirm its own irrelevance by decoupling its voice from its vote. In no time, the significance of the Obama presidency for many black mothers had started and stopped at *knowing that their sons could grow up to one day be President*. A fecund meme had set in, replicating itself like wildfire in no time.

The intellectual class then preoccupied itself with obfuscation, showing little bounds to its own cultivated deficient reasoning—an ingrained, near involuntary connivance. A prominent African American intellectual I'd engaged while developing this chapter told me the following:

> You should know that a black man cannot govern a white nation as if it were a black nation; you folks are confusing the USA with a black nation. He stood up for a black man [professor Gates] wrongfully arrested at his front door and lost white support for the rest of his two terms. Who could expect him to pay any attention to black folks after that? Are you suggesting that he should have used his first term majority to create programs for black people—programs that would

have ensured he would not be re-elected? Where is the politics in that? What kind of victory would that have been?

He certainly is no shrinking violet and is indeed a fierce advocate of his community, so the ease with which his class of blacks had come to value politicking in the big leagues over the politics of black improvement was perplexing, but yet again, just another element of "black exceptionalism." In speaking of President Obama's legacy on black America, a good friend—another African American intellectual who I also know to care passionately for his community, told me, "When you say Obama did nothing for blacks, you act like blacks have to be given something special. We are past the days of black folks getting any special treatment." He is also someone I know to still be an ardent defender of black interests and programs, including Affirmative Action.

But it wasn't just the intellectuals; the average man and woman in the street had also become overnight experts in civics, or so they'd believed, and they echoed the Sharpton talking points to near perfection. In questioning President Obama's commitment to black America in a Facebook post, I was asked by another African American, "You're are black? Right?" A member of my own family admonished me for even questioning whether or not the Obama presidency had brought black America any significant "change to believe in," beyond cosmetics:

> The president can't do anything without Congress. It is Congress that passes laws. He's not the president of Black America, you know. Why are black folks now looking for a handout from the government? You should know better.

Elsewhere, the foremost conniving force and master illusionist in black America—the pretentious black media—did its best to orchestrate the mirage. One public personality had no reservations in echoing the sentiments over the airwaves: "So what? Black folks have been silent for decades, and all of a sudden, they feel like they have a voice 'cause a brother's in the house?"

Such was the greatness of the Obama presidency that it had inspired much of the black intelligentsia to abandon overnight its long-treasured claims on the federal government, just because an African American was then in charge.

Through the conflation and false equivalences of surrogates like the Rev., the aspirations of the black masses had come to be seen—by black folk themselves—as the dreaded "special interest." At once, most had temporarily renounced lifetime beliefs in the need for specific government actions for their people. General affirmative actions that they'd championed up to 2007 and would return to championing after 2016 had become anachronisms during the years in between.

But the equivalences were false and at odds with the blame that black America had ascribed to, and the claims it had made of previous presidents. Ronald Reagan's policies were said to have decimated the poor, in particular, black America; the policies were Reagan's; he'd set the agenda and owned its execution. But according to the black intelligentsia and the man in the street, not so with Barack Obama. The election of the African American as president had seen the furtherance of blame still ascribed to white America—even for the black president's failure to articulate any specific issues within the black community. It was still the white man's fault; they'd even owned President Obama's tongue.

Reverend Sharpton, who'd spent much ink in *Pharaoh* denouncing the same behavior in both political and private arenas, was now busy denying his old self. Back then he'd had very harsh words for the Democratic Party, for President Bill Clinton, and for the Reverend Jesse Jackson for not demanding more of Clinton for the black community. In the private arena, he'd condemned the other Jacksons—the family of entertainers—for once having attempted to exclude African Americans (Sharpton himself) from economic participation in their concert tour. Recalling the time when he'd had to set Michael Jackson and the Jackson family straight about their obligations to the black community, Sharpton had told of seeking a role in the promotion of the "Victory Tour." When a member of the family had had the temerity to ask, "Why do we need black promoters at all?" He turned and asked, "You call this a victory tour? Whose victory is it? Is it a victory for all those kids who supported them when they were on the black chitlin'[*sic*] circuit?"[293]

Yet during the Obama years, the Rev. could not understand why African Americans, who'd consistently lagged at the bottom in every aspect of American

---

293 Al Sharpton and Walton, *Go and Tell Pharaoh*, 84.

life, who'd suffered the most in the last recession, and who'd held the highest hopes for an Obama presidency, would've wanted to closely engage the first black president on specific policy initiatives or other solutions to some of their issues. Once given the chance, Sharpton formed his own collective chitlin' squad of Obama surrogates and set out as contemporary paddy rollers to patrol and contain his community's exercise of a fundamental democratic principle—its freedom of thought and speech.

But a man capable enough to have been twice elected leader of the free world had needed no "black-prohibiting" barriers to inoculate him from the usual democratic interrogation by a segment of the people. Sharpton and others had made President Obama appear as an affirmative action president—put there by a mandate of the Electoral College and not having twice been popularly elected. With their *Maginot Line*, they painted the president and his presidency as implicitly weak. He was hardly in control, near incapacitated. Listening to them, it was easy to believe that the Republican Congress was running the executive branch and not the president and his cabinet. The powers of the Oval Office were suspended—as far as black America was concerned.

To their constituents, Sharpton and others represented the failure of exercising executive power as the absence of executive power, solely because a black man was the commanding executive officer. They erected a diminished capacity for the president by making him out to be less like himself and more like them. He was made to appear implicitly weak because he was black and explicitly subjected to reduced standards because he was one of them. They ended up imposing upon President Barack Obama, the curse of low expectations that they'd held of themselves. The president was made akin to just another member of the Congressional Black Caucus that has traditionally viewed black constituent accountability with disdain—as being beneath it. As Sharpton had condemned the Congressional Black Caucus as useless in *Pharaoh*, he'd now set out to render President Obama, albeit stealthily, just as useless to black America.

The Rev.'s payoff was big. He was now hosting the president and senior members of the administration at his National Action Network's Harlem compound or at his gala affairs. The entire Democratic electoral elite of New York quickly fell in line—all of whom, including a governor whose father and grandmother had once been on the receiving end of the Sharpton tongue and Secretary Clinton, whose husband had been equally treated, then became overnight Sharpton supplicants. Along with their visits while holding their noses, was likely donations, grants, program sponsorships, and so on.

In the end, the Rev. and President Obama's other African American surrogates had joined the black media in becoming master illusionists over the black community. They were able to convince black America of how far it had come by showing it how little it had mattered—nearly irrelevant in the concerns of a national government headed by a black man. It wasn't just a reduction of the president and of the presidency but also an abrogation of any belief in equality for black America.

In an ideal world, black America might stop voting for, or remove from office, black politicians who use racism as an excuse for their inaction on behalf of their communities. Because they run for offices on electoral contracts to *try* to effectuate changes in the face of racism in the first place. It's like hiring an "expert" plumber who then tells you, after taking your money, that your clog is too big for him to fix because your pipes are old. But that was your reason for hiring him in the first place—to fix difficult clogs caused by old pipes. For some African-American politicians, though, trying and failing would be a quantum leap; many don't even try because they can always ascribe blame to racism. It is in this sense that legitimate criticism of President Barack Obama should never be about what he was or wasn't able to do for black America, but instead, it should be about what he didn't even try to do.

Unintended Consequences

TODAY, THE SPECTACLE of seeing the Rev. and the black political class return to being energized by the threat to their employment and livelihoods come 2018 and 2020 is hypocrisy defined, though nonetheless amusing. Although they'd had no issue suppressing black voices, thereby abrogating the value of the black vote while a black man had sat in the Oval Office, Republican voter suppression is again being heralded as a threat to the democracy. To have spent an entire adulthood accusing previous white presidents—Democrats and Republicans—of nearly everything under the sun, only to become chief conniver during the reign of the black one, wasn't even a blip on the Sharpton radar. But in doing so, the Rev. has ironically advanced the bidding of those who see no value in ameliorating black America's condition. He has also lent credence to long-entrenched racist views that black America demands "the world" of others while asking almost nothing of itself.

For example, at the ninth annual State of the Union address in 1970, President Richard Nixon had this to say to Congress and to the American people:

> We have been too tolerant of our surroundings and too willing to leave it to others to clean up our environment. It is time for those who make massive demands on society to make some minimal demands on themselves.

Many in black America had taken it personally, as a slur against them. Some were offended and horrified and had deemed it racist. But some four decades later, the presidency of an African American would see Reverend Sharpton and this generation of black leaders somewhat validate Richard Nixon's edict (if it were indeed meant as a racist attack), by attempting to block even minimal claims by the black community on the black occupant of the Oval Office. They'd set out to ensure that black America had made no such claim of itself during its turn at the podium as it had traditionally made of white America. Again, it was an abdication of usefulness and as earlier stated, an example of that old acculturation from slavery. It goes back to that proscription of introspection, responsibility, and accountability that denies individual agency in deference to the masters who are seen as the ones holding the solutions—the only ones capable of solving the issues. Where some black folks had once looked to the master for protection, it appears that many in contemporary black leadership still believe that only whites in government can provide solutions to issues, and are therefore the only ones to be held accountable.

By defraying the costs of seeking to solve some of its own problems during the reign of the black president, the Rev. and others among the conniving black leadership had shown that inequality, as a phenomenon in American society, isn't just an imposition upon black America by white America. In truth, it's often a reserved imposition by internal forces and an accepted one by its black victims as well. Prevalent within contemporary black leadership is the mindset of reserved double standards and reserved inferiority for its people. Many among its leadership are often the last to believe in equality for their own and the first to re-impose conditions of bondage upon them.

This aspect of "black exceptionalism" has opened the door for the potential of significant unintended consequences for a long time to come. The precedent of connivance has left black America bereft of the moral legitimacy to demand accountability of a future female, white, Asian, or Latino(a) president. They will be under no natural obligations to respond effectively, knowing that black leaders had willingly ceded presidential accountability to women, LGBTQ, Latinos, and others within the Democratic coalition in exchange for maintaining their White House gate pass. So, the Obama-era Al Sharpton might have ended up negating not only the future Reverend Sharpton but also the future of black leadership as well. Any influence they or he (in his quest for future "greatness,") might have dreamed of wielding has been diminished along with the moral standing to make any future claims of white America. An appropriate yet regrettable Trump or future administration's response might simply be: *If you all didn't press your guy on these issues, why press my administration and me? Why press us?*

In the end, the greater and ultimate unintended consequences of the Sharpton-led black intelligentsia's Obama era connivance might very well be the negation of the wider black leadership itself. Feckless in its decades-long leadership through moral suasion and high-minded indignation, black leadership is now so tainted and morally stained by the Sharpton stench, that it is now dissonantly near dead in its tracks—empty and ineffective beyond the high-posturing likes of Congresspersons Maxine Waters and John Lewis. Black leadership had fashioned a Trojan horse that has since turned around and kicked it into an impending grave.

Progressive "Parvenu"

Earn a character first if you can. And if you can't, assume one.

—Mark Twain[294]

Middle-age possibilities and impossibilities, trophy girlfriend, eating for greatness, retroactive reincarnations, and one last attack on Jesse Jackson, had all rounded out *The Rejected Stone's* epic Al Sharpton.

There is an excellent scene in the old classic movie, *The Life and Times of Judge Roy Bean*, where outlaw Sam Dodd was brought before the nineteenth-century self-appointed West Texas frontier Judge, Roy Bean, for killing a Chinese man. Dodd's defense to the judge was that there was no law against killing Chinese [*paraphrase*], Indian, blacks [*paraphrase*], "greasers," and so on. Judge Bean responded, "All men are created equal before the law, and I will hang a man for killing anyone, including Chinese [*paraphrase*], Indian, blacks [*paraphrase*], or "greasers …I'm very advanced in my views and very outspoken." Well, the 1970s New York was no turn-of-the-century West Texas, but just like Judge Roy Bean, Brooklyn's Reverend Sharpton was seemingly also a man then ahead of his time—advanced in his views and very outspoken—albeit in a retroactive sort of way.

Original Feminist

In a period spanning nearly two decades, the Rev. had written two books that had mostly ignored women, yet in *Stone*, he told of being the "youth

---

294 "General Miles and the Dog" (speech) - *The Wit and Wisdom of Mark Twain*, 13.

director" for Congresswoman Shirley Chisholm's historic 1972 presidential campaign. As he'd never before shared such a history, it might be because it was false. Both of his previous books were pure machismo—tributes to the testosterone of James Brown, Jesse Jackson, Adam Clayton Powell Jr., Marcus Garvey, Dr. King, Bishop F. D. Washington, Alfred Sharpton Sr., and others. So, it was surprising to not only see an upfront dedication to his mother and three daughters in *Stone* but equally remarkable to see his incarnation as a *stone*-cold original feminist—not just a recent convert in 2013 but a retroactive one as well, mounting battles on behalf of the fairer sex as far back as 1972:

> It all brings to mind the battles I had when I was eighteen and was made the youth director of Shirley Chisholm's presidential campaign in 1972...Chisholm had been the first African-American woman elected to Congress in 1968...I was proud to be in charge of organizing young people in support of her presidential campaign. But that sentiment wasn't shared among the black leadership. Chisholm said that during her legislative career, she faced much more discrimination because she was a woman than because she was black. I can definitely attest to that because I saw it with my own two eyes.[295]

But for the child preacher groomed in the machismo of the black church, in particular, in the traditionally paternal patriarchy of the Holiness-Spiritualists (Pentecostal-COGIC) environment, being a cultivated teen feminist would've been an existential contradiction. In their study of the black church, religious writers C. Eric Lincoln and Lawrence H. Mamiya had told us as much:

> The Church of God in Christ ["COGIC"—Reverend Sharpton formative denomination]...had a high disapproval rate of 73.4 percent, who strongly disapproved of women as pastors...COGIC has an explicit denominational policy against the ordination of women as pastors. In COGIC women can become evangelists, an

---

295 Al Sharpton with Chiles, *The Rejected Stone*, 131.

official church, but not pastors. The few women who were pastors of churches in the denomination were widows who succeeded their husbands..."[296]

If the Pentecostals had disapproved of women being pastors as late as in the 1990s and possibly into the 2000s, they would've been downright indignant of a woman running for president in 1972—the very indignation that the black male leadership of the era had indeed doled out to Ms. Chisholm. But again, we were back to Sharpton the second or even third-rate forger. This story was a poor copy, a clear forgery, and we could see it the moment he'd signed it as "youth director."

The roving "youth director" role was a main vehicle for the Sharpton fabrications. He claimed to have been a youth director of many things under the sun, repeating the same pattern each time. He dropped himself in the midst of historical events for which most of the witnesses are either dead or too old to know of his claims, too old to dispute them or just too old to care. In that retroactive history, he was invariably a "youth director" of something important. For example, Sharpton had told us that in response to seeing a film on Dr. King's life in the aftermath of his death, he'd become youth director of Operation Breadbasket:

> I felt guilty, like I had let Dr. King down, that I wasn't doing my part. So I went back to Operation Breadbasket, and I asked Reverend Jones if I could organize a youth division, and he said he'd been hoping I would want to do that. He made me a youth director in 1969.[297]

To mayoral candidate Ruth Messinger, he'd expressed indignation—no longer based on just being youth director of Operation Breadbasket, but as youth director of Dr. King's actual Southern Christian Leadership Conference's (SCLC) New York chapter:

---

296 C. Eric Lincoln and Lawrence H. Mamiya, *The Black Church in the African American Experience* (Duke University Press, 1990), 292.

297 Al Sharpton and Walton, *Go and Tell Pharaoh*, 47.

I grew up in the civil rights movement. At the age of 14, I was appointed Youth Director of the New York Chapter of the Southern Christian Leadership Conference, [founded by, the Rev. Dr. Martin Luther King jr.], by the Rev. Jesse L. Jackson, (my lifetime mentor).[298]

By attempting to associate the Rev. with hyper-male, Minister Louis Farrakhan, Ruth Messinger had set out to discredit Sharpton not only among Jewish voters but also among women voters. Nothing would've been a more powerful way of shutting her down than to say, *How dare you? I was in the trenches with Shirley Chisholm*—if it had really happened? That in over two decades of writing the Rev. had forgotten about his youth directorship of Shirley Chisholm's campaign, it is likely because there was nothing to remember because he just wasn't. But he then continued to embellish his association with the African American pioneer with what appeared to have been background information gathered from a Google search or maybe from reading a book, but not as a witness to history. In fact, had the Rev. told us that, while in jail for his Vieques protest, he'd read Shirley Chisholm's life story, we could've believed him.

Next up for the retroactive progressive voyeur was a move to deny his old self by stereotyping and inculpating the black community and black males in the process, without realizing that he was attacking his own (sexist) church upbringing in doing so. As with his earlier "outing" of the black church choir in the same book, we again saw the master forger or at least a master of projection at work:

One of the things I have found disheartening throughout my career is the sexism in the upper echelons of leadership, particularly in the black community...Black male insecurity cannot continue to be the justification for asking black women to step back and let some insecure boys play out their manhood.[299]

---

298 Evan J. Mandery, *The Campaign Rudy Giuliani, Ruth Messinger, Al Sharpton, and the Race to Be Mayor of New York City* (Westview Press, 1999), 65.

299 Al Sharpton with Chiles, *The Rejected Stone*, 132.

Sharpton had rightfully described an aspect of the civil rights movement and pretty much the history of the patriarchal black church. But again, these were all factors of which he was both beneficiary and practitioner. He then described a meeting of black leaders in Gary, Indiana, at which the likes of bogeyman Jesse Jackson and others had denied Ms. Chisholm their support because she was a feminist—a denial of support that Sharpton had opposed. Sexist black men were treating a black woman poorly because they'd felt she was "into that feminism" and to her rescue had come the progressive young messiah:

> I attended the unprecedented gathering of black leaders and activists that happened that year in Gary, Indiana, and I was shocked that they would not endorse Chisholm. Jesse Jackson and the others were going with George McGovern. I think their problem with her was because they felt Shirley's into that feminism. But my response was, Well wait a minute, Shirley's a black candidate with our agenda in addition to a feminist agenda...Why can't we support her?[300]

The males had treated Ms. Chisholm so poorly that it had fallen to Sharpton— the seventeen-year-old super specimen and beacon of light—to have rescued her by reigning in the elderly big men of politics and the church because he'd felt her hurt and pain up close. This time, you could almost feel the river running through him. Again, given the dictatorial and patriarchal black church and political leadership of the era that was dominated by men of the church, this was sheer idiocy, especially when considered that Sharpton's very presence at those interactions in Gary, Indiana, was likely another fanciful arrogation:

> I saw the hurt and pain she went through having to fight black men...As her youth director, I felt the tensions. For a lot of these leaders, it was the first time I openly went against them. It was eye opening, and it was painful, because I had to make a personal choice. I had looked up to them and couldn't believe their view was that limited and that biased. There was no other way to put it. I knew there was considerable sexism in the church community...[301]

---

300 Ibid.
301 Ibid.

Reverend Sharpton was a youth. Although he might have felt himself an adult—having insisted on being called "the Reverend Alfred Charles Sharpton Jr." since childhood—had he, as a teen, really dared to oppose his church and political elders in any venue, he would've been squarely tossed out of the room. Again, his very presence at those events in Gary, Indiana, is doubtful and a likely invention crafted courtesy of a Google search. But the principal point remains; in his two previous books, the Rev. had carefully discussed the most mundane and intimate details of the people with whom he'd had contact, those with whom he'd been remotely involved, and of the events that he'd experienced on his journey. Except for one tangential sentence in *Al on America*, where he'd grouped Ms. Chisholm and Congresspersons Barbara Jordan and Adam Clayton Powell Jr. together as black leaders who'd done something for their community, there was never any mention of Shirley Chisholm. Neither was there any association with her historic 1972 presidential campaign—both of which would've elevated the Rev. to the stature of a true prodigy he'd worked so hard to convey in those two previous books.

Being associated with the first black woman to run for president of the United States would've been monumental for his resume at the time of writing his first book. Unless his true mindset and upbringing were sexist enough to have denied recognition of women as role models back then, had the status-seeking Sharpton really worked for Shirley Chisholm, it would have been front and center of his two previous books—in particular, the centerpiece of *Al on America*, which was a political manifesto for a presidential run. As for his statement regarding the sexist black leaders, this was the most well-known aspect of Shirley Chisholm's career in politics and of her presidential bid—again, to be easily found on page one of any Google search.

There is a small chance that the Rev. might have had some tangential involvement with Shirley Chisholm's campaign but likely as one of many young people helping out—sticking posters on public edifices or putting up signs in people's front yards. But the Shirley Chisholm "youth director" of *Stone* is more likely a Sharpton imposition on history than of history itself. Dropping himself in the middle of publicly known events to tell us that many black men didn't support Ms. Chisholm because she was a woman isn't a difficult invention to impose upon the past, as it is well-known historical fact.

In the process, the Rev. attempted yet again to show us the tenacious prodigy, the young messiah—Jesus-like in every way—who'd stood up to the elders and who had opposed their sexism. From this depiction, there was the expectation that at any time someone like a Hosea Williams might have just stood up and coldcocked this Sharpton kid, wondering, *Who the hell does he think he is?* But even for that to have happened, it would've required a presence in Indiana and on that stage in the first place which, while possible, is nonetheless doubtful.

All Roads Lead Back to Jesse

By now we've all seen that many things across the Sharpton books eventually find their origins in his obsession with discrediting Reverend Jesse Jackson, as the Rev. had sought to dethrone him. The Shirley Chisolm story seems to have been no different. The Rev. had made small mention in 2002's *Al on America* of the National Black Political Convention in Gary Indiana in May 1972—the first major gathering of black leaders and activists in the aftermath of the Voting Rights Act seven years before. That he was a seventeen-year-old high school student at that time is a fact he'd ignored in crafting these inventions. He told us that he dropped out of college but has never said anything about being a high school dropout as well. In any case, his mention of the conference then had nothing to do with Shirley Chisholm, nor was she mentioned. It was solely a hit job on Jesse Jackson in which Sharpton had shown us Jackson being heckled as a sell-out, telling us that Jesse was a sell-out "even then"—meaning Reverend Jackson was as much a traitorous race charlatan in 1972 as he was in 2002:

> But in the 1980s, there was a rift over my closeness to the nationalist crowd. Jesse would say, "What are you doing? That's not what you come out of!" Jesse used to catch a lot of flak from the nationalists because he carried on Dr. King's vision of integration. And they would call him a sellout and a tool of the party—even then. In 1972, the National Black Political Convention in Gary, Indiana, was the first place where I actually saw the tension between Jesse and the nationalists. I was eighteen years old, the youngest guy on the platform. They introduced Jesse

to speak, and Jesse was very popular nationwide. But he got booed soundly at the convention.[302]

While it would've been a near implausible oversight for any youth director of a historical pioneer-candidate to omit this experience in two previous books on his journey as a history-maker, for Reverend Sharpton, it would've been an existential impossibility not to have publicly hitched his wagon to Shirley Chisholm over the years since. Taken a step further, on its face, the Shirley Chisholm youth director might yet be one of the flakier Sharpton stories for a variety of reasons. These include the seventeen-year-old's doubtful presence or appearance on the platform among giants like Jesse Jackson and other pioneer religious and elected black leaders in Gary Indiana in 1972 and his own testimony (later chapter) to being wrapped up with singer James Brown out on the west coast during that time.

Finally, Shirley Chisholm was a feminist who'd run a campaign to break glass ceilings for little girls all over America. On her arrival as a congressperson in Washington, DC, one of the first things she did was to register a difference by hiring women staffers at all levels. It was therefore unlikely that she would've chosen to spread her message to young girls across the land—on whose behalf she'd waged a campaign—by having a male director of youth organizing.

Again, for readers of history or the history of theology, parallels in the Sharpton rhetoric to historical events are sometimes hard to ignore. His retroactive insertions into Shirley Chisholm's 1972 campaign and into Ali-Foreman's 1974 Kinshasa fight are almost worthy, not of Flavius Josephus himself but of the Septuagint's insertion of, "There lived Jesus, a wise man Jesus," in Josephus's *The Testimonium Flavianum*.

Eating for Greatness

Once we'd chipped away at the leadership and greatness memes, there was actually a segment of *Stone* that was well worth reading. The Rev. was candid about the calamitous diet of black America—a diet he'd once embraced—so

---

302 Sharpton with Hunter, *Al on America*, 193.

he echoed what many might not have wanted to hear but needed to hear: *Black America, you're no longer a slave, so stop eating like one.* Beyond that though, to write a book correlating leadership to weight was also a measure of the newfound dietary confidence of a man who'd once weighed in at nearly three hundred pounds. Accordingly, he'd come to believe that his diet was an important determinant of whether or not he was "serious about leadership."

As great leaders from Henry VIII through to Winston Churchill and beyond were large men in stature and form, this lien was sheer idiocy, especially for a man who told us of reading about and admiring Churchill; the Rev. had apparently never seen a picture of Churchill. But he—Sharpton, not Churchill—then tipped over the scale by stitching together parallels between Nelson Mandela, Dr. King, food, leadership, and himself that were all very hard to swallow:

> It dawned on me, reading about these great men [King and Mandela], that if I wanted to go to the next level, I needed to take control of my mouth—both what I put into it and what I allowed to come out of it…To me, that became a path to greatness; it was the only way I could go from being a famous leader to being a great leader.[303]

While he did have a potentially useful message for his readers, of healthy eating for healthy living, the Rev. ended up obliterating it with his usual buffoonery about "path to greatness" and "being a great leader." His journey from an unhealthy Sumo wrestler-like condition to a svelte looking 150-pound (or less) specimen was commendable and no doubt exhilarating for him. But even in discussing his weight loss, he found dishonesty his best companion. We can all imagine the words of his doctors warning him of his condition in the old days: *Rev., if you don't lose that weight, you will die.* Yet he was now concocting a story that his weight loss was the result of some kind of strategic decision made solely out of a disciplined purpose to transform himself into a great leader by eating less—by "eating for greatness." We were to believe that he'd lost half of his former self in his lone quest to become—not the next Jesse Jackson, but the next svelte Dr. King or Nelson Mandela.

---

303 Al Sharpton with Chiles, *The Rejected Stone*, 209.

Trophy Girlfriend

Nowhere were the mayhem and madness of that single substance engaged in dualist combat more pronounced than when the Rev. spoke of his girlfriend. His *he-man* credentials had shot sky high in late 2013 when it emerged that his companion was a beautiful stylist, twenty-five years his junior. This was baffling to anyone reading *Stone* because among the vast array of leadership advice Sharpton disseminated was that dating the classmates of your daughters wasn't being serious about leadership, and we know how seriously he feels about leadership. But he'd also noted such middle-age follies as "antithetical" to making a serious contribution to life:

> Carrying around those middle-age insecurities, needing a young woman to tell me I was still a man, all of that was antithetical to having a serious contribution to make in my life. From your diet to your friends to your social life, you have to say either you're going to be serious about leadership in all aspects or you're not going to be serious[304]

So how serious could his contributions to life have been, given that he had needed a young woman to tell him he was still a man? It appeared the cathartically-coded language of a subconscious sharing its belief that it had indeed contributed little or nothing to life while moving with time through the constellations. But this was the segment in which the dualist battle royal had descended into stratospheric comedy. In a book written during his relationship with his young companion, to whom he'd even made a spectacular dedication at the end, the Rev. also pointed out that dating a younger woman was an indication that a person was wracked by middle-age vanities. But accordingly, he supposedly wasn't:

> For instance, when I talk about women, I'm honest about the changes I went through after my marriage ended, when I was trying to date a lot of younger women, stumbling through the stereotypical middle-age crisis, trying to prove I was still young and vital. But one day, I woke up and thought, You can go out

---

304 Ibid., 214.

with a twenty-year-old girl, but you're certainly not twenty anymore. You're not fooling anybody but yourself…I can't concede and confess openly to foolish pride or worthless vanity or middle-age insecurity if I'm still wracked by them.[305]

The benefits had apparently outweighed the terrible costs Sharpton had listed because even as he'd written it, he was dating a woman half his age, which meant that he was indeed wracked by foolish pride, worthless vanity, and middle-age insecurities. He couldn't have "conceded and confessed" to things by which he was wracked, so instead, he chose not to concede or confess to them but to merely show us that he was indeed wracked by them.

Admittedly, dating a younger woman often causes the middle-aged man to say the silliest things, but in Sharpton's case, it had obliged a degree of confessional. It was indeed the highpoint dualist mayhem—seeing the author of things to avoid in life actively engaged in that which he was proscribing. As with his processed hair that no one had ever cared about, his insecurities manifested a constant need to explain away his reasons for not dating trophy dolls while in fact dating one. He gave us a rambling assessment of a middle-age crisis that was as unnecessary as it was confounding. As if with a compulsion to impress upon America that he was, in fact, dating a significantly younger woman, he endeavored to tell us precisely the opposite:

I was already separated when I started losing weight, so that meant I was on the dating market as the pounds were dropping off. I think I got caught up in the stereotypical middle-aged male mind-set—an old man dating young girls to try to affirm himself, prove he is still young and vital. But then I told myself, You need to stop this, What are you trying to prove? I knew I needed to settle down again.[306]

---

305 Ibid., 46.
306 Ibid., 214.

From all else, we were likely to conclude that the Rev. was very serious about leadership because he kept telling us that he was. But by his own criteria, he was anything but. By the end of the segment on dating, another whimsical Sharpton contradiction had firmly been established. He declared his beautiful companion and all women like her to be of no contribution to the goal of being a great leader and therefore mere distractions. Yet at the end of the book, he gave a warm dedication to that very distraction that was antithetical to serious contributions in his life, declaring, "Thanks to my companion and trusted friend Aisha McShaw, who helped me with this project."[307]

She'd helped out on a project that effectively declared her a nuisance, a distraction, "antithetical to having a serious contribution to make in my life," and a barrier to his most profound objective in life: "leadership." She'd helped in crafting her own portrayal as fodder, as arm candy for the stereotypical middle-aged geriatric-lite male attempting to reaffirm his manhood. Where the Rev. had asked America to begrudge him not his newfound status, middle-aged men across America were unlikely to oblige on this one. Indeed, What a woman!

End Act III

---

307 Ibid., 260.

Act IV: Free-Form Glider

Whenever you find you are on the side of
the majority, it is time to reform.

—MARK TWAIN[308]

---

308 *Notebook - The Wit and Wisdom of Mark Twain, 50.*

TOWARD THE END of the Obama era, the former jet-propelled machine was running out of fuel and steam. It was still attempting to move against gravity but lacking thrust and poorly guided, it had become a glider—no longer seeking the stratosphere but more of a projectile wobbling in free form. We could actually see the beginnings of its plummet; it was no longer a question of, "if" but rather, "when" and "how." Would it return to its known path or stray off course to wreak further havoc and widespread damage?

This was to be the era of *the reverted stone*—not quite *rejected* anew but forced to return to thrive in known pastures as opposed to prior ostentatious pretenses of boldly seeking to go where no man—not even Dr. King—had gone before. For those who'd mistakenly bought into the pomp and pageantry of the *newly minted stone* of gentry, a surprise was in store.

In those waning Obama years, no man in America must have questioned his future as much as Reverend Sharpton. But as the original genetic condition of that newly engineered species hadn't fundamentally changed its character, the old Sharpton knew he could've just walked right back into the bleachers and sat down to retake his rightful seat—the one that he'd always occupied among the commoners. And this he did spectacularly.

He'd used his time in the prime box seats to wreak havoc, to seek payback, and to affect revenge through gloating, but it was now time to return to bare-knuckle boxing. Nothing is worse than a threat to a man's livelihood. In addition to his earning potential, his prestige, stature, and self-worth are at all stake. So we saw the same old insecurities manifest in 2015 to fend off challengers and to defend his turf. The vituperative vicar had returned with vigor, vitriol, vulgarity, and vengeance. Elsewhere, he continued to amplify already magnanimous stories, but this time, choosing to use a known author as his vehicle of dissemination.

The Vituperative Vicar-Pimps, "Hoes," and Willie Lynch

Mark Twain said best: "When angry, count to four; when very angry, swear!" [309] Reverend Sharpton might have taken the latter part of that advice, but he'd certainly ignored the former. In 2015, two years after the publishing of Stone, the Rev. got into a brouhaha with a group of young activists, following the Ferguson, Missouri, riots in the aftermath of black youth Michael Brown's death.

Out of the events in Ferguson and from protests elsewhere across the country, a new generation of activists had decided to step forward to organize themselves from the grassroots—eschewing the Rev's toxic "celebritized" and exploitative activism for profit. Many had felt that they could no longer trust him. It was the same year that the *Smoking Gun,* through Freedom of Information releases, had outed the Rev. as a 1980s-era FBI confidential informant "CI-17," who, equipped with electronic devices, had taped his interactions with wise-guys from New York's varying crime families, and with others as well.

While some of the young activists had noted that the Rev.'s principles had fluctuated, others had come to see him as an outright hindrance. Though having lost much of his former self, in terms of poundage, this had little impact on Sharpton's esophageal capacity or lung efficiency. On entering a room, he still sucked the oxygen out of black leadership, out of black activism and causes, and often, out of black dignity as well. A few activists in New York, for example, were appalled at the way he'd welcomed back Bill Bratton for yet another tour as police commissioner under Mayor Bill de Blasio, given the fights they'd had with Bratton during his previous stint as commissioner under Mayor Rudolph Giuliani. Sharpton himself had been a visceral critic of Bratton in those days as well.

By the latter half of 2014, the activists had begun to be more vocal in their opposition to Sharpton. With victims' families like that of Akai Gurley—the innocent young black man killed by police in a Brooklyn stairwell—telling the Rev. to stay away, he'd felt his influence waning, his bread and butter

---

309 *Pudd'nhead Wilson - The Wit and Wisdom of Mark Twain,* 18.

threatened. This sent him hopping mad and into a full panic mode, and in early 2015, the Rev. finally decided to take on the young activists.

Capital New York captured the Rev. addressing the issue at his National Action Network in Harlem. On January 31, 2015, *Capital's* Azi Paybarah reported out Sharpton's rap-star-like invectives and tirades against the young generation of activists:

> They are pimping you. You're being tricked and you're trying to turn the community into tricks. And they are pimping you, to do the Willie Lynch in our community. It's the disconnect that is the strategy to break the movement. And they play on your ego. "Oh, you young and hip, you're full of fire. You're the new face." All the stuff that they know will titillate your ears. That's what a pimp says to a hoe. They tell them what they want to hear. They don't tell you "I'm going to turn you out." They tell you "You're beautiful. Nobody appreciates you like I do. Look at you. You deserve all these material things. You're not being in that London Fog coat. You should be in minks. You should have diamonds. You should have earnings [and] all you've got to do is come with me. We can have a brand new car together. We can buy a house in the suburbs together." And after they seduce you, they reduce you. And I'm not going to sit here and let them reduce our children.

It was reminiscent of the Rev.'s visceral attacks accusing Jesse Jackson of being at the beck and call of the "white supremacist" Bill Clinton. But this was an attack explicitly conveyed to a feminine target, with analogies of a prostitute subject to the seduction and abuse of a pimp. This was from a man who'd reinvented himself as a feminist and as a paragon of progressiveness in a book only two years prior.

For Sharpton, who after attending President Obama's second inaugural, had written of "dustbins of history filling up," it was a case of *plus ça change, plus c'est la même chose!* The more things had seemingly changed for him, the more they'd remained the same; he was still the same old vituperative vicar bearing much vitriol and vulgarity. Where he should've acted the part of elder statesman and mentored the young, he resorted to describing them as a "ho," as being "tricked," and being "pimped" out. It was the same "I'm not ok, you're not ok" masked as "I'm ok, but you all are not." As the father of two daughters had so "prolifically" spoken of the road to prostitution and of the pimping process with such ease and in such detail, it wouldn't have been a stretch to have asked even more questions of an already-nefarious past.

But there was also no denying his hypocrisy. In 2015, the Rev. had proven himself to be no better than the worst of the "gangsta" rappers he'd so indignantly condemned in his books. In *Al on America,* he'd decried the tone of rap music and its name-calling of black women. In *Stone,* he was just as prolific in his derision and indignation, telling us that he was at rap's beginning and had watched it co-opted by the record industry establishment and condemning rappers for using the same language he would use in 2015:

> We started with guys who were in touch with the streets, expressing their pain. And we wound up with guys assigned by the corporate music world to be politically non-threatening, to become in many ways minstrels who would entertain people at their base level and play into stereotypes of blacks— they want to have babies they won't raise, they want shiny jewelry and fancy cars without working for them, they want to call their women "bitches" and "hoes."[310]

Yet without hesitation, he attacked and insulted the integrity of young activists who'd just desired to play a role in their future, free of his stench. Above all, it was a stunning attack on the black woman, as his invectives were in forms traditionally used in her denigration. The Rev. had felt his authority being challenged and had reacted in the usual way by lashing out with the authoritarian paternalism, condescension, and sexist mean-spiritedness in his effort to command obedience.

In the broader context of the reserved and accepted inferiority of black America to which I earlier alluded, this was yet another example of where Sharpton's conduct didn't even register a blip in the general public

---

310 Al Sharpton with Chiles, *The Rejected Stone,* 87–88.

discourse. No black were women protesting his comments or demanding that he be fired from his television gig, no action from Comcast or MSNBC to fire or suspend him for his sexist remarks. If a white public personality had said or posted in social media, anything even remotely close—in either tone or substance—his or her public career would have been over. He or she would've been immediately fired from jobs, with all public associations cut. Reverend Sharpton would've been the one leading other black leaders in the hunt for blood.

But as this was an attack on African Americans, in particular, an attack on the black woman, nobody cared—not even the black woman herself. No *Black Women's Worth Matters* movement or hashtags had sprung up. And even today—the era of men dropping like flies for sexual abuse, harassment, and inappropriate behavior dating back decades—the standards by which black women are regarded and by which their mistreatment is mostly tolerated by society mean that Reverend Sharpton had little to fear of losing either his MSNBC job or his celebrity status for those remarks.

Understanding this reserved and accepted inferior standard has enabled Sharpton to be himself over the years. Like intra-communal criminals who prey on their own, the race leader knows he has a free rein to victimize his own with impunity, and so when in his comfort zone, young activists threatening his fiefdom are made out to be servile "hos" being tricked out by pimps. Nothing had changed about the "new man" who while at the presidential inaugural had come to believe that he'd no longer needed to be confrontational. On seeing the emergence of a new generation capable of challenging his supremacy, he saw them in the worst light—as aiding white racists, as aiding modern day "Willie Lynches."

Willie Lynch is a long discredited fictitious slave-era character and one of the great fake news artifacts of slave history. Supposedly, a sadistic slave owner and pioneer of slave brutality, Lynch was said to have instructed plantation owners in the South on the art of behavioral conditioning of their merchandise. A widely circulated Willie Lynch manifesto of brutality had accompanied the hoax, but scholars have long discredited this as a fantastic piece of fiction. Yet as late as 2015, this fantastic fiction had still owned much plantation space in the Sharpton brain, which he then conveniently tilled to delegitimize others.

The Rev. Goes to Hollywood

While the elimination of racist discrimination and other barriers against black participation in all aspects of American life is an essential measure of progress, black leadership has often been slanted toward prioritizing a type of high-level representation without accountability—the incremental participation of African-Americans at higher levels. They tend to view the expansion of the visual elite in municipal, state, and national government as a job well done. For example, while some emphasis is usually given to having more black officers on the beat in police departments, a higher emphasis is usually placed on having a few well-placed blacks as precinct commanders, captains, and the like. But this has often had little or no effect at all, as high-level representation doesn't automatically translate to high-level influence on necessary policy changes and enforcement to eliminate racial profiling, discrimination, and police abuse. The most visible example of this was the presidency of Barack Obama. As extensively discussed, it had no effect on police brutality across the land.

We've sometimes seen black leaders square the blame on black officers who perpetuate and participate in appalling and oppressive crimes against their own community, all while being tepid in calling for the head of senior African-American police honchos who otherwise condone or ignore the same. This means that calls for those officials to be put in high places often belie stronger desires for window dressing than for real changes. As such, with each new discovery of racism in industry or in areas dominated by whites (well, in all domains), the black leadership quickly heralds the absence of African Americans at the top as the reason, as if the presence of blacks at the top means the automatic suspension or elimination of racism. Yes, in some cases, as with the horrific and racist advertisements we've seen from Madison Avenue over the years, it is clear that an all-white environment lacking a high-level black face in the office or in the focus groups has indeed resulted in offensive disasters.

But again, having black faces in "important" positions have not always been a guarantee against catastrophe, because they're generally not fully empowered to make a difference.

So, with each inartful, insensitive, or genuinely racist behavior from the white establishment, we hear the usual demands for African Americans to be put in high positions. It's that desire for a lucrative social expansion of the black elite that often bears big payoffs in the form of donations to social organizations or in the way of social inclusion (honorific parties and image awards) for its champions in politics and activism.

This was the case in 2014 when Sony Pictures was hacked before the planned December release of *The Interview*, a controversial spoof of the North Korean leader Kim Jong-un. Hacked e-mails revealed that the company's co-chair, Amy Pascal, had traded racist e-mails joking about President Barack Obama with producer Scott Rudin. In another set of emails leaked, another producer even suggested that the studio not cast black actors, including mega-star Denzel Washington, in lead roles because they don't drive international ticket sales. Reverend Sharpton immediately hijacked any chance of the incident being a learning or transformative experience to effect real changes in Hollywood. Rather than meeting with black performers to apologize and to develop concrete plans to remedy the situation, which she might have preferred, an embarrassed and apologetic Amy Pascal was then dragged to meet with the Rev. and National Urban League president, Marc Morial, among others, for a December 2014 mea culpa in Manhattan. In a pre-meeting interview, the Rev. told a reporter that,

> Hollywood really reflects a lot of what was said in that conversation. There's no blacks with any real decision-making power; there's no diversity at the top. This could be the time to change Hollywood...Hollywood is like the Rocky Mountains; the higher up it goes, the whiter it goes.

He was none too impressed either that Sony was producing *Annie* with a young black actress in the lead. "That's product, that's selling to consumers," he said, in his call for black faces at the top. "Who makes the decisions? Who does the budget? Who writes the checks? That's where [*sic*] we wanna know." Of course, the budget person is also the one who often authorizes corporate donations as well. But according to the Rev., the racial makeup of twenty-first-century Hollywood had lagged decades behind the times. He described it as an environment that still resembled 1950's America, and at a press conference after the meeting, he went on to tell us that,

> We clearly are willing to deal with an immediate formula to see where we deal
> with breaking down the walls of inflexible and so far, immovable racial exclusion
> in Hollywood. But again, we're not going to be satisfied until we see something
> concrete done. Had Hollywood not had such an exclusionary, almost all white
> hierarchy; one could look at the context differently. We were very candid with
> her. I said to her at that time that the climate and environment of Hollywood only
> confirm the kind of language that was used in these emails.

But this was a slap in the face of the black public by Sharpton, who, along with his former mentor Jesse Jackson, had anointed themselves America's attention-grabbing black popes. Where the men of Rome had once believed themselves God's representatives on earth, Jackson and Sharpton have fashioned themselves as God's representative of blackness in America—regularly convening meetings with famous whites who've sinned against "blackness" and with famous blacks who've sinned in the name of "blackness." It's as if either man has held the keys to absolution for whites and redemption for moneyed blacks—for a price.

Where white racist conduct might be injurious to black America as a whole or where black celebrity conduct might be injurious to society as a whole, it's either man—likely through his respective organization—who gets a contribution for granting public absolution to the former or for facilitating public redemption of the latter. For example, when actor Michael Richards (*Seinfeld's* "Kramer") went on an N-word rant at a November 2006 "Laugh Factory" performance in West Hollywood, Jesse Jackson showed up to absolve Richards of his sins. Jackson even gave Richards airtime on his show to tell America how "sorry" he was for getting caught being himself.

Indeed, Jackson is an old hand at this. After former segregationist George Wallace had found either human decency, humility, or his comeuppance at the barrel of a gun, in a desperate bid to seek his endorsement in 1987, Jesse Jackson had rushed down to Montgomery, Alabama, to see the then reformed, yet ailing, Wallace. He gleefully led Wallace in prayer, in which he prayed to "the God of healing and health" for the old man's recovery. It was the ultimate absolution for Wallace, had anyone really doubted his reformation up to that point.

In any case, given Reverend Sharpton's history of corporate shakedowns, many had suspected that the "immediate formula" that he'd spoken of about Sony, had constituted some form of a desired donation to his National Action Network from either Amy Pascal, from Sony, or from both.

"Oscars So White"

Barely a month after the Rev.'s meeting with Ms. Pascal, the nominees for Academy Awards were announced, and not a single actor of color or female director was nominated for an Oscar by the Academy of Motion Picture Arts and Sciences in 2015. The hashtag, #OscarsSoWhite, exploded on Twitter when black performers, including director Ava DuVernay and actor David Oyelowo, were snubbed for *Selma*—a film that had entered the race as a strong contender for multiple awards, including for acting and directing. A year later in 2016, it was a repeat performance; no black actors were nominated, and all twenty actors nominated for an Oscar were white. It was deemed a "whitewash" by many, including some black industry figures. Comedian Chris Rock, the host of the eighty-eighth Academy Awards ceremony, effectively ended up doing an apology monologue for the absence of African-American nominees.

It was two years running, twice since the famous Sharpton meeting with Sony's Amy Pascal—proving yet again the ineffectiveness of Reverend Sharpton in the public arena. It seemed he'd achieved nothing with his discussions with Ms. Pascal or by his much-ballyhooed demands for real changes in Hollywood. Although she was out as a top executive at Sony soon after that, Amy Pascal could undoubtedly have relayed a message of needed change from her meeting with the Sharpton—had there been one. Further, had Hollywood any respect for the Rev., they would've probably kept Pascal on, if only to lead a credible diversity undertaking or at least for a window-dressing publicity campaign. But instead, it was left to the Academy of Motion Picture Arts and Sciences to deliver a response to Sharpton, and its response, twice affirmed, was a resounding, *Get lost!*

As the Rev.'s ineffectiveness was yet again on public display with the 2016 announcement of the nominees, he was forced to join the public protests to save face. The only weapon in his arsenal was the same old and tired rhythmic platitudes, as he huffed and puffed for the cameras anew, saying yet again that, "Hollywood is like the Rocky Mountains. The higher up you get, the whiter it gets and this year's Academy Awards will be yet another Rocky Mountain Oscars."

But the real issue was one that Sharpton couldn't touch. According to 2013 *Los Angeles Times* analysis, the Academy's membership—and therefore its voting base—was 93-percent white and 76-percent male. So, the previous year's awards given to Steve McQueen's *12 Years a Slave* might have seemed enough for this esteemed group, having felt it had satisfied its quota-for-the-decade requirements. Talk of Hollywood's "Rocky Mountains-like whiteness" and of the inflexible and immovable racial exclusions didn't even register where it had counted—with producers, directors, talent scouts, or the Academy's voting membership. But the Sharpton buffoonery was even further highlighted when public attention turned to Cheryl Boone Isaacs, a black woman who was a twenty-four-year governor of the Academy of Motion Picture Arts and Sciences—the governing body of the industry—and who was in her second term as its president. A black woman was sitting atop the body that had failed to recognize African American participation in any significant ways, two years running.

In January 2015, a month after the Sharpton news conference with Ms. Pascal, Cheryl Boone Isaacs was asked by *Vulture* magazine if the Academy had difficulty recognizing diversity. She said,

Not at all. Not at all! The good news is that the wealth of talent is there, and it's being discussed, and it's helpful so much for talent—whether in front of the camera or behind the camera—to have this recognition, to have this period of time where there is a lot of publicity, a lot of chitter-chatter.

The question then was, Why hadn't the Rev. publicly demanded a meeting with Ms. Boone Isaacs as well around the same time that he'd carpet-bombed Amy Pascal into meeting with him and others in New York? It goes back to the principal point of the desire among these black leaders for window dressing rather than for real change. Sharpton was stumped; he couldn't have seriously called for changes at the top when the top was already black. So instead he spoke of Hollywood in general. Additionally, as the narrative of racism is best served up with a white head on a plate, black accountability is off the table, so there were no initial calls for Cheryl Boone Isaacs' head. But equally important was that a weakened Amy Pascal and an embarrassed Sony Pictures would've also been more likely than Boone Isaacs to make a donation to Sharpton's National Action Network or to offer up some other kinds or remedies beneficial to the Rev. while doing little or nothing to change prevailing racism in Hollywood.

With the second snob in 2016, which had garnered more attention to the Academy's actual makeup, circumstances had cornered a Sharpton, now with egg on his face. The spotlight had turned to Cheryl Boone Isaacs, and so the Rev. was forced to go a little further. His National Action Network's Los Angeles political director, Najee Ali, then called for a "TV-tune out" of the Oscar telecast:

> The only thing the academy will listen to is ad dollars. There will be a lack of viewers, advertisers, and interest…The lack of African Americans and women excluded from the major categories of Oscar nominees is appalling…Cheryl Boone Isaacs, the African-American president of the academy, is nothing but a pawn, and the black face of Hollywood's system and culture that is racist, sexist and lacks true diversity.

Reverend Sharpton had finally been forced to take fellow African American Cheryl Boone Isaacs to task, and he ironically did so using the same words that entertainment mogul Byron Allen had used to describe him in Allen's 2014 suit against Sharpton's employer, Comcast. Like Byron Allen's Al Sharpton, Cheryl Boone Isaacs, was, per Sharpton's mouthpiece, a "pawn" in America's racist-industrial complex.

The Sharpton Infection

As shown above, there is no denying racism in Hollywood or any suggestion that it shouldn't be firmly tackled. But like racism in any other facet of American life, where exploited *a la* Sharpton or where recklessly trivialized—knowingly or unknowingly by others—efforts to combat it will lack the legitimacy required for success and therefore result in failure.

Although his impact on the affairs of black America has been decidedly negative, Reverend Sharpton's impact on the personalities of African Americans has been a little more difficult to gauge, as even in revulsion, many will still accommodate him as "leader," in per cultural norms and mandates of obedience and respect. But as his thinking and behavior have become so mainstreamed in certain quarters, there are times when others have echoed him without even recognizing it. This usually backfires because Sharpton being himself is kind of like tennis star John McEnroe being "John McEnroe" on the court back in the day; love him or hate him, he's most authentic in being himself. When others take a page from the Sharpton playbook, however, they invariably end up coming off like Ivan Lendl trying to be John McEnroe back in the day—somewhat inauthentic.

This was the case of a black actor in early 2017, who while having genuine concerns about racism in Hollywood, had failed epically to move the needle an inch and instead ended up causing himself much embarrassment with his blunder. In what seemed like a man on the verge of an overdose of "Sharpton juice," and reminiscent of the divisions encouraged among existing plantation attendants towards new arrivals from Africa, actor Samuel L. Jackson invented a form of nativist black-on-non-black uncivil disobedience in 2017. The actor publicly bemoaned the hiring of foreign black actors (mostly British) over African Americans in Hollywood. He had enjoyed African American director Jordan Peele's stealth success, *Get Out,* but was disappointed that British actor Daniel Kaluuya was the star. How does anyone enjoy a movie while feeling displeasure at the ethnic background of its lead actor?

We can almost call it "British black privilege," as in addition to an attack on Daniel Kaluuya and David Oyelowo, it was also an attack on the likes of Chiwetel Ejiofor, Idris Elba, John Boyega, Malachi Kirby, Trevor Noah, Naomie Harris, and David Harewood, among others. Whether he'd realized it or not, by inferring that a preference for foreign blacks to native African Americans was yet another type of Hollywood racism, Sam Jackson was channeling the early Reverend Sharpton. Sharpton had once told us that, "Caribbean blacks, West Africans, Latinos, twenty different white ethnic groups, all at each other's throats and all of them against African-Americans."[311]

The actor's remarks then led many African-American actors to chime in with varying demagogic-nativist excuses that our story in America can best be told by natives. They ignored that we're talking about "acting" and not teaching history lessons. After all, actors research their subject matters, prepare, rehearse, and "act." By comparison, it's hard to imagine white actors launching such an attack on non-American fellow white actors Javier Bardem, Nicole Kidman, Christoph Waltz, Liam Neeson, Kate Winslet, Daniel Day-Lewis, Hugh Grant, Hellen Mirren, Keanu Reeves, Jude Law, Christian Bale, Hugh Jackman, Robert Pattinson, Tom Hardy, Eddie Redmayne, Kate Blanchett, Colin Ferrell, and the like. Daniel Day-Lewis picked up his third "Best Actor" Oscar for playing Abraham Lincoln in the award-winning film about the American president. So why invent a double-standard to condemn black actors from abroad who are simply plying their craft like everyone else?

British actor David Oyelowo, who played civil rights icon Dr. Martin Luther King Jr. in super-director Ava DuVernay's *Selma* commemorative, was also in Sam Jackson's line of fire. Why hadn't Jackson made a personal appeal to Ms.

---

311 Al Sharpton and Walton, *Go and Tell Pharaoh,* 42.

DuVernay or publicly denounced her as well for perpetuating this form of racism in Hollywood—for violating his form of nativism? Instead, he attacked the British actors, inferring that they were little more than "scabs" taking jobs away from African Americans. It hasn't been that long a distance to past wherein racist whites had protested the employment of African Americans in certain Union jobs on the same basis Mr. Jackson had suggested of the British actors—that they were cheaply gotten.

In any case, Sam Jackson's argument was long defeated by none other than superstars Denzel Washington and Jamie Foxx. Mr. Foxx, in laughing at his fellow black actors, had even invented the hashtag #actbetter—if they wanted to win Oscars. His fellow Oscar winner, Mr. Washington, had once advised black actors to "get on stage," because that's where they "really learn to act." Most of the British "subjects" of Mr. Jackson's criticism had indeed started their careers on stage in England, and simply speaking, they can act, hence versatile and bankable. Yet Sam Jackson told New York radio station Hot 97 that, "I don't know what the love affair is with all that." In other words, he, the well-trained thespian since college, an actor in show business doesn't understand the industry's love affair with talent.

For some, Sam Jackson's comments were particularly disappointing because they'd come from him—an individual deeply rooted in civil rights activism since his college days. In fact, of the numerous black actors in Hollywood, Jackson stands out as a hero with a biography second to none, in terms of his college-days activism. But in mimicking Reverend Sharpton, he might have done more harm than good to his cause and genuine concerns, while showing yet again the poverty-in-thought that has inspired seeds of divisions within diaspora Africans since somewhere around 1445 BCE. His comments were yet another example of a societal cultivation in which, outside of attacking the white male, there is a belief among many blacks in a "free-pass" to attack those deemed safe and free of repercussion—others blacks. "It's the way they breathe," as Frantz Fanon would say. It's that same belief in sort of intra-communal impunity to which I earlier alluded in referencing Sharpton's 2015 attack-without-repercussion on young activists and young black women in particular.

To illustrate, had Sam Jackson made such remarks about another category of minority actors, such as Latinos or Muslims—both of whom can compete with African-American actors for roles—his career would be over today. For example, there wasn't any great fuss from Jackson when the light-skinned Latina actress Zoey Saldana had played the dark-skinned all-African-featured iconic Nina Simone—an even bolder move than Elizabeth Taylor as Cleopatra. It wasn't a matter of Saldana's inability to play Nina Simone; it was that she couldn't even look the part. But again, there was nothing then that was comparable to Sam Jackson's mega-bluster against British and other foreign black actors in Hollywood.

Finally, whatever the future holds for African Americans in Hollywood, it will depend on good writing, good acting, good directing, good producing, the courage to organize, and be resolved to privately and publicly challenge the studios and call out racism where it exists. In other words, as in all other domains of the American society where African Americans have excelled in spite of racism, prominence in Hollywood will come through excellent performance onscreen, hard work behind the scenes, and courage in all facets of work.

Early in 2017, as I sat in the theater and watched the credits roll for Denzel Washington's *Fences*, I couldn't help noticing that Mr. Washington's co-producer was the very Scott Rudin who'd shared those racist Obama e-mails with Amy Pascal. It was clear that Washington was solving his own problems, without any aid from outsider hustlers like the Rev.

In the end, in spite of much-useless bluster, Reverend Sharpton has and will continue to have zero positive impact on racism in Hollywood, just as he's had none in any other domain. Those who co-opt his demagogic approach will invariably be just as counterproductive.

Endnote:

As you read this, you might argue that I've attacked black leadership and black leaders here. So, what's the difference? But therein lies an issue of connivance and hypocrisy. I haven't attacked black leadership and black leaders to discredit them for taking jobs away from others. I've laughed them out of town because I believe that many do not work for the people who elect them and should, therefore, be removed for having done little beyond complaining and attributing blame elsewhere, while empowering and enriching themselves. Correctly stated, I've attempted to expose them by ridiculing them—precisely because I've recognized the awful job that many have done, and because I believe that their continued employment will be detrimental to the progress of the black community at large in the long run. A failure to arrest this phenomenon by ignoring it is the essence of connivance and hypocrisy. This is entirely different from targeting your own because there are limited opportunities in the sandbox in which you compete. The objective should be to jointly collaborate and work towards expanding that sandbox in order to make it a better environment for more opportunities for all.

Return of the Black Dantès

A little sincerity is a dangerous thing and a
great deal of it is absolutely fatal.

—OSCAR WILDE[312]

THE TITLE OF *The Rejected Stone* reflected the Reverend Sharpton's mindset that as *the stone the builder had refused*, he was now the *head cornerstone*—resolved to make those builders pay hell. This wasn't a case of betrayal of the innocent by the covetous, as in the case of Edmond Dantès, but who better to baseline the art of revenge than Alexandre Dumas' fictional *Count of Monte Cristo*?

As earlier pointed out, the insufferable cross of rejection at the hands of black elites has had a profound effect on the Sharpton life. The affinity and heredity he has claimed to this class had intensified his feelings of rejection over the years. Holding to the notion of an unceremonious ejection, supposedly occasioned by his father's departure, the Rev. has blamed the elder Sharpton for his forced exile into "negrodom"—that "all-black situation" in Brooklyn. He has also held middle-class and elite blacks in contempt for having permanently dislodged him into "negritude" in the years since. Since then he has seen his hereditary gentry's initial failure to recognize him as one of its own and its continued inability to accept him as a genius that rightfully belonged among it, as a treacherous betrayal to be punished.

This then fed a blind ambition that admitted no limitations for revenge. It is in this sense that Sharpton has shown much in common with Dantès, except that where Edmond was brilliant and his actions valiant, Al was a buffoon and

---

312 *Merlin Holland, The Critic as an Artist (Complete Works,* 2003, London), 1144.

his actions, cowardly. By act III of his public life, the black *Count* had offici-
ated the dethronement of the king of black America by slaying Jesse Jackson.
But even as crown prince, he continued to straddle the acceptance-rejection
continuum he'd straddled his entire life, burdened by the same insecurities and
drenched in the same pettiness. Over time, though, things started to work in
his favor as he began to be met with more acceptance and less rejection. But being accepted didn't amount to much without penalizing some of his own who'd
rejected him. In his mind, realizing a measure of acceptance was as much a
validation that he'd always been a nobleman as it was an affirmation that he was
wronged—a wrong to be avenged, but against whom?

Again, the fundamental difference between being denied acceptance by a
stranger and being rejected by your own lies in your ability to forgive the former
but not the latter; the stranger might not have accepted you because of misun-
derstandings or just from being unaccustomed to you or "your kind." Racists
hate you because you are black, brown, Muslim, and so on, because they're
indoctrinated that way and because they might not be accustomed to you, thereby having no chance to disprove their indoctrinated biases. But in most cases,
they don't hate you because you are *you*, as they don't know *you*—a point that
was beautifully articulated by writer Zora Neale Hurston. In the second to last
paragraph of her short autobiographical essay, she jokingly said, "Sometimes, I
feel discriminated against, but it does not make me angry. It merely astonishes
me. How can anyone deny themselves the pleasure of my company? It's beyond
me."[313] Indeed, many did deny themselves the pleasure and indeed discriminated against her, because they'd never had the pleasure of knowing the beautiful
Zora Neale Hurston in the first place.

As earlier stated, on the other hand, your own people reject you because
you're *you*—because they know *you*. They reject you in spite of or because of
knowing precisely who you are. It's, therefore, personal—the hardest to accept
and the hardest to forgive. This is the feeling we got from the Sharpton books.
Regardless of his outward manifestations toward white America, it was always
more an issue of finding acceptance and partaking of "white privileges" than of

---

313 Zora Neale Hurston, *How It Feels To Be Colored Me* (World Tomorrow, 1928, repr.
Applewood Books, 2015)

combating rejection on a personal level. But early black rejection was personal for the Rev., even where it shouldn't have been.

As he'd sat at the presidential inaugural recalling those who'd laughed at him as a child, he wasn't thinking about white people in that "all-black situation" in Brooklyn. He was thinking of better-positioned African Americans, who'd mocked and laughed at him for a variety of reasons—because of who he was—many likely owing to the ego that had insisted that fellow ten-year-olds address him as "the Reverend Alfred Charles Sharpton Jr." It would take him nearly forty years to get that sense of belonging. He'd started his literary journey in 1996's *Pharaoh* by crucifying the black elite and its agents, and by the writing of 2013's *Stone,* he ended up owning them. His blunt early reminders to the elites—of being "trespassers" in suburbia—had forced acceptance by those who'd needed no reminders of their existential conditions. They'd feared him and eagerly submitted to his emotional blackmail, much like Michael Jackson and the Jackson family had done in giving him his piece of the "Victory Tour" promotions pie. In the same way, by President Obama's second term, the Rev. was dominating the black elite and its agents—politicians, institutions, and celebrities, all of whose livelihood thrive on the massive vicarious-living black underclass out to pasture, of which Sharpton has long been the undisputed king.

But his job as an MSNBC television host alongside respected white subject-matter experts, black scholars, politicians, and celebrity guests alike, was his crowning moment of ultimate domination. The show catapulted him to the top of the black social echelons, over the heads of many others with all the bourgeois trappings of class, Ivy League education, and money—all things the Rev. has never had. He was dominating the stage and spotlight, working with "underlings" like the NAACP's Ben Jealous and the National Urban League's Marc Morial to craft the phantom black agenda for President Obama. But as the Rev. savored the moment, he was also laughing at Jealous, Morial, and others who'd needed his presence and "prestige" to get the ear of a president of the United States, after having subordinated their organizations and their usefulness to the Sharpton bulldozer. The Rev. was having a field day.

His newfound Obama era status was as much a story of "moving on up" as it was one of revenge—the pleasure of laughing at the many with education and stature who were now angling for a shot at being a guest on his show. Where the *Washington Post*'s Jonathan Capehart had once facilitated covert exchanges between Michael Bloomberg and the Rev. during a New York City mayoral campaign, Capehart was now elevating his own profile by being a regular guest on Sharpton's *Politics Nation.*

While Sharpton was "in like Flynn," many others, like Dr. Cornel West and television host Tavis Smiley, were forced to stand on the outside—out in the cold where they could but grumble at being ignored by President Obama. And so it was that in *Stone,* the Rev. aimed his cannon squarely at both without even naming them but with a clear reference to "a scholar" (West) and to "people in the black community" (West's elitist cohort and frequent Obama critic, PBS's Smiley). Dr. West, a former adviser to the Rev.'s nefarious 2004 public-relation stint as a presidential candidate, as well as the traditional representative of the black intellectual class, was never on the Rev.'s Christmas list from the outset. Sharpton had never liked West, having spent much ink mocking him in 1996's *Pharaoh* (Count West in as one of many who'd never read a Sharpton book).

In the meantime, as petty jealousies and jockeying for proximity to the president intensified, an internecine warfare enveloping the black men, or more appropriately, the African-American children encircling President Obama—those on the inside versus those who were shut out—then spilled out into the street for us all to marvel at the collective childish pettiness. It was almost incestuous, at times seeming more like a homoerotic battle for supremacy in gaining presidential attention and affection. Rather than diplomatically engaging as a collective on differences and similarities, these otherwise testosterone-driven men showed themselves as sensitive and vulgar in their attacks on each other—each regarding black America (and by extension the president) as his own fiefdom, in the old French sense of, *L'État, c'est moi!*

Dr. West and Tavis Smiley then declared war on the Rev. and other internal favorites for "carrying water" for President Obama. Sharpton then engaged the rhythmically enhanced Dr. Michael Eric Dyson as his chariot commander to take the gory battle to West and Smiley. It could've been described as "Onward black Christian soldiers, Marching as to War," as these very Christian men had set out to club and spear each other and themselves to death in the process. Credibility and reputations fell like victims to a Spartan archer when the war culminated or was officially declared with "The Ghost of Cornel West"—a brutal nine-thousand-word piece written by Dr. Michael Eric Dyson in the April 19, 2015, edition of *New Republic* magazine. As black America had waited with bated breath for the powder keg, otherwise known as Baltimore, to explode in the aftermath of Freddie Gray's "quartering" by forces of the law, Dr. Dyson, in another example of "Idols who were created to be destroyed," had found nothing better to do with his time than to take down Dr. West—his former mentor and idol.

The article eviscerated Cornel West as a *has-been* lunatic while promoting the Rev. as, of all things—a black "prophet," comparable to famed Hebrews of antiquity. In publishing the piece, Dr. Dyson had enjoined himself to the buffoonery of the century, as few in their right mind would associate Reverend Sharpton with the word "prophet" or with its pretentious cousin, mastered by West himself and often heralded by equally pretentious black scholars and theologians—"prophetic traditions." Even worse, though, who would undertake to write an article seemingly aimed at impressing Al Sharpton, even if the ultimate intent was to impress the First Reader in the Oval Office?

It was a sad spectacle to behold men with claims to political and "intellectual" leadership in black America devolving to such petty and garrulous conduct. William Golding couldn't have written it better. In this case, it wasn't just a Sharpton symptom, but instead, that *psychosis of deficiencies* and *inadequacies*—the emptiness of men that was on full display among all involved. They were fighting over President Barack Obama as if they were animals in a savage kingdom fighting for favors of the females among them.

On the receiving end, Dr. West and Tavis Smiley had been so forceful in their critique of the president that they'd managed to turn off many reasoned minds that might have otherwise been in sympathy with their positions. Cornel West then became a laughing stock on Dyson's revelation that his grievances with the president had had their origins in White House invitations and due deference that he'd believed were owed to him but were never forthcoming.

But behind it all, was a Reverend Sharpton laughing all the way to the revenge bank. The taste couldn't have been sweeter than to see two former friends and confidants of the intellectual class, neither of whom he'd cared for in the first place, at each other's throat. Dr. Michel Eric Dyson, a former mentee and friend of Dr. Cornel West, who'd even written Dyson a recommendation for his admission into the "Ivy Leagues," had set out, Sharpton style, to destroy his former mentor in favor of the Rev., who was now firmly in charge. Lost on Dr. Dyson was that the original *rejected stone* had had a bigger fish to fry and an even bigger score to settle for his rejection by Dyson's "own" class (Dyson still straddles the intellectual-downtrodden path as necessary). The Rev. couldn't have cared any less for the intellectual Dr. Michael Eric Dyson than he had for the intellectual Dr. Cornel West; both were Sharpton's "Isam" moment—his big fishes to be fried.

What Sharpton, who had long suffered from inferiority and insecurity to both men, had cared about, was seeing the former mentor-mentee tear each other apart. He'd set out to instigate the self-immolation of the class he'd long envied and detested and had provided the fuel while relishing the sight of each man scorch the earth out from under the other. In their pettiness, both Dyson and West had failed to realize themselves as "pawns" in Sharpton's machinations. But the damage was done, and it has left all involved, except the Rev., reduced in respectability and statue. Grown men were fighting among each other, tearing up old friendships, taking sides, and weakening their abilities to be effective as respectable commercial sirens or "public intellectuals"—as they call themselves—just as the Rev. had wanted and all while he'd stood by laughing. As went Reverend Sharpton so did black "public intellectuals" and black institutions in the Obama era, as reflected through Sharpton's relationship with National Urban League's Marc Morial.

Marc Morial wasn't among the fighting buffoons of the Obama era, but he was nonetheless one of the Obama jokers. His was not the crass conduct of the rest of the men, as the dignified Mr. Morial is obviously cut from more refined cloth. While Reverend Sharpton is the eminent buffoon of black America and Dr. Dyson, the buffoon in perpetual affinity to ghetto folk and rap stars, Morial was effectively the joker of the bourgeois experience during the Obama years. This ended up making him out to be one of the big losers of the inner group for his submission to the whims of Reverend Sharpton because Marc Morial should've known better.

After being part of the Sharpton conniving machine for President Obama's two terms, Marc Morial would wait until President Obama had left office to issue the "Obama Administration Scorecard" in January 2017. In its preamble, he was effusive in his praise of the president:

> President Obama is leaving office with an approval rating even higher than Reagan's, exceeded only by Presidents Franklin D. Roosevelt, Dwight Eisenhower and Bill Clinton. During Obama's presidency, the economy has added 15 million new jobs, and the jobless rate has dropped from 7.6% to 4.7%—and from 12.7% to 7.8% for African Americans. The high school graduation rate for African Americans has increased from 66.1% to 85%. There are 614,000 fewer long-term unemployed. Wages are up 3.4%. More than 16 million Americans who were uninsured now have health care coverage, with the uninsured rate for African Americans cut by more than half. Barack Obama's passion and steady hand made a huge difference in charting a progressive course and positively impacted the lives of ordinary Americans. Black Americans felt both the pride of his accomplishments and the pain when it was clear his opponents sought to diminish a great American. I am confident the long arc of history will judge him favorably.

But toward the end of the scorecard, there was a sneaky little observation that seemed to have indicated that President Obama had actually failed in some areas. One analysis claimed about a 57.5-percent rate of success to 42.5-percent rate of failure, but it was failure where it really counted:

> While we scored many of the administration's achievements with our highest rating, "Superior," President Obama's tenure as a whole had shortcomings due to some notable missed opportunities and outright failures, such as the economic development of urban centers, gun violence and the foreclosure rate and bank closure rate in communities of color and low-income neighborhoods. On these and other issues, we rated the Obama administration "Fair" or "Poor."

Marc Morial and the Rev. had headed the group of black leaders who'd supposedly pushed the five-point plan to the president for urban renewal, to no avail. With the cynical issuance of the Obama Scorecard, Morial showed the same credibility-gap as his fellow inside warriors Sharpton, Dyson, and others encircling the president; the report was effectively a big, *Oops, too late! These are now Trump's problems.* This highlighted the even more significant debilitating effect of the Sharpton "*denouement*" and its revenge quality—the National Urban League had also lost some credibility in the process.

So the battle for presidential affection was symptomatic of that broader effect the Rev. would end up having on the black elite, the black political establishment, and the oldest black institutions. Having orchestrated the obliteration of the respectability of those warring "public intellectuals," Sharpton then moved to contaminate the elites of the black institutions—nearly all of whom, including Marc Morial and NAACP's Ben Jealous, in fearing him—had sold their souls, silenced their consciences, and abandoned their usefulness and decency to the "celebritized" Sharpton of the Obama era. Instead of pushing President Obama on speaking to black America's despair, they instead followed Sharpton's lead in becoming "water carriers of silence" in demanding black America's obedience. In the case of Jealous, it might have all been too painful, so he admirably quit early—resigning from the NAACP in 2013.

In the end, the black establishment, including the Congressional Black Caucus, the NAACP, and the National Urban League, are now forever weakened, on life support for at least a generation to come—having lost credibility as effective advocates for its people by getting little or nothing from the black president while kowtowing to a "criminal buffoon" [Joe Klein] as the head of their connivance. As noted in Robert Kennedy Jr.'s diary, black leadership was forever tainted by the stench of Reverend Sharpton, but it's a stench that became radioactively corrosive during the Obama years. As the influence of these organizations and leaders continue to be buried in the Democratic coalition and negated by resolute Republican power, resurgent white nationalism (vocal and silent), and overall tribalism in the country, the man who'd once ran a mole Republican candidacy to weaken the Democratic nominee is now savoring the moment—having significantly weakened that elite black leadership.

As Reverend Sharpton had never liked the black elite, their agents, or their institutions—even in his earlier need to use the collective in his effort to elevate his stature—would he, who'd orchestrated the betrayal of one of America's two major political parties in his aim at self-promotion, have hesitated to betray those he'd so hated in the past? Additionally, in the advent of their weakness, the Rev. can now continue to secure himself a space, albeit with waning influence, to manifest and complain about the very epidemic he'd brought about—an even more weakened black leadership. He has left them all worse than he'd found them (or than they'd found him), and that's just the way he'd wanted it. As went the Rev., so did the NAACP, the Congressional Black Caucus, the National Urban League, and others of the Obama era's conniving machine.

Many who have declared themselves the intellectual, and to some extent, the political leadership of black America have repeatedly shown themselves as delirious weaklings who are primarily angry at white America for not inviting them over for Sunday dinners. Yet others are just frustrated from their failed efforts at imitating white America in order to be accepted. The Rev. was therefore on point in his *pharaonic* condemnations. He'd always known them to be mere tenuous "trespassers." So he promptly showed up as a Marshall with their eviction notices and showed them the front gate.

In the end, like that of Edmond Dantès, we'd witnessed the return of the Reverend Alfred Charles Sharpton Jr. to his "rightful" place among the black bourgeoisie—finally having his day mopping up the class of nobility that'd once forsaken him. As much of their conduct in the aftermath of the Obama presidency has shown, it was a cakewalk for the Sharpton. Many of that class were easy marks. Though not quite the return of Edmond Dantès, we'd nonetheless witnessed the vengeful return of the *rejected stone*.

James McBride, Al Sharpton, and James Brown

<hr>

Truth is stranger than fiction, but it is because fiction
is obliged to stick to possibilities. Truth isn't.

—MARK TWAIN[314]

Start of Truth, Continuation of Fiction

IN THE SPRING of 2016, nearly a year after completing my first draft of this manuscript, I was told that author James McBride had released a book on singer James Brown's life—*Kill 'Em and Leave, Searching for James Brown and the American Soul*—that relied heavily on Reverend Sharpton as a source. *Here we go again; they never learn!* I thought, reflecting on Jonathan Capehart's 2015 *Washington Post* article. I immediately recognized a portion of the title as a likely Sharpton contribution and was curious to see if the Rev., as a source, had followed the same fictional path as Sharpton, the writer.

As Reverend Sharpton had made *James Brown taught me this; James Brown taught me that* into a cottage industry in which he (Sharpton) was the big cheese—that all-important repository of all that was James Brown—for the naked eye, there could've been no better source for a book on Brown than Sharpton. So, under the circumstances, I understood it to have been natural that James McBride would've turned to the Rev. But when viewed through magnifying glasses, there was one problem to contend with: the Rev.'s real experience with Brown was never enough for him. Though holding a glove with a perfect fit, he'd always

<hr>

314 *Following the Equator - The Wit and Wisdom of Mark Twain*, 32.

insisted on planting a number of embellishments to further the milking of his super cow. So I ordered a copy.

In reading it, where James McBride made attributions to James Brown, intertextual reading was necessary in order to see where James Brown had left the room and the Rev. had remained—in other words, what Brown had actually said versus what Sharpton had invented and attributed to him. As I'd suspected, it didn't take much reading before the wheels fell off the wagon. It was pure comedy.

Meeting James Brown (McBride's Kill 'Em and Leave):

In McBride's chapter 10, "The Rev," the wheels didn't just fall off the wagon, they went careening with such momentum that you could hear the havoc of wreckage on structural integrities, smell the friction of burning rubber on contact with the pavement. Reverend Sharpton had always told us that James Brown was the father who'd given him legitimacy as a man, yet in a relationship so integral to, and so influential on his life, he gave three very different versions of his initial meeting with his idol. McBride's first Al Sharpton had initially met James Brown during Brown's function at the RKO Albee theater in Brooklyn, New York, to register black voters (1971) and to honor Brown's dead son, Teddy:

> "I met James Brown when I was seventeen," Sharpton tells me. The previous
> year, he says, PUSH fell apart, and so in 1971, he [Sharpton] started his National
> Youth Movement, a voter registration outfit. Brown's oldest son Teddy, joined
> that movement, and the two were friends for about a year until Teddy's sud-
> den death. At that time, a local DJ named Hank Spann introduced Sharpton to
> Brown during an event at the old RKO Albee Theatre in downtown Brooklyn to
> honor Teddy and get black youth to register to vote.[315]

---

315 James McBride, *Kill 'Em and Leave—Searching for James Browns and the American Soul* (Spiegel & Grau, New York, 2016), 108.

Of Brown's and Sharpton's initial conversations, the Rev. gave such vivid recollections three and a half decades later that James McBride described him as
misting sentimentally as he related his memories, which showed the mark of an
indelible impression left on Sharpton:

> Even now, forty years later, Sharpton, a master of the sound bite, a man who
> rarely shows his true face, who will keel over before he shows hurt in public,
> mists a bit sentimental as he pushes back into the memories of his first actual
> conversation with Brown. They met at a Newark theatre to discuss the upcoming
> voter-registration concert, before a scheduled Brown performance.[316]

Note that as he traveled down his misty memory lane, however, the Brooklynite,
Sharpton, was unable to even distinguish Newark, New Jersey, from Brooklyn,
New York. Here we got McBride's second Al Sharpton: an initial meeting
at Brooklyn's RKO Albee theater during a Brown voter-registration concert
quickly morphed into memories of a first conversation at a Newark theater to
discuss that very upcoming voter-registration concert in Brooklyn to honor
Brown's dead son.

Meeting James Brown (Sharpton's Go and Tell Pharaoh)

Pharaoh's Al Sharpton (written two decades earlier) had first met James Brown
before Brown's Newark, New Jersey concert (1973), not Brooklyn, as in the
second version of events told to McBride. But there's a twist: that Sharpton
was raising money for his National Youth Movement, and Brown had heard
of him and wanted to do a benefit concert for him—because Sharpton was
Brown's "kind of guy." James Brown was doing a concert to help out the
Rev.:

> In 1973 we were trying to raise money for the National Youth Movement, and
> James Brown heard about it and called a disc jockey I knew and offered to help us
> by doing a benefit. James had heard about me. He knew I was a preacher and an

---

316 Ibid., 108–9.

activist. James thought I was his kind of guy, and he had me brought to a concert in Newark to meet him. They took us backstage. I was awed.[317]

In that version, James Brown had supposedly contacted a disc jockey [Hank Spann] and offered to help, after which he'd had the Rev. brought to his Newark, New Jersey concert. Sharpton was left in awe after being taken back-stage to meet Brown, and of this encounter, the Rev. then elaborated by adding even more confusion in telling us of the circumstances:

> James had a show scheduled in Brooklyn, and he asked me if I wanted to help him. This would be a show for NYM [Sharpton's National Youth Movement]. Of course I said yes, and he said if I did exactly what he said, we could sell the place out…[318]

But this was a claim negated by its very construct (*"This would be a show for NYM"*). If James Brown had a show scheduled in Brooklyn for Sharpton's youth movement, why would Brown have been asking the Rev. to help him out, when it was for the benefit of Sharpton in the first place?

In summary, as related to James McBride, the Brown-Sharpton initial meeting was in the first instance during Brown's benefit voter-registration concert honoring his dead son at the RKO Albee theater downtown Brooklyn, New York. In the second instance, it was at a Newark, New Jersey theater to discuss the very same upcoming voter registration concert (presumably to be held at the same RKO Albee in Brooklyn) to honor Brown's dead son. Put another way, James Brown's performance to honor his dead son and to register youth voters at the old RKO Albee theater in Brooklyn was at once the venue at which Brown-Sharpton had made their initial acquaintance and, at the same time, the venue that had followed that initial acquaintance—this time, that initial acquaintance having taken place in Newark, New Jersey, many months before.

All in all, even after coverage by at least four books, we are still unsure of Reverend Sharpton's treasured first encounter with his idol James Brown,

---

317 Al Sharpton and Walton, *Go and Tell Pharaoh*, 66.
318 Ibid., 66–67.

as each account given has been a Sharpton narrative—invariably embellished, invariably fictitious.

"Ooh, Just 'Killing Them"

Where contradicting details of the Brown-Sharpton initial meeting might appear comedic, the rest of James McBride's chapter 10, "The Rev," was yet again, another Sharpton-scripted piece of propaganda—retroactively transposing his reputation *a la* 2016 back to the 1970s, as he'd done in his own book, *Stone*. It was a continuation of the Rev. advancing the Sharpton prerogatives, in particular, his usual undermining of Dr. King and his attacks on Jesse Jackson, whom he was still seeking to bury—even in 2016:

> Sharpton admired both King and Malcolm X; he shared common ground with all of the radical movements, yet fit with none of them. How do you follow God in a world that is gray? What do you do when black power turns out to be a cobweb of continual adjustment, where Baptists like King and Jesse Jackson looked down their noses at the Pentecostals like him—even as they needed a young voice like his? He saw no space for himself, so he created one. Guess who was the guy [James Brown] who showed him how to do it? [319]

Previous admiration for Jesse Jackson was now replaced by admiration for Malcolm X, who was never "admirably" mentioned in the Sharpton books—mentioned in passing only three times in his early books. But the long-converted Baptist was still carrying the insecurities of his "jack-legged" roots in the Pentecostal church. Many years had passed since he'd silenced New York's mayoral candidate Ruth Messinger by claiming affiliation to Dr. King's SCLC since age fourteen and declaring Jesse Jackson, a lifelong mentor. Yet even as the leader of black America in 2016, he was still holding resentment for what he'd perceived as having been looked down on with snobbery by Dr. King and Reverend Jackson, and out of his belief that "they" (Jackson) had needed his youthfulness to thrive.

---

319 McBride, *Kill 'Em and Leave*, 108.

James Brown had supposedly helped the Rev. overcome all of this, yet his obsession with Jackson had still remained. It was back to attacking Jesse, this time, using writer James McBride to squeeze in a few cheap shots at Jackson as a "status chaser"—in a book written about James Brown. "'Normal life didn't exist,' says Sharpton. 'Jesse and them's [*sic*] status was to get on the A-list. James Brown's status was there wasn't any A-list. He was the list.'"[320] Other digs at Jesse Jackson circa 1973 were even attributed to James Brown. According to McBride, in the Rev.'s back and forth in Brown's dressing room in between shows at the RKO Albee in Brooklyn (not Newark, New Jersey), Brown told Sharpton to cast off Jesse Jackson:

"I was a boy preacher, Mr. Brown."

"What does that mean?"

"I want to be like Jesse Jackson."

Brown cut him off. "No you don't," he said.

"You don't want to be the next Jesse Jackson. You want to be the first Al Sharpton...You can register voters, real young people, 'cause those guys out there in civil rights ain't got no heart."[321]

But this sounded much like the Sharpton of *Al on America*, where it was he, not James Brown, who was speaking:

Now I understand why God had me be around a man like James Brown. I would not have learned those lessons hanging around the guys in the Civil Rights' Movement. They didn't have that kind of fortitude and that kind of integrity and internal strength. They didn't have that kind of self-respect and internal strength.[322]

Additionally, it's unimaginable that 1973's James Brown, then Soul Brother No.1 wouldn't have been an ardent admirer of black America's number one

---

320 Ibid., 117.

321 Ibid., 110.

322 Sharpton with Hunter, *Al on America*, 211.

black leader—Reverend Jesse Jackson. It's further unimaginable that Brown would've belittled civil rights leaders as "heartless" in deference to a kid preacher from Brooklyn whom he was just meeting. But this was the Rev.'s often-ambiguous display of sentiments (to be or not to be?) toward Jackson. In 2013's *Stone,* Sharpton had bragged about his old meetings at Sylvia's in Harlem with his friends Gregory Meeks and David Paterson, telling us,

> In the early '90s I would have regular meetings at Sylvia's Restaurant in Harlem with two close friends of mine, David Paterson and Greg Meeks. All of us were in our thirties at the time, born within a year of one another, and we were all thinking about where we wanted our careers to take us next. One particular day, we conducted a little poll on where we saw ourselves headed…David went first…"I think I'm going to be the next David Dinkins, the next black mayor," David said. Meeks went next. "I want to be the next congressman from Queens," he said. They got around to me. I had already been through the wrenching ordeals of Howard Beach, Bensonhurst, and quite a few other high-profile instances of racial injustice in the city. I had just started my National Action Network to bring some structure to my activism and had recently run for the US Senate in New York. But up to that point, my work had mostly been contained in the city. "I want to do what Jesse does. I want to be the national civil rights guy," I said. They seemed surprised. "You don't want to hold elective office?" they asked me. I shook my head. "No I want to use running for office to drive voters to the polls, to drive policies, get in the debates, help push you guys through. I want to do what Jesse and Adam did."[323]

Even in ignoring for a moment that this "candor" was written or published in 2013 when he'd felt himself at the pinnacle of success and had given up running phony campaigns for public office, it's obvious that the Rev. hadn't taken Brown's 1973 advice (assuming Brown had indeed said that). Because up through the 1990s, Sharpton was still dying to be the next Jesse Jackson. With success in the Obama years, these old friends would regroup anew for an update:

---

323 Al Sharpton with Chiles, *The Rejected Stone,* 124–25.

Fast-forward about seventeen years. We were sitting in another restaurant, this time in downtown New York. David looked over at me. "Remember our meetings at Sylvia's?" he asked, a smile spreading across his face. "Yeah," I said, nodding my head. "I remember." "I think we did it," David said, his smile broader now. "I'm the governor of New York. Meeks is a congressman. And you're the national civil rights guy." It was a sweet moment. But what was interesting about it was that we all understood our roles, our different talents, and how we could make our contributions. I decided that I wanted to be the Jesse Jackson of my generation. Jesse decided before me that he wanted to be the Martin Luther King of his generation.[324]

All had realized their goals, including Sharpton—of being the next Jesse Jackson. The Rev. had indeed become the one who "ain't got no heart."

Pulling Up alongside a Cliff

By the middle of McBride's chapter 10, it started to feel like reading excerpts from *Pharaoh, Al on America,* and *Stone,* all cobbled together. We saw the point where the Rev. actually pulled up alongside a cliff, took a deep breath, looked left then right, then tossed himself headfirst.

First, according to McBride, after the show at the RKO Albee in Brooklyn, James Brown then left New York, only to return two weeks later to tell the Rev. to pack his bags—after which both men headed for Los Angeles for the start of a journey that would keep Sharpton out of New York City for fifteen years:

Brown left New York, returned two weeks later, and summoned Sharpton, telling him, "Pack your bags. We're going to LA." Sharpton packed his things, climbed aboard James Brown's private plane, and didn't come back to New York for fifteen years. He left New York City as Alfred Charles Sharpton, a seventeen-year-old boy-wonder preacher. He returned as Rev. Al Sharpton—the Rev—one

---

324 Ibid., 123–25.

of the most powerful, charismatic, controversial, and unique figures in African American history.[325]

If we conservatively accept the Rev.'s date of a 1971 initial meeting with Brown (elsewhere he's given the year as 1972 and 1973), then this would've kept Sharpton out of the five boroughs (NYC) until 1986. He would've therefore been missing in action for so many of his well-publicized fracases of the early to mid-1980s. He would've barely made it back in time for his December 1986 march to protest Michael Griffith's death in Howard Beach, Brooklyn, among others. He would've definitely not been in the city for his 1984 Bernard Goetz protest—for which he'd famously claimed "victory." In fact, half the events mentioned in *Pharaoh* could not have taken place, including this one with Brown in 1974:

> In 1974, James says to me, "Reverend"—when he was feeling good, he'd call me Reverend—"they won't let me play Madison Square Garden. They say my crowd's too rowdy. I want you to go down there and book it for the National Youth Movement. Tell them that if they won't let you, you'll picket the Knicks games." I did what he said and the managers laughed and said, "Look kid, it costs sixty thousand dollars to rent the Garden." I said, "I didn't ask you how much it cost. I want to rent it." They said, "All right, here's a contract. You have two weeks to pay the first twenty thousand. You've got to put up forty thousand two weeks after that." James gave me a certified check for $20,000 from Polygram Records, and I signed the contract.[326]

These had all taken place in New York City while the Rev. was out in Los Angeles and elsewhere preparing to return as one of the "most charismatic, controversial, and unique figures in African American history." Additionally, Sharpton, who'd turned 18 in the fall of 1972, had told us that he'd dropped out of Brooklyn College—not UCLA, Caltech, or Long Beach College—as a sophomore, which would mean somewhere around 1974, while he was out

---

325 McBride, *Kill 'Em and Leave*, 111.

326 Al Sharpton and Walton, *Go and Tell Pharaoh*, 68.

in California practicing charisma and controversy. But then there was also Shirley Chisholm's 1972 electoral campaign for president, for which Sharpton now claims to have been the "youth director." Was he organizing and directing youths from out there in Los Angeles as well?

Looking Left Then Right

Next up was a confounding story of the Rev.'s involvement with singer Michael Jackson. In 1996's *Pharaoh,* he'd given us the details of events surrounding Michael Jackson and the Jackson's 1984 "Victory Tour," in which Sharpton's on-and-off friend Don King had invited him to help mediate the Jacksons familial squabbles in Los Angeles. Then, James Brown wasn't mentioned anywhere as being involved in this. Thirty-two years later though, writer James McBride, who was then a reporter at the Jackson family press conference in Encino, recalls Reverend Sharpton then saying, "I'm here because of James Brown. I'm here to look after Michael Jackson's interest because James Brown sent me."[327] McBride tells us that back then, he thought, Sharpton was "full of it," but it "turns out what he said was true. He [Sharpton] had been sent there by Brown to help out Michael." [328]

This was the most challenging part of the McBride book, as it was the writer's validation of a Sharpton representation being put forward in his own book. But if Reverend Sharpton wasn't "full of it," why would he, in his own book, have written so eloquently of being Don King's emissary rather than James Brown's? Why would he have given such a detailed account of being summoned by Don King, even to the point of picking up tickets left at JFK airport by King for him to travel from New York to Los Angeles? As the Rev. had told us then, it was all Don King:

> My last big foray in the music business was the Jackson Family's Victory tour in 1984…Late one Sunday night, I got a call from Don King asking me to meet him in Los Angeles the next day. I was surprised, because we had been quarreling,

---

327 McBride, *Kill 'Em and Leave*, 120.
328 Ibid.

but he left a first-class ticket at Kennedy Airport and had a limousine waiting for me at LAX. The limo took me to Michael Jackson's house in Encino, where we had a meeting with everybody in the family, who were feuding. It had now developed that even the parents were being pushed out of the tour by the big-money people, and had turned to Don King.[329]

Given the way Sharpton had played up his relationship with the godfather in *Pharaoh*, had Brown really sent him to Los Angeles to help out Michael Jackson, it's hard to believe that the Rev. would've omitted mention of being dispatched as James Brown's fixer. Much like Shirley Chisholm's "organizer," this would've been yet another notch the Rev. had deliberately taken off his own belt, which we know to be uncharacteristic of Sharpton. But regardless of who'd sent him to help out Michael Jackson, there was yet another added twist to this story. If we accept McBride's premise of Sharpton having skipped out of New York for fifteen years with James Brown since 1971, then what was the Rev. doing picking up a ticket at, and flying out of, John F. Kennedy Airport in New York City in 1984?

Again, both stories can't be the truth. In this case, the Sharpton version given in *Pharaoh* seems the more acceptable, but with the Rev., who knows?

Taking the Plunge Headfirst

Unsurprisingly, in a book about James Brown, the *Rumble in the Jungle* would once more be offered up as evidence of Reverend Sharpton's closeness to the godfather. By now we know that the Rev. wasn't in Africa as part of James Brown's or anyone else's entourage for that 1974 fight. But his version in *Stone* was so tepid that it had left a little wiggle room for him to later say, *I was misquoted, taken out of context,* or something to that effect. But not so in the version told to James McBride. Here, there's no mistaking the context. Reverend Sharpton was in Kinshasa in 1974.

It's the lie told a few times that had now become "factual" yet even more confusing—the real hydra with multiple legs, arms, tentacles, and heads that

---

329 Al Sharpton and Walton, *Go and Tell Pharaoh*, 84.

had since sprung up to defeat itself. For example, all versions given in Sharpton's books had New York as the origination point for the trip to Africa and had placed him squarely in New York in 1974—not in Los Angeles during his supposed fifteen-year absence from the city starting in 1971 or 1972. So not only was the Rev. back in New York at that time but so was James Brown. This time around, though, a much larger and more embellished storyline was given, in particular, where the Rev. described James Brown's macho exploits in making a quick exit from Kinshasa, Zaire. They were heading "outta" Dodge, fast and furious; James Brown was *killing them and leaving*—a line that perfectly fits McBride's theme and storyline:

> When Brown played Zaire in Africa as part of the gala preceding the great Ali-George Foreman fight, with the world watching and the cream of black entertainment in tow, Brown knocked the socks off eighty thousand roaring and screaming fans. He told Sharpton after the performance, "Pack up. We're leaving." Sharpton didn't want to leave. He wanted to stay with the other entertainers who had come to revel in the pending fight, which was postponed because of an injury Foreman sustained. Besides, President Mobutu of Zaire, a country rich in diamonds, had made it known that he wanted to impart certain gifts to the performers. Brown had no interest.
> "But Mr. Brown," Sharpton protested, "we just got here."
> "Kill 'em and leave, Rev. Kill 'em and leave."[330]

The precision with which the Rev. invents merits attention here as either the maniacal or ingenious talents of an ingenious maniac. In addition to content, there is the repetition of themes and the provision of context with enough details to actually place the reader on the spot. Ignoring for a moment that Sharpton was actually in Queens, New York, at the time, the writer James McBride and his readers were taken back in time—placed right there in Africa, watching the impressionable twenty-year-old plead with his mentor for just one more day in the jungle so he could enjoy the rumble. But the godfather wasn't having any of it. Brown had already *killed them*, so he'd had to *leave*.

---

330 Ibid., 118.

On the upside, this version was much better researched than the ones given in Sharpton's previous books—noting, for example, the postponement of the fight due to George Foreman's injury. The Rev.'s previous renditions had had James Brown performing the day of the fight and leaving Africa that very day—skipping out, not on a basket full of diamonds but on house arrests for the entertainers who'd trashed former Zairian President Mobutu Sese Seko's hotels:

> The day of the fight, I get a call from James's secretary, saying, "Mr. Brown would like you to meet him at the airport. I couldn't believe it. The fight hadn't ended yet. But when I went to meet James and asked him why he didn't stay and enjoy the fight and he laughed. "Reverend, how many times do I have to tell you that this is a business? I did my show, I made my money, I got things to do." And strangely enough, Mobutu put everybody connected to the show and the fight under house arrest afterward because of high hotel bills, but James was here in the States, counting his money and booking new dates. All business.[331]

The "Kill 'em and leave, Rev" dialogue had followed a paragraph in which Sharpton told McBride's that Brown had once met President Richard Nixon with his .38 caliber revolver in his coat pocket. In other words, *The Godfather was a bad mother... packing heat, even at the White House.* So, if the Secret Service didn't faze him, Brown certainly wouldn't have been too impressed by President Mobutu and his diamonds down there in Africa—by inference, Jesse Jackson would've stayed back for the loot. Again, as we know, the only issue is that the Rev. was nowhere near Zaire in 1974, nowhere within earshot of James Brown telling him or anyone else to "Pack up. We're leaving; Kill 'em and leave, Rev. Kill 'em and leave." It was a fabulous piece of fiction—part and parcel of a James Brown legend formulated by the Rev. to support James McBride's narrative and likely the inspiration for the book's title—*Kill 'Em and Leave.* No lesser person than Reverend Sharpton would write books upon books of fiction only to then transmit the same inventions to the work of another writer, who appears to be his friend.

---

331 Al Sharpton and Walton, *Go and Tell Pharaoh*, 69.

In a later segment, James McBride unknowingly pointed us to the source of the hydra's evolution—Charles Bobbit, James Brown's long-time manager. Bobbit, also featured in McBride's book, emphasized James Brown's desire to "stay ahead" and to "control the conversation." In reflecting back to the 1974 fight in Zaire, at which he was present, Charles Bobbit gave McBride a picture of the events from someone who was actually there in Africa:

> They had chartered a plane for the performers. B.B King was on it and Etta James and Sister Sledge and Bill Withers. Brown wanted to bring his equipment. I told him, "You don't need to bring equipment. They're on a different current over there in Africa. They're 220. We're 110." But he insisted. They had to take a lot of his stuff off the plane because it was too heavy. He held the plane up. It was so loaded it barely got into the air. Oh my God, Bill Withers was so mad. They were late getting into Zaire because of Brother Brown...Mobutu [president of Zaire] was famous for giving diamonds as a gift. He sent word for all the entertainers to stay behind for a while when the music was finished. Mr. Brown said, "I ain't staying here."
>
> He came offstage, went into a room, changed his clothes, and went straight to the airport and sat there for four hours. And he could have gotten a bag of dia-monds as a gift. But he was a man that did what he wanted to do.[332]

The secret was finally out. The Rev. had heard the legendary story of James Brown skipping out on former Zairian president Mobutu Sese Seko and had spun his own variants—among which he had Brown skipping out on house ar-rest. Sharpton then infused himself in the "skipping out"—of an event that had seen him some sixty-four hundred miles away.

While the writer may bring us data points, propaganda, factoids, tidbits of information, or even synthesis of knowledge, new or old, original or unoriginal, it is the reader who interprets and makes the discoveries—she or he for whom it all falls in or out of place. When the writer or source is Reverend Sharpton how-ever, the reading experience soon starts to feel like beating a dead horse or be-ing kicked by a live mule; the contradictions bring on a kind of excruciating pain

---

332 McBride, *Kill 'Em and Leave*, 181.

that cripples and gets you nowhere. You're left understanding less of the subject matter and even less of the cosmic forces that facilitate or inspire such wanton buffoonery. As James McBride painted the picture of the young Sharpton pleading with his idol to stay at an event where he wasn't present, it was the live mule that kicked—unbearably painful and embarrassing just to read it.

In the end, how many people forget or confuse the location (different cities) and timing (months apart) of their first meeting with a superstar icon who is their lifelong mentor and who has taught them everything they know in life? In Sharpton's literary world, it was like having the same eye-witness standing in both Dallas and Houston at the fateful moment in 1963. In all fairness, Brooklyn and Newark was a reasonable stretch in comparison to Kinshasa and Queens.

Like the liberal press that has warmed up to the Rev., like the segment of black America that still sees him as its warrior-hero, like Jonathan Capehart and the *Washington Post's* editorial board that had given him enough credence as a source of expert advice, writer James McBride was equally duped in using Reverend Sharpton as a source for his book on the life of singer James Brown.

End Act IV

Earthbound! What Now?

Clothes make the man. Naked People have
little or no influence in society.

—MARK TWAIN[333]

The Biggest Loser

WITH A DETERMINED and emergent younger generation of activists nipping at his heels, the Sharpton star will likely fade in the near future even as the mainstream media continue to prop him up as the face of black America. But we'll still see the Rev. fighting for relevance and survival in a bid for renewal of old purposes because he fights whether he's up or down. But old purposes might be of little use, given that he's already rendered them futile and irrelevant by settling for little or nothing tangible to his "causes" from President Obama. But much could be dependent on the Trump presidency. President Donald Trump knows the Rev. even better than the Democrats who handle him. Trump confidant Roger Stone had once held the keys to the Sharpton chains; having long punched his ticket, Mr. Trump knows Sharpton's price. Besides, depending on the outcomes of the sprawling Russian investigation of the 2016 elections, a Reverend Sharpton looking at the wilderness might yet again avail himself as a *useful idiot* for purposes that others deem useful. So the president could also choose to resuscitate a Sharpton in decline—as a bogeyman to keep "dogging" the Democrats. Let's face it, as with President Obama, a Reverend Sharpton at center stage makes a President Trump appear grand at any hour of the day.

---

333 *More Maxims of Mark - The Wit and Wisdom of Mark Twain*, 3.

While those might be farther-fetched scenarios, we'll see blips and upticks along the Sharpton path in the near future. The Rev. might return to writing *"Pharaohesque"* monologues detailing further volumes of inventions and intimate encounters with the dignitaries and celebrities in his orbit. Or in a desperate bid for relevance, he might just return to cursing the Democratic Party and the black elite anew. Though still likely to be considered of use by statewide and local politicians, the Rev. has lost credibility with the younger generation of African Americans, in particular, with the activists and educated classes who have already shown their preference for engaging the Jewish senator from Vermont than being stained by the stench of the celebrity activist from Manhattan. The fact is that there would never have been a need to remind America that *black lives matter,* had the Sharpton life in political and social activism been of much use. So, in another election cycle or two, the voices of the young will be heard by governors, senators, congresspersons, and state and local representatives alike—unaffected by the endorsements of vote-brokering con men and women in their communities.

But this is still America, and unfortunately, African Americans will continue to suffer police abuse, profiling, brutality, and death—all of which will continue to fuel the Sharpton flame, somewhat. Let's face it, the Sharpton phenomenon is as much a product of *manifest-destinarian* ideals that seek domination and supremacy, that fuel racism, drive oppression, and deny justice—as he, Sharpton, is a product of oppression-driven neuroses. As tribal-racial divisions continue across the land, the media will continue to discredit itself by continuing to accredit the Rev., as his appearances, comments, and opinions will remain the gift that keeps on giving. Whether on radio or on television, a no less verbose Reverend Sharpton will likely remain on the scene for some time, although in decline. In social media, the buffoon will continue in ascendance.

Taking his usual stand in opposition might prove difficult with waning Democratic party support and a Republican party indifferent to the claims of a morally assuasive and pretentious black leadership. In 2013, as much as the Rev. had then felt himself to have been the *accepted stone*—post-rejection—he, too, might end up a mere tenuous "trespasser" by 2020, which means that circumstances might then force him to sit down and shut up. For a man who has already halved his daily caloric capacity, Reverend Sharpton might yet find himself the biggest loser in the near future.

Affirmation by Negation

Each race determines for itself what indecencies are.
Nature knows no indecencies, man invents them.

—MARK TWAIN[334]

IN MANY PARTS of black America, we can't ignore the evidence of people who wake up on Election Day to affirm themselves in the exercise of their democratic right to choose but who simultaneously negate themselves by selecting scoundrels to represent them. Others are even worse; they abdicate any obligation of that affirmation by not even bothering to vote, thereby suppressing and abrogating their own hard fought for rights as participants, to even more disastrous results—empowering those who might do them harm or others who are likely to exploit them. Although electoral apathy is in no way a black-only phenomenon, black America doesn't have the luxury to be democratically apathetic.

The Rev. has understood this very well—that he has long been indemnified and absolved of his transgressions by many in black America who prefer the racketeer to the racist. And this has perfected his hold on the black consciousness. That men like Reverend Sharpton are accepted by the masses is just a function of those same oppression-driven neuroses that cultivate the disaffected to value form over substance—a rhythmic *form* perfected in the church that strikes at emotions but is often exploitative. We see this each time men like the Dr. Michael Eric Dyson, Dr. Cornel West, and others get on stage. It's like watching President Obama in a South Carolina church singing "Amazing Grace." The soul is stirred with emotions, and we're weakened at the knees as the body melts.

---

334 *Notebook - The Wit and Wisdom of Mark Twain,* 18.

But when they step off the stage, it's like a psychedelic drug that wears off in no time. The living then goes back to thinking about its dead to be buried; the "uplifted" is left no better off than it was before, maybe even worse—if members had to buy a ticket to go hear these men speak. This is because they're usually not practical men offering practical solutions, and they fall short in holding out the possibilities of rebirth here on earth, salvation, or other holy causes, as the church does. Again, their initial appeal still goes back to the desire for a certain amount of anesthesia to aid renunciation of self or circumstance of their audience members. Promises to this effect are acceptable when offered by the church but echoes as empty and vulgar when from the mouths of laymen.

To march and protest, to be the loudest and most rhythmic voice screaming racism from a bullhorn often beckons neither genius nor the genuine. It just seeks appeal by speaking in "allowable" forms—repeating "permissible" narratives that are neither new nor imaginative. But this catapults them to the leadership of "issues" campaigns, causes, and movements that are essentially businesses and rackets. And therein lies the trap of the oppressed and disfavored in society: those movements that require genuine leadership are more than often led by racketeers in business for themselves—that "economic interpretation" to which I'd spoken in the opening of this book.

In black America, as with other disfavored minority groups elsewhere in the world, innate connivance and fear command the admiration, submission, and loyalty of the masses, and this cripple any form of internal resistance. A history of racism and white betrayal then ensures that those external to the black community, were they so disposed, are also limited in their efforts to arrest the community's exploitation by its own racketeers. It's a primary aspect of evolution: as Pavlov's dogs had evolved to be forever distrustful of the electric fence that shocked them, so have black folk—in becoming wary of whites who've traditionally betrayed them.

As a consequence, elements of reasoned and decent white America (Robert Kennedy Jr. *et al.*) that might take legitimate exception to the chicanery and subterfuge of Sharpton and others, would never dare to publicly criticize or admonish them, for fear of being lambasted for being either racists, paternal, or condescending. Hence the larger societal enjoinder that results in a general connivance that further suffocates the exploited black community at the hands of everyone. Taken a step further, in its rejection of white knights and saviors (Jesus, a notable exception), black America has been left with the black ones— the movement leaders who are in businesses for themselves. This is yet another variant of "black exceptionalism" that admits of its own denigration and its own negation in the form of its leadership.

Disqualifiers

Realistically, the modern American life isn't just an economic one in which wealth is preserved but also a fiscally aggressive and responsible one in which that wealth is first created. Reverend Sharpton's tax debts figure into the millions of dollars today. For a man who'd first pleaded guilty to tax violations back in the 1990s, the Rev. sits atop the leadership of a community in which many of its ordinary citizens have been imprisoned or further impoverished and ruined for much less. Being mired in continued tax infractions for so long should've been an automatic disqualifier from leadership, as such a person has proven himself fiscally irresponsible and is left malleable to selling out any cause to the highest bidders. How can you want to run for president when you've never put together a personal or social budget in over two decades? But as the Rev. and the larger black leadership have been expert exploiters of emotions, even the poor who suffer under minimal tax burdens, will interpret this disqualifier as ennobling—the belief that Reverend Sharpton is a victim of government persecution.

Another disqualifier is the persistent rumors of "Sharpton the Rat," who was once in service of the government, not only against criminals and mobsters but also against grassroots black liberationists and other African American public personalities, including his friend and former tutor, boxing promoter Don King.

Since the beginning of time, every culture in every corner of the planet has always looked upon enemy collaboration as acts of treason to be punished. At the national level, treason has traditionally been punishable by death. European citizens had treated collaborators to shame, disgrace, prison, and even to the gallows after WWII. After the fall of the Cold War, Eastern Europeans treated many of their "snitches"—East Germany's former "Stasi" collaborators, for example—to much the same punishment. In the raucous Middle East, subjects accused of collaborating with the enemy aren't even given a trial before being sent to paradise.

Yes, we live in a civilized society governed by laws and are above sinking to the latter. Additionally, collaboration with law enforcement can't be viewed in the same context as above, as it's often necessary to protect us and our communities from the scourge of criminal elements, nihilism, decadence, and complete anarchy. On the other hand, though, we do have a history in this country of oppressive and racist law enforcement's efforts to decapitate black leadership. This should naturally negate known "snitches" from black leadership or representation, regardless of their goody pretenses of acting out of civic duties. After all, how can you be a civic citizen if you don't even pay your taxes?

Why would Pavlov's dogs grow to trust those among them who'd consistently leaned on that electric fence without being shocked by it? Someone must have cut the current while they touched it, and there must have been a reason for that—beneficial to the those in charge of the experiment. There was the Brawley hoax, and the Rev. wasn't shocked. There was the infamous tape with law enforcement with and a "briefcase" on the table, and he wasn't shocked. There were the Crown Heights riots, and he wasn't shocked. There were the Freddie's Fashion Mart murders, and he wasn't shocked. There are his taxes, and he isn't being shocked. So it can't just be that the Rev is coated in Kevlar or like clothing. That he now sits atop the pack can only mean the existence of a *quid pro quo* somewhere.

Individuals who snitch for law enforcement, especially on their own people, do so because they're compromised and are facing some kind of prosecution for their own infractions. Nobody becomes an informant in America without first having been at least criminally indictable and facing the possibilities of prison time. Yet in black America, revelations of Sharpton's years as an FBI confidential informant—another example of a credibility gap that should've excluded him from leadership in any facet—has largely been ignored. What then might explain the difference between other cultures (including other black cultures) and black America, whereby the former abhors and rejects collaborators, while the latter sticks a suspect atop its leadership? The simple answer is that "reason" is the first casualty of direct forms of oppression.

The admission of an impaired black leadership is no different from the acceptance of, or a general belief in substandard housing, substandard policing, inferior fire prevention services, and poor healthcare, as existential norms of black life—in other words, the most that the black community deserves. The promotion of impaired men like the Rev. as leaders is, therefore, one of the most potent forms of racism by those who facilitate their ascension and empowerment and a most potent form of self-abnegation by those who acquiesce in submission, because they tolerate and facilitate their own oppression. For black America to have recognized Reverend Sharpton in any facet of leadership is indeed a sign of its abnegation of equality—of its embrace of an "unreason" that ultimately leads to its negation in its affirmation.

Indecencies

As many of the white detractors who've attacked the Rev. over the years were themselves no friends of the black community, it wasn't a stretch to have suspected that some of their attacks on him were sometimes deliberate strategies to strengthen and empower a weakling over his people. The result is the enfeebling of the black community in order for others to maintain their absolute supremacy. It isn't the so-called "race-baiter" that should've obsessed many in the white community but instead the man of little or no integrity, of little or no dignity, of little or no sense of decency—had they any. But many were mostly OK with those things. What had really irked them about the Rev. was that he had and continues to disturb their comfort zone—the presumed metaphysical obligation of every single African American with a functioning brain. Viewed through the prism of skepticism (or even paranoia), some might even view the Rev. as being in the employ of a kind of underground "confederacy in exile."

As there has never been any appetite for honest discussions on race in America, this has left a space wide open to demagoguery and despotism. It's a place of comfort and security for real racists and the real enemies of black America—black, white, and others—those who view the reserved inferiority imposed upon and accepted by the black masses as the justifiable norms of an inherently inferior people. There are yet others of the same views who just see money in the business of race. It is in this space that we find those most vested in having the ineffective Reverend Sharpton as the face of the downtrodden—the space permanently occupied by that illusory yet effective underground confederacy in exile.

It's therefore now a question of black America's need and courage to shift paradigm in order to move forward in the new millennium. Writer Mark Twain once told us that indecency is determined by those who invent it. This makes for a vicious cycle in a black culture long indoctrinated by W. E. B. Du Bois' idea of its "Talented Tenth" leading it out of the wilderness. That "Tenth" is sometimes an indecent and exploitative one, and it often determines its own indecencies—not the wider community. But another writer, George Orwell, had pointed out that however indecency is invented, it is nonetheless determined by the people, because, according to him, the people that elect corrupt politicians, imposters, thieves, and traitors, aren't victims but are instead accomplices. They enjoin and facilitate their own corruption and exploitation. Along the lines of Orwell but a little closer to home, Dr. Carter Woodson believed that racial exploiters of black America, while responsible for much of the corrupting indecencies of the black community, were nonetheless agents of the community itself, which bears the ultimate responsibility:

> The exploiters of the race are not so much at fault as the race itself...The race will free itself from exploiters just as soon as it decides to do so. No one else can accomplish this task for the race.[335]

In other words, it's useless for black America to sit around and ascribe sole blame to external forces for its subjugation and oppression when it actively tolerates and facilitates it. In Woodson's view, only the determinism of the community itself can arrest the damage being done to it by its own exploiters.

---

335 Woodson, *The Mis-Education of the Negro*, 65.

Down With "Prophets"

In his takedown of Dr. Cornel West, Sharpton-loyalist, professor Michael Eric Dyson affirmed his belief in Reverend Sharpton as black America's preeminent leader—implying as well that the Rev. was one of its foremost prophets. If this is true and these are its leadership and "prophetic" standards, then black America might be best served by having neither prophets nor leaders. But as this is likely not the case, the time for that next generation of black activists and leaders might be at hand—those in their twenties through forties. It's their turn to step up and courageously chart their own way forward, unimpaired, free of mind-prohibiting tutelage and proscription, free of the preachy condemnation that holds them hostages and prisoners to inutility and the willing deaf. New black leadership needs to free itself from the pretentious moral indignation endemic across the spectrum from the bourgeois classes to those who languish behind pulpits for the pitiful across the land.

No disfavored group or minority culture can advance in modern complex societies to see its humanity fully realized just by focusing on the external forces to which it is subjected or solely in imitation of the majority forces to which it is an object. None can advance or see its potentials fully realized while being led by contemporary vassals and exploiters with obligations and loyalties not to the group or culture at large but to themselves and to their social, political, or economic overlords. It's time to take down the prophets and put them on the shelves where they belong.

When to Hit It and When to Quit It

At times, examining the Sharpton life has been like a satirical musical compilation with each track being a "Best of"—according to the time period and subject matters covered. The comedy just never stops. As previously shown, unfortunately for others around the Rev., they often unwittingly enjoin themselves as subjects. Part II of James McBride's book on James Brown was entitled, "Hit It" and Part III, "Quit It." I couldn't help seeing the Rev.'s hands at work because chapter 5 of his own *The Rejected Stone* was entitled, "You Need to Know When to Quit It." There, he told of a great lesson he'd learned from his idol Adam Clayton Powell Jr.——not from James Brown——that had the same theme of "hitting it and quitting it." Accordingly, it was one of the greatest lessons he'd ever learned——yet another exercise in profundity that he'll never forget.

The Rev. had just learned of Adam Clayton Powell Jr.'s decision to throw in the towel and quit Congress as his troubles mounted in his waning years. Much like the way Sharpton had pleaded with James Brown to stay and enjoy the fight in Africa, he pleaded with Clayton Powell Jr., telling him, "But you can't leave us." According to the Rev.,

> He looked at me closely, He said, "Kid, one day, you're gonna grow up and be a great man. Always remember this: Know when to hit it, and know when to quit it."[336]

For the reasons mentioned above, there is little doubt that this was transmuted to James McBride as a lesson learned from James Brown, as it was used as section titles in a book on James Brown. Yet in his book, Sharpton attributes to Adam Clayton Powell Jr. In any case, cultural nuance is such that those outside the black community might not fully appreciate the funny and ironic sexual undertones to the "Hit it, Quit it" statement. But the sage of Brownsville who'd been consistent in making us laugh for over thirty years might have actually been onto something. Recalling Adam Clayton Powell Jr.'s advice, the Rev. then told us,

> When quitting time comes for me, I'm gone…If you see me slipping, losing my ability to get to that opening, like [Muhammad]Ali, then do me a favor——slide me a note to let me know that it might be time to quit it. But please, be kind.[337]

We can't always grant a man his full wishes in life, especially when he's likely to be ignorant of most of them. But where he has clearly articulated and delineated them and where they are possible with the minimum of efforts, decency

336 Al Sharpton with Chiles, *The Rejected Stone*, 32.
337 Ibid., 33–35.

mandates an obligation to grant them. It is this decency that now mandates an obligation to say,

Duly noted, Rev!
The note is under the door.
Mind your head on your way out.
In honor of Adam, you've already hit it.
Now it's time for you to quit it!

Epilogue–A Magisterium of Buffoons

The frustration engendered by the unavoidable sense of insecurity
is less intense in a minority intent on preserving its identity than
in one bent upon dissolving in and blending with the majority.

—Eric Hoffer[338]

Reverend Al Sharpton(L) and Michael Eric Dyson attend BET Networks Presents:
"Vote Like Your Life Depends on It" at the Apollo Theater on September 17,
2012, in New York City. (Photo by Brad Barket/Getty Images.)

---

338 Eric Hoffer, *The True Believer* (Harper Collins, New York, 1951), 50.

BY NOW YOU might have realized that this was not just the biography of a buffoon but rightfully the biography of *buffoons*. So, it would appear disingenuous to close without touching on that broader topic. The truth is that the racial racketeers of black America aren't just among the politicians and so-called leaders, but today they're as likely to be found among those who term themselves the "public intellectuals" of black America—not to be confused with real intellectuals.

The real black intellectuals are thought leaders seeking to harness the full potential of the black community to ameliorate adaptation and quality of life across the spectrum. They're the school teachers fighting ignorance and anti-intellectualism while struggling to keep inner-city students from dropping out of school. They're members of the clergy or civic groups who fight for social justice, criminal justice reforms, and even those who visit the prison systems to counsel and prepare the incarcerated for re-entry into civil society as productive human beings. They're activist and neighborhood organizers fighting crime and decadence one block at a time while taking direct actions to the power-structure to reduce discrimination and systematic abuse. The real black intellectuals are also those in institutions of higher education who prod their students to reason and intelligence. They do this not by dictating propaganda them or by telling them what to think and believe or how to do so, but by aiding in the development of agency and natural faculties to reason and think of their own free will. In their varying capacities, these intellectuals seek practical solutions to the issues of the day, prepare foundations for tomorrow, and they seek to promote self-advancement and the advancement of collective interests at all levels.

These individuals are different from the so-called "public intellectuals"—men and women who seek to appropriate legitimacy in their pursuits of self-interests by playing counterparts to the leaders who mislead black America. They aspire to lead mass movements—on Twitter and on Facebook—"not because they can satisfy the desire for self-advancement, but because they *seek to* satisfy *their own* passions for self-renunciation *through ideas of* movements that appeal not to those intent on bolstering and advancing the cherished self, but to those who crave to be rid of an unwanted self." [339]

---

339 Ibid., 12.

These public intellectuals are victims of a failed assimilationist mindset whereby comfortability cannot be found in acceptance of their "Africanness" in America. So they erect a certain fanaticism around ideas of "liberation" and "white privilege" when assimilation and imitation have been their lifelong struggle. It's "white privilege" because they're deprived thereof. Their "liberation" platforms and nationalistic rhetoric are essentially in reaction to their inability to welcomed as part of the "family" by white America. They seek to find acceptance and *equality* in the (still) foreignness of being black in America, which paradoxically is a real escape from freedom because it's a thing that will never happen—hence perpetual platforms and rhetoric primarily based in opportunism.

At the heart of these mostly black men who pretentiously call themselves "public intellectuals" (so far, I haven't heard of the self-styled native, white, Jewish, Asian, or Latino public intellectual), is an unfulfilled jack-leg country evangelist. But gone are the days of the backwater motels, the ordinary folks who used to accommodate them in their homes while on their journey to spread the *Word*, and the back-wood congregants who were the beneficiaries of their salvation. Today, these disappointed evangelists take up residence on social media. They monetize race instead of the *Word*, and they're "accommodated" by cable television networks, radio stations, and print journalism in pursuit of the same—the monetization of race.

Where these men once competed for back-wood congregants, they now chase the masses of angry-emotional Twitter followers, some of whom are just seeking a little guidance and a way out of their societal alienation, disenfranchisement, and despair while yet others with little or nothing better to do with their time. The business is no longer salvation through the *Word of Christ*. Today, its service offerings include the salacious bells and whistles of emotional exploitation—empty rhetoric, vast platitudes, anger-incitement, moral indignation & condemnation. Its products are primarily propaganda and fake history. Its goals run the gamut of seeking "liberation," demanding reparation, fighting "white supremacy," "whiteness," and "white privilege," and so on. And of course, its mission holds out a utopian promise land to be reached—if only there weren't whiteness, white supremacy, white privilege, and racism to deal with.

But in the real world, these public intellectuals scramble for a space in a small "sidebar" sandbox that offers slim paths to Ivy League professorships, wider public recognition, television appearances, radio programming, propagandist literature—books, internet web portals, and newspapers articles—and public speaking and associated fees from their now infamous "poverty," "reparation," and "empowerment" tours. They argue esoteric concepts and throw about intelligent sounding terms ending in "ism" to make themselves sound intelligent, all while parroting ideas taught to them by white America—in their condemnation of white America.

They imply instigations to revolutions that are likely to be fought in the Platinum Age—whenever that may arrive— all while they ignoring the need for tangible applicable solutions to the issues of the day, such as education and the discipline and skills required to excel in a modern complex society. Much like mainstream black leaders, you will hear condemnations of the education system from these educated "public intellectuals," but you will never hear a single one admonishing black parents for failing to prioritize their children's need to be in school. Nor will they use their positions to instill the value of education and training among the youths.

By "sidebar," try to imagine a court proceeding with a group of lawyers standing off to the side arguing their "emotions," not legal motions, as testimony, cross-examination, real legal motions, objections, and rulings—the entire court proceedings—continue unabated or uninterrupted. No one even notices them because they're completely irrelevant to the proceedings, except to the few spectators in the courtroom who themselves are largely irrelevant to the proceedings as well. This is the black "public intellectual" in America today—men and women of mostly irrelevant or outright nutty ideas—many of whom are just seeking an audience, trying to build a following that can be monetized.

I do mean to convey their irrelevance on public policies and social conditions because they are masters of futility who're experts at stirring up the anger and emotions of the young masses yet bereft of actionable ideas, strategies, or projects to harness those emotions to put anger and passions to a purpose or vice versa. Most are unimaginative—clueless about how to organize and fund think-tanks or resource centers that could one day become incubators of public policies or centers of original thought development for the next generation. This is because first and foremost, they too are racial racketeers with little value for institutions and institutional changes that might outlive them or that do not serve their immediate purpose of monetizing race. You'll never get a blueprint for the future from them because they're talkers, not planners or builders. Indeed, they're "liberators" with no value for concrete institutions to action and ensure their people's "liberty."

Not all are charlatans, and some are well-meaning men and women of integrity with a few good ideas. But ideas that aren't actionable soon become irrelevant. Ideas not backed up by institutions, thereby having no foundations on which to grow, become irrelevant in the long run. In black America, ideas that aren't introspective or those that skirt the primary social perils are futile over time. Those that do not seek to build frameworks to tackle existing decrepit foundations of poor education and social skills, widespread ignorance, poor health habits, licentious violence, teenage pregnancy and the single-parent phenomenon, self-hatred, dissonance and ostentation, and multi-generational dependence on public assistance, are definitely futile in the long run. Because they are ideas without foundations.

How can anyone seek to fight "liberation" wars without an army possessing the requisite skill and weapons to "liberate"? As Hoffer said, "people who see their lives as irremediably spoiled [*as the masses of the black underclass does*] cannot find a worth-while purpose in self-advancement. The prospect of an individual career cannot stir them to a mighty effort, nor can it evoke in them faith and a single-minded dedication."[340] In other words, the "family" or supposed "soldiers" can't even envision a battlefield because even as the disfavored, they fear change and have yet to arrive at the point where they see value in wars for change—beyond the usual indignation and complaints that follow retrograde racist irritations in society.

The army of liberators that are cultivated by these public intellectuals finds it hard to even make it to the polling stations on Election Day. In any social media space, you'll see a hurry to post videos of racism—as if a treasured prize proudly

---

340 Ibid., 12.

won in a contest. You'll find condemnations, heated discussions, and even "*thank you*" notes for posting. But for what purpose and to what end? It's as if there's a feel-good rush to "prove" to an indifferent white America that it's indeed racist. Admittedly, I too participate in some of the above at times. But roughly about a minute into any chain discussion online, it becomes evident that it's you're in the middle of a therapeutic exercise. The patients are there just to vent and to hear themselves vent but with neither capacity nor desire to listen to any therapist, to learn anything new or non-conforming, to organize, or to put passion to any type of useful purposes offline. It is "social" media after all. In any case, that's the extent of the mobilization to be harnessed among the masses of black America that comprise the supposed future armed forces of intellectual "liberation," as proffered by many of the black "public intellectuals."

So when these "public intellectuals" speak of fighting for the future direction of black America, like the Rev., they're really speaking of fighting for their own prominence and pre-eminence. There is nothing to "liberate" but the mind—the individual self—by first accepting it for what it is. And this they're neither willing nor capable of doing because it would first require the acceptance and discussion of some ugly truths—about themselves and of society in general. But as sirens and oracles in the black community often command some form of deification, these men and women end up captivating a sizeable part of the community's imagination in no time, because their emotional and otherwise rhythmic yet empty rhetoric speaks to the racism that the blind can see, and the deaf can hear. And that suffices.

So it was easy to see why these "Obama men" went scrambling and jockeying for positions and recognition during Mr. Obama's presidency. It was their moment in the sun. They'd seen the black presidency as the ultimate opportunity for the appropriation of legitimacy, and in doing so, they did what they've always done best; they continued to show their irrelevance by fighting among each other. Who else were they going to fight with—not white intellectuals, policy-makers, or real influencers? While politely "accommodating" them, the mainstream disregards them as irrelevant. So they have to fight with the only people who see them as relevant threats to their livelihood—themselves. Again, it's the way they breathe. With President Obama now gone, they've lost their platform, so their nonsense has intensified and will become even more so in the near future. As some of their public conduct has since been anything but coherent or sensible, Reverend Sharpton has been the beneficiary, still laughing at most of them from the sidelines, because again, he'd never liked any of them from the outset.

In returning to the savage kingdom analogy for a moment, Professor Cornel West is sort of the lion of the big cat group. Professor Michael Eric Dyson, Tavis Smiley, and others who mimic them or who're otherwise challenging them for supremacy, fall somewhere between the younger lions of the pride, the jaguars, or the cheetahs trying to claw their way to the top. As in any disfavored community, there are also the lower-tier fringe elements filling the vacuum for real people facing real suffering and for a younger generation lost as a result of decades of poor black leadership. In the wild kingdom of black intellectualism, these are hyenas in the hunt and their battle, an even more savage one.

Intellectual Effeteness

Emoting the rhythmic 1970s tonality of a street corner "cool kat" back in the day, Dr. Cornel West announces his "harmlessness," seduces, and disarms his fellow panelists and audiences in discussions by affectionately addressing them as "brothers" or "sisters." It's an updated version of the nineteenth-century "smiling black man" that we used to get from writers like Joel Chandler Harris. But make no mistake, like Reverend Sharpton, the West inner child stands ready to viciously attack others, including the younger generation that he deems a potential shade to his sunlight. He is the lion after all, but one whose meltdown at times seem to beckon the need for an intervention.

In 2016, Dr. West's stringent opposition to neoliberalism led him to endorse the Green Party's Dr. Jill Stein—the candidate he'd thought "most likely to win" the elections and therefore most likely to obliterate the global financial framework that Walter Lippmann, Ludwig von Mises, Friedrich Hayek, the Chicago and Austrian schools of economics, and the other men from Mont Pèlerin had dreamed up some seventy years ago. Since then, in article after article that Professor West has written, there's almost need to be a specialist in the works of eighteenth-century German philosopher Johann Goethe to make heads or tails of what Dr. West is talking about or what he would like you to think he's talking about.

West's partner in crime in the outer group from the Obama era, the faux-moralist, Tavis Smiley, is probably the most helium-filled hyperbolic windbag of them all. With his platform in television, radio, and literature, his "holier-than-thou" bluster often has him coming off as Tarzan—having found not only Jesus but the Holy Grail as well. Beyond high indignant condemnations over the years, the combative Smiley is a study in egos that defy gravity. Caught up in the recent wave of accusations of inappropriate behavior, which cost him his job at PBS, Smiley defiantly declared his belief that people working sixty-hours a week are left little choice. Office romances are the first refuge of the hard-working man—emphasis on "hard-working." He has declared his innocence and has since set out to prove it, but unlike others who've had the decency to either "prove" their innocence quietly or show some humility for the gravity of the situation, Smiley remains combative. He took to the airwaves to declare that he'd never ever groped or raped any woman. But his belief in himself apparently went beyond consulting public-relations professionals, and it showed. It also left America wondering: If Tavis Smiley had understood harassment and inappropriate behavior to be limited to groping or raping women, how could he have behaved appropriately in the first place?

Smiley is known for his empowerment and wealth creation ("poverty") tours that might have ended up leaving some of his people in the "sub-prime poor" category of the last recession. In 2016, likely as part of one of those tours or maybe during a detour, Smiley made an appearance at Lehigh University where a curious student asked him, "Mr. Smiley, do you believe that given the crisis of our democracy, we black folk could ever find ourselves enslaved again?" A reasoned mind or just a mildly-functioning brain would've politely explained to the student that slavery, as an institution, was first and foremost an economic phenomenon of its time that had then produced wider social evils in its defense and maintenance, but that civil societies have long moved beyond chattel-slavery, and that the circumstances of the day, while disconcerting to many, in no way portend a return to the nineteenth-century.

Tavis Smiley, though, as sure of himself as he's hyperbolic, answered the student in the affirmative. Where, as an adult, he should've educated the young student, the young student had educated him. The ostentatious Smiley then had the foresight to pen an October 16, 2016, *Time* magazine article under the banner "Why I Fear America Could Enslave Black People Again." Although admitting that legal scholars would find the question ludicrous and laughable, he wasn't beyond being ludicrous or laughable. He didn't think it was farfetched that the Constitution could be thwarted by President Donald Trump and the Republican Congress to re-enslave African Americans. This was his basis for writing of his "fear of a return to slavery."

But among the many problematic aspects of Smiley's "fear" that he didn't address was this one: What would Trump's Republican America do with forty-three to forty-four million millennial slaves? Would it dispatch them to raise produce and pick oranges in Florida, cotton and rice in Alabama and Mississippi, or peanuts in Georgia? Or would it subordinate their labor to a BMW plant in South Carolina?

Regrettably, as a result of Tavis Smiley's over the top posture, at least one black student at Lehigh University, maybe many, might now be anxiously bracing for a return to life pre-1863.

Of the inner Obama group, professor Michael Eric Dyson merits a special prayer. Rumor had it that Dr. Dyson was last seen bolting earlier in 2017—in the direction away from Studio 33 in Los Angeles when he was apparently called on to carry a pint of water for his friend, comedian Bill Maher, who had gotten into a little kerfuffle for his use of the *n*-word. The white Maher, whose proclivity for all things chocolate likely exceeds that of many black men in the Los Angeles area, had, in a moment of comfortability, exposed a critical aspect of black bourgeois decadence and hypocrisy—its quasi-prohibition of language in America, an unheard-of phenomenon in modern life. By definition, linguistic quasi-prohibition is either elitist or decadent unless you're in France.

To the chagrin of another generation of black thinkers like Dr. Frances Cress Welsing and others, who must be turning over in their graves, Dr. Dyson wrote a 2017 book, *Tears We Cannot Stop,* legitimizing a contemporary rhetoric of black decadence that declares white usage of the *n*-word as racist but black usage as romantic—an expression of brotherly-sisterly love—but not at all an act of self-denigration. Apparently, nothing stimulates black America's hormones like hearing those beautiful words, *"My nigga!"* It's romantic, according to Dr. Dyson—an intra-group expression of affection. Accordingly, the *n*-word is passionately off-limits to white America but allowed to be dispassionately flung about in a black America where its commercial exploitation rakes in hundreds of millions of dollars for an industry dominated black rappers who commoditize and sell the "non-degradation" of their communities to audiences—black and white alike.

As the champion of this thought is none other than Dr. Dyson, it had made perfect sense that he would've been called on to lend a hand to the other co-median—Bill Maher—in his time of need. But the good doctor copped out at the last minute, likely out of fear that a vocal defense of his written words might have echoed the same level of vulgarity as reading them. The Princeton University Ph.D. who told us this, of his graduating fellowship acceptance—"Mine was the only one in the Ivy League,"[341] and this, of his early struggles with his undergraduate college president—"This white man wasn't going to stop me from getting to the Ivy League,"[342] had nonetheless deferred to the lyrics of rapper Jay-Z to support his argument on the difference between the phonetically articulated and white-pronounced "nigger" (racist) versus the "ebonically" articulated and "nigga'dly"-pronounced "nigga" (romantic):

> Thus an offensive word became to many black folk an affectionate one…Nigga reflects self-love and a chosen identity. Nigga does far more than challenge the white imagination. Nigga also captures class and spatial tensions in black America. Nigga is grounded in the ghetto; it frowns on bourgeois ideals and spits in the face of respectability politics.[343]

It seems that Jesse Jackson had mistakenly pronounced the ending "er" instead of an "a," thereby sounding a little white and thus revealing a lack of affection

---

341 Michael Eric Dyson, *Tears We Cannot Stop* (St. Martin's Press, New York, 2017), 47.

342 Ibid.

343 Ibid. 163-4.

for then-candidate Barack Obama in that Fox television studio. Partly for this, Jackson was driven out of town.

In any case, in indicting white America for its ignorance on the subject matter, Dr. Dyson further elaborated his basis for the distinction. But it's a distinction to be recognized and accepted only by a decadent mind ravaged by oppression, or maybe by too many psychedelic stimulants:

> If more of you understood that nigger is a word apart from nigga, and if you understood how the different spelling and pronunciation —and the race of the user-changes its meaning, then some of you might not insist that you should be able to say it too.[344]

Poor Bill Maher couldn't have seen it coming. As a comedian, "spitting in the face of respectability politics" and its correctness is what he does best. Believing he was an honorary member of the tribe, he'd chosen to embrace a "chosen identity" that didn't exactly embrace him back. But in doing so, he'd also exposed a delirious double standard erected by a community that has spent a lifetime decrying the double standards to which it is subjected. Black America killed off the *n*-word in Webster's and in the Oxford dictionary but kept it alive and well in the Urban dictionary for its own private and commercial exploitation—an idea as preposterous and hypocritical as its condemnation of comedian Bill Maher as a racist.

That refusal to accept the distinction or to accept black America's first right of the "nigga" usage was just one of the many reasons for Dr. Dyson's condemnation of white folk in his book. It was written and addressed to the omnipotent and omniscient white America of his mind, whereby he effectively made the case that the very self-worth, dignity, humanity, and legitimacy of black folk are in the hands of whites. While the physical slavery of the Smiley imagination will likely stay where it belongs, the mental slavery of the Dyson mind prompted it to plead with its masters for unrequited love but only after eviscerating them for their "whiteness" and their "white privilege"—another "Sharptonesque" trick.

---

344 Ibid. 166.

Viewed through the prism of the *psychosis of deficiencies* that drive a sense of moral superiority and a right of righteous indignation towards others, men like Reverend Sharpton, Dr. Dyson, Dr. West, and Tavis Smiley are oblivious to the colossal planetary exhaustion with the holier-than-thou moralizing black preacher-"public intellectual"-politician. But as Eric Hoffer reminds us, "a man is likely to mind his own business when it is worth minding. When it is not, he takes his mind off his own meaningless affairs by minding other people's business. In running away from ourselves we either fall on our neighbor's shoulder or fly at his throat."[345]

And so it was that professor Dyson had written a book that reads like the rant of a disavowed family member in a drunken rage at thanksgiving, oscillating between menacing and condemning the rest of the family in one moment then begging its forgiveness and love in the next. "We cannot hate you, not really, not most of us," he says in the middle of dinner. "That's our gift to you."[346] But then he starts drinking again after dinner, and its back to condemnation. The family is the white America from which Dr. Dyson has gotten his fair-skinned complexion—of which he rarely fails to remind us, as in describing his daughter's fair skin that, "makes her appear to be what the film and television industry terms 'ethnically ambiguous.'" [347] Who in their right mind would write such nonsense, and to what possible end? It's classic assimilation rejection and a *mark of the oppressed*.

In any case, among the many other goodies of Dr. Dyson's sermon to white America were the following: "You can begin a film club for black children to attend movie theaters in more affluent areas where they might also enjoy a trip to the museum."[348] He advised white folk to sponsor and mentor a black child with all the accoutrements of "whiteness," as he termed it across his book. The idea of building healthy black communities with "affluent" theatres and of supporting the development of affluent community galleries and local museums is lost on the black "public intellectual." But again, it's just another form of self-renunciation, as it seems that he believes that it has to be white and in a white

---

345 Eric Hoffer, *The True Believer* (Harper Collins, New York, 1951), 14.

346 Ibid. 193.

347 Ibid. 25.

348 Ibid. 198-9

neighborhood for it to be good. It is in this sense that a book littered with the words "white privilege" and "whiteness" had breathed new meanings—frustration from a failure to mimic and imitate.

Dyson also advised white America of its need to get to know black folk by taking the time to read black literature, starting with James Baldwin—"Beloved, you must educate yourself about black life and culture…What should you read? I always start with James Baldwin."[349] As the black community is known for its "well-read" citizenry, it would've made very little sense for the Bible-thumping Dyson to "first cast the beam out of his own eyes" by writing a book extolling black folk to read and educate themselves on their own history. So, he did as would've been expected and preached the gospel to white folk instead. White America needed to read Jimmy Baldwin to appreciate its own moral destitution. If that fails, he believes that having a few black friends—beyond the token one or two—might ameliorate that moral destitution. It's evidently an issue that causes him profound distress:

> Not knowing black folk intimately exacerbates the distance between the white self and the black other. One solution is new black friends. It is distressing that so few of you have more than a token black friend, maybe two.[350]

White America also needed to attend a black church to listen to the black-expropriated Christianity it had given to black folk and to Dr. Tyson post-1700, in the first place. It's the usual battle-cry of the melanin tribe: *we took Christianity and made it better than you white folks; come see why we're the real Christians—the real followers of Christ*:

> Visiting a black church is just good for the soul…Of course, when you visit on a Sunday morning, you'll hear the magnificent music of our choirs, the thunderous ways they sing out the joy and wring out the blues by proclaiming faith in God through song.[351]

---

349 Ibid. 199.
350 Ibid. 206-7.
351 Ibid. 210-11.

The pretentious preacher-intellectual then also advised white America to set up IRAs—Individual "Reparation" Accounts. To buttress the laughing stock he is, though, Dr. Dyson demurred at demanding cold cash by suggesting that among other things, white America should pay its black workers a little more than it usually would:

> First, my friends, you must make reparations…You can hire black folk at your office and pay them slightly better than you would ordinarily pay them. You can pay the black person who cuts your grass double what you might ordinarily pay.[352]

But for those white folks who might be concerned about discriminating against their Mexican gardeners, Dyson also offered an alternative option: white America should pay for black folk to get massages, yes, *massages*—"As part of the IRA, you can also pay for massages for working class folk."[353] I'm confident that the professor will make the necessary adjustment in thought in his next book to call on whites to pay for psychiatric therapy for black folk as well, as it's clear that he would be a primary beneficiary.

But in Dr. Dyson's mind, the real white burden to be alleviated seems contrary to politics and all that was going on at the legislative level in the country that had just elected mega-capitalist Donald Trump as president. It's one thing to argue against wealth transfer by cutting taxes for corporations and the rich while squeezing the middle class and the poor but quite another to argue for raising taxes on both. Yet the progressive Dr. Dyson believed that it was time for white America to fess up and pay a "black tax"—even if it means assuming some aspects of "blackness":

> You can also pay a black tax, just as black folks do. The black tax refers to the cost and penalty of being black in America—of having to work twice as hard for half of what whites get by less strenuous means.[354]

---

352 Ibid. 197.

353 Ibid. 198.

354 Ibid.

It was indeed a doozy to read the "public intellectual's" prescription for white America, which ranged from command communism to a sort of *procession of the flagellants* for whites as a form of guilt-ridding reparation to African Americans. Not only does Dr. Michael Eric Dyson, a professor at Georgetown University in Washington DC, live in a country in which he's a stranger, but he also exists on a planet on which he's the same. Entrenched in the indoctrination of bourgeois decadence and ostentatious reverence, he's bereft of the most fundamental understandings of human nature, bereft of the most base-level psychology of human behavior. Would anyone in America—black, white, purple, or brown—pay anyone more than the job is worth, work twice as hard as they have to, or pay for their neighbor's massage to somehow outsource their guilt? Dr. Dyson can't even recognize or understand his own psychoses shown to us, yet he believes himself in a position to preach to white America about its own.

The comedy of it all is his dire belief in legitimization through the very "whiteness" he derides all over his book. Take this other jewel of an idea in his sermon to whites: white America should have a night of reverence at sporting events to honor civil rights veterans like Reverend Jesse Jackson, John Lewis, Eleanor Norton-Holmes, and others, just the way it honors military veterans. This is something that happens nowhere in black America, yet the scholar would never endeavor to first preach this to black folk because he believes that white America first has to start such a tradition to honor black heroes in order for black America to then follow suit as well. Only then can it become genuinely *bona fide*.

It was clear that this was purely intended to gain an audience and to maintain his relevance in that fertile pasture of activism for the downtrodden and the brainless—that "sidebar" sandbox earlier mentioned. His book is just to develop a following, so he can be accommodated as a "thought leader" on cable television, get speaking engagements, and continue writing even more propagandist nonsense. In listening to his sermon (reading his book), the irrelevance of he and others was again reaffirmed. If these are the ideas of an intellectual promulgator of black "thought," it is understandable why he and others are largely ignored by the wider society and why they've had no influence or impact on public policies—not even when a black man was sitting in the Oval Office.

Let's look at the poverty-in-ambition of an Ivy League-educated professor who writes a book based on Rap lyrics. The character of modern societies is charted by those at the top who define the intellectual and philosophical threads that underpin policy development, social and economic frameworks, and the political landscape, as well as by the massive working and middle classes that actually do the heavy lifting as the engine of the economic machine. Those at the bottom are generally a drag on progress. More than often, some defeat it outright because they're generally de-privileged and denied any stake in such collective progress. This might include both the intellectually and economically deprived that span the gamut of the uneducated and unskilled masses, the poor, the disaffected, outcasts, criminals, anarchists, nihilists, and other "*facinants*" of decadence among them. In other words, those who make the least or no contribution at all to progress in their communities or to society at large, and yet others who make negative contributions.

Overall societal progress is therefore mainly a function of moving people out of poverty, out of dependency, out of decadence in thought and behavior—out of the de-privileged underclasses and into the productive middle and working classes or above. Correspondingly, an essential factor in the retardation of progress is oppression—largely a function of "Selection." Those who are disfavored, based on different reasoning and criteria, are selectively isolated and kept right where they are at the bottom, thereby excluding them from competing in the economic marketplace, except as consumers, and ensuring that they remain a "tolerable" drag on progress for society. They're a "premium" baked into the stock of society.

On the intellectual side, the same applies. Progress is a function of indoctrinated mimetic aspirations to higher standards—levels of education, skillsets, knowledge, and wisdom, beauty, and aesthetics among many things. This mandates continually raising the bar and standards across all areas of art, science, research and development, and so on. But first and foremost, progress is human conduct—our interactions with each other, how we treat each other. Progress starts with arresting the proliferation of outright anti-intellectualism and mind-numbing idiocy, as well as anti-social conduct that may range from divisions based on race, religion, ethnic background, to crime and violence.

But progress doesn't come through resignation to the standards of, or the adoption of, values and wisdom of the unlearned and disaffected as the new baseline for all of society. This is a form of welcomed oppression as it isolates, rather than elevates, an even wider sector of society into the "idiots' column." We routinely call this the dumbing down of society—currently a delusional phenomenon of black life in America. As the society at large aspires to varying criteria of progress, ignorance, anti-intellectualism, nihilism, and decadence becomes the norm for more and more (per capita) of Dr. Dyson's people.

My cousin's son, for example, speaks to me of the "Illuminati" and of his favorite rap stars who are members of the Illuminati. I've exhausted myself trying to explain to him that the Illuminati and other secret societies of the world would never accept a person of African descent in a million years, regardless of their wealth because these are fundamentally racist societies based on medieval ideas of race and old bloodlines. They won't even allow *nouveau mega-riche* whites because they lack the bloodlines and pageantry of ancient history. But because he gets a large part of his education from rap artists, and they tell him that they are either with the Illuminati or being persecuted by it, there's no convincing him otherwise.

So, where intellectuals like Dr. Dyson and others brag about their Ivy League education, only to defer to rap artists to furnish the intellectual threads to society, there can be little surprise at the high levels of ignorance, anti-intellectualism, and decadence pervasive in many parts of black America. The intellectual top that should "define" and lead is now deferring to the wisdom of the bottom—some of which sells its own denigration and abnegation—just because that bottom is now a wealthy magisterium. Instead of wasting his time at Princeton University, professor Dyson could have developed the basis of his book by standing on any street corner in Detroit—the nexus of both rappers and preachers?

The *truths* spoken by the orators of rap music highlight today's unpleasant realities that society should be working to fix in order to realize a different and better tomorrow. But these *evident truths* shouldn't be enshrined as gospels for a permanence in encouraged decadence. Dr. Dyson and other black leaders, however, are encouraged by this permanence in decadence because their aim isn't to change things. They live to make cultural indictments and to further lay claims on white America—which while having no practical effect, nonetheless gains them an audience. Write hagiographies of rap stars or a book expropriating the lyrics of Jay-Z, KRS-One, or Tupac, and you get an audience. But ideas are infinity and unique to each individual. So, there's no reason why so-called well-educated "public intellectual" should not be held to derive his own original forms.

Rap music's vulgarity of poor self-worth, despair, meaninglessness, machismo, disaffection, and nihilism amidst the savage fight for existence among the de-privileged in America is a condition of black life that bourgeois black America likes to exploit but not to know about or to deal with. Your writer is not a critic of Rap stars or of their ingenious ability to reflect the brutal honesty of the lives they've known through music. Just as Nietzsche had viewed the Dionysian overrun of the refined Apollonian age in ancient Greece and other parts of Asia Minor, Rap is an actual *birth of tragedy*—a debaucherous revolt that demands attention and remedies for the entrapped and oppressed of the underclasses.

So, efforts to expropriate and trade off rap music's celebrity and wealth is yet another example of charlatanism among these "public intellectuals." I'm old enough to recall the 1990s when the elites of Dr. Dyson's class (although he'll deny being an elite) were the ones leading the charge against rap music's nihilism. Yet today they make a living teaching rap music in universities rather than educating students on the underlying fundamentals that gives rise to the revolt.

Demi-Demagogue

Finally, there was the hypocrisy and demagoguery of the Christian preacher-intellectual that was hard to hide, even though he'd tried. As if black America weren't in dire need of a sermon, Dr. Dyson, who has preoccupied himself in the past with white America's habit of voting against its economic interest, decided this time, to sermonize them. In doing so, he extolling white folk to love their native black brothers and sisters—though, not to waste their time on black immigrants who, "often have a leg up on native blacks, having lacked the common history of oppression that binds African Americans together." [355]

It seems hardly fair to call Dr. Dyson a demagogue, although he is. But his larger issue might just be a willful ignorance of slavery and colonialism in the Caribbean and in Latin America—in particular in the Portuguese territories, or of African slavery and colonialism—in particular, in places like "Leopold's" Congo. Dyson is also ignorant of the fact that many blacks in the Caribbean had started their journey as slaves right here in America, but even so, none of this really matters to the underlying issue. What matters is that he seems to suggest here that before profiling, abusing, or shooting a black man in the streets of America, police officers should first check to verify whether or not his great-grandparent had known Jim Crow in the South.

Where a "Duty of Care" become the object of your assimilation, it guarantees your licentious abuse across the spectrum because the underlying thread is no longer the pursuit of human and civil rights, or of justice and *equality*. Instead, it becomes the pursuit of "being taken care of." You remain either a slave or become a snowflake but not an emancipated individual. It's placing Damocles at Dionysius' table through the backdoor. But herein lies another trap of this line of black thought in America—often developed in its own echo chamber and often divorced from reality—in its escape from reality. In a country of immigrants, Dr. Dyson pleaded with white America to register an exception in thought to accommodate the notion that a set of new immigrants should be disfavored to an extended degree for having been taken to Latin America or the Caribbean rather than to South Carolina. This, even though they were brought to the Americas in the first place, by the same means of kidnapping and people theft that had brought him here. This nativism is a fallacy that achieves little beyond exposing the demagoguery at the heart of the failed assimilationist mindset. It goes like this, *My slavery was worse than yours; you didn't know Jim Crow.* But in reality, it is really saying, *I don't need any competition for my assimilation—for "their" acceptance.*

So, in what was a global phenomenon of inhumane atrocities for Africans everywhere, many choose to isolate their own experience as unique, thereby

---

355 Ibid., 209.

meriting special considerations from their respective white overlords. This then underpins that more extensive willful ignorance of diaspora experiences and serves to further alienate blacks in America from Africans in the rest of the world and vice versa. Native Africans are equally alienated from blacks in America, Latin America, and the Caribbean, as are Caribbeans and Afro-Latinos alienated from the rest because the colonial education elsewhere was the counterpart that inspired much the same divisions among diaspora Africans outside of America. It's an all-around indoctrination of divisions that results in further diaspora frustration from a wider alienation of brothers and sisters. A simple DNA kit might surprise many.

By contrast, many Irish natives were indentured servants in America and in the slave colonies of the Caribbean. They were treated a little better than slaves but in no way humane. After slavery, their inhumane treatment and discrimination on the labor front in areas such as coal mining had continued in America. Yet we've never seen contemporary Irish men and women seeking to disfavor new arrivals from Ireland, based on the distinction of a "common experience" suffered by early immigrants in America. An argument might be made that as whites and "non-slaves," the Irish have long been assimilated into the mainstream and no longer worry about competition. It's an argument odious, no less invalid.

It's as if in between those classes at Princeton, Professor Dyson, like Sam Jackson, had taken a few night courses in the Sharpton school of etiquette as well. The assertion of a "common experience" in America as the basis for discriminating against foreign blacks is a chauvinism that reflects old divisions inculcated during slavery. With that said, this applies equally in reverse as well—for Africans, Caribbeans, and Afro-Latino(a)s who may come to America without appreciating that very history of Jim Crow and how it has shaped black culture and particular sensitivities in America.

By this poverty-in-thought, Dr. Dyson discredits himself, especially relative to an earlier generation of African Americans who'd indeed fought for fairness in the immigration system to enable diaspora Africans to emigrate to America. But admittedly, his poor thinking is inherent to black life. As a teenager in New York City in the early 1980s, I'd witnessed first-hand the discrimination and persecution of Haitians, who'd shown the black and brown world how to revolt and claim their independence from colonial barbarity nearly a hundred and eighty years earlier. The new arrivals didn't face persecution from white America in their daily lives in my Brooklyn neighborhood. They'd suffered it from native blacks and from other Caribbean blacks endowed with the same biases Dr. Michael Eric Dyson has managed to put forth in his 2017 book.

Yet in early 2018, black America was up in arms when it was alleged that President Donald Trump had made disparaging remarks about certain African countries and Haiti, in particular. African American members of Congress dug out their Kente cloths from the closet to wear to the president's State of the Union address in protest. But the hypocrisy was palpable—further highlighted by the fact that on any given day, men like Dr. Michael Eric Dyson, Reverend Sharpton, and other black leaders are at the forefront of the fight for Latino ("immigration") rights. It's hard to accept that Latinos and African Americans share more of a "common history of oppression that binds" them together than African Americans do with fellow diaspora Africans.

The truth is that much like black leaders, these black "public intellectuals," might not necessarily love the Latino community, but this part of the "allowable" or "permissible" narrative of a safe path to a wider progressive audience. But here again, they serve to ultimately defeat the cause of black progress in America, not because Latino rights are mutually exclusive to progress but because internal divisions are. In a democracy, it's all about numbers. For the disfavored minority, division reduces the numbers and pushes progress farther into the future. Any chance for the numerical significance needed for the type of political organization that might one day acquire the power to change its conditions is dashed. For example, among those who're referred to as Latinos today are cultural backgrounds with little in common and even less mutual affinities beyond the shared Spanish language. Yet unification under a single umbrella has changed the political landscape and the effectiveness of Latinos and made them into a political force.

Ignorance on the street or in the Oval Office—no more forgivable—might nonetheless be "excusable." Where it comes from so-called intellectuals in the black community, however, it is neither. In the end, the most remarkable thing about these men who hog the medium calling themselves "public intellectuals," is that they're the only ones who fail to see what they manifest through their public discussions and writings. They're the only ones who fail to see their own confessionals. Written as a preachy sermon, Dr. Dyson's book is a big fat therapeutic exercise in which we see yet another—just as overt as Reverend Sharpton—straddle the acceptance-rejection continuum indoctrinated by a life lived in oppression. It bears out all the elements that Albert Memi and Eric Hoffer have long written about, and in this sense, Dyson, like others, consoles himself with the notion that as the disfavored in society, it's all because of the "white privilege" of which he's dispossessed.

Writer and jazz aficionado Stanley Crouch once said, "The real deal is that few intellectually sophisticated black people are ever seen on television discussing issues." But I would add that where black faces on television are those of men and women who also sit on the faculties of prestigious Ivy League universities, it's almost a given that they are simpletons at heart. Otherwise, they'd be busying themselves with building think-tanks or with doing the heavy lifting of shaping the next generation of their people in the classrooms of Historically Black Colleges and Universities (HBCUs) that still guard the frontier against decadence for many students in many parts of the country.

On reading *Tears We Cannot Stop*, I couldn't help but to somehow feel vindicated by my son Romain's decision to get his education in Chicago and not in Washington DC.

Postscript

ALTHOUGH YOU MAY have found much to laugh about, Biography of a Buffoon was never conceived as an effort to embarrass the Reverend Al Sharpton or others mentioned. Indeed, they're just symptoms of the decadence endemic to black leadership in general and to the intellectual and showbiz types who stir and exploit black America's emotions in their efforts at brand marketing through all means necessary, including running for president. Social scientists do admit that charlatanism is to some extent indispensable to effective leadership, and for that reason, it is understandably tolerated. But as idiocy has never known any such indispensability and as both have become so mainstream in American society—almost a new norm black America—it might be time to emulate past Greek and Roman playwrights by laughing at those who make fools of us, in the hopes that we may slow their progress. We need not be right in all of our arguments in order to make them. We just need to laugh while making them.

The End

About the Author

PAUL SINCLAIR IS a native of Kingston, Jamaica, who was raised in New York City. He received his bachelor's degree in business administration and his master's degree in finance. In the last twenty-five years, he has lived in the United States, France, England, Switzerland, and Holland.

Disheartened by the state of affairs in politics, culture, and race relations on his move back to America in the mid-2000s, he identified the inefficacy of current black leadership and the culture of chicanery as an existential threat. He hopes that his work will start dialogues dedicated to changing this current climate.

Today, his work is focused on issues of sustainability and well-being (which he believes poses an even greater threat to black communities). He is the proud single father of a son, Romain, a strategic consultant in New York City.

Index